R127

Education in Ireland: Challenge and Change

Education in Ireland: Challenge and Change

Edited by Sheelagh Drudy

Gill & Macmillan

Gill & Macmillan Ltd
Hume Avenue
Park West
Dublin 12
with associated companies throughout the world
www.gillmacmillan.ie

© Sheelagh Drudy, Deirdre Raftery, Judith Harford, Dympna Devine, William Kinsella, Joyce Senior, Máirín Barry, Gerry Mac Ruairc, Lelia Murtagh, Marie Clarke, Maureen Killeavy, Anne Moloney, Elizabeth O'Gorman, Audrey Bryan, Paul McElwee, Bernard McGettrick, Conor Galvin 2009
ISBN 978 07171 4767 0

Index compiled by Helen Litton
Print origination in Ireland by O'K Graphic Design, Dublin

The paper used in this book is made from the wood pulp of managed forests. For every tree felled, at least one tree is planted, thereby renewing natural resources.

A CIP catalogue record for this book is available from the British Library.

CONTENTS

PART 1: THE CHANGING SYSTEM

PART 2: DIVERSITY AND INCLUSION IN SCHOOLS

PART 3: TEACHER EDUCATION FOR CHANGING TIMES

ACKNOWLEDGMENTS

As editor, I would like to acknowledge the help and support of many people in the production of this book. First, and most importantly, I owe the contributors to the book a great debt of gratitude, not only for the chapters they have contributed with the results of their research but also for their cheerful collaboration and for meeting the various deadlines that were imposed on them. I also owe all of them my appreciation for their years of support as colleagues in the School of Education in University College Dublin. I am very glad to share with them our celebration of the centenary of the establishment of Education in UCD, of which this book forms part.

At an early stage of the planning of this volume, it was decided that it should meet the standard of an international peer-reviewed publication. We owe our readership no less. Therefore, as part of the editorial process, a national and international panel of reviewers was assembled and all agreed to undertake a blind peer-review of chapters. I would like to thank all of them for so readily agreeing to what is, in fact, quite an onerous task. Their generosity in factoring this into very busy work schedules of their own is greatly appreciated. All engaged in the process with consummate professionalism and, like the contributors, all met their deadlines. In alphabetical order our expert panel of reviewers comprised: Professor Madeleine Arnot, University of Cambridge, England; Professor Tuula Asunta, University of Jyvaskyla, Finland; Professor Dòra Bjarnason, University of Iceland, Iceland; Professor Patrick Clancy, University College Dublin; Professor John Coolahan, National University of Ireland, Maynooth; Dr Jim Gleeson, University of Limerick; Dr Seán Griffin, St Nicholas Montessori College, Dublin; Dr John Harris, Trinity College Dublin; Professor Lorraine Ling, La Trobe University, Australia; Dr Anne Lodge, President, Church of Ireland College of Education; Dr Jean McNiff, International Education Consultant; Dr Maeve Martin, National University of Ireland, Maynooth; Professor Jim O'Brien, Moray House, University of Edinburgh, Scotland; Professor Marie Parker-Jenkins, University of Limerick; Ms Susan Parkes, Fellow Emeritus, Trinity College Dublin; Dr Margaret Reynolds, formerly Head of Education, St Mary's University College, Belfast; and Dr Roland Tormey, University of Limerick. I am extremely grateful to all of them for their expert advice and comments. Naturally, if there are any remaining errors or infelicities they are our own, and not attributable to the reviewers.

The chapters in this book contain much original research. This was obtained not only through the efforts of the researchers, but also through the co-operation of many thousands of respondents—principals, teachers, other educators, pupils, students and some parents, who generously co-operated with the surveys and interviews and allowed us to share parts of their lives. We are deeply appreciative of them all. A number of the research projects were funded by external bodies. To these we also wish to express deep appreciation.

The staff of Gill & Macmillan were very professional and supportive in the publishing of this volume. While the production staff comprises many people, I am sure that no one would object if I single out for particular praise three people: Ms Marion O'Brien, Publishing Executive for College, Further Education & Training and Ms Aoife O'Kelly, Managing Editor at Gill & Macmillan, and Ms Claire Rourke of Bookends Publishing. They were always most supportive, helpful and ready with advice. Emma Farrell of Gill & Macmillan was also very helpful at an early stage of the planning for the book. Grateful thanks are also due to the Chancellor, Registrar and Senate of the National University of Ireland for the award of a grant towards scholarly publication.

Sheelagh Drudy, Editor
Professor of Education
University College Dublin
August 2009

LIST OF CONTRIBUTORS

Máirín Barry is an Assistant Co-ordinator and Lecturer in Inclusive Education and Special Educational Needs at the School of Education, UCD. She has extensive experience as an educator working in inclusive settings, supporting students with a range of special educational needs, including autism, Down syndrome, dyslexia, ADD, language disorders, and both mild and moderate general learning difficulties. She is Vice-Chair of the Irish Learning Support Association and editor of their professional journal *Learn.* Her current research focuses on dyscalculia and early interventions for students with learning difficulties in Mathematics.

Audrey Bryan, PhD, teaches comparative, international and development education in the School of Education, UCD. She obtained her doctorate from Teachers College, Columbia University, where she received a President's Grant for Student Research in Diversity; a Dean's Grant for Student Research; and an Interdisciplinary PhD Conflict Resolution Research Award. She has published internationally in the areas of intercultural and anti-racist education, development studies, and the experiences of sexual minority youth. Her current research interests include representations of international development and international educational development policy and practice.

Marie Clarke, BA, MA, HDip in Ed, PhD, is Head of the School of Education and a member of the UCD Governing Authority and Academic Council. She is Joint Director of the PGDE and MA in Education (Mentoring). Her research and publications include the areas of teacher education, history of education and higher education. She is a member of the Executive Council, Association of Teacher Education in Europe. In 2007, she was a Visiting Scholar at Teachers College, Columbia University. She was formerly a post-primary teacher with City of Dublin VEC, Liberties College.

Dympna Devine, PhD, is a Senior Lecturer in the School of Education, UCD. She lectures in the sociology of education and childhood and directs the Structured PhD programme. She has published internationally in the areas of children's welfare and identities, ethnicity, migration and schooling, gender and educational management, and school and teacher effectiveness. She is General Editor of *Irish Educational Studies.* Her book *Immigration and Schooling in*

Ireland will be published with Manchester University Press in 2010. In 2006, she held a Marie Curie Fellowship at the Norwegian Centre for Child Research.

Sheelagh Drudy, PhD (Cantab), is Professor of Education at UCD and was Head of School 2000–2007. Her research and publications focus on: gender; social class and disability in education; and the sociology of teaching. She has been involved in policy development, having been a member of the National Education Convention Secretariat, the Higher Education Authority, the Senate of the NUI, the Task Force on Autism, the Tuning Educational Structures in Europe Project and the Teaching Council. In 2008, she was a Visiting Fellow at Lucy Cavendish College, Cambridge University.

Conor Galvin, BA MA (Kent) MPhil PhD (Cantab) is a Lecturer at UCD School of Education. He holds the President's Award for Teaching Excellence and speaks regularly at national and international events on public policy, ICT/digital literacy in higher education and 21st-century schooling. His interests include policy change, professional knowledge and lives, the social and political context of teaching, and the cultural politics of higher education. Before joining UCD, Dr Galvin worked at University of Wales, Swansea, and University of Cambridge, England.

Judith Harford, BA, MA, HDipEd, PhD, is Director of Teaching and Learning and Joint-Director of the Post-Graduate Diploma in Education at UCD. She has published internationally in the areas of gender and education, history of education and teacher education policy. She is a member of the Board of the Teacher Education Policy in Europe Network and a Convenor of the Teacher Education Research Network of the European Educational Research Association. She is series editor for Peter Lang ('Re-Thinking Education' Series) and a Visiting Research Associate at the Institute of Education, University of London (2009–10).

Maureen Killeavy, PhD, is Director of the National Pilot Project on Teacher Induction Post-Primary at the School of Education, UCD. Her research interests are wide-ranging and her publications include studies of teacher professional development, values education, learning and teaching, and mentoring. As Senior Lecturer and Senior Research Fellow, she served on a range of ministerial commissions and policy bodies. She has served on the Governing Authority of UCD and is a former president of both the Association for Teacher Education in Europe and the Irish Federation of University Teachers.

William Kinsella, BA, BSc(Psych), MA(EdPsych), HDipEd, HDip Remedial and Special Education, is an educational psychologist and lectures at the School of Education, UCD. He is Course Director of the MA and PhD Courses in Educational Psychology. He also lectures on other courses relating to teacher education and has a particular expertise in the area of special needs education. His areas of research include educational provision for pupils presenting with Autistic Spectrum Disorders and the inclusion of students with disabilities and special educational needs in mainstream schools.

Gerry Mac Ruairc, PhD, is a former primary-school teacher and member of the DES Inspectorate. He directs the Masters in Education programme and has recently been awarded a University Fellowship in Teaching and Academic Development. He is committed to providing insight into the reproduced patterns of inequality that persist in the education system through his publications and teaching. He maintains a theoretical and analytical focus on the complexity of the issue and the deeply embedded nature of the marginalisation in the structures and practices that constitute the education system.

Paul McElwee, PhD, has lectured in UCD in Science Education since 1980. He has published research in both science and science education and has been a visiting scholar at the University of New South Wales, Arizona State University and the University of Florida. As Head of Education and Senior Lecturer in Education in St Catherine's College of Education, he developed his interest in teaching methodologies that encourage students to think for themselves especially in the area of science.

Bernard McGettrick is a registered psychologist and an associate fellow of the Psychological Society of Ireland. He joined the School of Education, UCD, in 1986 and has lectured on a wide range of courses in the school and supervised research at postgraduate level. He was involved in the establishment of the MA in Educational Psychology and the MEd in Special Educational Needs. He was subsequently Director of the MA in Educational Psychology. Action research, reflective practice and the facilitation of student learning and development have been his areas of special interest.

Anne Moloney is Researcher Co-ordinator with the National Pilot Project on Teacher Induction Post-Primary. Her professional background is in teaching and she has previously worked with the National Council for Curriculum and Assessment and with the Primary Curriculum Support Programme. She has also worked in instructional design. Her main research interests are in teacher learning and the knowledge society. She is a member of the Ireland Executive Committee of the International Professional Development Association.

Lelia Murtagh is a Lecturer in the School of Education, UCD. Her main interests are first- and second-language acquisition, literacy, language assessment and research methods. She worked for many years as a researcher in the psycholinguistics section of the Linguistics Institute of Ireland (ITÉ), conducting national surveys of achievement in Irish and generally researching and publishing on the teaching and learning of Irish. Her doctorate, from Groningen University, published in 2003 focused on the attrition of second-language skills. She is currently engaged in a follow-up study.

Elizabeth O'Gorman teaches, lectures and facilitates workshops in the areas of teacher professional development, inclusion and special education needs. She is currently seconded as Lecturer to the School of Education, UCD. In addition to working in Ireland, she has worked in the United Kingdom and Hong Kong as both teacher and teacher educator. She has co-ordinated national and international research projects and is an invited peer-reviewer for journals in the fields of inclusive and special education with invitations to contribute to symposia and conferences worldwide.

Deirdre Raftery, PhD, is Deputy Head of the UCD School of Education and an international expert in the field of history of education. Her many publications include *Women and Learning in English Writing, 1600-1900* (1998) and (jointly): *Emily Davies, Selected Letters, 1861-1875* (2004); *Choosing a School: Second Level Education in Ireland* (2007); *Female Education in Ireland, 1700-1900: Minerva or Madonna?* (2007); *Gender Balance, Gender Bias: International Perspectives on Education* (2009). She is joint editor of the international journal *History of Education* and an honorary Life Member of Girton College, Cambridge.

Joyce Senior, PhD, is an educational psychologist and lecturer in psychology and inclusive education at the School of Education, UCD. She is Director of the Graduate Diploma and Masters Degree in Special Educational Needs. Her particular research interests are social and emotional behavioural difficulties and genetic and neurological conditions. She is author of the seminal study on epilepsy, *Educational, Medical and Advisory Provision for Children with Epilepsy in Ireland*.

INTRODUCTION

Sheelagh Drudy

This book presents research in a number of key areas of education. It has as one of its central propositions that education is essential to understanding the changes and challenges which Irish society faces. Irish education has undergone unprecedented change in the past two decades. Today, schools and other education institutions are very different places from what they were at the beginning of the 1990s, and are very greatly changed from the 19th and early 20th centuries.

This book begins with a historical perspective to provide a lens through which we can see the roots of the present system at a much earlier time. It then takes the early 1990s as a point of departure when schools had fairly homogeneous pupil populations. For example, while the second-level system was stratified, to a degree, along social-class lines, into secondary, vocational and community/comprehensive schools, within these strata, teachers encountered reasonably similar pupil profiles. Today, both primary and post-primary mainstream schools serve pupils from a much wider variety of individual needs and backgrounds.

Since the late 1990s, government policy has favoured the inclusion of children with disabilities in mainstream schools and classes, while still retaining a continuum of provision of special schools and classes to meet, in particular, the needs of children with more significant disabilities. Recent research indicates that the proportion of children with *assessed* disabilities (and thus in receipt of special supports) in mainstream schools varies from just over 5 per cent among the post-primary pupil population to slightly less than 4 per cent among primary-level pupils. This figure does not include the many children in mainstream schools who may have special educational needs but do not have an assessed disability. While acknowledging this, a small proportion of both primary and post-primary schools have much larger numbers with assessed disabilities/special educational needs and report that over 20 per cent of their pupils fall into this category (O'Gorman & Drudy, 2009).

In addition, schools now cater for children from a variety of cultural backgrounds. In some schools, there may be up to 20 nationalities and linguistic backgrounds, and children from a wide variety of religious backgrounds. By 2007, some 10 per cent of primary-school pupils were from immigrant or 'newcomer' families, of whom over three quarters were non-English speakers (Smyth et al., 2009, pp. 44–5). At second level, some 6 per cent of pupils were from immigrant families, of whom 70 per cent were non-English speakers. Again, some schools have a much higher proportion of their pupil populations comprising immigrant children. At primary and second level, there are some schools with over 20 per cent of their pupils in this category (ibid.).

In the early 1990s, no teacher had to work with another adult in the classroom. By 2009, not only is 'team teaching' much more common than previously, there are now more than 10,500 special needs assistants (Special Group on Public Service Numbers & Expenditures, 2009), compared to less than 300 in the late 1990s, and some 8,450 learning support and resource teachers, many of whom work alongside the mainstream teacher (Hanafin, 2007). In addition, teachers now have many young adults as pupils in their classrooms. The percentage of 18- and 19-year-olds in full-time education has increased from 51 per cent and 34 per cent respectively to 61 per cent and 45 per cent, some of whom are still in second-level and some in third-level institutions (Department of Education & Science, 2009b). However, in spite of more pupils staying on in education into early adulthood, there still is a significant problem of educational disadvantage based on social class and socio-economic status.

The skills and competences required to teach this diverse pupil population effectively, and to teach successfully with other adults in classrooms, are very different from the skills and competences which were needed at the beginning of the 1990s. As the current financial turmoil and consequent economic downturn begin to have a serious impact in Ireland, it is contended here that a significant route out of difficulty will be to develop Ireland as a 'knowledge economy'. This means raising student achievement at all levels of the system. Research has shown that student achievement is closely correlated with teacher quality and qualifications and this makes teacher education and the professional development of teachers an essential and important part of the creation of the knowledge economy. However, the challenges presented by the recession from 2008 onwards, and the resulting drop in the public finances, present a major test of the contribution that education can make. If all of the recommendations on cutbacks in education in the report of the Special Group on Public Service Numbers and Expenditure Programmes (2009) are incorporated into government policy, it is very difficult to see how Ireland can achieve a position at the forefront of innovation in Europe or even to make any kind of reasonable progress in that direction. Nor is it easy to see how education can contribute significantly to economic recovery.

Education policy making is, of course, the prerogative of government rather than of any expert group, specifically of the cabinet member designated as having particular responsibility for education, assisted and advised by his or her department, and approved by cabinet (Harris, 1989, p. 7). Nevertheless, while the ultimate maker of policy is the government, in modern democratic societies policy making is a more widespread and complex phenomenon. In education, it involves the ability of particular groups and mediators to affect national policies. In Ireland, these normally include the middle and upper-middle classes, the Churches, employers' representative groups, the teacher unions, educational management bodies and parent bodies (Drudy & Lynch, 1993, pp. 113-33). One must also include the influence of international organisations on Irish policy, especially the Organisation for Economic Co-operation and Development (OECD) and the European Union. Within Ireland, the wider range of groups with a legitimate interest in education became apparent in the early 1990s when a rather unique consultative process was established by the then minister as a prelude to the 1995 white paper on education and the first comprehensive Education Act in 1998. This process, the National Education Convention, involved the coming together of 42 representative bodies (including parents, employers, educational management bodies, teacher and other unions, the unemployed, farmers, students and many more) to make formal presentations on their positions and to debate issues in education (Coolahan, 1994).

In recent years, there has been a great deal of emphasis internationally on the need for 'evidence-based' policy making. There have been two dimensions to this. In one, prominence is given to the need for randomised and rigorously matched experiments evaluating replicable programmes and practices in order to form a basis for policy and practice in education (Slavin, 2002). In the other, weight is placed on utilising rigorous, high-standard, qualitative research in policy-making (Freeman et al., 2007). In fact, the educational research community should ensure that appropriate quality criteria are available for all approaches (Whitty, 2006).

In the light of the foregoing, *Education in Ireland: Challenge and Change* provides research evidence on key changes that have taken place in Irish education, especially in relation to inclusion and diversity, and on the forms of teacher education and professional development required to respond to the changes and challenges in the system. The policy implications of the changes are indicated in its different chapters.

The book assesses the ways in which Irish education has changed, how it deals with diversity and inclusion in schools, and teacher education: three extremely important agendas in the light of the growing demands of a knowledge economy. There is a focus on three central and very important themes: the changing system; diversity and inclusion in schools; and teacher education. The research presented under these headings outlines the changes and challenges that have happened in Ireland in a number of different educational areas, and their implications. All of the findings and their implications have to be assessed in the light of policy and legislative change, and possible future directions.

The book approaches its subject matter from two different but complementary perspectives. On the one hand, there is a strong thread which examines education from an egalitarian perspective and, on the other, there is a considerable focus on quality and professionalism in teaching. The challenge of creating inclusive schools from a system which has, in the past, been inherently unequal is one major dimension of the research reported here.

The second major aspect of the research in this book focuses on the recruitment and professional formation of high-quality teachers. While acknowledging that education alone cannot bring about social and economic change, the two components of egalitarian, effective and inclusive schools and a high-quality, well-educated teaching force form the bedrock on which a socially cohesive society and a knowledge economy can be built.

Part 1 focuses on significant changes that have taken place in the Irish education system at three different phases in its history—the 19th century, the early 20th century and the turn of the 21st century.

In order to provide a background and to lend perspective, in Chapter 1 Deirdre Raftery outlines some of the key legislative changes that have left a legacy to Irish education, especially at primary level. She also notes how the failure to enact certain changes had an important influence on Irish education, and comments on how the education system evolved and how policy was made which accommodated both legislated and 'unofficial' contexts and changes. The historical theme is also developed in Chapter 2 by Judith Harford. She explores, in particular, the opening up of the Irish university system to women in the latter part of the 19th century and up to the middle of the 20th century. In Chapter 3, Sheelagh Drudy focuses on the late 20th century and early 21st century. She considers education's role in building a knowledge economy and addresses the equally important issue of equality. This chapter is concerned with the educational policy challenges facing Ireland in a period of economic downturn.

Part 2 of the book analyses the changes in Irish schools arising from the inclusion of more diverse pupil populations. Given the changing patterns of immigration in the Republic of Ireland, in Chapter 4, Dympna Devine considers how factors related to ethnic and gender identity mediate children's interaction with one another in a newly multi-ethnic primary school. In chapters 5, 6 and 7, the challenges of the inclusion of children with disabilities in mainstream schools are explored. William Kinsella charts the organisational changes that are demanded in order for mainstream second-level schools to become inclusive. Joyce Senior focuses on a poorly understood learning disability, Attention Deficit Hyperactivity Disorder, and examines the school experiences of a cohort of students with ADHD. Máirín Barry identifies and examines features of inclusive education in two primary schools, one in Ireland and one in the state of Virginia in the United States. Through comparative analysis, she explores effective inclusive educational policy and practice. Gerry Mac Ruairc puts the crucial area of social class and socio-economic disadvantage under the microscope in Chapter 8. His discussion focuses on one element of social class and cultural practice, i.e. language and linguistic variation, by examining the manner in which different groups of children engage with standardised testing in schools. In Chapter 9, Lelia Murtagh addresses an aspect of linguistic diversity in schools in her exploration of the learning of Irish in primary and second-level schools. She looks at the place motivation plays in relation to students learning Irish in the school system by reviewing studies which have tried to measure the level of students' attitudes to learning Irish, the impact of socio-cultural and educational factors on motivation and the association between students' motivation and their achievement in Irish.

Part 3 of the book explores research on teacher education at all stages of the teaching career and discusses how teachers can adapt to the challenges of change. In Chapter 10, Sheelagh Drudy focuses on recruitment to primary teaching in both parts of Ireland. Particular emphasis is placed in this chapter on the relatively small proportion of males entering primary teaching. Marie Clarke focuses on the characteristics and experiences of recruits to second-level teaching on postgraduate diploma in education programmes in five universities. Maureen Killeavy and Anne Moloney analyse the importance and the process of the induction of newly qualified teachers. In Ireland there is not, as yet, an entitlement to systematic and resourced induction. Some of the results of a national pilot project to develop models of induction are described and findings from initial and ongoing research in the programme in relation to the supports and challenges for newly qualified teachers in Ireland are presented. In Chapter 13, Elizabeth O'Gorman presents evidence relating to the continuing professional development of teachers who support pupils with disabilities and special educational needs. She draws on an account of a large-scale research project that was conducted to explore the work of learning support and resource (LS/R) teachers in Ireland. The particular focus here is both the roles of LS/R teachers and the professional development which LS/R teachers seek in order to execute these roles effectively. In Chapter 14, Audrey Bryan explores teacher education relating to a more ethnically diverse pupil population. She highlights some of the complexities of teaching against racism for teacher educators and second-level teachers alike, and considers the implications for the ways in which teacher education can best prepare students to address issues of racism, inequality and discrimination in their own classrooms, and to work with culturally diverse student groups. Science education has been identified as a vital element in the creation of a knowledge economy and, in Chapter 15, Paul McElwee explores constructivist approaches and argues that they satisfy important criteria in relation to the teaching of science. Acknowledging the international drive towards making teaching a research-based profession, in Chapter 16, Bernard McGettrick argues that training in action research has the potential to substantially facilitate teachers to work in ever changing and complex situations. Finally, in Chapter 17, Conor Galvin illustrates that there are insights to be gained from considering the position of policy practitioners and thought leaders in the education policy process and the roles of a variety of actors and institutions at the supranational, national and sub-national levels in the policy process.

This book is published at a time of severe social and economic crisis. It provides the results of research and analysis that will contribute to the understanding of the education system and its importance to Ireland's social and economic development and well being. It provides information which illustrates the complexity of many of the challenges facing the education system and the need for policy makers to enable the education system to deliver on its mission of social, economic and cultural development, of providing a quality education, of facilitating greater participation and egalitarianism and of enabling all young people to achieve their potential.

Part 1
The Changing System

1

THE LEGACY OF LEGISLATION AND THE PRAGMATICS OF POLICY: HISTORICAL PERSPECTIVES ON SCHOOLING FOR IRISH CHILDREN

Deirdre Raftery

BACKGROUND

Our understanding of contemporary education in Ireland is greatly informed by gaining some insight into contexts and changes in the past. From such an endeavour, it is possible to see that no contemporary context has emerged within a vacuum, rather our education system has evolved. This process of evolution reflects the passing of a series of pieces of legislation, the impact of which can be seen today. The purpose of this chapter is to provide this book with the background to education change in Ireland that will be discussed in subsequent chapters, and it is perforce summative rather than comprehensive.

Subsequent chapters reflect research in areas such as education psychology and sociology, engaging with contemporary developments, and the book serves a unique function in bringing diverse disciplines together. The diversity to be found in this book anticipates somewhat the wide range of readers that will use this text. What is not attempted in this chapter, therefore, is an engagement with readers already deeply familiar with Irish education history, or with the discipline of history of education; such work is more suited to a specialist text or an academic journal published for scholars working in the history of education. There follows, instead, an attempt to paint on a broad canvas in a way that will help readers of this book, while not compromising the richness of the primary and secondary material used. The chapter includes references to a range of material that both students and general readers will find useful in pursuit of widening their understanding of the history of Irish education.

INTRODUCTION

The chapter outlines some of the key legislative changes that have left a legacy to Irish primary education. While many historians of education have referred in passing to education legislation in support of their studies of national, intermediate and higher education, there has been a tendency in historical research to privilege the social context of education and the experience of schooling rather than dwelling on the legislation itself.[1] One exception is Coolahan (1981, p. 4) who has noted that Ireland had 'a long tradition of state legislation [in] relation to education'. This chapter examines some of that tradition, noting the impetus for some legislative changes, scrutinising some relevant acts and describing some of the ways in which they found expression.

The chapter will also note how the failure to enact certain changes had an important influence on Irish education and it will comment on how the education system evolved and how policy was made that accommodated both legislated and 'unofficial' contexts and changes. What will become clear is that education laws and policy initiatives came about to 'make' contexts and not just in response to them. The Penal laws on education are example of this: they imposed restrictions in education to facilitate political and economic control.[2]

The chapter draws mainly on legislation introduced between the 16th and 19th centuries, and it also makes some reference to bills and official reports. These can give some indication of legislative changes that were proposed, even if they were not enacted; additionally, reports from commissions of enquiry and from official bodies can illuminate for us how the enacted legislation was realised.

For the 19th century and up to 1920, many official reports, and the findings and recommendations of parliamentary commissions set up to examine education in Ireland, are contained within the British Parliamentary Papers. Taken together, acts, bills and reports are the very bedrock for research into the history of education in Ireland, and their legacy for education is everywhere, even today.

The legislation under scrutiny here mainly dealt with primary education, and it illuminates the issue of Church–state relations in education in Ireland. Extracts from many other documents, including legislation, reports and recommendations of commissions of enquiry, can be sourced easily in Hyland and Milne's *Irish Educational Documents,* Vol. I. Extracts in this chapter which have been taken from this text are referenced verbatim (Hyland & Milne, 1987). Another most useful research tool is Parkes's *Irish Education in the British Parliamentary Papers in the Nineteenth Century and After, 1801–1920* (Parkes, 1978).

THE LEGACY OF LEGISLATION: PENAL TIMES

In Ireland in the 21st century, there is sustained public interest in the role of the Churches in schooling.[3] It is worth reflecting on the history of the labyrinthine connections between the Churches, the state and schooling in Ireland. In Ireland, the notion that there is a role for the Churches in education dates back at least to the sixth century. Foreigners had bestowed upon Ireland the title of *Insula sanctorum* (island of saints), and Colmcille had founded the monastery at Iona from which Christianity was carried to Scotland, the Orkneys and the Shetlands. Missionary work spread through northern England and to the continent, and Columbanus founded several major monastic settlements in Europe.

However, centuries of invasion brought about the destruction of the monasteries and introduced English and continental influences into Ireland. Nonetheless, medieval records show that education remained under Church auspices. By the 16th century, Tudor policy included that schools should facilitate spreading the influences of the Reformation in Ireland, and this viewpoint was very firmly consolidated during the Penal period, when a series of laws were enacted to proscribe Catholic education and to harness schooling in the support of Protestantism and loyalty to the crown. The Catholic Church lost its public role in education, and the Church of Ireland claimed that role.

The Penal laws that eroded Catholic education require some scrutiny, as they illustrate the view in which the government held the Irish Catholic population. The passing of these acts indicates a government view that the Catholic clergy and Catholic teachers posed a threat to the crown, and that only the threat of severe punishment could break the Catholic hold on Irish education. In 1695, An Act to Restrain Foreign Education was passed. It prohibited Catholics from sending their children abroad to be educated at centres of Catholic education in countries such as Spain and France, and from having their children educated anywhere by 'any Jesuit, seminary priest, friar, monk, or other popish person'. It also forbade that any money should thereafter be given to any Catholic 'priory, abbey, nunnery, college, school, or any religious house whatsoever'.[4] The final blow to Catholic education in Ireland was dealt by the absolute prohibition on Catholics running schools, as the law stated that 'no person whatsoever of the papist religion shall publicly teach school, or instruct youth in learning' (ibid.,

p. 48). In 1703 and 1709, threatening severe penalties, further pieces of legislation ensured that it was highly dangerous for any 'person of the popish religion' to send their children abroad or to be found teaching.[5]

One of the most significant outcomes of the Penal period was the emergence of an illegal and secretive system of schooling: the hedge schools (also called Pay Schools). Because hedge school masters moved regularly from town to town and were always wary of being reported to the authorities, they have left few records of their work and of the schools they operated. However, from the accounts of travellers in Ireland in the 18th century and from some official reports, it is possible to gain much insight into how this unofficial education system operated (McManus, 2002). By the end of the 18th century, there were some 9,000 of these hedge schools in existence catering for the majority of the Irish school-going population: the Catholic poor. So high was their reputation, that some Protestant families sent their children to them. The subjects provided included astronomy, land measurement, Greek, Latin, the English language, science and Mathematics. Such was the proficiency in the classical languages attained by some pupils at hedge schools that many of them spoke Latin and Greek on a daily basis. One contemporary recalled that some former hedge school pupils would 'meet at the fairs and buy pigs from each other without ever using a word but Latin'.[6]

The hedge schools were to have a lasting influence on education in Ireland. Emerging in direct response to harsh legislation, they were clear evidence of a native initiative to take control of schooling—even at the risk of punishment or deportation. Though the hedge schools were not, strictly speaking, a 'system', they formed the largest type of schooling in Ireland until the establishment of the national system in 1831. In 1782 and 1793, the Catholic Relief Acts removed the Penal laws relating to education. Up to that time, Irish Catholics continued to go abroad in pursuit of higher education, especially to study theology, and they had developed their own foundations in Spain, Italy, France and the Low Countries. It is perhaps not surprising that hedge schools, with their extraordinary legacy, have found their way into literature, drama and art, and indeed the defiant nature of their existence has added to the perception that the Irish people deeply valued education and that they were as much a land of scholars as a land of saints.

THE PROBLEM OF THE NATIVE POOR: SCHOOLING AND SOCIAL CONTROL

Throughout the late 17th and 18th centuries, there were repeated 'official' efforts to provide schools for the poor that would be an alternative to the hedge schools. Though no legislation was passed on this issue, governments showed a sustained interest in education by establishing a series of commissions of enquiry, the findings and recommendations of which provide researchers with considerable data.

In 1791, an Irish Education Enquiry was set up, which surveyed provision in the country at the end of the century, including parish schools, royal schools and diocesan schools. The report was not published until 1858, perhaps because of its radical proposal that there should be a central state board established to reorganise and manage the existing schools. The task of the commissioners was continued in 1806 after the Act of Union. Detailed accounts of Irish education can be found in the 14 Reports of the Commissioners of the Board of Education in Ireland that resulted. There is information on teaching, curriculum, attendance, daily routines, children's diet, discipline and labour undertaken by children in some schools. The reports were ordered by type of educational provision, so, for example, there are volumes on the Blue Coat Hospital, the Hibernian School, the schools founded by Erasmus Smith, and the 'classical schools of private foundation'. There is also a volume on the charter schools, the emergence of which reflected increasing interest in the education of the poor within hedge schools and a desire to establish a Protestant alternative.

The success of the hedge schools gave considerable concern to the hierarchy of the established Church. The Protestant Bishop of Killala had complained that in his diocese 'the popish schools [were] so numerous that a Protestant schoolmaster cannot get bread' (Cahill, 1940, p. 121). Archbishop Hugh Boulter argued that the only solution was to establish an education system supported by the government, with the aim of instructing 'the children of the Irish Natives ... in the English tongue and the Fundamental Principles of the true Religion'.[7] The petition, sent in turn to King George II, resulted in a charter being granted for the founding of the Incorporated Society for Promoting English Schools in Ireland. Its schools later became known as charter schools, and they were established with the expressed aim of raising children in the 'pure Protestant faith', and rescuing them from the 'dangers of superstition and idolatry' in which it was believed the Catholic 'natives' lived. The only substantial study of the charter schools is Milne's (1997) work, *The Irish Charter Schools, 1730–1830*, though some scholars have examined elements of charter school education in shorter works.[8] The aims of the charter schools merit some scrutiny as they illustrate how Irish Catholics were viewed at the time. These aims were:

> ... to [train] up the children of the papists ... before the corruptions of popery have taken root in their hearts; ... to strengthen his majesty's government, and the protestant interest of Ireland, by increasing the number of protestants ...; ... to cure by degrees, that habit of idleness, which is too prevalent among the poor of this kingdom ...; to introduce and spread, gradually, through the kingdom, the English spirit of improvement; ... [to dispense] charity in feeding, clothing and comforting many poor distressed children, orphans and foundlings ...
>
> Incorporated Society for Promoting English Protestant Schools, 1737, pp. 4-5

The charter also revealed the view that schooling for the 'native poor' should have a strong vocational element. The schools were to give children a practical training; small farms and factories were to be attached to the schools at which girls were taught to spin, knit and do domestic work, while boys learned 'husbandry and agriculture'. The pupils were to be given every encouragement to remain loyal to Protestantism and avoid turning back to Catholicism. For example, they were apprenticed to Protestant masters and mistresses, and they were given a premium of £5 if they completed their apprenticeships and married a Protestant. To remove the possible influence of Catholic homes, children were 'transplanted' to schools far from their homes and had little contact with their families again.[9] This was a policy that continued for over a century.

Pupils at charter schools had such a poor sense of their backgrounds that their evidence to the Commission of Irish Education Enquiry (1825) was to cause concern. They often had no idea of their age, when they had first entered the charter schools or how long they had been institutionalised, though they were able to give vivid accounts of some of the brutal treatment that they suffered at the hands of the school masters.

The First Report of the Commission of Irish Education Enquiry (1825) is a source that merits some scrutiny for its inclusion of children's evidence and for the stark honesty with which the brutal regime of the schools was reported. At Sligo charter school, the use of the birch rod, leather strap and wooden stick ensured that children laboured particularly hard at weaving; one pupil from that school testified that the master 'used to get hold of the [pupils'] neck, and knock their heads against the boards … and give them clouts in the jaw'. Another pupil gave an account of how the teacher would beat the children with a whip, and then 'seize them by the throat, and hold them till they were ready to faint' (Commission of Irish Education Inquiry, 1825, p. 159). Commenting on Kevin Street charter school, it was recorded by one pupil, Frances Coyle, that girls were beaten severely, and sometimes they were stripped for beatings. Coyle replied to the questions of the Commissioner that: 'The provost ordered one of the girls to be beaten, to get a horsewhip; she was a very bad girl, and she was stript and beat' (ibid., p. 256).

The charter schools drew criticism, both for the cruel treatment of children and because they did not facilitate the spread of literacy. The commissioners in 1824 were dismayed at the ignorance of pupils in the charter schools. Little school work was undertaken and the unhealthy conditions, together with the emphasis on labour, meant that children made poor progress. The schools became so unpopular with Catholics that their numbers fell dramatically in the second half of the 18th century. Commissioners' reports noted that children were being sent in increasing numbers to the hedge schools, even when such schools were very overcrowded and ill-equipped. For example, a charter school built at Newport to cater for 40 pupils, had only 12 pupils in 1824, while 96 children—including 38 Protestants—were attending the local, overcrowded hedge school (McManus, 2002, p. 21).

The strong involvement of Catholic diocesan priests in the education of Catholic children can be dated from about this time. While the Banishment Act of 1697 had greatly reduced the number of Catholic religious in the country, some diocesan priests availed themselves of the Registration Act, 1697 (United Kingdom, 1697a, 1697b). This allowed them to register with the civil authorities, and pay two sureties of £50, whereupon they could continue to minister if they demonstrated good behaviour.

Diocesan priests responded to the dangers of proselytism that the charter schools presented, and the influence of the hedge school masters, by taking firm control of schooling. They established a system of parish schools, which they themselves controlled, with the support of a fund set up in Rome. Priests consolidated their influence in local schooling in the early 19th century by supervising the work of the hedge school masters and by co-operating with them where possible, and they also provided the necessary 'approval' needed by a schoolmaster if he was to gain employment and be accepted by parents. The

Parochial Returns of 1824 show that teachers were either appointed by priests or they 'taught with the sanction and approbation of the priests, who visited the schools and superintended the instruction of the children' (Brennan, 1935, p. 62).

As McManus (2002) has noted, priests had no option but to work with hedge school masters and mistresses. There were 2,627 Catholics to every priest at the start of the 19th century, and since catechesis was the main objective of these priests, they relied on the co-operation of hedge school masters. Many masters were also involved in the Confraternity of Christian Doctrine, a Catholic revival movement that encouraged its members to attend chapel on Sunday and promote Sunday schools for Catholic children.

By the late 18th century, the repeal of relevant Penal laws on education and the increased involvement of religious in schooling, brought changes in the management and control of Irish education. A seminary was founded in Maynooth in 1795 to train candidates for the secular clergy while, at the same time, increasing numbers of religious congregations were establishing themselves in Ireland and opening schools. Catholic religious operated initially at a time when government funding for schools continued to be channelled through Protestant voluntary societies. One of these societies—the Kildare Place Society (KPS)—had been founded with a view to becoming the main provider of schooling and teacher-training, in order to 'afford the same facilities for education to all classes of professing Christians without any attempt to interfere with the peculiar religious opinions of any' (Society for Promoting the Education of the Poor of Ireland, 1820, p. 60). While the KPS enjoyed some popularity, and developed an elaborate and efficient system of provision of school supplies and training of teachers, it eventually fell into disrepute and was accused of discriminating against Catholics by allowing the Bible to be read 'without note or comment' within schools. Daniel O'Connell was at the forefront of the opposition to the KPS, arguing that this situation was unacceptable to Catholics. The increasing confidence of the Catholic Church meant that its rejection of the KPS as a possible national system of education was heeded. The schools were criticised by Dr James Warren Doyle, Bishop of Kildare and Leighlin, for instances of proselytism.

A victory for Catholic bishops was the setting up of the Commission of Irish Education Inquiry in 1824, which was established to investigate the state of schooling, including that provided by the KPS. While the reports of the commissioners did not lead to an instant resolution of the problem of mass education in Ireland, they certainly provided ample evidence that the various denominations had firm ideas on the principles that they believed should inform education, and indicated the limits of public tolerance on the question of denominational education.

The reports of the 1824 commission are a most important source in the history of Irish education. Even allowing for contemporary tastes and possible bias in accounts, the reports contain much detail on the different types of school and on education providers. The reports also are a useful point of reference when attempting to assess the relative success of subsequent provision, and they help to create the education context leading up to 1831, when the government of Earl Grey supported the establishment of a state-funded national system of education.

LITERACY FOR ALL: NATIONAL SCHOOLING

It is noteworthy that when the considerable machinery of the national system was put in place in 1831, there was no act to legislate for this major initiative in state-funded, mass education. This probably reflects the conservative position of the architects of the system, who were aware than it might have to be recalibrated at intervals and that it was something of an experiment. The experimental nature of the system has been noted by scholars such as Akenson (1970) and Coolahan (1981). As Coolahan has commented, 'Ireland, as a colony, could be used as an experimental milieu for social legislation which might not be tolerated in England ... thus education was one of a series of social policies such as an organised police force, improved health services, a Board of Works, which were introduced into Ireland in the 1830s' (Coolahan, 1981, p. 4).

The nature of the 'experiment' devised in 1831 was laid out in a letter written by the chief secretary of Ireland, E.G. Stanley, to the Duke of Leinster. In the letter, Stanley informed the duke of the intentions of the government to 'constitute a board for the superintendence of a system of national education', and invited him to become president of this new board. The letter became known simply as the 'Stanley Letter'.[10] While the Stanley Letter is a blueprint for change rather than a piece of legislation, it reflects both the experimental nature of the innovation and the emerging awareness that previous efforts at a state-supported, mass system, such as those of the KPS, had foundered on the 'denominational issue'. Examining this blueprint, it is possible to see how it had been created in a way that anticipated some resistance from parties, but it also showed commitment to spreading literacy among the 'native poor' and developing an effective system of teacher training.

The aim of the national system was to provide 'if possible a combined literary and a separate religious education … a system of National Education for the lower classes of the community' (ibid.). At the time of its inception, out of a population of some 8 million people, 6.5 million were Catholic, and there was pressure on the National Board to develop the system as one of non-denominational schooling, rather than to revert, once again, to supporting schooling via Protestant agencies. Over decades in which the system faced criticism and many challenges, it nonetheless increased in popularity; in 1831 the national schools enrolled over 100,000 children, and this number increased to almost 1 million within 40 years.

The establishment of the national system involved creating several administrative layers and a detailed reporting mechanism. As a consequence, there are many records of national schooling in Ireland with which the scholar can work. An unpaid National Board of Commissioners was formed, and the annual reports of this board contain much data gathered on schools, enrolments and attendance, books and materials, and the training and payment of teachers. The titles of the schools were vested in trustees, though some were non-vested, and each school had a patron, usually the local bishop or ecclesiastical authority, who took the initiative in setting up the school. The patron appointed a school manager, also often a local clergyman, who, in turn, employed the teachers and managed the school. The record-keeping attendant in managing a national school has left school registers and roll books, discipline books and inspectors' report books.[11] The practice whereby national schools were obliged to use textbooks created and supplied by the Commissioners for National Education has resulted in a significant number of such books remaining in libraries and repositories, from which scholars can get a good idea of the academic diet of the school children.[12]

These sources combine to give a sense of the changing face of primary schooling after 1831. While the initial plan was that the system would support non-denominational schooling, it quickly became denominational. The different Churches expressed antipathy to elements of non-denominationalism, that, initially, threatened to destroy Stanley's plans. The Presbyterian objection was to the denominationally mixed nature of the board, and the powers this board had over schoolbooks and teachers. There was additional hostility to the fact that the Bible had been removed from the centre of education and to the rule that religious instruction was to take place separately from literary instruction. The Church of Ireland also objected to the latter regulation, and to the weakening of its control in education. The Catholic Church had a complex relationship with the system; while it initially tolerated it for any potential benefits to Catholic children, it became hostile to the principle of mixed education. By 1836, the Christian Brothers had openly demonstrated their concern with the influences of Protestantism and British culture, and they withdrew their schools from the system.

The national system made slow progress in the early decades of its existence. Nonetheless, the machinery of the system continued to be developed and promoted. Most particularly, the 'five graded reading books' produced for use in schools continued to be modified, produced and distributed into schools in an attempt to provide a solid education that avoided instruction in the Irish language, history and culture, and made a modest use of Protestant religious tracts.

The aim of the first and second reader was to introduce children to simple words and short sentences, while the advanced readers had short lessons on the history of the British monarchy, the geography of England and some natural science. There was also occasional use of extracts from works by evangelical writers such as Hannah More and Sarah Trimmer, and there were special 'female reading books' for use by girls, that delivered lessons on domestic economy, and the need to be meek and humble. The *Reading Book for Use of Female Schools* appeared in 1854, and was followed by the *Girls' Reading Book for Use of Schools* (1864). In 1869, the commissioners added the *Manual for Needlework* and, in 1885, they produced *Short Lessons in Domestic Science*, both directed at girls. The *Manual for Needlework* advised its young readers that: '… a practical knowledge of plain needlework is, probably the most important acquirement for females, especially for those attending the National Schools of Ireland' (Commissioners of National Education in Ireland, 1869, preface (unnumbered)).

The all-pervasive tone of the reading books produced by the Commissioners for National Education in Ireland was that children should learn self-control and obedience to their elders and betters; additionally, a message of social control permeated the books, leading many scholars to argue that the reading books— and indeed the schools—facilitated the British cultural assimilation policy for 19th-century Ireland. Indeed, Goldstrom (1972), in the only substantial examination of national school textbooks, adopted the perspective that the textbooks facilitated 'social control'. The relative failure of the system to contribute effectively to that policy is, in part, because progress by pupils was very poor: there were high levels of absenteeism and early school withdrawal, and there was also the impact of famine which resulted in disease, death and mass emigration. It is perhaps unsurprising that during the first 50 years of the national system, the majority of Irish children did not progress beyond the second reader (see Goldstrom, 1972; Coolahan, 1981; Raftery & Parkes, 2007).

Reflecting a commitment to gathering and analysing 'useful facts' that was characteristic of the Victorians, it was decided in 1868 to appoint a commission, under the chairmanship of Lord Powis, to assess the state of national education in Ireland and to determine whether or not the system was providing value for money. Once again, it is possible to see how detailed gathering of information, bound and catalogued within the British Parliamentary Papers, provides scholars and readers with a legacy of source material on schooling in Ireland. Some of the recommendations of the Powis Commission would have far-reaching effects on schooling, literacy levels and on the teaching profession. One of the recommendations was the introduction of a system of payment-by-results, whereby national school teachers were paid 'results fees', in addition to their salary, depending on the performance of their pupils. A scale of payments was devised for each subject at each level (see Table 1.1). By the end of the century, 'a teacher's salary could vary from £30 (for a female assistant teacher) to over £70 (for a male first-class teacher)' (Hyland & Milne, 1987, p. 129) and the additional payments on the basis of pupils' results were calculated and added to the basic salary.

The introduction of payment by results contributed significantly to increasing the reading and writing proficiency of pupils, and it is fair to say that this kind of progress was to lead to a need for a system of intermediate (or second-level) education. When the Intermediate Education Ireland Act was passed in 1878, it provided young men and women with a route into civil-service jobs and the universities, opening up well-paid careers and the 'learned' professions to Irish Catholics.

Table 1.1: Results fees paid per pupil for each subject at each level

Ordinary and optional branches—fees for passes								
	Infants Class	First Class	Second Class	Third Class	Fourth Class	Fifth Class 1st stage	Fifth Class 2nd stage	Sixth Class 1st & 2nd exams
Subjects	s d	s d	s d	s d	s d	s d	s d	s d
Infants' course	3 0	–	–	–	–	–	–	–
Reading	–	2 0	2 0	2 6	2 6	2 6	2 6	2 6
Spelling	–	1 0	1 0	1 0	1 0	1 0	1 0	1 0
Writing	–	1 0	1 0	1 6	1 6	1 6	1 6	1 0
Arithmetic	–	1 0	2 0	2 6	2 6	2 6	2 6	1 0
Grammar	–	–	–	1 0	1 6	1 6	1 6	1 6
Geography	–	–	–	1 0	1 0	1 6	1 6	1 6
Bookkeeping (optional for boys & girls)	–	–	–	–	–	2 6	2 6	3 0
Needlework 1 (for girls)	–	–	–	–	4 0	5 0	5 0	5 0
Agriculture	–	–	–	–	4 0	5 0	5 0	5 0
Vocal music (optional for boys & girls)	–	–	2 6	2 6	2 6	2 6	2 6	3 0

Source: Commissioners of National Education in Ireland, (1872). In: Hyland & Milne, Irish Education Documents, Vol. I. p. 129.

CONCLUDING COMMENTS

Though it is beyond the scope of this chapter to discuss the far-reaching consequences of late 19th century legislation and policy in Irish education, it is possible to see strong points of connection between many of the major education innovations from Penal times to the mid-19th century, and to tentatively suggest that the legacy of policy and legislation can be clearly seen today.

The most obvious legacy is the ongoing debate about whether or not the

Churches should have a role in managing schools. As seen in this chapter, the relationship between Church and school was formally recognised as early as Penal times, when the position of the Anglican Church in Ireland was supported through education legislation and through the efforts of the proselytising agencies involved in education.

From this time too, and perhaps even more obviously in the 19th century, there was a clear recognition that schools could be used as agents of social control. The long and often painful history of the relationship between schooling and control spans centuries in which the Irish language and culture were almost erased, and a state-supported, national system of schooling was established to promote literacy in the English language.

The tendency to privilege 'academic' education and memory work can also be traced to the founding stages of the national system, though, as this chapter has indicated, the indigenous hedge schools also promoted scholarly pursuits and education in the Classics. With an explicit favouring of rote-learning and drill, the payment by results era, that was ushered in following the findings of the Powis Commission in 1870, would cast a long shadow on the organisation of schooling and would give status to the use of terminal assessments. A superficial examination of the payment by results scheme also shows how the formal curriculum was becoming 'gendered'. Traditionally 'male' and 'female' subjects were valued differently, as was the work of men and women teachers. While needlework attracted a modest payment of 2s 6d for every successful fifth class girl, the 'male' subject of agriculture drew a payment of 5s at the equivalent level, and male teachers were paid higher basic salaries than their female counterparts.

Considering some of these issues at this early point in this book will allow the reader to remain mindful of the fact that the history of education can help us to understand and contextualise better many of the concerns of educators and education researchers today.

ENDNOTES

1   Useful studies which examine the social context of education include Goldstrom (1972), Akenson (1975) and Titley (1983).

2   An act to restrain foreign education (7 Will. c.4 (1695)); an act to prevent the further growth of popery (2 Anne c.6 (1703)), see Hyland & Milne (1987).

3 In 2009, the Catholic Church was patron of 2,899 of the state's 3,282 of primary schools. The Catholic Archbishop of Dublin, Diarmuid Martin, signalled that the time had come to review this position and to bring about a change whereby some schools would be handed over to the state.

4 An act to restrain foreign education (7 Will. c.4 (1695), see Hyland & Milne (1987) p. 47).

5 An act to prevent the further growth of popery (2 Anne c.6 (1703)); an act for explaining and emending an act entitled. An act to prevent the further growth of popery (8 Anne c.3 (1709) see Hyland & Milne (1987) p. 48-9.

6 R. Herbert, 'Four Limerick hedge schoolmasters' *Irish Monthly* (1944), as cited in McManus (2002).

7 Report made by His Ggrace, the Lord Primate to the House of Lords Committee, 226-7, quoted in Jones (1938).

8 See, for example, Coleman (2001). The charter schools are also discussed in Robins (1980).

9 For a map showing the location of the charter schools see Milne (1997) p. 172.

10 Letter from the Secretary for Ireland to His Grace the Duke of Leinster on the formation of a Board of Education; 1831–2 (196.) XXIX. 757.

11 For an examination of inspection see O Héideáin (1967); see also Akenson (1970).

12 For a detailed examination of the national system of education see Akenson (1970). The national system is also discussed in Atkinson (1969) and Daly (1979).

2

'WORDS IMPORTING THE MASCULINE GENDER INCLUDES FEMALES':[1] WOMEN AT UNIVERSITY COLLEGE DUBLIN IN THE FIRST DECADE OF THE 20TH CENTURY

Judith Harford

I t is perhaps difficult to conceive of a time when women in Ireland were excluded from entry into university solely on the basis of gender. This, however, was the case until the closing decades of the 19th century. Women gained access to the Royal University of Ireland in 1879, to the Queen's Colleges from the 1880s and to Trinity College Dublin in 1904 (Harford, 2008).[2] The opening of universities to women in Britain and the growing strength of the women's lobby internationally meant that, by 1908, University College Dublin (UCD), one of the three constituent colleges of the newly established National University of Ireland (NUI), had no alternative but to open its doors to women on equal terms as men.

While those women who passed through the doors of UCD in the first decade represented a minority of middle-class women whose social, cultural and economic position enabled them to benefit from reform of higher education, their participation in higher education had wider social implications. It shattered the Victorian ideal of womanhood which confined women to a life in the private sphere and, for the first time, allowed women access to the professions, previously a male preserve, thus extending the potential and capacity for women's involvement in wider social and political arenas. Gains were slow and tentative, however. The scale of opposition to reform was considerable, with public discourse objecting to the admission of women to universities on religious, moral and physiological grounds.

The reform of women's higher education in the latter part of the 19th century did not occur in a vacuum but was part of a wider climate of reform which sought to improve the social, economic and political status of women (Evans, 1977). Similar movements were also emerging across Europe and the United States, where educational reform became part of a wider movement for economic and political autonomy. Demands for improved educational and employment opportunities led to a series of further demands, including property and child-custody rights for married women, female representation on public boards and local authorities, the right to vote in local elections, and, ultimately, the right to the parliamentary vote (Cullen Owens, 2005, p. 4). This process was paralleled in most Western countries, and is described by Evans as 'the history of a progressively widening set of objectives' (Evans, 1977, p. 34). The reform campaign also took place against the backdrop of the wider 'Irish university question' which had dominated the political agenda since at least the 1850s. The key 'question' which successive governments had failed to answer was how best to accommodate the demands of lay Catholics to a university education in line with Catholic principles while promoting a non-denominational policy agenda. The politically charged nature of the 'university question' was such that it was never purely an issue of educational provision. As Coolahan (2008, p. 3) has noted 'the university question was never purely an educational issue; it was interpenetrated by political, religious and economic considerations'. Although the focus of interest was unapologetically on Catholic males, Catholic, and indeed all, women profited from aligning their campaign to the wider university question.

What were the objectives of those women lobbying for reform in higher education in the latter half of the 19th century? In the early stages of the campaign, demands for educational reform were based on conservative and socially acceptable arguments, namely that access to higher education would better equip women to carry out their role as wives and mothers. At this point, those advocating reform argued for the endowment of single-sex, denominational women's colleges in which women would receive an education comparable to their male counterparts. The pioneering women's colleges were the Ladies' Collegiate School (1859), later renamed Victoria College Belfast, and Alexandra College Dublin (1866). The former was founded by Margaret Byers, Presbyterian educationalist and temperance activist, while Anne Jellicoe, prominent Quaker and educationalist, was the vision behind the latter. Both colleges shared much in common with the ideology and ethos of new academic schools and colleges for middle-class girls emerging in England at the same time, which promoted the study of Latin and Mathematics, in an effort to bring the education of girls in line with that of boys (Dyhouse, 1981; 1995). Central to their mission was the securing of the right of girls to participate in the public examination arena, including the recently established examinations of the Intermediate Board and the Royal University of Ireland. Success in such examinations meant the acquisition of valuable cultural capital which could, in turn, be transferred to the field of employment (Jacobs, 2007).

Catholic women's colleges were slower to emerge because of the Catholic hierarchy's opposition to the new direction in the higher education of women which, it warned, could damage the moral fabric of the family. The Catholic Church was the dominant force in Irish social and political life at this time and was a key agent in shaping educational policy and provision at all levels. While it diligently pursued the goal of providing for the higher education needs of Catholic males, it initially dismissed the appeals of Catholic women for access to higher education within a Catholic setting (Harford, 2005). However, when it emerged that Catholic women were prepared to source higher education in non-Catholic establishments, the hierarchy was left with no alternative but to revisit its policy and cater for the needs of Catholic women in the higher education arena. Motivated by the perceived threat of proselytism, the hierarchy supported the establishment of a series of Catholic women's colleges from the 1880s, the most successful of which were St Mary's University College, Merrion Square (1893), operating under the auspices of the Dominican order, and Loreto College, St Stephen's Green (1893).

The women's colleges were highly significant to the wider reform movement for a number of reasons. They were established with the purpose of targeting the more prestigious and valuable domains of knowledge, which resulted in participating women students having access to a range of high prestige cultural and social capital (Harford, 2007). They provided teaching in the liberal arts, exposing women for the first time to a rigorous academic curriculum and to participation in the public examination arena. They also promoted participation in student societies, which advanced women's capacity to fulfil a more public and active role in 19th-century Irish society. Many of the prominent women activists of the period, including Mary Hayden, Agnes O'Farrelly, Alice Oldham and Hanna Sheehy Skeffington, were students and subsequently teachers at these colleges. Although the colleges did not enjoy the status and prestige of the older universities, they provided a structure and a framework to the embryonic women's higher education campaign at a critical and formative juncture.

Notwithstanding the success of the women's colleges, by the turn of the century, women were no longer content to be 'shut up in women's colleges'. Despite the views of a minority of women that women's experience of higher education both as students and as academics would be more positive in women's colleges, by this stage, the majority of women desired full and unequivocal access to the university domain, on equal terms as their male counterparts. Trinity College Dublin's decision to finally admit women in 1904 following decades of trenchant opposition sealed the fate of the women's colleges and gave further momentum to the campaign for full access to the university domain. In the end, it proved expedient to admit women rather than to risk the recognition of Alexandra College Dublin as a women's college within the University of Dublin, in which Trinity had been, since its foundation in 1592, the sole constituent college. Such a framework might have led to the recognition of a Catholic college within the University of Dublin which would have been staunchly opposed by college authorities (McCartney, 1999, pp. 25–6).

Following numerous attempted settlements, a final solution to the university question was reached under the Irish Universities Act of 1908. Under the terms of the act, the Royal University of Ireland was dissolved, Queen's College Belfast was elevated to the status of a university in its own right and the National University of Ireland, with its three constituent colleges—University College Dublin, University College Cork and University College Galway—was established (Coolahan, 1981, p. 123). Non-denominational and state-funded, there was a prohibition on religious tests and 'no test whatever of religious belief' was to be imposed on professors, lecturers, fellows, scholars, exhibitioners, graduates or students. However, although both universities were theoretically non-denominational, the act was, in many ways, a clever compromise, conceding to the demands for denominational education on both sides without overtly supporting it. As Pašeta (2000, p. 282) notes, 'covertly sectarian', the act ensured that Queen's University Belfast catered for Presbyterians, while the NUI catered primarily for Catholics.

Although non-denominational by statute, in December 1914, UCD was considered 'thoroughly Catholic in its actual tone' (*National Student*, 1910–15). One of the objectives of the new university was to fulfil its potential to be 'national' and the driving force in the shaping of a new Ireland. The early decades in the life of the university were shaped both by its Catholic identity and its nationalist stance. Many of the early graduates would become, to cite Kate O'Brien, novelist and playwright, and a student of UCD in the period 1916–19, 'strong torches, across the dark field of this extraordinary period' (O'Brien, 1955, p. 3). Many of the early academics and students would significantly shape the consciousness of the emerging nation. Prominent women associated with UCD in this embryonic phase of its development included Mary Colum, Louise Gavan Duffy, Mary Hayden, Kate O'Brien and Agnes O'Farrelly. Described in

May 1910 as 'an engine of national culture' (*National Student*, 1910–15), the university represented a literary and political nucleus at the very core of an emerging nation. The literary movement, the Gaelic League and the Sinn Féin movement were all part of its evolution. It was synonymous with what Pašeta refers to as 'the rising Catholic university elite' (1999, p. 53).

The 1908 settlement had, in many ways, presented women with numerous possibilities. Unlike those women who entered Trinity College in 1904, women entering UCD were part of a new beginning. As a result, they were less subject to the kind of rigorous monitoring and control to which Trinity women were subjected. As a method of limiting women's impact across the university, women students attending Trinity College were required to leave the campus by 6 p.m. each evening and women academics were prohibited from using the Common Room (Parkes, 2004, p. 55). Their hall of residence, situated in Dartry, was also a significant distance from the university which also meant their movements were restricted. Commenting on the relative freedom of women attending UCD, Mary Ellen Murray, a student of UCD in the 1920s, noted:

> Grafton Street in the 1920s was a pedestrian precinct and during the fashionable hours it was crowded with smartly dressed people strolling along at a leisurely pace, window shopping, stopping to chat with acquaintances, and dropping in for afternoon tea to one of the many cafes. During term a considerable portion of the throng was composed of university students from both UCD and Trinity College. The Trinity students on parade were almost exclusively male. The reason for this may have been that the Trinity Hall of Residence for women was in Dartry, a considerable distance from the college, but there was also the fact that at this period Trinity was very much a male preserve and women were excluded from many college activities. The Trinity men students were easily distinguishable from their UCD counterparts. They were usually better dressed, seemed more mature and self confident, and many of them spoke with an English accent. We eyed them with interest and curiosity as if they belonged to a different species![3]

As Murray notes, the location of the women's residence and its proximity to the college was a key factor in the experience of women students. When it officially opened in November 1909, UCD was divided across buildings at Earlsfort Terrace, St Stephen's Green and Cecilia Street, all within walking distance of the city centre. The majority of women students attended lectures at St Stephen's

Green, where the Faculty of Arts was located and Cecilia Street where the Faculty of Medicine was located. A reading room, cloakroom and sitting rooms for female students were also provided at 82 St Stephen's Green. The majority resided at either Loreto Hall or St Mary's Dominican Hall, both located on St Stephen's Green and hence just a short distance from the hive of university activity. Both residences offered extra social and cultural activities for women students, including the production of plays and musicals as well as society meetings. The residences also attracted many prominent members of the Catholic intelligentsia, including the poet and novelist Katharine Tynan and the author Shane Leslie.

Nonetheless, although subject to less rigorous control than women attending Trinity College, women attending UCD were subject to a strict code of discipline designed to safeguard propriety in the co-educational university. A 'Lady Superintendent', E.H. Ennis, was charged with responsibility over students' 'general conduct outside the precincts of the College' (*University College Dublin Calendar, 1910–11*, p. 83). Within lecture settings, a 'Sunday school atmosphere' and a 'frigid decorum of behaviour' were said to prevail (*National Student*, 1910–15).

A series of rules was also drawn up to monitor the movements of women students. These included the following: students were forbidden from organising or attending any entertainment in lodgings which may encourage the attendance of both men and women students; women students not residing with their parents were required to obtain permission of their Officers of Residence before accepting invitations to dances 'or similar entertainments' and; men and women students were not permitted to reside in the same lodging house, except in the case of members of the same family, and in cases approved by the Officers of Residence.

Poking fun at the code of discipline, the *National Student*, the college magazine, proposed alternative rules for students in its December 1915 edition. Among the rules proposed for 'lady' students were 'no Lady Student is to have hair the same colour as any male student' and 'no Lady Student is to have feet of the same size as any male student ... Lady Students are debarred, under penalty of rustication, from appearing without at least four chaperons within three miles of St Stephen's Green' and 'if a Lady Student sees a male student in the College she is to do penance in sackcloth and ashes for the space of the calendar month' (*National Student*, 1910–15). Nonetheless, despite the frivolity of the editors of the *National Student*, the code of discipline was strictly enforced. Students who breached the rules of discipline, particularly in relation to the unauthorised mixing of male and female students, were immediately reprimanded. A perceived breach of the code of conduct by two women students who had held a dance in their lodgings in March 1914 resulted in the president of the college requesting a full apology and writing to the students' parents.

Yet, despite the limits imposed on the freedom of students, the new life of the university provided excitement and stimulation for both men and women. Kate O'Brien recalled her time at Loreto Hall as follows:

> Granted we had to be indoors at eleven—but some of the greatest men of the thirteenth and fourteenth centuries had to accept a nine o'clock curfew in Paris and Salamanca. After 'lights out' we lit candles in our cubicles and heated up Bovril and crept downstairs and stole Mother Eucharia's honey and brown bread. We were always hungry and seem to have been always impelled to talk and argue half the night.
>
> O'Brien, 1955, p. 6

It is perhaps not surprising that the majority of women students attending UCD in 1909 enrolled in Arts, since women had historically concentrated their efforts in this field. Of the 42 women who entered in this year, 29 enrolled in Arts, the remaining 13 enrolling in medicine. The majority of women students who had gone through the Royal University of Ireland were successful in the area of Arts, and modern languages in particular. As Mary Colum, the writer and literary critic, noted 'myself and nearly all my fellow students among the girls were going in for the same sort of degree in modern languages and literatures—the girls at the time in Dublin rarely went in for a classical or mathematical degree' (Colum, 1947, p. 81). However, not all parents viewed an Arts degree as an appropriate choice of discipline for their daughters. Mary Lavin, short-story writer and novelist and a student of UCD in the 1930s, recalled her father Tom Lavin bringing along 'a big wad of cash' when enrolling her, and on hearing what the Arts degree fee was, he reputedly asked, 'What kind of a degree is this Arts anyway, Mary, if it's so cheap?' (Walsh, 2005, p. 123).

Women continued to dominate in the field of Arts and in the area of social science which emerged in the 1960s. The propensity of women to gravitate towards Arts and shy away from fields such as Engineering and Architecture reflected the long-term legacy of the gendered nature of the curriculum, both formal and hidden (Lynch, 1989a; Kehily, 2002).

Quite a significant number of women students who registered in the session 1909–10 went on to work as teachers. The names of eight women students enrolled in Arts in 1909 appear on the first Register of the Intermediate School Teachers in Ireland, published in 1919. Teaching was an obvious career choice for female graduates in Arts, as it was in many ways a continuation of the nurturing role (Blackmore & Kenway, 1993; Drudy et al., 2005). A teaching diploma had been introduced in 1899 in the Royal University of Ireland and UCD subsequently introduced a Diploma in Education under the direction of Professor Timothy Corcoran, Roman Catholic priest and educationalist.

The number of women enrolled in the Faculty of Medicine is perhaps more surprising in that medicine was one of the oldest professions dominated by men. However, by 1909, women had already made significant inroads into the medical profession in Ireland. One of the most important dates in the history of women's involvement in the medical profession in Ireland was the decision in 1876 of the Royal College of Physicians of Ireland to open its examinations to women (Finn, 2000). In 1885, the Royal College of Surgeons in Ireland had decided to extend its privileges to women and, by 1896, the medical schools of the Queen's Colleges and the Medical School, Cecilia Street, were also open to women students. By 1919–20, women numbered one in six of the medical students at UCD (McCartney, 1999, p. 82).

Women embraced the opportunity to become involved in student societies and used the social network represented by the societies to advance their role in the college and in wider society. Among the societies in which women were active in the early years were the Scientific Society, the Chorale Society, the English Literary Society, the Medical Society, the Gaelic Society and the Literary and Historical Society (L & H). The admission of women to the L & H was a significant breakthrough, following decades of resistance when the society was part of the former Catholic University. Their admission was, however, not universally welcomed:

The entrance of ladies marked an epoch in our history. Whether we wished for their presence or not was shown by the fact that by an unfortunate instance of 'rules run mad' *they* voted *themselves* into the rights of membership. They have added practically nothing to the speaking force, yet they take up a good deal of room, and one is sorry to see that from such a deal of impressiveness so little should have come.

July 1911 (*National Student* 1910–15)

Women students and academics also became actively involved in external political organisations such as Cumann na mBan (the Irish Women's Council) which was founded in 1914 as a women's auxiliary to the Irish Volunteers (Cullen, 1997, p. 271). Prominent UCD women associated with the organisation included Louise Gavan Duffy and Agnes O'Farrelly.

Gavan Duffy, a founder member of the organisation, was one of the more prominent UCD women to take part in the 1916 Rising. She graduated with a BA in 1911 and an MA in 1916. In January 1914, prior to completing her Masters, she was appointed to the post of Assistant in the Education Department, working alongside Timothy Corcoran. She subsequently taught at St Ita's School before co-founding Scoil Bhride, an Irish-language secondary school for girls, in her own home at St Stephen's Green in 1917. The school later transferred to Pembroke Road and then on to Earlsfort Terrace, where it was used by student teachers in the college's Education Department (Walsh, 2007, pp. 332-3). O'Farrelly, also a prominent member of Cumann na mBan and a member of the executive of the Gaelic League, was one of the first women appointed to a lectureship in UCD in 1909. She was subsequently appointed Professor of Modern Irish Poetry following the resignation of Douglas Hyde in 1932. Deeply committed to the revival of the Irish language and Irish culture across the college, she was active in the Gaelic Society and was also behind the establishment of a Camogie Club in May 1914. Commenting on her experience in the Camogie Club, one student noted:

> We have a Camogie Club here. We refused to play that horrid English game-hockey; besides, you have to run too much in it ... Our superiors told us it was not a lady-like game—fit rather for the masculine woman. We go out to Terenure on Thursdays and Sundays. The boys are not allowed out on those days, although some hang around, pretending to play football!
>
> June 1914 (*National Student*, 1910–15)

As McCartney (1999, p. 83) notes, 'the ratio of women to men among the academic staff had started out on a promising note'. The original appointment of statutory staff under Statutes I and II provided for the establishment of 45 professorships and six statutory lectureships. Three women were appointed to professorships and one to a lectureship. Yet, despite the significant number of women appointed to senior academic posts, it must be remembered that their number, as a proportion of the entire university staff, was small. Furthermore, all senior appointments were in the Faculty of Arts, and this remained the trend for some time. Women appointed at this level included: Mary Hayden, Professor of Modern Irish History; Mary Macken, Professor of German; Maria Degani, Professor of Italian and Spanish; and Agnes O'Farrelly, lecturer in Irish language. Of these women, Hayden was without doubt the most formidable. The daughter of Thomas Hayden, former Vice-President of the Royal College of Physicians and member of the Senate of the RUI, she had been educated at the Ursuline Convent, Thurles, before studying at both Alexandra College and St Mary's University College. She was nominated as the only woman member of the Senate of the NUI, in 1909, and was appointed Professor of Modern Irish History in 1911. She was also Vice-President of the Irish Association of Women Graduates (IAWG), an organisation founded in 1902 to 'promote the interests of women under any scheme of University Education in Ireland, and to secure that all the advantages of such education shall be open to women equally with men' (IAWG to the Chancellor and Senators of the National University, n.d.). Although its central focus was university reform, the IAWG also became involved in the debate over teacher registration and worked to advance employment opportunities for women. A student attending Hayden's lectures in the early days at UCD recalled her as 'brisk and matter of fact without being fussy. Far from expecting to be waited on, she stepped up on a chair, hung up her map, and started work without a trace of ceremony' (*The Lanthorn*, December 1942). Nonetheless, the presence of women academics among the senior layer of the academy did not last and, by 1949, there was only one woman professor on staff, Kathleen Cunningham.

Perhaps what is most surprising about the unconditional admission of women to University College Dublin in 1909 was the lack of upheaval to college life, following a period of intense struggle and resistance. When examining the official records of the college for this period, the absence of any comprehensive engagement with the admission or inclusion of women students is remarkable. In part, this was due to the gradual and fragmented way in which women had gained access to the wider university domain during the previous decade, however, it was also due to the collective acceptance of the inevitable integration of women into the university sphere.

By the end of the first decade of the 20th century, the argument for a single-sex college was no longer to be heard. The integration of women into the life of the university was facilitated, in no small part, by a strong, resilient cluster of women academics, keen to provide women students with a positive and fruitful experience of university education. Hayden and O'Farrelly, in particular, were highly active and visible members of the university, and particularly vocal in relation to issues affecting women students and academics. Their presence ensured a voice for women students and they were highly regarded in the academic community. However, while the first decade of women's admission was largely a success, particularly in relation to the number of senior academic posts occupied by women, the history of UCD has not always been so supportive of women academics. This struggle continues today, as the battle of women academics to obtain equal participation at all levels within the university structure remains active.

ENDNOTES

1   *University College Dublin Calendar for Session 1910–11*, Archives Department, University College Dublin.

2   This research has been supported by a grant from University College Dublin. This support is gratefully acknowledged.

3   I am grateful to Conor Ward, Professor Emeritus of Social Science, University College Dublin, for providing me with a copy of his first cousin's recollections of her time at UCD.

3
EDUCATION AND THE KNOWLEDGE ECONOMY: A CHALLENGE FOR IRELAND IN CHANGING TIMES

Sheelagh Drudy

INTRODUCTION

Since the 1960s, education has been seen as central to social and economic development in Ireland and, over the past decade, policy has focused in particular on education's role in building a 'knowledge economy' and enhancing social cohesion. This chapter focuses on policy choices relating to these themes in order to provide a basis for understanding the link between education and sustainable social and economic development.

First, it looks at a number of background issues, including economic growth, inequality and recession. The chapter then considers the concept of the knowledge economy and the related idea of the knowledge society, outlining what these concepts imply. It also addresses the equally important issue of equality. Equality is directly linked to other important policy goals—those of social cohesion and the improvement of the quality of life for the genuine enjoyment of fundamental human rights and the respect of human dignity (Council of Europe, 2009). The chapter is also concerned with the educational policy choices now available to Ireland in a period of economic downturn, including choices relating to teacher education.

THE BACKGROUND: ECONOMIC GROWTH, INEQUALITY AND RECESSION

If becoming a knowledge economy/society is a legitimate goal for Ireland (and there is some debate about this), then we need to consider progress over recent years. A country's progress can be measured in many ways. One commonly used measure is the rate of national economic growth (or income) as measured by Gross National Product (GNP) or Gross Domestic Product (GDP). The latter measure, which includes the income generated (some repatriated to parent countries) by multinational firms, is used extensively in the European Union.

GNP is a somewhat better measure as it relates to the income accruing to the country, as opposed to GDP which, in many cases, masks significant repatriation of profits. However, both measures are subject to serious criticism and should be regarded as inadequate indicators of progress because of their failure to take account of the distribution of income and the prevalence of poverty as well as key indicators of 'development', such as educational achievement, health care and housing provision. Nevertheless, because of the use of these measures by most countries, reference will be made to them below, bearing in mind these cautionary comments.

In this chapter, there is an emphasis on material inequalities as represented by the distribution of income. It is particularly important for any assessment of Ireland's education system to be contextualised within a framework of material inequalities, as it is not possible to understand the operation of the system without reference to the distribution of income, wealth and life chances (see Drudy & Lynch, 1993). This is, of course, equally true of all education systems and there is an extensive international literature on education and equality. There are global inequalities and national inequalities which shape all education systems (Baker et al., 2006, pp. 413–14). Material inequalities, such as income inequalities, however, make up only some of the important inequalities in industrialised countries and in the world as a whole (ibid.). Baker and his colleagues point out that there are also important inequalities of respect and recognition: inequalities in the relative status of members of different groups, expressed in the varying degrees of esteem and contempt that they show towards one another and that social institutions and structures embody (ibid.). In this chapter, space does not permit a consideration of all these, and so the focus is mainly on income distribution and a number of international, social-cohesion indicators.

On the narrow measure of economic growth, Ireland undoubtedly performed well over the period from 1993–2007. During the 1990s, it was the fastest growing economy in Europe (European Commission, 2008). However, income inequality remained a feature of the economy and, in fact, was exacerbated by the state's own budgetary policy in the 1990s—although the lowest income groups gained slightly in the budgets of 2000–2005 (Callan et al., 2005).

Income inequality is exemplified by the 'Gini index' which is a measure used by many national and international agencies (Central Statistics Office, 2007, p. 9).[1] The CSO figures show that, for example, in 2006 the Gini index for Ireland was 32.4. Income inequality may also be illustrated by looking at the distribution of income among the different fifths (quintiles) of the population, from highest to lowest average incomes. The 'quintile share ratio', was 5.0 per cent in 2006. This meant that the income of the top 20 per cent of the population was five times that of the lowest income fifth (ibid., p. 9). In fact, Ireland remained an outlier among rich European nations in its high degree of income inequality, though still falling well short of the level seen in the United States (Nolan & Smeeding, 2005). These issues were particularly serious in their consequences for young people and for the education system. The implications for the knowledge economy are considered later.

Following this period of dramatic economic growth (yet enduring inequality), Ireland's economic circumstances changed drastically in 2007–2008. From the position of having one of the highest annual economic growth rates anywhere in the world, Ireland moved very rapidly into a period of recession, deflation and economic contraction. Economic decline accelerated in 2008 and in the first half of 2009. Initial estimates of Gross Domestic Product (GDP) and Gross National Product (GNP) for the first quarter of 2009 showed strong declines in both measures. Compared with the corresponding quarter of 2008, GDP at constant prices was 8.5 per cent lower while GNP was 12.0 per cent lower (Central Statistics Office, 2009a). Towards the end of 2008, in the face of the imminent collapse of the banking sector, the government provided guarantees to the financial sector of more than 250 per cent of GDP (International Monetary Fund, 2009). By the middle of 2009, the seasonally adjusted, standardised unemployment rate was almost 12 per cent for the first time since the early 1990s (Central Statistics Office, 2009b).

This economic turnaround had immediate effects on education. The 2008 October budget set out a programme of cuts in services which included an increase in class sizes in primary and post-primary schools (and a consequent loss of teaching posts), cuts in the allocations to teacher professional development, cuts in higher education funding and cutbacks on a range of schemes designed to support disadvantaged and marginalised pupils (Department of Education & Science, 2008a). In 2009, the Special Group on Public Service Numbers and Expenditures recommended additional wide-ranging and Draconian cutbacks to be implemented at all levels of education.

Both the economic collapse and the education policy response to the budget raise a number of fundamental questions. For some considerable time, in policy terms, the Irish state, public commentators and policy makers, and the university system, had espoused the objective of the development of the 'knowledge economy' as a key plank of public policy. This chapter raises the question of whether the groundwork was sufficiently well laid during the period of high growth to continue this trajectory in any meaningful way. A further question is whether the goal of a knowledge-based economy as a route to economic recovery is a viable option at a time of severe economic and educational retrenchment.

THE KNOWLEDGE ECONOMY AND THE KNOWLEDGE SOCIETY

The World Bank sees the knowledge economy as essential for countries to compete effectively in today's dynamic global markets (World Bank, 2009). It defines it as:

> A knowledge-based economy is defined as one where knowledge (codified and tacit) is created, acquired, transmitted and used more effectively by enterprises, organizations, individuals and communities for greater economic and social development.
>
> Dahlman & Andersson, 2000, p. 13

The Organisation for Economic Co-operation and Development (OECD) has defined knowledge-based economies in very general terms as being based on the production, distribution and use of knowledge and information. Central to this is the importance of digital technologies, the internet, computers, information and the globalised networks these technologies enable (Carlaw et al., 2006; Bullen et al., 2006). In its recent response to the economic downturn, the Irish government defines the knowledge economy—which it refers to as the 'smart economy'—as follows:

> The Smart Economy combines the successful elements of the enterprise economy and the innovation or 'ideas' economy while promoting a high-quality environment, improving energy security and promoting social cohesion.
>
> Government of Ireland, 2008a, p. 7

Other definitions suggest that the key component of a knowledge economy is a greater reliance on intellectual capabilities than on physical inputs or natural resources (Powell & Snellman, 2004). While knowledge was a key factor in economic change from the time of the industrial revolution, what is new today are the technologies in which the economy and society exist—digital technologies, built around information and communication technologies, i.e. ICTs (Carlaw et al., 2006). It is arguable that, corresponding to the knowledge economy, a new society is also emerging with pervasive information capabilities that make it substantially different from an industrial society: much more competitive, with an emphasis on democratic political systems, less centralised, less stable, perhaps better able to address individual needs and even perhaps friendlier to the environment (ibid.).

Key factors for a successful transition to the knowledge economy are improved education, appropriate funding for research and development in basic and applied sciences and, in particular, appropriate mechanisms of technology transfer from laboratories to companies (Musyck & Hadjimanolis, 2005). According to Hargreaves, in knowledge societies, wealth, prosperity and economic development depend on people's capacity to out-invent and outwit their competitors, to tune in to the desires and demands of the consumer market, and to change jobs or develop new skills as economic fluctuations and downturns require. He argues that, in knowledge societies, these capacities are not just the property of individuals, but also of organisations which have the capacity to share, create and apply new knowledge continuously over time and in cultures of mutual learning and continuous innovation. Knowledge society organisations develop these capacities by providing their members with extensive opportunities for lifelong upskilling and retraining. Knowledge societies are learning societies (Hargreaves, 2007, p. 224). As regards schools, the curriculum in knowledge societies incorporates content and process that engages schools and teachers in professional creativity and knowledge generation (Looney & Klenowski, 2008). So, how did Ireland perform in its progress to the knowledge economy/society during the recent 'boom' period?

POLICY FIELDS: KNOWLEDGE INFRASTRUCTURE AND EDUCATIONAL PERFORMANCE

In the mid-1990s, Ireland was positioned at the bottom of the top band of the knowledge-economy index, just behind the average for Western Europe (Dahlman, 2004). In order to assess Ireland's performance on building a knowledge infrastructure, this chapter uses four indicators:

1. Ireland's general position on knowledge competitiveness in relation to a number of other countries/regions;
2. the investment in the digital technology base;
3. Ireland's investment in education; and

4. general educational performance.

These will be examined in turn.

The *World Knowledge Competitiveness Index* is compiled by the Centre for International Competitiveness (Huggins et al., 2008). Its focus is primarily on the performance of different regions. In the case of Ireland in 2008, it presented data on just the Southern and Eastern region.[2] To provide an overall measure of knowledge competitiveness, the indicators include: GDP; economic activity; the number of managers and employees in IT and computer manufacturing; the number of high-tech employees and employees in other knowledge-based industries; per capita expenditure on R&D; and per capita expenditure on the different levels of education. The performance of the Southern and Eastern region of Ireland on the overall knowledge competitiveness index is assessed by this instrument. It indicated that, in 2008, this region compared moderately well with other European regions but was not at the top level. On this overall measure of knowledge competitiveness, Ireland's knowledge performance was roughly in the middle of all of the regions included in the index—approximately halfway between Latvia and Sweden (ibid.).

Regarding investment in the digital technology base, there is one important single measure which is included among many others in the competitiveness index, i.e. the ICT infrastructure (the number of internet hosts and the availability of broadband). On this measure, Ireland's performance was not impressive in comparison with other European countries and with a number of countries outside Europe. On the measure of the number of internet hosts per 1,000, Ireland ranked poorly—on a par with Hungary, Latvia, Lithuania, the Czech Republic and Spain and far behind the Nordic countries—Sweden, Denmark, Norway, Finland, Iceland and their associated territories (ibid.).

Another important element to facilitate the development of a knowledge economy is broadband access. In 2008, the percentage of enterprises in Ireland with a broadband connection (83 per cent) was slightly above the EU27 average of 81 per cent. However, the percentage of households with a broadband connection (68 per cent) was poor compared to the EU average of 80 per cent (Central Statistics Office, 2008a). Thus, Ireland's performance on the broadband indicator is relatively poor and ranks alongside Lithuania and Hungary, rather than the high performing knowledge economies such as Finland (Huggins et al., 2008). In relation to schools, data produced by the OECD show that Ireland failed to invest significantly in ICT resources in second-level schools. In the mid-2000s, the mean number of computers per student in schools in Ireland (0.11) was below the OECD average of 0.16 and below the means for the United Kingdom (0.23), the United States (0.30), Finland (0.17) or Denmark (0.19) (OECD, 2006, p. 414).

As regards investment in education, during the period of economic expansion from the mid-1990s to the mid-2000s, the Irish state continued to increase its overall investment in education on an annual basis, with the most significant increases occurring at first and second level and more modest ones at third level. However, in comparison with other OECD countries, this was from a relatively low base and Ireland continued to be below the OECD average on all of the indicators. See Table 3.1.

The data in Table 3.1 refers to the period 1995–2001/2002. What it illustrates is that Ireland's expenditure on education was lower than the OECD average, well behind the Nordic countries but also behind the United Kingdom, Austria, Germany and the United States. Ireland's expenditure as a percentage of GDP was in the middle band, most similar to that of the Czech and Slovak republics, Japan and Spain. However, in the period 1995–2001, Ireland did increase its educational expenditure significantly. This increase was one of the largest of all the OECD countries, second only to Turkey, but, like Turkey, the increase was from a low base in relation to many of the northern European countries. The figures on per capita educational expenditure at primary, secondary and tertiary levels reflect the general tendency in most of the countries to spend more per capita on higher education, less on second-level education and least on primary. There are strong social and educational arguments for increasing expenditure on primary education as, of course, it provides the basis for all further education and also virtually all citizens of the state participate in it. On the other hand, third-level education is very expensive and is widely viewed as being essential to economic and social development. The spending per capita on tertiary education shows Ireland with a slightly lower spend than the OECD average and falling in the middle band of expenditure. The most recent year for which comparative OECD figures are available (2005) shows that Ireland continued to invest less per capita than the OECD average on primary, secondary and tertiary education at €5,732, €7,500 and €10,468—the latter figure includes research and development activities (OECD, 2008a, p. 218). Department of Education and Science (2009b) figures for the year 2007 showed a further slight rise in that year to €6,161, €8,864 and €10,901 respectively.

Table 3.1: Comparative expenditure on education 1995–2001 (OECD countries)

		Annual expenditure per student 2001 (US dollars)[1]			Index of change in annual expenditure per student 1995–2001 (1995=100)	
	Public and Private % of GDP	Primary education[2]	Secondary education[2]	Tertiary education[2]	Primary and Secondary education	Tertiary education
Australia	5.97	5,052	7,239	12,688	131	96
Austria	5.78	6,571	8,562	11,274	...	109
Belgium	6.36	5,321	7,921[c]	11,589	...	...
Canada	6.14	...	...	...	...	...
Czech Republic	4.58	1,871	3,448	5,555	96	63
Denmark	7.10	7,572	8,113[d]	14,280[d]	121[d]	124[d]
Finland	5.84	4,708	6,537	10,981	109	101
France	5.98	4,777	8,107	8,837	114	113
Germany	5.26	4,237	6,620	10,504	103	111
Greece	4.06	3,299[a]	3,768	4,280	144[a,e]	131[e]
Hungary	5.18	2,592[b]	2,633[b]	7,122[b]	115[b]	92[b]
Iceland	6.70	6,373	7,265	7,674	...	...
Ireland	4.49	3,743	5,245	10,003	145	139
Italy	5.31	6,783[b]	8,258[b]	8,347[b]	112[b,e]	120[b,e]
Japan	4.63	5,771	6,534[d]	11,164[d]	122[d]	117[d]
Korea	8.20	3,714	5,159	6,618	...	...
Luxembourg	3.64	7,873[a]	11,091[c]	...	...	...
Mexico	5.87	1,357	1,915	4,341	125	90
Netherlands	4.90	4,862	6,403	12,974	124	105
New Zealand	...	...	...	...	...	...
Norway	6.37	7,404	9,040[c]	13,189	94[a,e]	94[e]
Poland	...	2,322[b]	...	3,579[b]	157[b,e]	89[b,e]
Portugal	5.85	4,181	5,976	5,199	166	111
Slovak Republic	4.11	1,252	1,874[c]	5,285	115	101
Spain	4.89	4,168	5,442[c]	7,455	129[e]	133
Sweden	6.46	6,295	6,482	15,188	103	101
Switzerland	...	6,889[b]	10,916[b]	20,230[b]	100[b,e]	128[b,e]
Turkey	3.51	...	...	...	147[b,e]	159[b]
United Kingdom	5.48	4,415	5,933[c]	10,753	106	96
United States	7.34	7,560	8,779	22,234[c]	114	109
Country mean	5.62	4,850	6,510	10,052	...	...

Notes:
...   not available or negligible.
1.   Financial and human resources invested in education, 2001 data, unless otherwise stated.
2.   Converted using Purchasing Power Parities for GDP.
a.   Includes pre-primary education.
b.   Public institutions only.
c.   Includes post-secondary, non-tertiary education.
d.   Includes part of post-secondary, non-tertiary education.
e.   Public expenditure only.

Source: StatLink: http://dx.doi.org/10.1787/650383071321. OECD, 2004a; 2004/2005.

The progress outlined above is reflected in the commentary of Ireland's National Competitiveness Council (2009) which has argued that education has been at the centre of Ireland's economic and social progress. The NCC has signalled significant achievements—for example, in 2008, 34 per cent of the Irish labour force aged 25–64 had completed some form of higher education, compared to 4 per cent in the early 1970s. Similarly, the number of those holding a primary education or less has fallen from circa 60 per cent to 14 per cent over the same period (ibid.).

As the NCC emphasised, these strong educational outcomes were produced with relatively modest public financial resources. However, it acknowledged that much needed to be done to enable Ireland to be comparable with the highest performing competitive economies in Europe and elsewhere in the world. With regard to expenditure on research and development (a core element of the knowledge economy), despite significant increases in public and private investment over the decade 1998–2008, the Chief Scientific Advisor has pointed out that Ireland ranks modestly at 18th out of 28 OECD countries (Cunningham, 2009).

This section has looked at Ireland's performance on each of three indicators of the knowledge infrastructure—i.e. the general position on knowledge competitiveness in relation to a number of other countries/regions; investment in the digital technology base; and investment in education. Ireland has made some progress towards becoming a knowledge economy but is not as well positioned as might be wished, as far as knowledge infrastructure is concerned. In fact, the government's Chief Scientific Advisor has described Ireland as a 'follower' rather than a 'leader' in the area of innovation and behind such 'target' leader countries as the United Kingdom, Austria, Denmark, Sweden and Finland (Cunningham, 2009).

Since Ireland's knowledge infrastructure made faltering progress during a period of high economic growth, by the end of the first decade of the 21st century, the country faced a major challenge as it slid further into recession. These factors have profound implications for the educational participation and outcomes of the population as a whole and for educational policy making at a time of deepening recession.

We will now turn to look at indicators of general educational performance. The OECD is generally regarded as playing a significant role in framing and steering education policy at a European and global level (Grek, 2009). One key measure that has been of great international interest over the past decade has been the relative level of performance of 15-year-olds on the Programme of International Student Assessment (PISA) in three areas essential to all economies and societies: literacy in reading; Mathematics; and science. PISA and its effects have been seen as a useful tool in the project of building the new European education area of competitiveness and cohesion (ibid.).

Irish 15-year-olds performed well on the PISA reading tests (ranked fifth out of 31 countries), just above the average on science (ranked 14th out of 32 countries included) and at the OECD average in Mathematics (16th out of 32). However, taking the example of another small European country, Finland, their 15 year olds, by contrast, were ranked second for reading and first for science and Mathematics. While there have been many debates about the value of such rankings (Grek, 2009), they provide an indicator (albeit a limited one) of general education performance and suggest that Ireland's 15 year olds were not yet performing at the top level in comparison with a number of other countries (OECD, 2007). On an equally important indicator, i.e. the literacy of educationally disadvantaged children, a recent report by the Irish school inspectorate has shown, inter alia, that despite some good practice and initiatives, nearly half the primary-school children in disadvantaged schools evaluated had very low scores in reading, while almost two-thirds of children scored poorly in Mathematics (Department of Education & Science, 2005a; Hyland & Moore, 2009). This has problematic implications for the future performance of a significant segment of the pupil population.

POLICY FIELDS: EQUALITY AND TEACHER EDUCATION

Given the international agreement that the key factors for a successful transition to the knowledge economy are improved education and appropriate funding for research and development in basic and applied sciences (Musyck &

Hadjimanolis, 2005), it is quite clear that education has to be a key part of the solution to the economic difficulties now facing this country. It is also clear that it cannot adequately contribute to a resurgence of the economy and to a stable and democratic society unless a number of important choices are made by Ireland as a society. One of these choices relates to the issue of equality and social cohesion.

As a general indicator of equality, the measure used here is the distribution of income. Where does Ireland 'fit' in comparison to other countries? This is not an easy question to answer, not least because comparing international databases needs to be done with a degree of caution. Internationally, analysts have tended to contrast neo-liberal systems[3] with social-democratic ones. However, there is an argument that we need to modify the customary models of political economy to include four, not just two, types of the knowledge economy in the developed Western world (Green, 2006). These include: the 'neo-liberal' or market model of the United States and some other English-speaking countries, sometimes referred to as the 'Anglo-Saxon' model (US, UK, New Zealand, Australia, Canada and, arguably, Ireland during the boom); the social market model of countries in 'core Europe' (i.e. Austria, Belgium, France, Germany and the Netherlands); the southern European group of economies (sometimes unflatteringly called the PIGS—Portugal, Italy, Greece, Spain and, perhaps, Ireland in recession) and the social democratic model of the Nordic states (ibid.).

A calculation of the average Gini index for each of these groups of countries from the most recently available comparative data produced by the World Bank (2004) in the *2005 World Development Report* shows differences in the level of inequality, with the 'Anglo-Saxon' group having the highest average Gini index of 36.2; the 'southern European' being next in terms of inequality at an average of 35.6; 'core Europe' had an average of 29.7. The Nordic group of countries emerged as by far the most egalitarian at an average of 25.6. Ireland, with a figure on the Gini index of 35.9 ranked slightly behind the United States and the United Kingdom in terms of inequality at 40.8 and 36.0 respectively, and very close to the average for the southern European states (World Bank, 2004, pp. 258-9).

However, the survey year in this report is indicated as 1996. The World Bank 'development indicators' for 2007 give its most recent Gini figure for Ireland for the year 2000 of 34, indicating a reduction in inequality of income at the end of the 1990s (World Bank, 2007). As seen earlier, the most recent figure from the CSO (2007) of 32.4 indicates that this reduction in inequality of the distribution of income continued to the mid-2000s. This most recent figure still compares unfavourably with the Nordic countries and with countries such as Austria and Germany. The best comparison is with the distributions of the southern European economies (Portugal, Italy, Greece and Spain). Thus Ireland's progress, measured in terms of its performance on the income distribution measure, has improved somewhat but it is still relatively inegalitarian.

Other indicators of equality and social cohesion used by the OECD show that Ireland, by the end of the 'boom' period, ranked well above the OECD average on the poverty rate and on measures which indicated poverty among children (OECD, 2009a, pp. 91–3). The country was on the lower end of the range on the indicator of average public social spending and of net social spending (ibid., pp. 97–9). Attitudinal data indicated lower 'life satisfaction' scores among Irish people than the OECD average (ibid., p. 121) and the crime victimisation reportage was the highest in the OECD (ibid., p. 11). Thus, Ireland made relatively poor progress at the time of its highest prosperity on measures of social cohesion.

These indicators of inequality in the general population are closely interlinked with educational inequalities. Indeed, it has been argued by many sociologists that education both maintains and reproduces social class and socio-economic inequalities. The persistence of educational inequalities relating to socio-economic background are well documented and have persisted throughout the period of Ireland's economic prosperity (Lynch & Moran, 2006). For example, the most recent figures on the economic status of school leavers (Byrne et al., 2008) show that school leavers from professional backgrounds have a high share of further education places relative to those from other socio-economic backgrounds. Those from manual and non-manual backgrounds were more likely to go straight into employment. Those from unemployed backgrounds had similar labour market participation levels as these manual and non-manual groups, but a greater share of these young people were themselves unemployed (ibid.).

Another important factor in assessing the impact of social class and socio-economic inequality on educational performance has been the level of segregation or stratification of the different elements of the school system. The results of the OECD's Programme for International Student Assessment (PISA) show that in a number of different countries, the effect on student performance of a school's average economic, social and cultural status is very substantial and that socio-economic differences at student levels are much less predictive for performance than the school's socio-economic context (OECD, 2004b, pp. 189–90).

As regards the Irish system, it has been observed that the institutionalisation of invidious status hierarchies between different post-primary schools has served to reproduce existing status hierarchies (Clancy, 1995, p. 490). This succinctly summarises one of the key features of the Irish second-level system—i.e. its division into a hierarchy of four strata. Stratification of school types is, of course, observable in many education systems. In the Irish case, fee-paying voluntary schools are at the 'top', followed by non-fee-paying voluntary secondary schools, then community and comprehensive schools and, lastly, the schools in the vocational education sector. Vocational schools have the highest proportion of students from poor and unemployed family backgrounds (Smyth, 1999). Fee-paying schools have the highest proportion transferring to higher education and vocational schools the lowest (ibid.). These status hierarchies between different types of school also serve to make it difficult for schools to become more inclusive or egalitarian. The PISA report argues that more inclusive schooling systems have both higher levels of performance and fewer disparities among students from differing socio-economic backgrounds (OECD, 2004b, p. 197). Thus, a more inclusive school system[4] has to be part of the solution to Ireland's economic difficulties and to increasing social cohesion.

It is acknowledged here that, from the early 1990s, the state had begun to incorporate inclusion and equality into policy and legislation. During its period of strong economic growth, the development of the social agenda was reflected in a number of pieces of equality-related legislation, including parts of the Universities Act 1997, the Education Act 1998, the Employment Equality Act 1998, Equal Status Act 2000, Human Rights Commission Act 2000, European Convention on Human Rights Act 2003, the Education for Persons with Disabilities Act 2004, the Equality Act 2004 and the Disabilities Act 2005 (Government of Ireland, 1997, 1998b, 1998c, 2000b, 2000c, 2003, 2004a, 2004b, 2005). The Combat Poverty Agency, a quasi-independent, non-governmental organisation focused on poverty, had already been established at the height of a previous recession in the mid-1980s under the Combat Poverty Agency Act 1986 (Government of Ireland, 1986).

The education acts cited above were the result of a number of years of intense public consultation and innovation in education from the early 1990s to 2005. The period began with the publication of a report by the OECD on the Irish education system in 1991 (OECD, 1991). This was followed by the publication by the government of a Green Paper on Education, *Education for a Changing World* (Government of Ireland, 1992), the establishment of the consultative National Education Convention in 1993, with 42 national bodies represented, and its subsequent report (Coolahan, 1994), the White Paper on Education, *Charting our Education Future* (Government of Ireland, 1995), the *Report of the Commission on the Status of People with Disabilities* (Commission on the Status of People with Disabilities, 1995), the Green Paper on Adult Education, *Adult Education in an Era of Lifelong Learning* (Government of Ireland, 1998a), the White Paper on Early Education, *Ready to Learn* (Government of Ireland, 1999) and the White Paper on Adult Education, *Learning for Life* (Government of Ireland, 2000b). The consultative reports and the passing of these acts meant that Ireland had begun to take the equality agenda seriously, both in education and in other spheres of life.

From the middle of 2008, when the looming recession was apparent, it became a matter of public concern to many people that the agencies set up under these acts were being very seriously hampered in the performance of their statutory functions either through severe cuts in their budgets or through being absorbed into the civil service (see, for example, Manning, 2009a). Likewise, the commencement/implementation of important sections of the Education for Persons with Disabilities Act 2004 and the Disabilities Act 2005 were deferred for resource reasons.

At the time of writing this book, the Report of the Special Group on Public Service Numbers and Expenditure Programmes recommended an extremely radical array of cuts to education spending at all levels of education (2009). The future of education, and of its capacity to deliver on the agenda of the knowledge economy, depends on the policy response to this report's recommendations and on whether policy and investment pay much more attention to seriously supporting and progressing social inclusion and equality, rather than cutting back and weakening them. Policy makers also need to implement and build on the very substantial body of policy developed during the 1990s and 2000s and to utilise key development indicators, such as education and knowledge infrastructure, rather than placing an undue focus on crude measures of economic growth, necessary though economic recovery is at a time of spiraling unemployment.

Thus, at the end of the period of prosperity, the issue of educational inequality remains intractable in spite of a range of government policies designed to combat educational disadvantage (Department of Education & Science,

2005b). Furthermore, Ireland is not as well positioned as either core European or Nordic countries on general measures indicative of social cohesion, including the relative level of income inequality and other social indicators.

A second policy choice facing policy makers if education is to be a strong element in economic recovery is the quality of teaching and teacher education. Teacher recruitment and teacher education are now internationally understood as having an extremely important role in the provision of high-quality education, in the quality of pupil learning outcomes, and in social and economic development (Darling-Hammond, 2006; National Competitiveness Council, 2009). The importance of teacher recruitment and education have also been recognised by the EU Commission from the early part of the 21st century. Through the Lisbon Agreement (2000), the European Union set out to make Europe the most competitive, digital, knowledge-based economy in the world by 2010, and it also aimed to bring about greater social cohesion through economic reform. The Lisbon Agreement made specific mention of teachers and aimed to use community programmes to foster and remove obstacles to their mobility, to bring about greater transparency in the recognition of qualifications, and to attract high-quality teachers (paragraph 26). The link between the economic and democratic projects of the European Union and teaching was most clearly established at a European level by the work of the Education and Culture section of the European Commission in the development of common European principles for teacher competences and qualifications and its statement on teacher quality (European Commission, 2005, 2007). The commission envisaged that teaching should be a high-status, high-reward, well-qualified profession in which every teacher should have the opportunity to continue studies to the highest (i.e. doctoral) level. Teachers, it argued, should be lifelong learners. They should be able to understand the factors that create social cohesion and exclusion in society and be aware of the ethical dimensions of the knowledge society. Furthermore, teacher education should be an object of research.

All of the above policy statements would suggest a form of teacher education that is reflective, analytical and critical and that would be on a par with advanced studies in any of the professions. The analytical, research-based work of teacher educators would, the European Union envisages, be conducted in partnership and collaboration with schools and other stakeholders. While there is an evident, genuine concern to attract and retain high-quality people in the profession, much of the language of these documents, e.g. *Teachers Matter* (OECD, 2005), is substantially that of neo-liberalism, performativity, performance indicators, standards, evaluation and appraisal and may, of course, be critiqued from a more holistic perspective (Drudy, 2008a).

Nonetheless, the evidence available from these and from a number of sources is that high-quality teacher education from initial education, through systematic induction programmes and on to continuing professional development, is fundamental to a high-quality profession and to pupil learning (Darling-Hammond, 2006; Westbury et al., 2005; Killeavy & Murphy, 2006; Clynes, 2008). Thus, if progress towards enhanced educational achievement and outcomes for a much more diverse pupil population is to be sustained, and if the overall participation and achievement of the population as a whole is to be further improved to the highest international standards, then substantial investment in initial and continuing teacher education is essential.

The Teaching Council, established under the Teaching Council Act 2001, has a statutory role with significant powers to ensure the quality of teacher education at all stages on the continuum of teacher education from initial teacher education through induction and continuing professional development (see www.teachingcouncil.ie) for further details. However, decisions on the resourcing of teacher education rest with the state.

CONCLUSION

The international evidence suggests that education should be a central mechanism for Ireland's economic recovery. However, the analysis here illustrates that, in spite of having the development of the knowledge economy and the building of social cohesion as central policy platforms for over a decade, Ireland invested only moderately in its knowledge infrastructure in comparison with other OECD countries. In addition, from the early 1990s, considerable policy development and legislation was developed in relation to a wide range of educational issues. Nevertheless, data shows that, by 2009, Ireland rated relatively modestly, especially in relation to the Nordic countries, on measures of knowledge infrastructure, educational performance and income equality. This has left the country facing major educational challenges, as well as economic and social ones.

From an educational policy perspective, it will be extremely important to protect the budgetary allocation for education to the maximum extent possible as the country struggles with recession and the fallout from the banking crisis. Social cohesion objectives are at odds with the form of education policy which results in cuts affecting the least well-off and the marginalised. This occurred in the October 2008 budget and represented the first reaction of the state to Ireland's economic collapse. The measures included cuts to a range of supports targeted towards the support of economically disadvantaged groups (Department of Education & Science, 2008a). These cuts achieved little in savings but were potentially very damaging to the disadvantaged. Additional, and much more extensive, cuts to all levels of education, including cuts to the building of the country's research infrastructure, were recommended by the Special Group on Public Services and Expenditures in 2009 and, if implemented in full, would undo much of the relatively modest progress made during the time of economic prosperity on developing knowledge infrastructure and social inclusion in education. The proposed expenditure cuts also have the potential to seriously impede progress towards the establishment of Ireland as a knowledge economy.

Education, it is argued here, is vital to Ireland's economic recovery and to social cohesion. The evidence to date suggests that, given the decline in manufacturing, the decline in the numbers employed in agriculture (although agriculture will always be a crucial element in Ireland's economy) and the collapse of construction as an economic driver, Ireland has little choice but to invest all possible resources in its development as a knowledge economy. To take just one example, in agriculture—traditionally one of Ireland's principal industries—Professor Rudy Rabbinge of Waginingen University, speaking in a European context, has argued the following:

> In the EU as a whole, a policy directed towards research programmes stimulating scientific excellence and greater coherence in the European knowledge system would greatly strengthen agriculture's competitiveness and contribute to food security and sustainable development.
>
> Rabbinge, 2009, p. 21

If Ireland is to move to higher levels of research and innovation as part of its central strategy for economic recovery, it faces a considerable challenge in the light of its modest progress in this direction during the time of economic prosperity. Ireland cannot compete with low-cost economies. Even though the country faces severe cutbacks in public expenditure, strategic educational investment will be a key ingredient from the primary and pre-primary levels through to postgraduate studies and research and innovation. Social cohesion is a core policy platform for Ireland.

This chapter has identified the need for sustained measures to address educational inequalities in order to enhance social cohesion. These are particularly important in the light of the persistence of inequality in society and in education, and in the light of state responses to the economic downturn. Proposals for cutbacks in the public services in the light of the recession have significant potential to weaken the capacity of agencies with equality-related responsibilities and are, themselves, a major challenge.

Finally, if Irish society wishes to pursue its policy goal of becoming a knowledge economy, to become 'an innovation and commercialisation hub' (Government of Ireland, 2008a, p. 8) in the move to economic recovery then it must invest much more in knowledge infrastructure, in education generally, in research and innovation and, not least, in high-quality initial and continuing teacher education. High-quality teacher education will be an essential ingredient of the knowledge economy, as evidence from a number of countries shows that high-quality teaching is central to improved educational outcomes. Educational policy makers need to build on the policy innovation that took place in the 1990s and early 2000s and be prepared to see educational development as a core, and absolutely essential, part of social and cultural development and of economic recovery, lest the stated policies of the smart economy and social cohesion metamorphose from targets to mere aspirations.

ENDNOTES

1   The Gini index is the measure most frequently used to give a measure of income inequality. A Gini index of 0 = perfect equality; a Gini index of 100 = perfect inequality (World Bank, 2005, p. 268).

2   The relatively prosperous Southern and Eastern region covers the southern and eastern half of the country. If the less prosperous Border, Midland and Western region in the west and north-west were included, the overall index for Ireland as a whole would most likely be lower.

3   'Neo-liberalism' is a set of economic policies that have become widely espoused, even dominant, particularly since the early 1980s (Martinez & Garcia, 2000) and is a movement towards the notion of a pure and perfect market which is made possible by the politics of financial deregulation (Bourdieu, 1998). In the public sector, including education, neo-liberalism involves privatisation, liberalisation and the adoption of commercial criteria.

Competitive success is to be achieved through loosening formal systems of control (Ball, 2006, p. 10). A new form of 'managerialism' arises which views traditional bureaucratic control systems as unwieldy, counterproductive of efficiency and repressive of the enterprising spirit of all employees. Thus the managerial discourses in the public sector become those of excellence and effectiveness (ibid.) but without a regard for holistic or communitarian values. Ironically, surveillance is also a key element of neo-liberal systems but it is accompanied by the illusion of individual autonomy and has been described as a move 'from morality to moralistic audit-driven surveillance' (Davies, 2005, p. 12).

4   Inclusion, of course, involves more than including children from different socio-economic groups. It also involves the inclusion of children of immigrants and ethnic minorities, and students with special educational needs/disabilities (see Drudy & Kinsella, 2009). These issues are dealt with in a number of other chapters in this book.

Part 2
Diversity and Inclusion in Schools

4
DYNAMICS OF INCLUSION AND EXCLUSION IN CHILDREN'S SOCIAL WORLD IN SCHOOL

Dympna Devine

Increasing and rapid immigration into Irish society has resulted in schools and classrooms becoming more ethnically diverse spaces, hence spaces where there is a growing number of children who are from religious and cultural traditions different to the norm. Children no less than adults are embedded in this changing social landscape, their social world enlarged through engagement and interaction with others who are ethnically and culturally different.

Given the changing patterns of immigration in the Republic of Ireland in the past 10 years (Central Statistics Office, 2008b), this chapter considers how factors related to ethnic and gender identity mediate children's interaction with one another in a newly multi-ethnic primary school. The chapter foregrounds the exercise of power in such relations, and how discourses related to what is considered normal and 'other' cut across the dynamics of inclusion and exclusion in children's peer relationships. Recommendations in relation to classroom and school practice are made with reference to the need for teachers to take account of the complexity of children's social worlds and the dynamics of power and control that operate within it.

THE IMPORTANCE OF CHILDREN'S SOCIAL WORLD TO THE EXPERIENCE OF SCHOOL

When we think about the impact of schooling on children, influences on academic learning and cognitive development tend to come to mind immediately. However, a considerable amount of time spent in school involves social learning. In the company of peers, generally but not exclusively of the same age, a considerable amount of time in school is spent by children interacting and learning socially and culturally about one another (Devine, 2003). This has a significant impact not only upon how they see, understand and define themselves, but also how they see, understand and define others. In other words, schools as institutions may be considered not only as physical spaces in which formal learning (as defined by the curriculum) takes place, but also as social spaces in which children, through their interactions with significant others (peers and teachers especially) work out aspects of their social identities (Devine, 2007, 2009). Such processes of social identification and meaning-making also influence children's learning and achievement, as they position themselves along a continuum of positive–negative affiliation towards school. When children experience a sense of belonging, recognition and inclusion in school, it contributes to feelings of self-efficacy and motivation to learn. Alternately, if children are isolated or alienated, this can lead to withdrawal and an experience of disconnection from school life. The importance of the social aspect of everyday life for children can be gauged from the high rating given by nine-year-olds to the importance of friends in their lives (Government of Ireland, 2009) and of the identification of 'time with friends' as the most 'liked' aspect of being at school (Devine, 2003).

It is important for teachers to be aware, then, not only of the effort children engage in the formal learning environment of school, but also of the considerable effort involved in the social aspect of their school lives. One way of considering children's social world in school is through the lens of child culture—a distinct social and cultural world that exists between children—that comprises its own rules and regulations, patterns and structures that is frequently outside of teachers' awareness. Perhaps Harre (1993) best encapsulates child culture, when viewed through adult eyes as that which:

> … exists in the giggling conversations which cease when adults appear, in the knot of struggling boys on the other side of the playground, in the whatever is happening upstairs when we hear the sound of feet across the ceiling.
>
> Harre, 1993, p. 113

Today, there is a considerable amount of work within the sociology of childhood which challenges overly passive views of children and childhood, and highlights the very active and reflective manner in which they negotiate their everyday lives (Brembeck et al., 2004; Devine, 2003; James & James, 2008; Zeiher et al., 2007). Such analyses draws attention to the complex processes of negotiation that children work through in making and keeping their friends (Adler & Adler, 1998; Corsaro, 2005). Within this perspective, children are deemed to be active negotiators of both culture and identity, manoeuvring and positioning themselves in order to attain recognition, status and an experience of intimacy and belonging with peers. This is not an isolated/individualised process, but is deeply intertwined with broader discourses related to gender, ethnicity/race, sexuality and social class, as the children both position themselves and are positioned, either negatively or positively, with peers.

THEORISING DYNAMICS OF RACE/ETHNICITY IN CHILDREN'S SOCIAL WORLD IN SCHOOL

The social space of school can be considered, then, as an arena of struggle in which children seek to position themselves with others, including peers and teachers. Drawing on the work of Foucault (1979, 1980) in relation to the exercise of power, we can say that children's interaction is deeply implicated in processes of power and control, dynamics of inclusion and exclusion in their social world framed in the context of what is considered as normal or 'other' in the society at large. As this applies to inter-ethnic relations in school, research consistently draws attention to the prevalence of children's racialised attitudes and how these influence their interaction with one another in ethnically diverse classrooms (Aboud, 2009; Bigler et al., 2009; Devine et al., 2008; Gillborn, 2006; Connolly, 2004; Troyna & Hatcher, 1992). However, the consistently hidden aspect of racial conflict in schools is also noted in research, with name-calling, racist bullying and fighting occurring most frequently out of sight of teachers (Pilkington, 1999; Henze et al., 2000; Varma-Joshi et al., 2004). Indeed, what teachers may see taking place in the yard or school classroom is often the 'tip of the iceberg' of the incidence of racism in children's lives (Connolly, 1998; Troyna & Hatcher, 1992). Furthermore, with respect to newly arrived immigrant and refugee children, research indicates a general acceptance by children of their refugee/immigrant peers on the surface, but evidence of hostility and racism underneath (Pinson & Arnot, 2007; Myers, 2003; Rutter, 2003; Tomlinson, 2005). In Ireland, research points to the prevalence of racial prejudice toward Traveller children (O'Keefe & O'Connor, 2001), along with relatively essentialist constructs of Irishness (Bryan, 2008; Waldron & Sikes, 2006) which can lead to prejudicial attitudes toward those who differ from the norm (Devine et al., 2008; Devine, 2009; Smyth et al., 2009).

Racism has its roots in discourse which defines those from differing ethnic groups as 'other', stereotyped according to a set of negative dispositions (lazy, dirty, aggressive, etc.) which appears to justify their exclusion from full participation in the society. Embedded within discourses of difference are also those of normality—to define someone else as 'other' is to have a clear sense of oneself as 'normal'. Where the dominant discourse classifies 'Irish' as being white, sedentary and Catholic, this positions those outside this norm (Traveller, black Irish, Jews) as 'other' with all the consequences this implies for participation and recognition within the peer group. Discourses related to gender, sexuality, dis/ability, and social class intersect with those of ethnicity, creating alliances between children based on their emerging social identities. One way then to consider children's interaction patterns is along a continuum of 'sameness' and/or 'difference' and how this influences their level of inclusion and/or exclusion in school. This is illustrated in Figure 4.1.

Figure 4.1: Dimensions of pupil social interaction and ethnicity in school

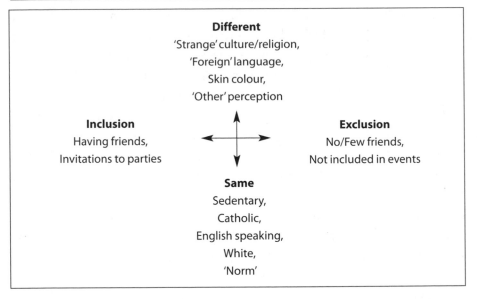

As we shall see, children can be positioned in any one of the quadrants. Minority-ethnic children may be different to others but nonetheless be included in friendship groups, or they may be different and be excluded. Similarly, they may be the same and be included (as in the case for example of friendships within an ethnic grouping), or they may be the same (ethnically) and excluded. In this sense, the children's social positioning is predicated on the signifiers of status/intimacy that are dominant within the peer group (e.g. sport, ability, interests) and the degree of difference that they present or suppress in their relations with one another. Identity work is central to these processes of inclusion/exclusion as children's ethnic identities intersect with their positioning as gendered, classed and abled beings.

METHODOLOGY

This chapter draws on findings from case-study analysis of a primary school which has undergone considerable demographic change over the past eight years. Pseudonyms are used throughout the analysis. Oakleaf primary is a designated disadvantaged, co-educational primary school located in a large, urban centre on the outskirts of Dublin. Currently, over one third of the school population is classified as minority ethnic. Housing in the local area comprises a mixture of council and private housing, as well as a locally built Traveller halting site. While the school is Roman Catholic by designation, the religious profile has changed significantly with increasing immigration, with a considerable number of children from the Muslim community, as well as other Christian denominations among its numbers. The school benefits from a highly committed principal, Mr Robinson, and two full-time language support teachers, Ms Macken and Ms Farrell.

This case study derives from intensive ethnographic research in the school over one year, followed by repeated annual visits by the author in subsequent years up to the present time, interviews with seven classroom teachers and a selected sample of children (94 in total) drawn from Grade 2 (children aged seven to eight years) through to Grade 6 (children aged up to 12 years). Interviews were also conducted with a sample of parents who attended an open day organised by the school and by more recent interviews conducted as part of an ongoing project in relation to the involvement of immigrant parents in Irish schools (Devine, in press: 2010). In conducting the research, clear ethical guidelines (Alderson & Morrow, 2004; Fraser, 2004) were followed. Pseudonyms are used throughout. The analysis is also supplemented by observations of classroom practice and socio-metric analyses of the children's interaction over one school year in Mr O'Reilly's classroom.

NORMALITY AND 'OTHERNESSS' IN CHILDREN'S ETHNIC RELATIONS

While there is often a perception among teachers that race and racism is not a problem among children (Devine, 2005), analysis of the data revealed complex processes of interaction that highlighted the significance of children's constructs of 'norm' and 'other' to their social relations. In their discussions, it was clear the majority-ethnic children focused on difference as a form of 'deficiency' in their minority-ethnic peers. This was most evident in their narratives about children who came from the Middle East and Africa as the following quotations show:

> Maura: Muslims are different.
> Kate: They go on fast.
> Jane: That means you are not allowed eat.
> Kate: The Muslims they do fasts.
> Maura: *That's all that's wrong with them.*
>
> Grade 2, majority-ethnic girls, emphasis added

> Laura: Americans are just like us, *they're real normal,* but Africans they're just more different.
>
> Grade 4, emphasis added

Initial accounts from the children seemed to suggest that racial abuse was experienced infrequently in school and this was something that was confirmed by the teachers. However, a more detailed examination indicated that the children had available to them a wide repertoire of racially abusive terms which they clearly had both used and experienced in their school lives. In order to tease through these experiences, the children were encouraged to talk about the conflicts which took place in the course of their everyday lives and the incidence of teasing and name-calling in the course of such conflict. Their talk revealed the prevalence of name-calling in their interaction with one another and how it was firmly located in the context of difference and/or perceived 'deficiency' in a child. Martha, a 10-year-old, majority-ethnic girl put this aptly when she said: 'If you are tall, short, fat, thin, you get called names.'

The children's sensitivity to difference must be considered in the context of their understanding of what it means to belong and, for majority-ethnic children, a privileging of 'whiteness' (Gillborn, 2006) as the ethnic norm. Skin colour was a very visible marker of ethnic difference, and one which the children drew upon in highlighting instances of overt racism through name-calling:

> Interviewer: What sorts of names are used calling someone who is a different colour?

Siobhain: Chocolate Face. Mongolian. Chalkies. If someone has really dark skin they call them Charcoal.

Majority-ethnic, female, Grade 5

Interviewer: Are there some names that people are called that hurt the most?

Shakil: Yeah, they calls us the black people, Chocolate Boys.

Yusuf: Yeah, Chocolate Boys.

Interviewer: Is that sixth class boys?

Shakil: Yeah. And fifth class and second class too.

Nigerian male, Grade 2

Sonya: Louise doesn't like black people, she said it to my face. I was crushed. I'm not that black, I'm tanned.

Libyan girl, Grade 5

Naomi, who was born in Libya, questioned the very basis for name-calling arising from colour and the contradiction of only labelling those with black skin 'coloured':

Everybody has a right … it's just a colour. I don't know why they call black people coloured. White people when they get sick they get blue and pink. When they die they get pale and when they feel sick they get purple. Black people don't do that. I don't know why they are calling us coloured, they are the ones who turn all different colours.

However, just as 'otherness' by virtue of skin colour carried with it the threat of exclusion from certain peer groups, some children also interpreted it as the basis for inclusion in peer groups with a shared ethnic/cultural identity. This highlights one aspect of sameness focused on by the children in their constructions of friendship, but appeared to particularly apply when a child was new to the school or classroom (as would be the case for many immigrant children). In one interview, for example, children (both majority and minority ethnic) spoke of the ease of a new child settling in if there were other 'coloured' children present:

Joanne:	Say one coloured person was in your class, it would be really hard because it's just one coloured person. Say there's three coloured people in their class, cause they've got coloured people to play with them.
Interviewer:	But Anthony [Lithuanian boy] plays with all people.
Katherine:	Yeah, but John and Luke only play with one person. *They like playing with their own colour* [emphasis added].
Joanne:	Sometimes, we discuss this in our class during circle time.
Interviewer:	And what do you say?
Joanne:	It's real hard if a new coloured person coming in as there's so many white.

Majority-ethnic, females, Grade 2

While the children were sensitive then to colour-based difference, this was not the only ethnic identifier which could lead to patterns of exclusion. Cultural racism[1]—i.e. prejudicial attitudes which stem from cultural-based differences (Gillborn 2008; Modood, 2007)—was also prevalent. It was exemplified in the negative attitudes towards Traveller children, spoken of in terms of their culture and lifestyle:

Interviewer:	Why are Traveller children picked on so much?
Martha:	Because they don't change their uniform, and they usually have scruffy nails and face and ears.
Grainne:	And they go around in tracksuit bottoms with hooker boots on and everything.

Grade 2

Such patterns gave rise to uncertainty among Traveller children themselves in terms of how they would define and present themselves at school. Very much aware of their Traveller identity—'we talk different, we keep horses, we live in trailers'—two of the Traveller children interviewed spoke of their denial of their Traveller identity in order to be accepted among their sedentary peers:

| Lisa: | Girls in my class don't know I'm a Traveller ... I'm shamed, I don't want to tell them. |
| Tom: | They don't even know we are Travellers. |

Similar patterns were evident among immigrant children, positioned as the ethnic 'other'. Their coping strategies, involving a considerable degree of ethnic self-monitoring that centred on minimising, embodied aspects of cultural difference related to accent, dress and diet especially:

> Paul: I like to use an Irish accent … if you speak *normally* they don't slag you.
>
> Nigerian, Grade 5

> Suanne: Whenever my friends come over we don't eat traditional Zimbabwean food.
>
> Zimbabwean, Grade 6

Active participation in extra-curricular activities that were distinctly Irish (such as GAA[2] clubs for hurling, football and camogie, as well as Irish dancing) was evident among children who had multi-ethnic friendships, their competence in these activities was a form of cultural capital which symbolised their 'Irishness' and willingness to be the same:

> Suanne: [To belong you have to] make friends with the class and be nice to everyone … get more involved in athletics.
>
> Zimbabwean, Grade 6

Religious identity was also a defining feature of 'otherness' and, therefore, a marker for potential exclusion from dominant peer groups:

> Patrick: I wouldn't like to be a Muslim in any school.
> Interviewer: Why?
> Patrick: I just don't want to get picked on by anybody. I wouldn't like to be a Protestant either.
>
> Grade 5

INCLUSION AND EXCLUSION: THE INTERSECTION OF ETHNICITY, GENDER, SOCIAL CLASS AND 'ABILITY'

Clearly, the children, both minority and majority ethnic, were sensitive to differences that existed between them. What is important, however, is to consider how significant this was to their friendship patterns and the extent to which processes of inclusion/exclusion were also underpinned by dynamics related to gender, ability and social class. An intensive case-study analysis of patterns in Mr O'Reilly's class (Grade 4) gives us some indication of how dynamics of inclusion/exclusion are tied to perceptions of sameness and difference that may be culturally/ethnically based, but also of how these are mediated by gender and ability. Socio-metric analysis indicated changing patterns of friendship among the boys, with significantly greater inter-ethnic mixing by the end of the year. Sporting ability was especially important here in patterns of integration—especially the playing of soccer, with considerable enhancement of the status of boys who were good at sport, but also susceptibility to racial abuse when tensions were high on the sports field:

> Marcus: Please people who are listening to this, pick up some sport or you get slagged. You have to be good at sport.
>
> Minority-ethnic boy, Grade 5

> Tony: Racism mainly takes place in sport … sometimes white people are picked first or if a coloured person hacked you or side tackled you then you could give them a punch.
>
> Majority-ethnic boy, Grade 4

Ability was also a precursor to acceptance into peer groups and we see this in the integration of Sam, a boy from Nigeria, into a group of majority-ethnic boys (Sean, Tom and Patrick) on the basis of their work together on a classroom project:

> Sean: I always play with Sam now after school. People from different countries are great to get to know because you learn all different games and all about their country.
>
> Grade 4

However, a different pattern was evident among the girls in Mr O'Reilly's class, with the initial popularity and acceptance of 'new girls' into high-status female groups giving rise to more polarised patterns by the end of the school year. By the end of the year, the three minority-ethnic girls in this class (Sarah, Elizabeth and Sharon) were a distinct cluster, separate from their majority-ethnic peers. A number of factors gave rise to this pattern—including the subsequent 'new' arrival of a majority-ethnic girl in the middle of the school year who supplanted

Sarah's popularity. However, just as being good at sport was an important aspect of high-status masculinity (Reay, 2006) among the boys, within the girls' groups high-status femininities revolved around being able to participate in romance and fashion/physical appearance talk. This had implications for minority-ethnic girls who differed substantially in their physical appearance and modes of self-presentation to traditional Irish girls and is reflected, for example, in Lisa's comment earlier where she speaks about being 'ashamed' of her Traveller status and denies it in school, as well as Elisabeth's (a Nigerian girl) perception that she was not liked because of negative comments about her hair and skin colour. Cultural norms related to gender gave rise to Sarah's reluctance, as a Muslim girl, to engage in romance/boy talk that was becoming an increasingly important aspect of bonding among girls generally in the class. Significantly, also, none of these girls were considered as high achievers (another marker of status) by Mr O'Reilly. While Elisabeth and Sharon struggled to maintain friendships with majority-ethnic girls in the class, Sarah sought out Muslim girls in other classes during break-time and noted them as her friends in her socio-metric choices. The confusion and absence of 'belonging' is also borne out by Salma's comment below, as she reflects on her positioning in the social world of school:

> Salma: First I didn't know where I belong ... now I only like to be friends with Arabs cos I tried to be friends with Irish but it just didn't work ... they have really different stuff they do that we don't do [especially for girls].
>
> Palestinian

While there was evidence of ethnic clusters emerging within friendship groups, especially among girls, it would be a mistake to assume this was the case for all girls from minority-ethnic groups. Intra-ethnic conflict was also evident that was based on levels of adherence to norms within particular religious/ethnic groups and the differing orientations the children took to the extent to which they would assimilate into 'Irish' ways of being and doing (Devine, 2009). We see this in the contrasting experience of Karina and Karla—both Muslim girls in Grade 5 —who hold differing views on the extent to which they will adhere to Muslim practices and traditions. Karina receives some negative comment from her two Muslim peers who, in interviews, are critical of her lack of adherence to dietary and clothing requirements within Muslim culture and traditions:

> Narina: Last Thursday she [Karina] brought that chicken … Well me and her were telling her, you know that's not allowed in our religion … and her mum doesn't wear Hijab like our mums.

Karina actively works through and negotiates her own positioning—she is excluded from the intra-ethnic cluster of Narina and Karla and seeks to regain her own status and sense of belonging by pointing to her 'difference' from them and her simultaneous 'similarity' to her indigenous Irish peers:

> I'm a Muslim but my mum was brought up not wearing scarves and all the Muslims jeer me because I'm not like them … Sometimes, I wear scarves when I go to the Mosque. Since me and Karla used to be friends because we are both Muslims and everyone used to think we had loads of things in common.

Dynamics of inclusion and exclusion that are intertwined with those of sameness and difference are reflected in this excerpt as Karina speaks of the competitiveness among peers for friends as well as the isolation in being excluded:

> Since Narina came, she took Karla away from me. They use to leave me out because I wear dresses and don't have a scarf, they just wouldn't let me in.

The excerpt also indicates how simple stereotypes regarding ethnic and cultural identity ignore the hybrid forms this can take in differing cultural and social contexts, resulting in dynamics of inclusion/exclusion based on sameness/difference within ethnic groups as much as between them. In her effort to secure her status in school, Karina aligned herself to high status forms of femininity (Reay, 2001; 2006) through active participation in Gaelic football as well as a willingess to engage in the romance and fashion talk of her female peers. Karina's positioning with her Irish peers was facilitated not only by her own ambiguous positioning within the Muslim community, her football capacities (she was a member of the school girls' football team that had recently won a prize and she was very proud in showing me the photo displayed on the school wall) but also by her explicit identification with Irishness, as she proudly related that she held an Irish passport.

Social class was also a key part of the children's positioning (Devine, 2009) and must be considered in terms of the contrasting social-class positioning of many of the immigrant children (whose parents worked as medical professionals in a local hospital), relative to the working-class background of many of their indigenous Irish peers in Oakleaf primary. Underpinning Karina's positioning for example was also a sense of place (Lareau, 2003; Mac Ruairc, 2009) that derived from her middle-class position, her 'posh' background providing her with increased symbolic status among her indigenous female peers:

There are certain parts in Dublin ... places that are common and some are more posh. Where you live [Karina] is grand[3] ... it's private and it's really clean ... I don't think you'd get jeered a lot.

DISCUSSION

Children's social world in school is one which is simultaneously fun and risky, within which they invest a considerable degree of effort building alliances and friendships that are open to fluctuation and change. In so doing, they highlight their competence as active and social negotiators, mobilising whatever resources they have at their disposal in an effort to secure status and recognition in school. While this social positioning is an active process, it is also deeply embedded in the politics of recognition (Fraser, 2000) that derives from ethnic and gendered norms that prevail in the society at large.

Children, no less than adults, exercise power with one another, drawing on dominant discourses of normality and 'otherness' in their inclusionary/ exclusionary practices. While this analysis has highlighted the children's perception of difference, and the way that, for majority-ethnic children this is firmly embedded in cultural stereotypes about what it means to be 'Irish', the data also demonstrates the strategies that minority-ethnic children employ in coping with these norms. Such strategies are mediated by both gender and ability and, although it is not significantly developed in this paper, social class (Devine, 2009).

For minority-ethnic boys, dominant/high-status constructions of masculinity which revolved around being good at something, but especially sport, facilitated the successful integration of these boys into distinct male peer groups. This, coupled with the tendency for boys to play in large groups during playtime, appeared to provide them with significant opportunities for mixing and networking with their male peers. A question arises, however, as to the potential integration of minority-ethnic boys who do not conform to dominant masculine norms.

For newly arrived minority-ethnic girls, their initial high status among female peers gave way to different experiences of inclusion and exclusion, dependent upon their ability to find common ground with others and to negotiate their entry into relatively exclusive friendship groups. Identity work was clearly involved in these processes as cultural and gendered norms conflicted. High-status femininities especially an emphasis on 'boy' talk, fashion and appearance (but also in the case of Karina sporting prowess) within the talk of majority-ethnic girls, rendered it difficult for minority-ethnic girls who differed from this norm. While Sarah played with two Muslim girls in another class (in so doing heightening her 'other' status among majority-ethnic peers in her own class, but providing her with feelings of inclusion in school), Elisabeth and Sharon struggled at the fringes of the female peer network—their ethnic 'otherness' clearly positioning them in exclusionary terms. In two other classes, the successful integration of both Karina (Muslim) and Lisa (Traveller) into female peer groups coincided with their overt affiliation with dominant ethnic and gendered norms, giving rise to some criticism from within their own 'ethnic' groups.

The implications of such findings for policy can be considered on a number of levels. At a broader level, the analysis highlights the complexity of the children's social world and challenges any benign interpretation of children's interaction that draws on overly paternalistic and individualistic assumptions about their behaviour. As competent agents (Brembeck et al., 2004), children know what they do and why they do it—responding to the challenges and opportunities of peer group membership in the context of the cultural, social, emotional and material resources they have at their disposal (Devine, 2003). Policy must take account of this complexity as well as children's competency, acknowledging the multi-layered strands of identity that influences their positioning with one another in school.

At the level of implementation, whole school planning for equality, diversity and social inclusion needs to be undertaken that is relevant to the particular context of each school, while sensitive to national guidelines and best practice in the area. Particular attention should be given to the inclusion of newly arrived children to the school and the establishment of support structures (e.g. a 'buddy' system) to facilitate their integration. A charter of social relations should be included with an emphasis on respecting all forms of diversity in peer and pupil–teacher relations. The inclusion of the voices of parents and children from minority as well as majority-ethnic groups should be central to such planning. This, in itself, requires a commitment to the development of trusting and supportive relations between school personnel and members of the broader parent community and was something which both Mr Robinson and Ms Macken in Oakleaf Primary were committed to doing. However, racism and anti-racism needs to be confronted and named in such planning, moving beyond the tendency to tackle prejudicial behaviour solely within an anti-bullying framework and failing to acknowledge issues related to power, identity and the politics of difference in social relations in school. Such planning should also seek to empower children to name and confront all forms of prejudicial and exclusionary behaviour.

At the level of classroom practice, inclusive pedagogies need to be developed that provide an increased awareness of cultural diversity without stereotyping and further labelling minority-ethnic children as different and outside the norm. Teachers need to undergo their own identity work in this respect (e.g. What does it mean to be Irish? What are the norms I adhere to?) in order to be able to incorporate sensitively the experiences of a diverse group of pupils into effective classroom learning. Furthermore, while strategies such as co-operative learning and group project work, such as those employed by Mr O'Reilly, were effective in promoting positive inter-ethnic relations, teachers also need to be sensitive to how particular constructs of masculinity and femininity mediate children's interaction with one another. Developing an awareness of and sensitivity to the dynamics of child culture and the actual friendship patterns among children in the classroom is an important element here, enabling teachers to plan more effectively for the needs of children who are positioned at the margins of children's social world.

ENDNOTES

1   Gillborn (2006) remarks that while 'old racism' was based on a prejudice linked to feelings of superiority and inferiority, a new form of racism has emerged in recent years. Adopting notions of ethnicity and cultural difference, such racism rejects the 'influx' of those who are ethnically different, outside of what is considered 'normal', in the interests of social and

national cohesion. However, either form of racism rests on the power to define and impose particular representations of ethnic groupings, with resultant implications for their rights, status and participation within the society. Such representations are communicated through discourses which provide the logic with which our common-sense view of the world is structured and maintained.

2   There is a very strong tradition within Ireland of youth participation in 'Irish'-based games, organised on a voluntary basis at community/parish level by the Gaelic Athletic Association.

3   That Karina did not feel she needed to hide her middle-classness may be understood in the context of the increasing overall prosperity in Oakleaf estate—a working-class estate that was now shifting from social to private housing and relatively full employment, creating opportunities for upward mobility in a rapidly expanding economic environment. Conversely, it could be expected that with economic decline, a much more hostile attitude towards immigrant groups and resentment towards their higher class positioning would be expected, especially in areas most likely to be hit by economic recession.

5
ARE INCLUSIVE SCHOOLS POSSIBLE? STUDENTS WITH DISABILITIES AND SPECIAL EDUCATIONAL NEEDS IN SECOND-LEVEL SCHOOLS

William Kinsella

INTRODUCTION

The topic of inclusion of students with disabilities and special educational needs is at once the most topical, probably the most challenging and, possibly, the most significant, in terms of potential for change and development within the Irish education system today. It is contended that it is at second-level that the operationalisation of the ideal of inclusive education is likely to prove most challenging and, because of some unique characteristics of the Irish second-level system, it may prove even more challenging in Irish second-level schools than in other jurisdictions. The evolution of thought on the education of students with special educational needs, both internationally and nationally, has constituted an ideological journey from a segregationist, through an integrationist, to an inclusionist perspective. This constituted a change initially from separate provision in specialist settings to the integration of these students into mainstream education in the form of special classes or 'remedial' withdrawal programmes. The focus was on the nature of a student's difficulties and the level and nature of support required for that student to access the mainstream education system.

From the inclusionist perspective, the focus is no longer exclusively on students' individual needs, but is on also on the education system, at school and at national level, to determine if and how the system needs to change in order to meet the diversity of students, who are trying to access it. This reflects a shift from a medical model to a social model of disability. The impetus towards inclusive education has been accelerated by sentiments contained in the policies of international organisations—such as the Convention on the Rights of the Child and Convention on Rights of Persons with Disabilities (United Nations,

1989, 2006); Salamanca Statement (UNESCO, 1994); and the European Union (EU Council of Ministers' Charter, 1990, in Griffin & Shevlin, 2007)—and these sentiments have been translated into the legislation and policy of many national jurisdictions, including Ireland. The related developments in Irish education policy and legislation are outlined in detail by Griffin and Shevlin (2007).

This chapter reports some of the key findings from research that adopted a case-study approach, working closely with four second-level schools, to identify the challenges involved in developing more inclusive practices in schools.

RATIONALE FOR INCLUSION

According to Thomas and Vaughan (2004), the rationale for inclusive education represents the confluence of several streams of thought, namely social, political and educational. They state that it has arisen from: demands for greater social justice; calls for civil rights; prohibition of discrimination in legislation; educational research; and from the voices of service users of special education services. The theoretical and advocacy perspectives, which underpin the demand for more inclusive schools, include: equality; needs; rights; and participation.

Baker, Lynch, Cantillon and Walsh (2004) emphasise the importance of equality in education, stating that educational equality is articulated in a number of international legal instruments, that education is a conduit in the realisation of other rights, that proficiency in literacy and numeracy is essential for participation in the information society, that education impacts on personal development and that education, being mandatory in developed societies, is an intrinsic part of the lives of children for a very significant part of their childhood. However, the equality principle, in itself, is not considered sufficient as a guarantor of inclusive education, because equality is often compromised by the meritocratic principles inherent in society, such as 'survival of the fittest'. This is likely to provide the more talented with more status, resources and power both during their education and afterwards, while ensuring that only the successful are given a real opportunity to develop their capacities and to realise their potential (Gaden, 1993). While equality is essential, then, as a starting point in advocating for any potentially disadvantaged group, it is not sufficient to just treat all people equally, because equality does not mean treating everyone the same, as all people's needs are not the same, and some facilitation and accommodation is therefore required based on the concept of people's need.

The notion of need has dominated the discourse in disability education since the Warnock Report (Warnock, 1978) in the United Kingdom, as a consequence of which the term 'special educational needs' replaced the notion of 'handicap'. However, the concept of need may also be problematic as a foundation cornerstone of an inclusive education system, because the notion of need is value-laden, deficit-based and can be relative, thus varying according to context (Roaf & Bines, 1989). Furthermore, the needs of the less powerful and the disadvantaged are usually determined by persons who are more powerful and more privileged. This means that needs can be socially constructed, with the result that provision can be deficit-oriented and charity driven, granted as a concession rather than as of right. Therefore, while the concepts of equality and need are important in the context of educational provision for persons with disabilities or special educational needs, they are not, in themselves, sufficient in this regard.

According to Roaf and Bines (1989), the polices and practices of an education system should be based not on needs but on rights, as articulated in the UN Convention on the Rights of the Child (United Nations, 1989). They state that rights and equalisation of opportunities are a better way of framing the education of children who are experiencing difficulties in school. This right must go beyond the right of students with disabilities and special educational needs to merely access mainstream schools. It must extend to them the right to participate meaningfully in mainstream education, such a right to be reflected in the quality of their learning experiences, the learning credentials attained by them and their levels of participation in the totality of school life, including participation in extra-curricular activities.

The concept of rights has been the most contentious issue in relation to the disability legislation enacted in Ireland since 1998. This legislation is regarded as being both comprehensive and progressive and reflects a genuine attempt on the part of legislators to provide a legal framework for the inclusive participation of pupils with disabilities and special educational needs within the Irish education system (Baker et al., 2004). However, its main lacuna is that it does not constitute full, rights-based legislation, as demanded by disability advocacy groups in Ireland, as provision of services for persons with disabilities is subject to exchequer budgetary constraints. Similar criticisms have been directed at the legislation in other jurisdictions, such as the United Kingdom (e.g. Allan, 2008). In contrast, Roaf and Bines (1989) contend that the US system does not formally treat resource limits as constraining what can be provided for pupils with special educational needs and places the burden of adjustment on the ordinary school.

A crucial issue in the debate on inclusive education refers to the potential conflict of rights between students with special educational needs and their class peers. This potential conflict has not been resolved within the Education for Persons with Special Educational Needs Act (Government of Ireland, 2004a), which is the most pertinent piece of Irish legislation relating to special educational needs (SEN) provision. While advocating inclusive education, the act states that a child with special educational needs should be educated in a mainstream school except where this would not be in the best interest of the child or would be inconsistent with the effective provision of education for children with whom the child is to be educated. This proviso could give rise to conflicting interpretations and, possibly, future litigation proceedings.

RESEARCH QUESTION

The aim of this study was to explore, firstly, at whole-school level, the issues, challenges and opportunities for development in relation to the inclusion of students with disabilities and special educational needs in second-level, mainstream schools. The second aim of the study was to explore, with mainstream classroom teachers, the challenges involved at classroom level in effectively including students with special educational needs. A particular aim of the study was to identify if the core issues, difficulties or challenges identified by the participants could be explained or addressed at the micro-level of individual students and teachers or would more appropriately be addressed at the macro-levels of the whole school and the broader educational system.

RESEARCH PARADIGM

The central tenet of inclusive education is the requirement to shift the attribution frame of disabilities and difficulties from the individual to the environment and to the nature of the interactions between the two, in other words to shift from a medical model to a social model of disability. This involves a change from the concept of 'individual pathology' to 'organisational pathology'.

Skrtic (1991) contends that the institutional practice of special education is an organisational artefact that emerged to protect the legitimacy of a non-adaptable, bureaucratic education system. From this perspective, special education, special schools, special classes and compensatory withdrawal programmes have arisen not only on the basis of the severity of the needs of the pupils who avail of these services but as a consequence of the failure of the 'ordinary' education system to respond to the needs of all those attempting to access it. Inclusion theorists, such as Booth (1996), Ainscow (2000), and Thomas and Vaughan (2004) have continually called for the exclusion of some pupils to segregated specialist settings to be recognised as a form of institutionalised discrimination and a denial of human rights. Special education structures and arrangements may, therefore, be serving the needs of organisations and of professionals working within them more than the individual students assigned to such specialist provision. If the locus of causality of student failure and student disaffection is to be found, at least, partly in the context of the organisational structures of the educational system, then at least part of the solution must also be sought within these structures. The conclusion of this is that the organisation of special educational needs provision and the development of more inclusive practices in schools must also be approached and researched at the level of the organisation. For this reason, the research methodology adopted in this study has been informed substantially by the Organisational Psychology paradigm, with a focus on how schools function as organisations and how organisational structures can impact on educational provision for students with additional needs.

PREVIOUS RESEARCH

The study was also informed by a study undertaken in the United Kingdom by Clark, Dyson, Millward and Robson (1999). These authors selected four second-level schools, that were perceived to be inclusive, in order to observe what was happening 'on the ground', to establish if 'the practice matched the rhetoric'. Their stated aim was not simply to report the rhetoric of senior managers and policy documents, but to identify practices through which these approaches were, or were not, realised, to examine how teachers within the schools understood special needs and to investigate the schools' responses to special needs. They identified a number of difficulties encountered by schools, as attempts were made to implement more inclusive educational practices.

The first difficulty reported by these authors was the resistance of some teachers to the inclusion of some pupils, especially pupils with problematic behaviour. The second difficulty was that the 'technology' of inclusion, i.e. the systems, structures and procedures for enabling inclusion to occur, was inadequate. There were difficulties with the in-class support systems or team-teaching, in that there was not enough support to cover every class in which there were pupils with SEN. In other instances, there were relationship issues between classroom teachers and supporting teachers, roles were unclear and effective planning of the support partnership was largely non-existent.

Another major difficulty reported by the authors related to what they termed the 'resilience of the special education paradigm'. They concluded that the basic structures and assumptions of special education were residing not far beneath the surface, even within schools that were apparently inclusive. These included ability groupings and streaming, which were regarded by the authors as another form of segregation. In some cases, a special class had been created in a separate building. Sometimes, there was a different curriculum for students with special educational needs and a return to an emphasis on basic skills in literacy and numeracy frequently delivered outside mainstream classes in withdrawal settings, similar to 'remedial programmes' which have traditionally characterised special needs provision in mainstream schools. There was an ambiguous role for special educators, with a constant stream of referrals to the special educational needs co-ordinator of students excluded from their ordinary classes. According to these authors, the practices of special education appeared to be capable of resurrecting themselves in new guises in inclusive schools.

Another difficulty was perceived as arising from national educational policy, namely the fact that schools were constrained by the prescriptive National Curriculum introduced in 1987 and by the need to compete against each other for students in an education 'marketplace'. It was found that the inflexibility of the curriculum limited teachers' ability to respond to the diverse characteristics of their students, leading to the impossible demands of a diversity of students on the one hand and a tightly prescribed, content-heavy curriculum on the other. It was perceived that a school's reputation for 'being good with students with special needs' made it less attractive in the marketplace, while attracting increasing numbers of students with difficulties. This led to teacher resistance to the admission of more students with SEN. Clark, Dyson, Millward and Robson (1999), therefore, concluded that the movement towards inclusive schooling was difficult to manage, the direction was unclear and the movement was at least as much circular as it was linear.

RESEARCH METHODOLOGY IN PRESENT STUDY

This research project adopted a case-study approach of four second-level, mainstream schools. Three of these schools were urban-based and were participating in the Department of Education and Science initiative known as *Delivering Equality of Opportunity in Schools (DEIS): An Action Plan for Education Inclusion*, which replaced the label of 'disadvantaged' status (Department of Education & Science, 2005b). The fourth school was located in a provincial town and was not involved in this initiative. Three were voluntary-secondary schools, while one was a community college and was thus under the governance of a Vocational Educational Committee (VEC). Two of the schools were co-educational, while the other two were single-sex schools, one an all-boys' school and the other an all-girls' school. The schools ranged in size approximately from 400 to 800 students. The aim was to explore, in depth, with principals, special educational needs teachers and classroom teachers in the participating schools the issues and challenges involved in the inclusion of students with special educational needs in their schools. In-depth individual interviews were conducted with the principals and the special educational needs co-ordinators. Questionnaires were completed by a total of 140 teachers distributed across the four schools. Focus group interviews were conducted with teachers of one specific mixed-ability first year class group in each school. A total of 44 teachers participated in the focus-group interviews. The study adopted a developmental approach in that the emergent findings of the study were periodically discussed with the principals and the special needs personnel in the schools. Furthermore, meetings of the four principals were also organised and comments from these discussions and meetings were also incorporated into the findings of the study.

The advantages of this case-study approach were that it facilitated an in-depth analysis of the views of the participants and a detailed exploration of relevant issues at whole-school and at classroom level. The limitations of the study reside primarily in the small number of schools involved and, hence, the relatively small number of participants. Consequently, the sample of schools cannot be considered representative of Irish second-level schools and the generalisability of the findings is thus limited.

RESULTS

The teachers who participated in this study were generally in favour of the principle of inclusion, citing both academic and social benefits of inclusion and such benefits were not perceived as being confined to the students with special educational needs. However, not all participants were convinced of the merits of inclusion, while others would advocate it with some reservations, these reservations relating mainly to class size, the nature of the presenting disabilities, the spectrum of ability within particular classes, the nature and extent of challenging behaviour and the level of support available. Of the presenting conditions and difficulties, emotional behavioural difficulties were identified as presenting the greatest challenge to the second-level system. Discussion of this issue often occurred in the context of a possible conflict of rights between students with emotional behavioural difficulties and their class peers, whose educational experiences might possibly be impacted upon by the behaviour of these students.

As this study developed, a conceptual model of inclusion emerged based on the literature review and informed by the findings of the study. The core elements of this model refer to: the expertise that exists in schools to meet the needs of students with special educational needs; the resources available; and structures that are in place to operationalise that expertise and deploy the resources. While the expertise, resources and structures are considered necessary for the development of an inclusive school, it is hypothesised that there are certain over-arching processes of inclusion, which also need to operate if a school is to become more inclusive. Such processes would include: school planning and review procedures; modes of communication; and opportunities for consultation and collaboration. The processes would relate to how well the school functions as a system and as an organisation and would equate broadly to what Clark, Dyson, Millward and Robson (1999) referred to as the 'technology' of inclusion.

Expertise

Expertise, in the context of inclusive education, relates to the availability of specialist expertise in the school in relation to teaching students with special educational needs in the form of personnel who have received formal qualifications in this regard, to classroom teachers' competence in teaching such students and the availability of, and teachers' participation in, continuing professional development initiatives relating to SEN.

There was quite a diversity in both the availability and deployment of specialist SEN expertise in the four participating schools. In two of the schools, the person charged with responsibility for co-ordinating SEN provision held specialist SEN qualifications while, in the other two schools, this role was performed by a deputy principal and career guidance teacher. In only one of the schools was all additional SEN teaching provided by qualified SEN teachers. In two of the schools, up to 30 per cent of the staff were involved in additional special needs provision. The arrangements for providing extra tuition were sometimes as much a factor of teacher availability at a given time within a student's timetable as the nature of the student's needs.

The issue of the challenge of teaching a broad curriculum to increasingly diverse groups of students gave rise to a debate about mainstream teachers' levels of preparation for this task in relation both to initial and to in-career teacher education. The principals strongly advocated a review of initial teacher education to prepare teachers for the current reality of second-level schools. It was felt that this review would need to address, inter alia, the duration and content of teacher education courses and the nature and number of teaching placements undertaken as part of these courses.

The perceived shortcomings of the initial education received by teachers currently in the system gave rise to discussions about the effectiveness or otherwise of in-career teacher education. It was generally agreed that there had not been sufficient 'in-service' available in relation to special needs education and it was further stated that the inputs that had been provided were generally ineffective and were not sufficiently practical. In a number of instances, such inputs were regarded as pushing a particular agenda on behalf of school management. Teachers stated that the most useful inputs were those that were subject-specific, such as those provided by subject-associations, but they objected to the fact that these had to be availed of in one's own 'free time' and at teachers' own expense. The principals felt that in-career education should be compulsory and should be organised outside of the school timetable, with appropriate remuneration for teachers, if necessary. They contended that the system of in-career teacher education was in need of critical review, in relation to organisation, content, mode of delivery, level of co-ordination between the multiplicity of agencies involved and its overall effectiveness in forging change at classroom level.

The principals were anxious to point out that there was also need for professional development opportunities for principals and management personnel in relation to SEN provision and the management of the change that is inevitable in schools becoming more inclusive.

Resources

In parallel with, and following from, the equality and disability legislation which has been enacted in this country, there has been an exponential increase in the allocation of resources for pupils with disabilities and special educational needs, such resources constituting human, physical, therapeutic and technological supports, and this was generally acknowledged and welcomed by the participants in the study. Some concerns were expressed that perhaps the available resources were not always being used to maximum advantage, as SEN resource materials tended to remain within the remit and the responsibility of SEN personnel, and were rarely found in mainstream classrooms where they could be used for the benefit of all students.

It was also stated that resources were sometimes underutilised due to lack of time on the part of teachers and lack of training in how to use them. The principals acknowledged that the resource application and allocation system had improved considerably, but also recommended that the whole resource system be evaluated to determine its effectiveness in terms of enhanced performance by the students who are in receipt of the additional support and resources.

Structures

With regard to the co-ordination of special educational needs provision, there is no specific post of responsibility for such co-ordination in Irish schools such as exists, for example, in the United Kingdom, in the form of special educational needs co-ordinators (SENCo). Under the Code of Practice (DfES, 1994, 2001), there is a SENCo appointed in each school. There were varying arrangements for the co-ordination of such provision in the schools participating in this study. In two of the schools, there was a reasonably tight departmental structure in relation to special needs provision, involving a co-ordinator and four or five teachers, who were predominantly, though not exclusively, involved in special needs teaching. In the other two schools, the arrangements were much 'looser', with greater deployment of mainstream class teachers in the provision of additional support. This usually involved class teachers being allocated a few hours each week to teach pupils with special needs in their specialist subject. This posed considerable challenges in relation to the co-ordination of this support. The predominant mode of delivery of additional support in three of the schools was individual or small-group tuition on a withdrawal basis, while team-teaching was used to a considerable extent in the fourth school as well as small-group withdrawal.

The efficiency of the system of provision for students with special needs will be influenced not only by the structure of the SEN system in the school but also by the overall class structures that pertain in the school. The single most contentious issue that emerged during this study was the issue of mixed-ability teaching and learning. Management in three of the schools had, relatively recently, moved from some system of streaming or banding of students, according to ability, to mixed-ability class settings and this was meeting with some resistance in each of these schools. In the fourth school, the principal said that his school had been operating a mixed-ability system for over 20 years, but conceded that students were still streamed in English, Mathematics and Irish from various stages in first year. Another principal had been attempting to retain mixed-ability settings until Junior Certificate, but had just yielded to severe pressure from teachers of the 'core' subjects, English, Mathematics and Irish, to set up 'bands' within these subjects in second year.

The concern was that adhering to a strict mixed-ability system up to Junior Certificate would negatively impact on Junior Certificate results. One of the principals stated that it might impact on the Junior Certificate results, but the experience in his school was that the real positive impact of mixed-ability settings really only became evident at Leaving Certificate level, with improved school retention and increased school completion. The other principal stated that 'it would be difficult to hold the nerve' and that 'staff would not have the patience to wait that long' for the positive effects to become evident. For some of the principals, the survival of their schools into the future was dependent on the maintenance of academic standards and the retention of the perception of being an 'academic' school.

The mainstream class teachers articulated both advantages and disadvantages of mixed-ability settings and any reluctance to embrace this approach was frequently borne out of a concern for their students, their subjects and for academic standards. There was a concern that the students at both ends of the disability spectrum could be disadvantaged, due to a teacher tendency to 'teach to the middle'. This concern was accentuated by the fact that the range of diversity within the classes was perceived as widening. Other teachers were conditionally in favour of mixed-ability teaching, citing class size as the main determinant of its feasibility. Many teachers recommended that mixed-ability settings should only operate in first year. Time constraints were identified as the main barrier to effective mixed-ability teaching, an issue that was all the more pertinent because of the failure to address and reform other related key elements, such as the breadth and depth of the curriculum and how it is examined. The teachers queried how they should examine material for students taught in mixed-ability settings. It was contended that while teachers were being exhorted to embrace mixed-ability teaching, no attention was being paid to mixed-ability assessment and the Department of Education and Science was persisting with examining students at two or three levels in practically all subjects:

> It would be different if you were going towards a common paper, but you're going towards Higher and Ordinary. The Department are confusing everybody, because they even set three standards in some subjects. I just can't understand that the Department are saying one thing and they're doing something else.
>
> Teacher

The teachers felt that when one attempts to differentiate curriculum content and meet the needs of all students within a diverse classroom, one must inevitably move at a slower pace, with the result that it takes more time to cover each topic. Consequently, according to the respondents, there is a real risk of not covering all the topics on a curriculum—a curriculum that has not been reviewed to take account of the new teaching and learning contexts of inclusive mixed-ability settings.

The challenges of effectively teaching students in mixed-ability settings identified by the class teachers in this study were, therefore, the interrelated factors of a wide spectrum of ability, with a consequential wide range of needs in terms what students needed to access within the curriculum, broad curriculum content, assessment-led demands and time constraints. It was the interrelatedness and the interaction of these factors in particular which were emphasised by the teachers as constituting significant challenges for them. One teacher, who had been trained in another jurisdiction and who felt that he had been very well trained in the differentiation of teaching and assessment for mixed-ability settings stated: 'I can differentiate the curriculum, I can do mixed-ability teaching, I can teach a comprehensive curriculum, but I cannot do all three together.'

Processes

The two issues of time and co-ordination repeatedly emerged in this study as being the key factors in the development of more inclusive practices in schools. It was perceived that there was a lack of co-ordination within second-level schools, especially in relation to the organisation of provision for students with special educational needs and the incorporation of that provision into the general operation of the school. This lack of co-ordination was mainly due to structural deficits, such as the lack of a special educational needs department co-ordinated by a dedicated person, and by organisational issues, such as time-constraints and timetabling issues, as manifested in timetabling constraints resulting from the organisation of the school day and the school year. There were calls for more co-ordination at all levels within the education system, and between the education system and other key agencies. Issues arose pertaining to the transition of students from primary to second-level schools which emphasise the need for considerably improved levels of communication and collaboration between the various levels of the education system.

Teachers' concerns about the perceived poor literacy levels of students entering first year were confirmed by the literacy scores of, albeit, a small sample of students examined as part of this study. These literacy levels would give rise to serious concerns about the accessibility of second-level textbooks for a certain proportion of students entering first year. This concern would be accentuated by the fact that, in most instances, there were ineffective procedures in place for informing mainstream classroom teachers about the literacy difficulties of the students in their classes.

IMPLICATIONS AND CONCLUSIONS

The aim of this study was to explore, at whole-school level, the issues, challenges and opportunities for development in relation to the inclusion of students with disabilities and special educational needs. Informed by the social model of disability, which aims to deflect the focus from the individual deficits of students to the structure of the learning environment, the study was informed by the Organisational Psychology paradigm, which prompted a focus on possible organisational deficits of schools and the national education system in which schools operate. The first aim was to describe what was happening in the participating schools in relation to SEN provision. A striking aspect of this description was the diversity of practices, structures and policies that were in operation in the four schools, which would suggest a lack of a cohesive model of inclusive education in second-level schools. This diversity manifested itself first and foremost in the personnel involved in organising and delivering special educational needs provision in the schools.

The issue of the nature of provision for students with special needs at second-level and the nature of the personnel involved in this provision raises fundamental questions about the aims of special-needs teaching at this level. It prompts a debate about whether the aims of such inputs should be to improve overall academic performance, through development of literacy and numeracy skills, or should aim to increase accessibility of the mainstream curriculum through providing inputs in individual mainstream subjects. The outcome of that debate has implications for the initial training of both special needs teachers and mainstream teachers. If substantial inputs for these students are delivered by mainstream class teachers in their own subject specialisms, there may be a danger of special needs teaching becoming, in part, an institutionalised 'grind' system for lower achieving students and the delivery of provision may be determined as much by organisational expediency, in terms of teacher availability, as by student need.

This study has been informed by previous research undertaken in the United Kingdom by Clark, Dyson, Millward and Robson (1999). These authors postulated that a number of dilemmas were at work which rendered the inclusion of students with special educational needs difficult to implement. Very similar dilemmas were found to operate in the schools in this study.

One such dilemma was the possible conflicting tension between the need to maintain and, where possible, raise standards and, at the same time, cater for an increasing diversity of student within mainstream schools and, where possible, to teach these students in mixed-ability settings. This dilemma becomes all the more pertinent when the future survival of a school is perceived as depending on the maintenance and improvement of academic standards, as was the case with some of the schools in this study. This has been articulated as the equity-excellence dilemma and, referring to the UK context, Black-Hawkins, Florian and Rouse (2007, p. 1) state:

> High levels of inclusion can be entirely compatible with high levels of achievement; combining the two is not only possible but essential if all children are to have the opportunity to participate fully in education.

However, these authors do acknowledge that doing so can make great demands on those who work in classrooms and schools. The difficulty in resolving this dilemma has also been acknowledged by statutory bodies such as the House of Commons Select Committee:

Regardless of the theory, in practice the evidence clearly demonstrates that Special Educational Needs and the raising attainment agenda sit very uncomfortably together at present.

House of Commons Select Committee Report, 2006, p. 66

This dilemma raises fundamental questions about the nature and aims of second-level education.

This study has also been informed by the rights and participation agenda. The participants in this study were found to be struggling with these issues, firstly due to the possible conflict of rights between students with disabilities and special educational needs and those without such difficulties. They were struggling to ensure the appropriate participation of all students within their classrooms, especially in the context of mixed-ability teaching and learning environments. They were concerned that they were not giving sufficient time and assistance to the less able students, while not sufficiently challenging the more able students and not covering the curriculum at a level that is possible in more homogenous groupings and that is demanded by the state assessment system. There was a sense of a lack of 'joined-up thinking' between the demands for mixed-ability teaching and learning while at the same persisting with traditional forms of assessment at two or three different levels in most subjects, the curricular content of which makes high demands on students and teachers and which has not been reviewed in the context of the new reality of second-level mainstream schools and classrooms.

The overall conclusion is that while very significant efforts were being made in the participating schools to cater for students with disabilities/special educational needs, there was no consistent model of integrated or inclusive practices evident across the schools. It does not appear that the schools had undergone the restructuring that is required to effectively meet the needs of all pupils who are presenting with difficulties. The indications are, therefore, that the practices generally adopted to respond to the needs of pupils with disabilities and special educational needs are derived more from the integrationist rather than from the inclusionist perspective and, consequently, the attitudinal shift and the changes in the ethos, culture and practices that are required for the effective inclusion of such pupils do not appear to have been realised yet in these schools or, quite possibly, in the majority of Irish second-level schools.

The findings of this study are contextualised within a hypothesised model of inclusive education incorporating the expertise, resources, structures and processes that are regarded as requisite for the development of an inclusive school.

Fundamental issues and questions have been raised in the course of this study, which can only be addressed at the structural level of the school and the wider national education system. Some of these questions are central to the nature of education as a whole; such as those pertaining to the aim of second-level education in general and to the aim of special needs education at second-level in particular. The related issue of the need for a critical review of initial and in-career teacher education is a macro-educational issue. There are organisational issues which need to be addressed at school and at national level in order to achieve more co-ordination and communication between different sectors within the education sector, including between primary and second-level schools, and between different personnel within schools, especially between SEN personnel and mainstream class teachers.

The lack of co-ordination at school level, evident in this study, was mainly due to a lack of organisational structures for SEN provision and a lack of time, resulting from the constraints of daily and yearly school timetables. This lack of organisational structures and lack of time for consultation and collaboration between school personnel is likely to inhibit the development of more inclusive practices in schools, because consultation and collaboration are the core elements of the processes of inclusion or what Clark, Dyson, Millward and Robson (1999) termed the 'technology' of inclusion. Without these processes, the substantial expertise and resources that are currently available in Irish second-level schools in relation to the education of students with special educational needs are likely to be less than fully effective. In the absence of appropriate consultation, the 'inclusion agenda' is regarded as being imposed on mainstream classroom teachers and thus is less likely to be embraced by them.

These are issues that can only be resolved at the macro-level within the education system, involving consultations between key stakeholders, such as the Department of Education and Science, teacher unions and managerial bodies. This means that the development of more inclusive practices in schools will only be realised in the context of the interaction between the strengths and needs of individual learners and the organisational strengths and needs of schools and the national education system. The indications from this study are that, to date, the focus has been predominantly on the former rather than on the latter and that there is need for a change of focus in this regard.

6

ADHD: INCLUSION OR EXCLUSION IN MAINSTREAM IRISH SCHOOLS?

Joyce Senior

ADHD: A CONTESTED CONCEPT

In many professional circles, Attention Deficit Hyperactivity Disorder (ADHD) is a contested concept in that the diagnosis of a 'psychiatric disorder' is based on a range of aspects of behaviour which are subjectively measured by professionals with considerable reliance on behaviour checklists. The *Diagnostic and Statistical Manual of Mental Disorders* (DSM-IV) (American Psychiatric Association, 1994) includes ADHD as a discrete member of the class of 'Disruptive Behaviour Disorders' and states that it is characterised by persistent inattention and/or hyperactivity/impulsivity which occur across several settings and more frequently and severely than adults judge to be typical for children of the same chronological developmental stage.

In the broad context of learning difficulties in general, the interest that ADHD evokes is quite remarkable. Wilkinson (2003) claims that all other childhood difficulties combined have not generated the prolonged and intensive scrutiny given to ADHD. While much has been written about the condition, it remains a frequently misunderstood disorder. According to Kewley (1999), ADHD is one of the most overlooked and misunderstood of all childhood difficulties. Yet it is one of the most frequently occurring conditions amongst school-going children. According to the Department of Health and Children (Department of Health & Children, 2001), the prevalence of ADHD in Ireland can be estimated between 1 per cent and 5 per cent among school-age children (i.e. aged five-15 years) which is in line with the research findings in other European countries. According to the DSM-IV (American Psychiatric Association, 1994), the disorder is much more frequent in males than in females, with male-to-female ratios ranging from 4:1 to 9:1, depending on the setting (i.e. general population or clinics). The prevalence rate for severe ADHD in Ireland can be estimated at approximately 1 per cent of the school-going population (Department of Health & Children, 2001). The children diagnosed are those severely affected, who are usually also comorbid for other disorders, e.g. depression, conduct disorder, learning difficulties or dyslexia.

The increasing incidence of ADHD has given rise to scepticism that so many children in our cognitively and educationally affluent societies should be afflicted with a disorder rarely, if ever, mentioned in Irish schools even 15 years ago. According to Weiss and Hechtman (1993), ADHD has clearly become the most-researched and best-known of the childhood behaviour disorders in the past 20 years. They feel this is due to a number of reasons, including the fact that it is the most common single condition for which children are referred to child psychiatry clinics, and also because the condition is severe enough to be very distressing to teachers and parents and to the children themselves. Despite this high level of interest, ADHD remains an elusive disorder. Wilkinson (2003) contends that further study of ADHD is essential because, despite the ever-increasing research and public debate about attention problems and hyperactivity, ADHD still defies precise definition and specification, particularly as these relate to the behavioural and medical management of the condition at home and in school. Despite increasing public debate and concern about ADHD, there is a dearth of research information and baseline studies on ADHD in Ireland.

Stead, Lloyd and Cohen (2006) contend that ADHD is a global phenomenon, spreading rapidly as a result of the increasing dominance internationally of US psychiatric models, the need for new markets for major pharmaceutical companies, the increasing use of the internet by parents and professionals and changing approaches to schooling. It is interesting that not all countries have embraced the ADHD construct. While it is well established in many countries, including the United States, Canada, Australia, Norway, Sweden, Denmark and the United Kingdom, it is notable that great international disparities exist in the use of stimulants as treatment for ADHD. It is estimated that 97 per cent of the global sales of drugs for ADHD were derived from the United States, with the rest being from Europe (CNS Drug Discoveries, 2004). However, certain countries with high rates of adult psychiatric drug use, such as Italy and France, appear to have resisted using stimulants with children in any significant manner (Cohen, 2000). In fact, Bonati (2006) reports that Methylphenidate (Ritalin) was withdrawn from the Italian market in 1989 by the manufacturer due to low sales and because of the increasing illicit use of the drug.

While methodical explanations for international differences in the ADHD construct is lacking, it is possible that the 'reality' of ADHD might assume different forms in countries just beginning to embrace the construct. It is notable that the established prevalence rate of ADHD among Italian school-going children is 1–2 per cent (Bonati, 2006). Since the 1970s, Italy has had a national policy of integrating nearly all students with disabilities into the general education classroom. As a result, many advocates of inclusion have identified Italy as an excellent example of how wide-range inclusion can be accomplished (Begeny, 2007).

In the Western world, an increasing recognition of the political and social construction of disability combined with moves to inclusion have been paradoxically paralleled by ever-increasing use of psychotropic medication for children (Lloyd & Norris, 1999). The irony of the increasing medicalisation of behaviour in school is the resultant 'inclusion' of students who may otherwise have been excluded from school. Conversely, it may also be argued that the label ADHD provides schools with an alibi to explain why they regularly fail to facilitate some children in the only societal institution designed exclusively for children.

Although a prolific number of publications in relation to ADHD exist, few take a critical view of the concept and associated practices, particularly in relation to the educational experiences of children in schools. Despite the considerable contested construct of the ADHD and its associated labelling and the alleged widespread (ab)use of stimulant medications, the fact remains that, for many students with ADHD and their families, life, and in particular the school-going years, is a struggle.

Drawing on 10 case studies, this chapter offers insight into the reality of the difficulties experienced by both the person with ADHD and their families in relation to their educational experiences.

OVERVIEW OF THE STUDY

The general aim of the empirical aspect of the study was to obtain, from in-depth, structured interviews with 10 young people with a formal diagnosis of ADHD and their parents, a comprehensive view of the medical, educational and behavioural characteristics of ADHD, as well as the provision afforded them. A developmental psychopathological approach was employed in order to examine the complex pathways from earliest childhood into adolescence in order to identify critical factors which may have inhibited or exacerbated the characteristics associated with ADHD. Bee (2002) contends that even for a disorder such as ADHD, which appears to have major biological causes, the severity and persistence of the disorder can be best understood in terms of the child's cumulative patterns of interaction as well as the child's own internal models of relationships. According to Masten (1989), investigations of children's responses to specific risk factors, and of resilience and vulnerability, are one 'window' on the process, since they enable close observation of processes that are normally so gradual or subtle that they defy observation.

The next section of this chapter will draw on one aspect of the study which was an examination of the school experiences of the 10 students. The sample, which constituted a total of 10 sets of parents and their children who were living in the Greater Dublin area, was derived from two sources: the patient files of a Dublin-based consultant paediatrician (who co-operated while strictly observing the ethical and data protection guidelines); and the membership file of the Hyperactive/Attention Deficit Disorder (HADD) Family Support Group in Dublin. Of the 10 families, eight were in the middle-class socio-economic category while two were in the lower socio-economic class. Consequently, it cannot be claimed that the views reported in this study are representative of all parents of children with ADHD in Ireland, since the sample consisted of families who had variously availed of, or who had access to, the best services and facilities available for children with ADHD, whether in terms of the advisory and support services provided by HADD or the paediatric services provided by the consultant clinician who collaborated in the selection of the sample or indeed in relation to school choice.

Because of the fact that there was only one female who fulfilled the age criterion in the initial sample, and because of the established 4:1 prevalence of males to females with ADHD (American Psychiatric Association, 1994), the study was limited to males.

In order to make the case studies more representative, it was decided to include children from as many stages as possible in the education system, i.e. from upper primary school through to post-Leaving Certificate. Of the final sample, four of the participants were in the 10 to 12 age range; four were in the 12 to 18 age range, while two of the respondents were in the 18 to 21 age range. Four children were in primary school, while four were in second-level education. In two cases, the students had completed secondary school and were in part-time salaried occupations. One had just completed the Leaving Certificate (Applied)

Examination and was working in a temporary job while the other had taken a year out of a third-level degree course and was also working while studying for repeat examinations. Tragically, this student committed suicide the following year.

'ADHD? OH, YEAH I THINK I'VE HEARD OF THAT': PARENTAL EXPERIENCES OF SCHOOLS' DISPOSITION TOWARDS STUDENTS WITH ADHD

The parental interviews clearly showed that there is an urgent need for greater recognition of ADHD and its associated difficulties in the Irish school system. Although the majority of the parents in the present study said they had received an initial favourable reaction when they told school principals about their child's condition, only four of the parents reported that the principal was willing to cater for their son's needs on an ongoing basis. When enrolling their son in second-level school, one set of parents said that when they told the principal their son had ADHD, he just commented, 'That's interesting', but allegedly used the information prejudicially in subsequent dealings with the student. By this, the parents meant that the principal used any excuse to refer to the boy's ADHD both in public and private, and allegedly requested a letter from a psychiatrist to state that it was 'safe' to allow the student to remain in the school. The conflicting discourse used by principals in relation to enrolment versus the extent to which they (and by implication the schools) were prepared to cater for the children's needs are illustrated in the following comments:

> The principal's reaction was favourable, he said he had heard of ADHD but he wouldn't enrol him if he wasn't taking medication.
>
> Secondary school

> We received a good reaction from the principal, but he wasn't confident that admitting him to the school would be a long-term solution. He said he'd had children like this before and from his experience it wouldn't work out.
>
> Secondary school

> The principal said, 'Oh yeah, I think I've heard of that.'
>
> Primary school

The principal just said, 'Ah, we're used to that. It's no big deal.' He didn't want me to think he was ignorant about the matter.

Primary school

The reality, however, was that placement in mainstream schools did not, of itself, guarantee inclusion. Although all of the parents discussed their child's condition with their child's class or form teacher(s), six of them reported that teachers' reactions were unfavourable. As is evident from the following parental comments, there were mixed levels of support at teacher level, with some feeling that mainstream schools could not cater for children with ADHD.

Yes, I tried to discuss it with them [the teachers] but they just didn't want to know about it. They said he should be on Ritalin and attending a psychiatrist.

Secondary school

When I met his form teacher, she told me that I'd no right to send a child like that to boarding school, and that I'd never told them that he had ADHD. The information wasn't passed on to the teachers by the principal.

Secondary school

She [form teacher] just wasn't having it; she was not interested! She said that Ritalin was given to children whose parents couldn't manage them and that he would be better placed in a special school where they could cater for kids like him.

Secondary school

Yes, I discussed it with all the teachers. Some were receptive enough, while others advised me to take him out and put him in a special class.

Primary school

A central and somewhat disconcerting theme when examining the parents' narratives in relation to discussing their child's condition with school personnel was the underlying views of both principals and teachers that enrolment or subsequent placement in the school was dependent on medication and/or psychiatric treatment. Parents commented that although the teachers knew of the condition, they allegedly knew very little about its management. Only three parents reported that their child's teacher(s) asked them for more information about ADHD and its management. In general, the primary-school teachers were said to have been more understanding and supportive than teachers at second level. The medical deficit model, as opposed to a systemic view of learning and behavioural difficulties, was apparently entrenched in certain schools.

All of the parents indicated a sense of powerlessness and lack of autonomy regarding their child's schooling. As parents, they felt that their child's education was a constant struggle as they had to tirelessly advocate for their child and make major decisions regarding issues such as school choice, psychological assessments and subsequent battles to obtain additional learning support (both in terms of in-school support and private tuition), medication and even finding alternate school placements. Despite having a formal diagnosis of ADHD and experiencing educational difficulties, many of the parents spoke of their personal struggle, often without the support of the school, in obtaining additional learning/resource support for their child.

I had to take a legal case against the DES to get one [a resource teacher].

Primary school

The principal wasn't supportive at all. We had to change school in fifth class on the advice of the psychiatrist who said our son was very unhappy in school. I had to hound the Department of Education to get three hours with a resource tutor in second year, but it didn't work out because some days the tutor didn't turn up—it was very scrappy.

Primary and secondary school

The parents also spoke of the dilemma they faced in relation to being 'grateful' for the school placement versus their unhappiness that their child was frequently stopped from participating in school-related activities, such as tours, outings and sports.

There is always a threat there—for playing rugby, football matches, going to movies, on school trips, it's always hanging over him.

Secondary school

There were also more overt cases of exclusionary practices in the form of suspension and expulsion. In studies by Barkley, Fischer and Edelbrock (1991), and Wilson and Marcotte (1996), significantly more adolescents with ADHD were suspended from school than their non-ADHD peers. Mannuzza, Klein, Bessler, Malloy and Hynes (1997) have also reported that children with ADHD were found to have completed less formal education and to have achieved lower occupational levels than control groups. In the present study, six of the 10 students had been suspended from school at some stage, with four of them being suspended more than three times, and one student being suspended 15 times in one year. The four students who had not been suspended were still in primary school. Reasons for suspension included: fighting; messing and accidentally throwing a bag out a window; writing graffiti which was targeted at the principal; shaving his head; setting another student's hair alight; stealing mobile phones and a wallet; verbally abusing teachers; and smoking.

Having been suspended a number of times, one of the students was expelled a few months before he was due to take the Junior Certificate Examination. His parents could not find a place for him in another school so he did not sit the examinations.

Another parent had to take a legal case against the Department of Education and Science to get her son back into a school. After he had sat the Junior Certificate, they received a letter from his school saying that they could not offer him a place on the Senior Cycle course. They applied to a number of other schools but were refused a place. The Department of Education and Science then offered him a place on a Youthreach programme, which they did not accept as they wanted him to complete the Leaving Certificate. After lengthy negotiations, the Department of Education and Science finally secured a place in a Community College to which he had to get a taxi because of its distance from his home. However, the school then said that they could not meet his needs and asked him to leave. His parents subsequently took the case to the High Court for judicial review. He was offered a place on Youthreach again, but his parents would not accept this on its own, so he was given a part-time tutor (nine hours tuition for English and Mathematics) as well as part-time Youthreach training. Finally, his parents secured a place in a school in which he passed the Leaving Certificate Applied Examination.

In summary, when asked if they felt that the school system had met the needs of their child, all of the parents emphatically stated that it had not. Reasons included lack of knowledge and understanding about ADHD among the teaching profession, lack of resources and facilities in schools, lack of awareness of just entitlements, difficulties in getting appropriate assessments and in securing learning support, even in cases where their children were officially entitled to such resources. Due to the alleged unwillingness of the Department of Education and Science to meet their obligations, two of the parents in the present sample were forced to take legal action to secure the type of education to which their child was entitled. The following parental comments illustrate their general feelings of dissatisfaction with the Irish educational system and the ongoing struggle and hardship with which they were faced:

No, it has not met his needs. If I had not been in a position to pay for all the assessments and subsequent grinds and tutoring, he wouldn't have got this far. School was such a miserable time for him—he was miserable in school, he rarely smiled. Maybe if he'd had Ritalin then, his life would have been so different.

Secondary school

No, it has definitely not met his needs. They don't know anything about the condition and they don't want to know about it either—they think it's used as an excuse.

Secondary school

I had to enrol him in a private, fee-paying school and even at that there have problems getting appropriate help for him.

Secondary school

No, it hasn't met his needs, but it's not the school's fault. The system needs to be revised for children who have conditions such as ADHD.

Primary school

No way, it most definitely has not. The system is at fault; we have had difficulties trying to get the nine hours of tuition that he's entitled to [because he was expelled from school and they were having difficulties finding another school in which to enrol him].

Secondary school

No, definitely not, especially if a child is not of average ability. They don't cater for children who learn at a slower rate. Look at how I had to take a legal case in order to get a resource teacher. I could have put all the time and energy that took into looking after my sons.

Primary school

No, not yet, because mainstream schools do not yet have enough resources and facilities to include these children enough.

Primary school

Absolutely not. There's no support or interest. We had to pay for [our son] to be assessed in England; that involved four visits in one year but it was worth it. Now we're not getting anywhere trying to get support for him in school. The principal says there's just nothing available; they haven't even been assigned a psychologist yet and he says he can do nothing until then.

Secondary school

'TROUBLEMAKERS AND MESSERS': STUDENTS' VIEWS ON THEIR SCHOOL EXPERIENCE

While the nature of the school experiences of the children appeared to depend on the ethos and inclusive nature of the setting, it was clear from the students' articulate narratives that the majority of them felt that the school, and in particular the teachers, did not know how to deal with the difficulties associated with ADHD. Seven of the 10 students felt that their teachers had no understanding of the difficulties associated with ADHD, while six of them said that there was allegedly nothing done to help them with their difficulties. Two students commented that by having a diagnosis of ADHD, they felt they were labelled as 'troublemakers' or 'messers', and that this affected their teachers' opinions of them.

It was also clear from the student narratives that they experienced tremendous exclusionary pressures in the form of negative attitudes and stigmatisation. Nine of the 10 students said that they had been called names, such as pigs, 'muppets', idiots, and/or had been told that they were lazy, stupid or apathetic. It was noteworthy that a number of parents expressed relief when their child was actually diagnosed with ADHD, as it confirmed their contention that their child was not 'stupid'. Questions relating to school experiences evoked a palpably emotional reaction from nine of the 10 students, and the embarrassment and hurt that they felt was evident in the manner in which they spoke about their experiences. The comment by one student that he was 'totally demoralised in front of the class' by some of the teachers was reflected in many of the other students' comments. The following are some of their comments regarding how they were allegedly treated by some of their teachers:

I was often told, 'You're lazy', because there were certain times that I could do really well in exams and other times not, but they didn't understand the reasons for this variance in performance.

Post-secondary school, age 19

Yes, I got called names a lot and told I was lazy. In first year, the vice-principal hit me for doing nothing. I lost a lot of respect for teachers after that.

Secondary school, age 17

I was often told that I was apathetic. Other teachers totally demoralised me in front of the class.

Post-secondary school, age 21

Loads of them gave out to me, especially when I wasn't taking medication. I'd become annoyed and answer them back and then get in trouble again.

Secondary school, age 17

Yeah, I've been called lazy a few times. Some of the times it was because I wasn't paying attention in class, but other times it were just because I find it so difficult to listen all the time.

Primary school, age 12

Yes, I've been called a muppet, an idiot and stupid. He'd physically take me and lift me by the arm out of the seat and drag me up to the top of the class and say, 'Look at this boy, he's an idiot.'

Primary school, age 9

She kept on telling me that I was lazy and that I wasn't paying attention, even when I was. I felt like punching her in the face.

Secondary school, age 16

Two of the students and their parents referred to alleged physical abuse by the teachers; one boy was allegedly hit by the vice-principal, while another nine-year-old boy was lifted out of his chair by his arm and dragged up to the top of the classroom, where the teacher instructed the other children to, 'Look at this boy, he's an idiot.'

The students also referred to other exclusionary pressures, such as inappropriate teaching methodologies, failure to respond to diversity and learning styles and overall lack of commitment to inclusive education. When asked what kind of things were particularly unhelpful or upsetting in school, the students cited: taking down a lot of work from the blackboard; impatience; not explaining material adequately; lack of consistent discipline practices; lack of encouragement; being over strict; and not being given an opportunity to explain their actions. The following comments give an insight into their experiences at class level:

> There was such a lack of patience. The least helpful teachers were those who just sent you out of the classroom. I missed out on a lot of subjects because I was sent outside the door so much.
>
> Post-secondary school student, age 21

> The year head was very strict and terrorised my mother about me not keeping up in class. I nearly had a breakdown over him. I was suspended every year, apart from first year.
>
> Post-secondary school student, age 19

> I found it hard because they didn't explain things properly and expected us to take down things quickly. If I asked them to repeat a question, they'd become impatient and think that I wanted to cause trouble.
>
> Secondary school student, age 16

> The worst teacher was X. He never encouraged me. He picked on me constantly for two years. Every time I'd try to please him he'd say, 'Hm', and throw my copy on the desk without looking at it and then pick up someone else's copy. If I asked for help, he'd ignore me. He gave me a lot of punishment, for example, lines for doing small things. I never did PE, not once during the whole year.
>
> Primary school student, age 12

> The most upsetting thing is when teachers don't let pupils explain themselves, for example, when they get in trouble. I understand that it's a problem because they often don't have enough time to listen to the pupils, but they should try to give them an opportunity to explain.
>
> Secondary school student, age 16

The students themselves suggested strategies which would have been helpful in maximising their learning opportunities in the classroom. These included: the provision of notes by teachers so that they did not have to copy material from the blackboard; explaining things well; making their subjects interesting; being less confrontational; and generally displaying some understanding that students with ADHD approach and complete work in a different way from other students.

CONCLUSION

Undoubtedly, students with social and emotional behavioural difficulties, including ADHD, present a major challenge to schools on the journey to becoming inclusive organisations. However, frequently, the solution to the problem of how to include and engage these children is to 'refer' them on and entangle them in a bureaucratic process characterised by waiting lists and delay and conflict, with devastating consequences for themselves and their families and at an unacceptable cost to society (Hayden & Dunne, 2001).

Medicalisation of ADHD

In the present study, the loss of voice and isolation felt by both parents and their children in relation to the education system was juxtaposed to the power and control of the 'professionals', including teachers, psychologists and psychiatrists. Analysis of the narratives of both parents and the students showed while the schools were generally open to enrolling students with ADHD, such overt inclusionary practices were often paradoxically paralleled by demands that the students were assessed and labelled, taking medication, and/or attending a psychiatrist. It may be necessary to change the emphasis, or at least readdress the balance between addressing the needs of the individual child in school, and critically examining the systems which are supporting and perpetuating increasing diagnoses of ADHD and the resulting medicalisation of the behaviour of children.

The power of the 'new medical' and 'biopsychosocial' model (Slee, 1998; Cooper & O'Regan, 2001; Thomas & Loxley, 2001) and how it impinges on teacher attitude, curriculum and pedagogy and disempowers educators, parents and students from responding to a diagnosis of ADHD in a non-medicalised paradigm also requires attention. The reality is that the current system of resource allocation in Irish schools is compounding the medicalisation of ADHD.

The linking of resource entitlement to individual assessment has been found to encourage assessment, identification and labelling resulting in considerable resources being expended on the assessment procedure itself and, by extension, on litigation procedures and appeals when the sought resources are not forthcoming (Kinsella & Senior, 2009). Correspondingly, the resource allocation model for low-incidence disabilities (under which ADHD is categorised) is also focused on the characteristics of the recipient at an individual level. Winter, Fletcher-Campbell, Connolly and Lynch (2006), in a review of models of resource allocation in operation in Ireland and internationally, state that resource allocation based on individualised assessment contradicts the ethics and principles of inclusive education since students with special educational needs must be explicitly identified, i.e. labelled, in order to access the very supports which will enable them to participate within the school system on a par with their 'non-disabled' peers. This is particularly applicable to ADHD, as under the Department of Education and Science *Circular SP.ED 02/05*, children who come under the category 'Emotional and/or Behavioural Problems', are entitled to 3.5 hours resource teaching (Department of Education & Science, 2005c). However, in order to qualify for additional support there is the caveat that '… such pupils are being treated by a psychiatrist or psychologist'.

The reality is that even when a child actually receives a formal diagnosis of ADHD, there may be long waiting lists for Child and Adolescent Mental Health Services (CAMHS) so their entitlement to additional resource teaching is further delayed. Despite a Health Service Executive (HSE) review of waiting times in February 2007 and an in-depth analysis of waiting times and service usage in November 2008, the figure has not changed in the past two years (Shanahan, 2009). According to Shanahan (2009), the HSE has confirmed that waiting times for mental health services for children and adolescents range from 22 to 36 months. Those on waiting lists range from children with acute psychiatric problems to children with behavioural, emotional and educational difficulties.

A specific ADHD pedagogy?

As the 10 case studies drawn on in this chapter clearly show, placement in mainstream schools does not, of itself, guarantee inclusion. The main barometers of inclusion appear to revolve around the levels of differentiation and the quantity and quality of the additional resources provided (Kinsella & Senior, 2009), many of which were allegedly not provided by the schools. Both parents' and students' comments about teachers' knowledge and understanding of

ADHD showed that there is still a significant lack of awareness among the teaching profession as how best to maximise the learning opportunities of pupils with ADHD.

Without this support, children with ADHD are likely to be at greater risk for school adjustment problems (e.g. homework problems, issues with teachers, possible disciplinary action, truancy). Wilkinson (2003) contends that staff knowledge and understanding about ADHD and its management is one of the factors in the successful inclusion of pupils with ADHD in mainstream school curriculum. The findings of the present study support this contention and show that such understanding and support by the school system may be a critical factor in the developmental psychopathology of the condition.

Undoubtedly, ADHD may be a very difficult and testing condition for the teacher. As Wilkinson (2003, p. 32) rightly points out, it is certainly the classroom teacher who 'bears the brunt of ADHD because in the classroom children are expected to wait their turn, remain seated, listen, be academically productive etc.', activities which can be difficult for some children with ADHD. While it is imperative that teachers are provided with training on how to recognise ADHD, as well as how to deal effectively with the associated educational, behavioural and emotional needs, it is also important to move away from the notion that there is specific ADHD pedagogy. The prolific literature on strategies for teaching children with AHHD makes very strong claims for specialist intervention. Yet, Cooper (2005) claims that when these are examined, they almost always identify issues and practices that are not particular to diagnoses of ADHD and, in fact, will benefit all students.

There are no 'ADHD' students; there are individual children with varying abilities, interests, competencies and learning styles. Effective and inclusive educational provision should be concerned with constructing appropriate and meaningful learning experiences, and not about the labelling and medicalisation of children.

The present study on ADHD comes at a crucial time in the debate on the definition, aetiology, treatment and prognosis of this under-recognised condition which, in some professional circles, is still considered to be a result of 'poor parenting' or as something that the child will 'grow out of'. Yet the reality is that ADHD is increasingly being recognised within the international research community and by national education, health, criminal justice and social-welfare systems as constituting one of the most important predictors of psychiatric and social difficulties in adulthood.

7
INCLUSION IN PRIMARY SCHOOL: EXPERIENCE IN IRELAND AND THE UNITED STATES OF AMERICA

Máirín Barry

INTRODUCTION

This chapter looks at inclusive practice and provision in primary schools for students with special educational needs, with reference to two case-study schools—one in suburban Dublin and the other in the greater suburb of Washington DC, in the state of Virginia (Barry, 2003). The purpose of the study was to identify and examine features of inclusive education in both schools and through comparative analysis, it sought to acknowledge effective inclusive educational policy and practice and to identify aspects which might benefit from practical recommendations for improved delivery for students with SEN and for all students.

Since the mid-1990s, a great deal of change has occurred in perceptions and attitudes within Irish society and within Irish education in relation to students with special educational needs (SEN) and disabilities. Changing beliefs about equality, openness to a fuller understanding of disabling conditions, strong international influences, economic improvements, greater parental involvement in education, significant legal challenges and changes in legislation have brought about a climate in which inclusive education has found many committed theorists and proponents.

While Ireland is a relative newcomer to inclusion, the *Draft Guidelines for Teachers of Students with Mild Learning Disabilities: Introduction* (NCCA, 2002a) tell us that:

> ... the inclusive school is concerned with meeting the diverse needs of all students. Within the inclusive school everyone belongs, diversity is celebrated and everyone has some valuable contribution to make to the school community.

> NCCA, 2002a, p. 2

The United States of America was considerably ahead of Ireland in the move to inclusion, having enacted the pre-cursor of much inclusive legislation (the Education for All Handicapped Children Act—EACHA) in 1975 and consequently schools within the United States have been involved in inclusive educational practice for many years.

THE MOVEMENT TOWARDS INCLUSIVE EDUCATION

The education of students with SEN and with disabilities alongside their peers in mainstream classrooms, has been in practice and under discussion internationally, for more than 40 years (Goldstein et al., 1965; Dunn, 1968; Hegarty & Pocklington, 1981; Hall, 1992; Swan, 1994). Variously known as mainstreaming, integration and, most recently, as inclusion, it has received strong support in the literature (Booth & Ainscow, 1998; Clark et al., 1995; Carpenter et al., 1996; Nolet & McLaughlin, 2000). Prior to the advent of inclusive theories, it had largely been the practice, if children had particular difficulties in school, to put them together with other children, whose needs were perceived to be similar. According to Thomas and Loxley (2001, p. 21), many considered such segregation positively and saw 'a rationale for it ... built on arguments about the best interests of the separated children'.

However, research dating as far back as the early 1960s, has found that the levels of academic progress achieved by students with SEN who remained in mainstream schools were similar to the levels achieved by those attending separate, special schools (Johnson, 1962; Dunn, 1968; Birch et al., 1970; Lipsky & Gartner, 1987). Galloway and Goodwin (1979) critically examined the view that children benefit educationally from attending special schools rather than ordinary ones, but did not find evidence to support it. Anderson and Pellicer (1990), Carson (1992), Hegarty (1993), and Thomas and Loxley (2001) all found similarly. Additionally, studies have identified gains in social, emotional, life-skills and language development for students with SEN who attend mainstream schools (Forest & Pearpoint, 1990; Steele & Mitchell, 1992; Wilgosh, 1992).

It has been found that pupils 'benefited in terms of social and emotional development from taking part in integration programmes' (Cohen & Cohen, 1986, p. 100). There were 'great gains in the socialisation and independence skills of children involved in integration' according to Steele and Mitchell, (1992, p. 16). Wilgosh (1992, p. 8), identified the greatest advantage of integration as presenting pupils with better opportunities 'to be prepared for living and working in society as adults'. Baker, Wang and Walberg (1995, p. 14) held that 'there is no separate knowledge base for teaching children classified as mildly retarded or learning disabled'. Thomas and Loxley (2001) further suggest that while it is maintained that students are 'educated separately for their own benefit' (ibid., p. 21), it is also seen as being 'for the benefit of the majority' and the 'children who are difficult to teach, have become, by default, special children' through their removal from the regular environment (ibid., p. 26). Others see the problems relating to SEN and disability as located, not in the child, but in the expediency and convenience that seeks to facilitate the majority society (Fish, 1985; Foucault, 1991).

Internationally, inclusive education is widely supported and endorsed by countries as diverse as the United States (McLeskey & Waldron, 2000); Italy (Buzzi, 1995); South Africa (Naiker, 1999); Australia (Slee, 2005); and Ghana (Ainscow, 1999). The United Nations' World Programme for Action Concerning Disabled Persons (United Nations, 1983), the Salamanca Statement (UNESCO, 1994) and the *Dakar Framework for Action* (UNESCO, 2000), with their resolute commitment to Education for All, reflect and sustain this worldwide movement towards inclusion, supported by the network of UN agencies. In the United States, the EACHA Act (United States, 1975) and the Individuals with Disabilities Act (IDEA) (United States, 1990, 1997) established the rights of all students to public education in the least restrictive environment. Originally advanced as early as 1959, the concept of 'normalization' (Bank-Mikkelsen, 1976) proposed that people with disabilities should be allowed to live as normal a life as possible. 'Normalization', therefore, focuses on commonalities between children rather than their differences.

The influence of the 1994 Salamanca Statement (UNESCO, 1994) was highly significant in education development in many countries including Ireland, impacting particularly on policy and practice in inclusive education, stating the rights of all children to inclusion and outlining terms of access to education. Concerns about human rights, equal opportunities and the rights of disabled people, taken together with disquiet in relation to the negative effects of educational exclusion, have led to the development of inclusion policies within many European education systems (Evans et al., 1999). Inclusive policy in Ireland was reflected in the recommendations of the authoritative *Report of the Special Education Review Committee* (SERC) (Government of Ireland, 1993), which proposed 'as much integration as is appropriate and feasible with as little segregation as is necessary' (ibid., p. 22). SERC outlined a continuum of provision in meeting the individual needs of students, ranging from help within the classroom, to special classes attached to mainstream schools, to segregated special schools (ibid., p. 24). This was, again, reinforced in the *White Paper in Education: Charting our Education Future* (Government of Ireland, 1995), giving special recognition to the role of parents in their children's education. The *Draft Guidelines for Teachers of Students with Mild Learning Disabilities: Introduction* (NCCA, 2002a), describe inclusive education as being, 'concerned with creating quality education for all students, including those with a disability' (ibid., p. 2) and declared that 'the inclusion of students with mild general learning disabilities in mainstream schools is supported by all legislation relating to special education provision' (ibid., p. 2).

DEFINING INCLUSION

Inclusion is a complex, abstract, dynamic concept involving principles of equality, justice, community, diversity, democracy, commitment and respect. While inclusion is difficult to define precisely, it can be observed in the features that characterise it: features that would typify an inclusive school and would form part of the aspirations and goals of the community involved. They have been identified as including: collaboration and a shared framework; a feeling of ownership and involvement of all teaching staff, family and community; good planning and use of support staff; good, relevant evaluation procedures; self-belief and high expectations; good communication; full participation and equality of opportunity; and a strong leadership advocating and facilitating all of these (Booth & Ainscow, 2002).

Inclusion implies a student with SEN attending the school that they would have attended, in the absence of any significant special need (Mittler, 1999, p. 11). It is distinct from the term 'integration', although often used interchangeably (Thomas et al., 1998, p. 11). The onus is on the school to adapt and change in order to accommodate the student's needs, rather than the student being required to fit in with the school's established systems and expectations. The focus of inclusion is not on the students with special needs and their assimilation into mainstream schools, but on the schools themselves becoming places where all children with varying strengths and needs and from all kinds of backgrounds are valued. The mere presence of students with special needs is not enough—it has to lead to participation and that participation has to be guided by notions of equity and of the development of a shared community (Ainscow, 1999; Dyson & Millward, 2000).

OUTLINE OF THE COMPARATIVE STUDY

In order to provide a comparative context to explore the progress of inclusive educational practice in Ireland, a school in the suburbs of Washington DC, in the state of Virginia in the United States, was selected as a case-study school. The opportunity to study this school arose through a visit sponsored by the Irish Department of Education and Science (DES), under the Memorandum of Understanding between the United States government and the Irish government (Government of Ireland, 2000c). The visit established links between Irish teachers working with students with SEN and their counterparts in the Washington DC area. The school was identified as an example of best practice by the US Department of Education (DoE) where inclusive education was well established. It had a long-standing commitment to inclusive education and a history of facilitating parents, educators and others interested in observing practice and had received numerous awards and commendations from the State Department of Education, Virginia. The Irish school selected for this comparative study was one where the researcher had access to documentation, to staff and students and to the observation of educational practice with the full permission of the Board of Management. As with many Irish primary schools in the early 2000s, it was in the process of developing policies on inclusive education and dealing with a number of new initiatives in this period of change (NCCA, 1999a; 2002a; 2002b; Department of Education & Science, 2002a; 2002b). The schools were matched for size of enrolment, pupil age and socio-economic background. However, the Irish school was a girls' school, while the American school was co-educational. The Irish school had 16 students with identified SEN in its mainstream classes and the Washington school had 31.

The issues examined included: the resource provision for students with SEN; the assessment procedures employed to identify students with SEN; the whole-school involvement in working with students with SEN; the planning and implementation of Individual Education Plans (IEPs); the delivery of other professional services and supports; the involvement of parents; and the role of the principal and management in enabling inclusive SEN education. While the comparative approach proved to be a very fruitful one, the fact that the two schools were at different stages of development in relation to inclusion must be borne in mind in interpreting the findings.

The research tools, carefully matched in both schools, were: classroom observation; an in-depth examination of documentation relating to requirements and procedures pertinent to the provision of services to students with identified SEN; interviews with key personnel and parents; and questionnaires for all class teachers. The data was combined to gain a holistic picture of inclusive education provision in two schools in different jurisdictions. Ethical guidelines advocated by UCD School of Education were strictly adhered to and confidentiality was assured. Fictitious names were ascribed to the schools involved: Thompson Elementary in the United States and St Mary's in Ireland.

OVERVIEW OF INCLUSIVE EDUCATIONAL PROVISION IN THE CASE-STUDY SCHOOLS

Comparison of context and historical perspective

In the past, both jurisdictions made predominantly segregated provision for students with disabilities. Both had experienced the influence of court challenges on educational legislation and practice and while the effects of population diversity appeared more evident in the United States, such cultural difference had become apparent in Ireland. In the United States, unlike Ireland, special education teachers and regular elementary teachers have separate initial teacher education programmes. In Ireland, all primary teachers must qualify as general education teachers and some may then go directly into special education without further specific qualifications.

National policy on SEN and inclusion

In the United States, the Education for All Handicapped Children Act (EACHA) (United States, 1975) and its subsequent amendments, enshrined in law the entitlement of students with SEN to Free Appropriate Public Education (FAPE) in the Least Restrictive Environment (LRE) and to an Individual Education Program (or Plan) (IEP). The 1990 Individuals with Disabilities Education Act (IDEA) (United States, 1990, 1997) made significant changes in terminology and identified additional groups with disabilities, such as autism and traumatic brain injury, and extended provision to them. It introduced the requirement for multidisciplinary teams and stipulated that an IEP team was necessary for placement decisions. The IDEA was amended in 1997, further strengthening its provisions and entitlements. The reauthorisation of the IDEA in 2004 revised the statute to include provision for early intervention elementary school programmes and to align it with the requirements of the 2001 No Child Left Behind Act (NCLB) (United States, 2001). NCLB allows financial incentives to states who improve their special education services and general education standards and services.

While still in the developing stage, Irish national policy and legislation has increased significantly in recent years. The Education Act, the 1998 and 2004 Equality Acts, the 2000–2004 Equal Status Acts and the 2000 Education (Welfare) Act (Government of Ireland, 1998, 1998b, 2000a, 2000–2004, 2004) have all strengthened the constitutional rights of children to education, including children who have a disability or other special need.

At the time of writing, the suspension of the rollout of the Education for Persons with Special Educational Needs Act (EPSEN) (Government of Ireland, 2004a) has been imposed. EPSEN is a critical piece of legislation which, along with the Disability Act (Government of Ireland, 2005), has created a framework to empower those with special needs and disabilities. Some encouraging progress has been made. The potential within the EPSEN Act to put the education entitlements of children and young people with SEN on a statutory basis is clear. The prescribed mechanisms, which include: appeals procedures; appropriate, comprehensive assessment; transition supports for students; and collaborative IEPs, remain advisory.

Involvement of the courts

Courts in both jurisdictions have been called upon to establish and clarify the entitlements of students with SEN to education and both have done so with reference to their respective constitutions. The *Board of Education v. Rowley* (1982) in the United States established that an appropriate education exists when a programme of special education and related services is provided such that the individual benefits and due process procedures have been followed in developing it (Ysseldyke et al., 2000, p. 64). In Ireland, the judgment in the *O'Donoghue* case clearly established the constitutional obligation on the state to provide free basic elementary education to all children and broadened the interpretation of the term 'education', stating that it involves 'giving each child such advice, instruction and teaching as will enable him or her to make the best possible use of his or her inherent and potential capacities, physical, mental and moral, however limited these capacities may be', (*O'Donoghue v. Minister for Health* (et al.), 1996). Despite these similarities, the existence of extensive legislation in the United States continues to provide far greater protection of rights, clarity of interpretation of detail, guidelines on the operation of SEN provision and access to redress where pertinent.

Policy implementation and planning for SEN and inclusion

At school level, the study found marked differences in the implementation of SEN policy and planning. In the United States, the IDEA (United States, 1990, 1997) mandated an active policy of seeking out children at pre-school stages (Child Find) in order to affect early intervention strategies. On entering school at age five, compulsory screening of all children was carried out and a multidisciplinary team—including a school-based psychologist, speech and language therapist and occupational therapist—began planning students' IEPs, where needs were identified. All required services were specifically itemised and it was the Local Education Authority (LEA) that had responsibility for ensuring that the IEP was implemented fully. The IEP was (and is) required to be re-evaluated at least every three years (State of Virginia, 2009, p. 47) and more frequently if parents request it. This process is an obligatory one and involves a great range of services and expertise. It also provides a means of maintaining continuity throughout the individual child's education and allows parents a clear view of the programme their child would follow and the expectations appropriate to it.

In the Irish system, some families had independently identified children's special needs or disabilities through private assessment or through the agencies of the Department of Health, prior to attending school. Otherwise, an educational psychologist with the National Educational Psychological Service (NEPS) became involved, at the request of the school, when a pupil did not appear to make progress *vis-à-vis* their peers, or when their behaviour gave cause for particular concern. At the time of the study, St Mary's School had not been allocated an NEPS psychologist and so private educational psychological assessment, funded by the Department of Education and Science (DES) on a quota basis, was allowed instead. However, before that assessment could take place, the school had to demonstrate that appropriate intervention and support within the school had been tried to no avail. This continues to be the case (National Education Psychological Service, 2007). As of yet, there is no established team of professional expertise involved in assessing student needs, nor is an IEP required by law. The *Guidelines on the Individual Education Plan Process* (National Council for Special Education, 2006a) have provided an adaptable framework for schools to develop IEPs for students, recommending the specification of learning goals, over a set period of time, and the teaching strategies, resources and supports necessary to achieve them (ibid., p. 4).

They advocate developing an IEP through a collaborative process involving the school, parents, the student (where appropriate) and other relevant personnel or agencies, such as occupational therapist, speech and language therapist, or social worker. According to these advisory guidelines, the school principal is required to ensure that a suitable IEP is drawn up. The regional Special Educational Needs Organiser (SENO), under the direction of the National Council for Special Education (NCSE), does not take responsibility for this process, but may assist in facilitating it. The establishment of NCSE on 1 October 2005 marked the beginning of implementation of the EPSEN Act, 2004. The NCSE was charged with drawing up a plan for implementing EPSEN. This *Plan for the Phased Implementation of the EPSEN Act* (National Council for Special Education, 2006b) was completed by October 2006. According to the plan, it had been envisaged that the EPSEN Act would be fully implemented by 2010. However, Budget 2009 saw the announcement that the implementation of the requirements within the 2004 EPSEN Act was to be halted. Responsibility for certain aspects of SEN and disability lie with the Department of Health and since 1 June 2007, the provisions of the 2005 Disability Act in relation to assessment of need have been implemented in respect of children aged under five (Department of Health, 2007, p. 4). Implementation of the 2005 Disability Act in respect of five to 18 year olds was to be introduced by the end of 2010 and in respect of adults in 2011 (ibid., p. 4).

Comparing local structures for the administration of education

The system in the state of Virginia in the United States, involved a professionally qualified, educational board at county level overseeing all schools, thus ensuring continuity of educational policy and a co-ordinated service. Meetings and discussions, decisions made and actions taken were disclosed on an ongoing basis through the public access county education board website. Also available to the public were the qualifications and experience of board members, detailed information on how the education system operates, specific entitlements of students and parents, names and points of contact of those responsible for all aspects of educational provision and procedures to follow where required, including redress and due process.

The voluntary Board of Management in the Irish primary school had no formal training in educational provision, nor any required background in education or related fields. All board of management meetings were regarded as confidential unless otherwise stated and while the parents' annual general meeting was given a formal short report by the board, there were no channels of easy access to the ongoing concerns and operation of the board.

Comparing planning for SEN in the case-study schools

Access to educational psychological assessment was the key for many students in identifying their specific needs in Irish schools, whereas the Child Find and early-screening policies in the United States lead to earlier identification and thus enabled earlier intervention at pre-school age. Assessment in Irish schools tended to occur at a later stage than in the United States and many students would not have been formally prescribed help until well into their third year in St Mary's, at age seven or eight.

The planning of the student's IEP in the Irish system appeared to lie largely with the resource teacher, while an in-school multidisciplinary team was required in Thompson. Parents were involved in planning their child's IEP in the US school, as stipulated by law. Irish teachers, at the time of the study, believed it would be appropriate to inform parents of the plan that the school would put in place. The whole-school approach, which operated in Thompson, with a specific SEN inclusion plan, was effective in ensuring a high-quality service and emphasised the importance of all the roles required in its delivery. Teachers did not work in isolation and the collaboration and sharing of ideas across the multidisciplinary team facilitated and enhanced learning about SEN within the school itself.

In Ireland, many new resource teachers, at the time of the study, were unclear as to their role and class teachers saw the resource teacher as someone to take responsibility for their difficult students, rather than a colleague to work with on a collaborative basis (Coyle, 2001, p. 50). Unlike its American counterpart, St Mary's, at this time, had no school plan for SEN or inclusion, no scheduled planning time for conferences with teachers or parents, nor any clear vehicle or channel through which collaboration could be fostered. The introduction of the General Allocation Model (Department of Education & Science, 2005c) has given schools greater flexibility in responding to student needs and allows for some support to be put in place prior to diagnosis (see below). It also advocates the concept of an in-school, team approach to student support.

Since 2003, the provision of support by the Special Education Support Service (SESS) through school-based and professional-development services and the postgraduate studies programmes for teachers, funded and supported by the Department of Education and Science, have contributed to the development and promotion of good practice in SEN and inclusion.

Students supported

In comparing both schools, it was clear that greater numbers of students identified with SEN were in Thompson Elementary. Almost 3 per cent of students at St Mary's were identified as being entitled to resource teaching to facilitate their SEN in an inclusive setting, while, approximately 5.5 per cent of students in Thompson received similar support. This greater incidence may be due to: earlier identification by Child Find; comprehensive mandatory screening of all students within the initial period of starting school; and access to evaluation services based on *need* in Thompson, rather than the *quota* of assessments per year available in St Mary's. It is important to note that it is a frequently observed phenomenon that more boys than girls tend to be identified as having SEN (Croll & Moses, 2000, p. 40; Ysseldyke & Algozzine, 1995, p. 347), and therefore it is in keeping with this to find more students with SEN in a co-educational school than in a girls' school. A further factor influencing the lower numbers identified in St Mary's may have been the stringent requirements of *Circular 08/02* (Department of Education & Science, 2002b) which allowed, for example, resource teaching to students with dyslexia only if they scored at or below the second percentile in reading, writing or Mathematics. The largest grouping of students with identified needs in both schools was that of dyslexia, making up 50 per cent of the students identified with SEN in St Mary's and just over 48 per cent of those in Thompson.

Since this study was completed, the introduction of the General Allocation Model (Department of Education & Science, 2005) in Irish primary schools now allows for more flexibility in the work of teachers with responsibility for students with learning support needs, SEN and disability. Rather than having to establish student need before accessing extra teaching provision, it allows for a stable permanent number of special education teachers to be granted to schools based on factors of enrollment, student gender and social disadvantage. Additional teachers may also be sought for students with conditions seen as 'low incidence' (i.e. involving a more significant element of disability) and thus requiring specific extra support. The formation of special education teams of learning support and resource teachers within a school is also advocated in this model, as is in-class support to augment the more common student-withdrawal model.

The staged approach to student learning difficulties, outlined in the NEPS guidelines for schools, *Mainstream Primary Schools and Special Education Needs—A Continuum of Support* (National Educational Psychological Service, 2007) continues as national policy.

IMPLICATIONS AND CONCLUSIONS

The findings of this comparative analysis (Barry, 2003) indicated that, in comparison to Ireland, the structures promoting inclusive education in the US school were well developed and comprehensive. The provision of a wide variety of supports and services which facilitated planning and collaboration with a range of professionals, with parents and learning support personnel, as well as amongst teachers themselves, promoted and facilitated inclusive education practices.

The existence of specific legislation provided the mandatory framework within which the US school operated (United States, 1975, 1990, 1997, 2001). The public dissemination of information relating to the legislation reinforced and maintained inclusive practice, ensuring appropriate and consistent IEP provision and implementation. The strong local support provided by the LEA advising, monitoring and funding the US school, ensured that legislation was properly interpreted and complied with, and that parents were fully appraised of their entitlements. At the school level, policies reflected a deep commitment to, and a thorough understanding of, educational needs, in terms of individual students with SEN and inclusive education.

The study found that inclusive structures in the Irish system were then at an emergent stage. Student assessment needs were great and while the NEPS was in the process of development, it was anticipated that the service would advance rapidly. The NEPS has grown and has delivered assessment, support and advice professionally and effectively to schools, teachers, parents and students throughout the country. However, the full complement of educational psychologists has not yet been reached and there are still waiting lists for student assessments. The Disability Act (Government of Ireland, 2005) has begun to have an effect on assessment needs as, since 2007, it is being implemented through the Health Service for children aged under five. This helps to address some concerns in relation to early identification to facilitate early intervention.

Despite the range of legislation which has been introduced since the late 1990s, the suspension of the EPSEN Act 2004 (and of the Disability Act 2005) leaves a major gap in terms of the rights of children and young people with SEN and disabilities to access a range of professional supports and services and an appropriate education in an inclusive environment along with their peers. Until the acts are fully implemented these rights will not be vindicated.

Working closely with parents in planning IEPs was the norm in the US school but the Irish school, at that time, believed it sufficient to keep parents 'informed'. Parental involvement is identified as a necessary component of inclusive education (Fullan, 1991; Wolfendale, 2000). The centrality of parents in decision making relating to their children formed part of the recommendations of the *Task Force on Autism* (Task Force on Autism, 2001, p. 350) and in the *Guidelines on the Individual Education Plan Process* (National Council for Special Education, 2006a) parental participation is strongly advocated.

The study found Irish teachers, in a time of substantial and rapid change, unsure of procedures and lacking confidence in their knowledge of appropriate approaches to SEN planning and collaborative work practices. Roles and responsibilities in these areas had not been clearly defined. A range of support services have now been put in place to support Irish schools, giving rise to guidelines, circulars and access to teacher professional development which all contribute to greater dissemination of knowledge on SEN. Chief among the services are the NCSE, with their regional SENOs, and the NEPS, which continues its expansion to all schools. The SESS provides useful information on SEN and direction to professional teacher-development courses and further qualifications.

In comparing SEN supports at regional and local levels, it is evident that they differ in structure and character. In the United States, in the state of Virginia, LEAs co-ordinate and maintain provision in a number of schools: sharing knowledge and skills acquired through and across regional experience; devising IEPs; and identifying and sourcing appropriate supports and expertise. In Ireland, each individual school has its own Board of Management with responsibility for all school policy. There is the regionally based NEPS with a designated educational psychologist for groups of schools, and a local SENO to assist co-ordination, but other relevant professional services and supports are not available in this manner. Collaboration in the IEP process is less structured and still advisory and there is no prescribed participation required of support services. The *Task Force on Autism* (Task Force on Autism, 2001, p. 364) strongly advocated multidisciplinary team approaches to these services. While the expression of intent is similar, the enabling process and support mechanisms substantially distinguish the two systems.

There were strengths to be found in both schools and common elements in terms of: the commitment and professionalism of staff; the desire to achieve better outcomes for all students; a willingness to engage in collaborative practice and to take on new responsibilities. Clear, specific legislation to ensure prompt provision of appropriate education continues to be the most critical requirement to ensure access to inclusive education. The required legislation (EPSEN Act, Government of Ireland, 2004a) has been passed but to date significant sections have not been implemented.

8

LANGUAGE, SOCIO-ECONOMIC CLASS AND EDUCATIONAL UNDERACHIEVEMENT

Gerry Mac Ruairc

INTRODUCTION

The highs and lows, triumphs and despairs that have characterised the recent economic landscape of Ireland have been the subject of much debate and deliberation. Throughout this period of growth, expansion and rapid decline, the mechanisms of social class continued to function as a significant defining framework with respect to lifestyles and life chances for the different socio-economic groups living on this rollercoaster. Nowhere are the manifestations of socio-economic class more evident than in the field of education, where despite a successive range of policies, initiatives and investment, significant inequalities with respect to educational outcomes continue to prevail between socio-economic groups. Many would argue that the 'cultural labour' among middle classes, during the Celtic Tiger years, in an effort to appropriate for their children the range of cultural capital redolent in different educational trajectories, added to the levels of inequality that existed previously (Lynch & Moran, 2006).

This chapter deals specifically with the persistent patterns of educational inequality and marginalisation that prevail in the primary-school sector. The analysis will draw on the recent cultural turn in social-class theory (Devine et al., 2005) to provide a range of conceptual tools that facilitate a more in-depth and powerful exploration of class inequalities (Apple, 1996, 2001, 2002; Giroux, 1983, 2001; Giroux & McLaren, 1994; Lareau, 2000, 2003; Reay, 1999, 2000, 2004, 2005). Within this perspective, cultural practice, in all its forms, can be critically examined for the purpose of revealing how patterns of consumption in everyday life serve to classify individuals and groups (Certeau de, 1984; Certeau de et al., 1989; Reay 2004, 2005). The discussion will focus on one element of culture practice, i.e. language and linguistic variation, by examining the manner in which different groups of children engage with standardised testing in schools.

The purpose here is not to provide a critique of testing *per se* (this has been done elsewhere: Mac Ruairc, 2009; Haertel & Lorié, 2004; Shohamy, 2001a, 2001b) but rather to problematise one aspect of cultural practice in schools that has retained enormous credibility in defining and measuring educational outcomes (Shohamy, 2001a). In this way, it is possible to look beneath the asymmetrical patterns of reading attainment by highlighting the patterns of continuity and discontinuity between different linguistic codes and registers and the vocabulary tested in reading tests. In the case of codes—i.e. the linguistic system of communication (Thomas et al., 2004)—research has revealed that there are marked differences between the social groups with respect to key features of linguistic codes in practice (Bernstein, 1996; Labov, 2001; Vaughn-Cook, 2007).

Although there is considerable evidence that points to the linguistic equality of many well developed, co-existing code systems (Chambers 2003; Thomas et al., 2004), the sociological differences in terms of the prestige of one code over another continues to prevail (Vaughn-Cook, 2007). This is particularly the case in schools where the role played by education in the management of linguistic variation is well documented (Stockman, 2007; Maybin, 2007). The school code, including the content and format of language assessment, does not resonate with all social groups equally and privileges those for whom this code is consistent with other linguistic experiences. In the case of linguistic register,[1] a similar pattern is identifiable where the *field* and *tenor* components of the register often result in patterns of linguistic continuity and discontinuity for children between the linguistic expectations and demands of school and the prevailing patterns of linguistic practices outside school.

SOCIO-ECONOMIC CLASS AND PATTERNS OF PARTICIPATION AND ACHIEVEMENT IN EDUCATION

There is a significant body of literature, both nationally and internationally, that points to the high level of correlation between educational attainments, longevity in the education system and socio-economic background. A number of reports are produced, almost annually, detailing national research on this issue identify the extent of the socio-economic divide with respect to opportunity, participation and outcome in the education system both within and across levels and disciplines (Clancy & Wall, 2000; Clancy, 2001; Cosgrave et al., 2001; Cosgrave et al., 2004; Osborne & Leith, 2000; Sheil, 2006; Higher Education

Authority, 2007, 2009). Research has consistently identified widespread underachievement in reading in schools with a significant representation of pupils from disadvantaged backgrounds presenting in the lower achievement bands. Over 10 years ago, the 1998 National Assessment of English Reading concluded that there had been no change in the performance of low-achieving pupils in English reading attainment and that the majority of these students in crisis were located in areas of socio-economic deprivation (Cosgrove et al., 2000). The persistence of these patterns has been confirmed by the most recent National Assessment of English Reading carried out in 2004 which concluded that:

> The results of the assessment indicate that the mean scores obtained by Fifth class pupils in the 1998 and 2004 assessments are almost identical. Further, scores on the three domains (narrative, expository, and documents) vary little across the two assessments, indicating that no change in 'national reading standards' has occurred since 1998. Indeed, based on linkages between this and earlier assessments, it can be inferred that overall standards have not changed since 1980.
>
> Eivers et al., 2005, p. xv

Another recent publication on this issue *Literacy in Disadvantaged Primary Schools* (Eivers et al., 2004) reveals that the single most significant causal factor in relation to both achievement and underachievement is socio-economic status. A recent study of 40 schools carried out by the Department of Education and Science in 2004 (Department of Education & Science, 2005a) provides further evidence of this problem. The overall consensus in the data strongly indicates that quantitative measurement of attainment levels in schools in working-class areas is showing a persistent resistance to change. Recent literature on this issue has explored how the structure and organisation of the school system contributes to the persistence of this problem (Tormey, 2007). This chapter explores one dimension of the range of cultural and linguistic practices that are mediated by these structures and develops recent work with respect to language variation in schools (Mac Ruairc 1997, 2004; Creegan, 2007). It challenges some more traditional approaches to educational research, which produce descriptive data, often articulated as universal and ideologically neutral, taking little account of the heterogeneity of the values, mores, experiences and practices that exist in society. It is common in aspects of this approach to research to 'control for' factors such as socio-economic class for the purpose of statistical analysis (Wrigley, 2008). Class is relegated to part of the overall 'noise' or 'outside background factors' that need to be stripped away in order to reveal the true impact of school factors (Angus, 1993, p. 361). To challenge this limiting, reductive view of the impact of fundamental categories such as socio-economic class, it is necessary to take into account the complexity of the school population and focus directly, rather than 'control for', the manner in which educationally marginalised groups participate and engage in the process and practice of schooling.

EDUCATIONAL DISADVANTAGE POLICY IN IRELAND

Since the early 1980s, many government-led measures have been introduced to alleviate the problems of disadvantage in primary schools (for a summary of initiatives see Department of Education & Science, 2005d). These initiatives, and the policies that underpin them, have been characterised by ongoing, if somewhat narrowly focused, reviews (Kellaghan et al., 1995; Weir et al., 2004) and are often strongly positioned within a functionalist, meritocratic perspective.[2] While many of these initiatives have had a positive impact on schools in terms of the overall quality of provision, it is the contention of this author that many do not adequately take account of the complexity and diversity of issues encompassed in the term 'educational disadvantage' when formulating policy. An example of this can be identified in the targets included in many policy documents. These targets are often hopelessly aspirational. They may arguably serve to prevent the setting of more measured, attainable targets. Examples include 'halving the proportion of pupils in designated disadvantaged schools with serious literacy difficulties by 2006' (Goodbody Economic Consultants, 2001, p. 24) or 'having regard to the assessment of their intrinsic abilities, there [should be] no students with serious literacy and numeracy problems in early primary education within the next five years' (Combat Poverty Agency, 1997, p. 18). Another factor has been the quantitative nature of many initiatives emanating from government which have focused on the important issues of extra teachers, extra financial resources and a range of schemes and programmes but lacked an overall cohesive vision on how to make a meaningful difference at school, classroom and individual levels.

The most recent initiative to deal with educational disadvantage *Delivering Equality of Opportunity in Schools* (DEIS) (Department of Education & Science,

2005b) went some way towards reframing practice in this area. In addition to providing enhanced funding for schools, the DEIS framework acknowledged the need for a new, co-ordinated approach to dealing with disadvantage. This initiative introduced the School Support Programme (SSP) with the prime focus on integrating and developing the range of existing initiatives. Despite the fact that it was implemented very late in our economic success cycle, there were a number of strengths to this new model. A key dimension of the rationale underpinning DEIS was the increased autonomy given to schools. Although schools and teachers in the Republic of Ireland have always been very autonomous in many aspects of the educational provision on the ground, autonomy with respect to financial resources has often been much more limited. The DEIS model shifted the paradigm somewhat. Schools were encouraged to engage with the process of DEIS planning at a local level and identify their own targets and priorities based on an analysis of evidence of local needs. This was recognition for the first time of the need to respond in a measured and appropriate way to the different shades of the overall complexity of the field of educational disadvantage and marginalisation, depending on the type of school or community. The overall structure was set centrally but the 'one size fits all' straitjacket of previous initiatives was somewhat loosened enabling locally specific plan and practices.

In addition to the enhanced funding and the more liberal approach to how it was spent, schools were supported by the Primary Curriculum Support Programme (PCSP), which assigned a DEIS Cuiditheoir (support co-ordinator) to the targeted DEIS schools, and the School Development Planning Initiative (SDPI), the main task of which was to assist schools in the development of DEIS action plans. Both of these support structures were combined in 2008 into the Primary Professional Development Service (PPDS). Schools were supported in setting clear targets in key areas identified within the DEIS action plan. The focus on improving literacy and numeracy and the renewed focus on enhancing attendance, education progression, retention and overall attainment are particularly notable. Research carried out by the author on school leadership in DEIS schools (pending publication) indicates that evidence in relation to the efficacy of DEIS was positive.[3] The targeted nature of the support and the freedom to respond to locally identified priorities were noted as particularly important and progressive elements of the initiative (Mac Ruairc, forthcoming). However, the DEIS model has been short lived as a result of the recent economic downturn. Funding for DEIS has been reduced in a number of areas, leaving schools in very vulnerable positions with respect to plans and targets formulated during different economic conditions.

This recent decrease in funding will impact on efforts to evaluate the long-term impact of DEIS. However, this is not the only problem to be identified in the overall model. The move towards increased autonomy for schools is the focus of international policy making at present (Pont et al., 2008). As a model of schooling, 'autonomy' is now embedded in the broader political and ideological domain. International evidence strongly indicates that the recent neo-liberal shift towards school autonomy is regularly combined with high stakes models of accountability (for a definition of neo-liberalism see Chapter 3). Evidence from the United Kingdom and the United States reveals that this has proven to be particularly regressive (Apple, 2001; Ball, 2006, 2008; Cambridge Primary Review, 2009). In Ireland, we are recent participants in this accountability trajectory (see Gleeson & Ó Donnabháin, 2009). The introduction of a range of recent measures—including the introduction in 2008 of mandatory standardised testing, the publication of Whole School Evaluation reports from 2006, and the media-driven league tables on the school origins of third-level students—provides evidence of the nature of the Irish policy response to the increasing demand among the public at large for evidence of the quality of school performance.

The pressure on schools to be seen to do well is understandable and can lead to some positive reflection and review. However, it can also lead to a range of undesirable practices that are justifiable because of the need to deliver at a local level or face the consequences. Practices such as: the exclusion of undesirable students; the commodification of other students (i.e. where students are viewed in terms of the impact they will have on how the school is perceived); teaching to the test; back to basics improvised curricula; and the extensive use of streaming/banding or setting, sometimes in early primary, are all identifiable in research both internationally and nationally. Will this policy trajectory lead to a greater abdication on the part of governments for issues such as low levels of attainment in certain schools? It has been argued that the impact of increased autonomy becomes a mechanism for the distribution and delegation of blame (Apple, 2009a) and is a practice that allows failure to be located at individual school level, thereby detracting from political and broader societal responsibility for the problems.

Two factors are identified as part of what is required to address the persistence of educational failure and to prevent a further deterioration in the outcomes of schooling for lower socio-economic groups as a result of the impact, both realised and potential, of recent neo-liberal policies. First, a critical, more nuanced approach to educational discourse in order to inform policy development is vital. This will require a deliberate move away from a reliance on the safe, functionalist discourse of the past. The lack of debate in relation to the recent introduction of mandatory standardised testing is testament to the prevalence of this functionalist approach to policy development and to the paucity of critical debate that prevails in education circles. There were a number of issues related to the well-documented, contested field of mandatory standardised testing that were not considered. One of most notable omissions in the discourse was the failure to take account of the problematic nature of standardised testing with marginalised and disadvantaged students (Delpit, 2006; Lam & Bordignon, 2001; McNeil, 2000; Meier, 2000; Shohamy, 2001a).

In addition to a more robust model of policy making, a significant investment in teacher education and leadership development is necessary in order to enrich the profession in critical and theoretical domains. This author contests that by drawing on developments in social-class theory (developed below) and by acknowledging and dealing with, rather than reproducing, the outcome of the cultural struggle within education, school systems can begin to act on the persistent problem of educational disadvantage in a truly sustainable way. In this way, educational leadership at a broad level and school leadership at a local level can contribute to this emancipatory endeavour. It will be difficult. It will require sustained advocacy at all levels of the system. Some of the canons of our current model of schooling will be exposed as divisive. Many well-established and highly valued practices will be revealed to legitimise and validate some students while at the same time invalidating others. This author contests that it is not longer possible for governments, policy makers, leaders, teachers, academics and communities to participate in a system that continues to deliver the current degree of inequality at all stages in the schooling process, particularly in relation to school engagement and patterns of participation and attainment.

THE CULTURAL TURN IN SOCIAL CLASS

Recent scholarship in relation to social class has reframed the concept 'as a dynamic mobile aspect of identity that continues to permeate daily interactions despite its marginalisation in prevailing contemporary discourses' (Reay, 1998, p. 259). What now prevails is a greater understanding of the complexities of class in contemporary society (Reay, 1998; Charlesworth, 2000; Woodin, 2005). This understanding makes problematic the relationship between material circumstance and cultural discursive resources. This is in order to attempt to explain why, in a pluralist society when many multiple ideals are available and accessible, certain ideals prevail, though they have no inherent superiority.

The concept of class has been extended from economic capital alone to cover human capital, social capital (Putnam, 2000) and cultural and symbolic capital (Bourdieu, 1977, 1984, 1986, 1991). This broader focus of class theory examines how cultural and symbolic resources function to position people in a similar way to economic resources. The cultural symbols of the working-class population, who are marginalised economically, are also the subject of a lack of prestige culturally because their cultural options are considered to lack knowledge and taste and become associated negatively as 'the problem' with the working-class (Lawler, 2005). 'Class is being configured in terms of culture and identity, and damaged or faulty identities are conferred on the working-class people ... they are vilified ... for having the wrong kind of life and the wrong kind of identity (ignorant, desperate, inept)' (Lawler, 2005, p. 803).

The developments in this field have provided a theoretical framework which makes it possible to examine specific aspects of cultural struggle embedded in the overall socio-economic context. Cultural struggle manifests itself in many ways in society and this is particularly evident within the field of education. Over the years, more radical theorists have provided a range of conceptual tools and frameworks for the critical analysis of education (Apple, 1996, 2001, 2002; Ball, 2006, 2008; Devine, 2000, 2003; Giroux, 1983; Giroux & McLaren, 1994; Lynch & O'Riordan, 1996; Lynch & Lodge, 2002). Against the conservative claim that schools transmit objective knowledge, we now look at areas of hidden curricula, as well as ideologies that identify the specific interests underlying different knowledge forms. Many theorists argue that school knowledge is a particular representation of the dominant culture, a privileged discourse constructed through a selective process of emphases and exclusions. To search for a radical pedagogy informed by cultural politics involves the task of creating theoretical models that provide a critical discourse of schools as socially constructed sites of contestation actively involved in the production of knowledge, skills and lived experiences. Central to this is the need to understand how pedagogical practice represents a particular politics of experience, i.e. 'a cultural field where knowledge, discourse and power intersect so as to produce historically specific modes of authority and forms of moral and social regulation' (Giroux & McLaren, 1989, p. 141).

There is a need to examine how schools individualise failure and legitimise inequalities within a structure where failure is attributed to inborn facilities or where 'cultural deficits relayed by the family ... come to have the force of inborn facilities' (Bernstein, 1996, p. 13). Such an approach makes central the need to analyse how human experiences are produced, contested and legitimated within the dynamics of everyday classroom life (Giroux & McLaren, 1989). It is concerned with the ways in which 'oppression is structured and legitimated in the taken-for-granted norms, habits and rules of institutions' (Barton, 1996, p. 10). By focusing on some of the implications of class-based language registers for different socio-economic groups in schools, this study seeks to relocate social-class positioning and socio-economic status (SES) to the centre of the analysis while in no way endeavouring to minimise the impact of race, gender, ethnicity, etc. on life experience. It is the contention of this author, as a result of the evidence that exists in relation to failure and participation rates, that the issue of socio-economic class is fundamental to inequality in schools.

TALES FROM SCHOOLS

Two parts of a larger, in-depth study of school experience are presented here. The first part provides a comparative analysis of the standardised test results of sixth-class pupils in English reading collected from a total of 24 schools positioned at opposite ends of the socio-economic spectrum. The categorisation of schools is based on the classification developed by the Department of Education and Science in 2000. The schools which formed the middle-class and working-class elements of the sample were selected on the basis of the statistical information from the Irish Census of Population 1996 and 2001, Small Area Population Statistics (SAPS) data. In the case of sample schools in each socio-economic grouping, the parental occupation (of both parents where possible) was provided by the schools from their records. The patterns established by the school records were checked against the SAPS data. This analysis confirmed the 'ideal type' classification of the schools used in this sample.

The data from the second phase of the research is part of a larger, year-long study consisting of a series of in-depth discussions with a total of 53 children from two working-class schools and one middle-class school. The short vignette cited here is drawn from a friendship focus-group discussion on how different groups of children engaged with the standardised reading test. The discussion explores participants' views of test content and the strategies used to complete the different test items. A simple, non-phonetic style of scripting is used in order to best represent the children's pronunciation (e.g. 'dis' for 'this', 'sayn' for 'saying'). Where included, the language variety used by the researcher will be transcribed in a similar fashion. Explanatory comments will be inserted in square brackets in order to clarify colloquial and other local terminology.

TEST RESULTS

The results of standardised English reading tests from a sample of 1,053 sixth-class students (511 working-class areas and 542 middle-class areas) are presented in Figure 8.1. An examination of the patterns arising from these results reveals the extent of this contrast between the students on the basis of socio-economic status. Almost 36 per cent of students in working-class areas are in the lowest quintile while only 8 per cent of their middle-class peers present in this band. Almost 32 per cent of the middle-class children are in the top quintile while only 9 per cent of the working-class children are included in this high-achievement category.

Figure 8.1: Comparative performance on standardised reading tests

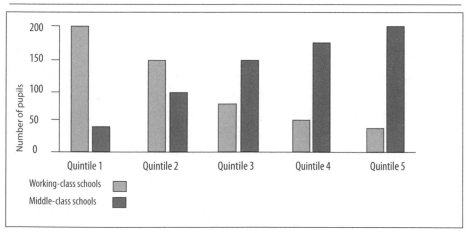

The data reveals a starkly contrasting picture in terms of the attainment levels between the different socio-economic groups. There are a number of interpretations that could be applied to the data. It could be read in a similar way to many international and national studies which suggests that there are significant problems with the children in working-class areas with respect to reading. It could also be argued that the test is successful in categorising reading attainment and that, in this way, the objective of the test is achieved. However, to confine the analysis to these patterns of results ignores a number of factors. These include a number of highly complex issues related to the extent to which reading is a cultural practice not equally dispersed in social groups with consequent implications for engagement with reading (Smagorinsky, 2001), the overall bias in the tests used to assess reading (Gipps & Murphy, 1994; Gallagher, 2003; Haertel & Lorié, 2004) and a key contextual issue which is the subject of this chapter, i.e. the linguistic register of the test when considered in the context of the linguistic register of the test takers.

There is considerable evidence in the literature that the analysis of patterns of reading attainment fails to take account of the complexity of the issue, serves only to stigmatise further children and schools in working-class areas and, by implication, apportion the blame on the schools and on the quality of the teaching therein. The brief selection from discussions with the children (reported below) explore the content and language register of the test items and reveal difficulties for children who are not at ease with the linguistic register of the test in completing the test items. The range of strategies used provides an insight into how this discontinuity contributes directly to the asymmetrical patterns of attainment on the test. (For a broader discussion on these strategies see Mac Ruairc, 2009.)

The most salient of the findings for the purpose of this consideration of language and socio-economic class was the manner in which the different groups of children used the strategies of checking the word in context and checking to see if the word 'sounded right' as a way of selecting the correct answer. When children were unsure of their answer, they often read the key word and the distractors into the sentence to check for sense. In the case of the middle-class children, this was often a simple and successful checking strategy to confirm the suitability of their answer. For the working-class children, this did not occur. In many cases, the language in the test did not resonate, in a meaningful way, with the children's linguistic experience. As a result of this, both the key word and the distractors were viewed as making sense. There were numerous examples of incorrect answers arising from this strategy in the data (pseudonyms are used to protect the children's identities).

Working-class response: Drumcondra test

> **She is a very <u>competent</u> person.**
> *lazy*
> *quiet*
> *proud*
> *able*

Frank: It's what suits it. Yeah, go … she is a very lazy person … she is a very quiet person … she is a very proud person … she is a very able person. And, yeah, see which one sounds best and the one that sounds best is 'proud'.

In some cases, the children tried to draw on their own experience of the use of the word in order to try to figure out which option to choose.

> **The action we took was <u>appropriate</u>.**
> *suitable*
> *considerate*
> *profitable*
> *necessary*

Rachel: But appropriate means, like … that … like … my ma would say. You need to wear appropriate clothes so it means suitable.

While there were some incidents of success for working-class children in their search for a context for the word, it was in the use of this strategy that the degree of linguistic discontinuity between the test and the linguistic repertoire of the children in the schools in the working-class areas became most evident. The level of experience among the working-class children of the type of words used in the test was not part of their linguistic comfort zone. Their views in relation to the language used in the test clearly indicate the gap that exists between the children and the linguistic register of the test instrument.

Peter: They're very hard to understand.
Sandra: They're big weird yokes … I never really heard any of them before.
Emma: Hello, have you stumbled? [hypercorrect voice/mocking tone]

Sandra: You wouldn't hear them unless you were going in for one a them
           meetings and ye'd have to wear a little suit an' all like an' high
           heels.
Emma: Ye'd have them in a real posh school.

It is not surprising, therefore, that seeking a familiar context for the language in
the test was regularly unsuccessful. In some cases, the children's use of the
strategy revealed fundamental misunderstandings about the meaning of the word
as a direct result of the particular context in which the child had, or thought they
had, experienced the use of the word.

They were unable to <u>subdue</u> him.
quieten
rescue
assist
replace

Declan: They were unable to subdue him ...
James: I put 'rescue' cause I thought subdue meant to ... like ... get
           him back.
Pat: I thought he was stuck down the hole and you get him back.
James: To subdue him back to your gang, yeah, that's it.
Matt: I wrote 'quieten' cause subdue means to calm him down.
Frank: I put 'replace' ... cause in work if some fella left and you couldn't
           get another fella for the job then you couldn't replace him.

Are dogs <u>domestic</u> animals?
foreign
friendly
tame
sensible

Shelly: I picked friendly because domestic means clean from Domestos
           the bleach and clean ... well ... that's good and so is friendly.
Ali: I picked 'friendly' cause they are ... dogs are friendly.

In the case cited below, the boys completely ruled out the correct word and found the idea that this choice could be appropriate as a source of amusement.

You have made one <u>*obvious*</u> *mistake.*
evident
careless
silly
slight

Jack: I put 'silly'.

Fred: I put 'careless'.

Kevin: I think 'careless', 'silly' and 'slight' all make sense with it cause you can make a slight mistake.

Robert: What about 'evident'?

Fred: Evident … [laughing] no that wouldn't make sense that's legal stuff … evidence.

Middle-class response: Drumcondra test

There was a marked contrast in the experiences of the children in the middle-class school who were notably more at ease with the language in the test. This 'search for context' strategy resonated with their linguistic habitus[4] (Bourdieu, 1986, 1991). The responses from this group of children ranged from a significant level of familiarity to a 'gut feeling' based on a view that they had heard the word used before. This provided a degree of familiarity that often was enough to successfully guide their choice of answer.

Are dogs <u>*domestic*</u> *animals?*
foreign
friendly
tame
sensible

Derek: 'Domestic' means to do with the house, to do with where you're living. It's like a domestic appliance … so 'tame' is supposed to be the correct answer. It's really stupid, none of them are the correct answer but the one you'll get the marks for is 'tame'.

> ***Ann answered the question <u>courteously.</u>***
> *correctly*
> *immediately*
> *politely*
> *cleverly*

Researcher:	Why did you choose 'politely'?
Jackie:	'Courteous' kinda means 'nice', kinda you know … polite.
Eva:	I don't know why I knew the meaning. I've heard it like loads of times before.
Eire:	You read it in books.
Stephanie:	You … kinda … hear it around the place.

> ***The <u>confrontation</u> lasted three hours.***
> *argument*
> *ceremony*
> *lecture*
> *conference*

Emma:	I don't know … I thought … I have heard the word 'confrontation' before but I can't remember. I thought it meant something about … like … arguing. You know confronting something, like, you know? I thought it meant 'arguing'. I wasn't too sure.

CONCLUSION

The link between socio-economic class and education is complex, resistant to change and persistent in terms of the impact it has on life chances. Exploring the reproduction of patterns of success, failure, engagement and alienation in schools requires the critical deconstruction of the fabric of school life. This is a difficult task and one which has the potential to disrupt the distribution of well-established patterns of power, prestige and outcomes within the field of education. Consequently, it is a focus of enquiry which is often marginalised in the discourse framing educational debate (Apple, 1996; Ball, 2006, 2008; Giroux & McLaren, 1989).

The brief vignette cited above provides an example of the type of issue that needs to be raised. It provides an insight into one aspect of the kinds of unchallenged practices that occur in schools which, at times, can have far-reaching consequences for particular social groups.

When the different strategies used by the students in completing test items are interrogated, significant differences between the socio-economic groups in terms of the efficacy of each strategy emerge. While this indicates differences with respect to the workable reading strategies within and between groups, it also points to the marked difference in the linguistic habitus (Bourdieu, 1991) and its associated linguistic capital (ibid.) between the two groups of students. The level of resonance between the language used in test items and the middle-class linguistic repertoire positions the middle-class student in a notably privileged position in terms of the potential for higher levels of attainment on the test. This high level of linguistic resonance permeates through the whole test experience for the middle-class child, with the result that each of the strategies used, including simple guessing, have a great likelihood of success. The testing experience for the working-class child on the other hand, is characterised by varying degrees of struggle with the linguistic challenges that the tests presents. It could be argued that repeated use of this form of testing provides a context for the further erosion of many children's self-efficacy in meeting the demands of schools and serves as a clear reminder of the inferior position of the working-class linguistic repertoire on the linguistic hierarchy that prevails within schools and in society.

If the use of tests of this type is examined from the perspective of the dominant majority, the issue is not so contestable, because, in general, what is being tested is what should be tested. The language in the tests is based on the dominant/standard linguistic code and the high level of continuity between the language validated by the school, the vocabulary tested in the reading test and the linguistic experience of the children from the dominant group provides a solid framework within which to test the attainment of this group of children. What is being tested is one dimension of the linguistic heterogeneity that prevails. In many ways, therefore, the school and the system/policy agenda that promotes the use of these tests is clearly validating the dominant linguistic register and rewarding those who are immersed in this register for their success in acquiring literacy of their own linguistic world. In this case, the results of the tests are useful to teachers as a basis for informing differentiated pedagogy, useful to the school in terms of target setting and useful to parents and the broader system as an objective measure of children's reading.

What, then, is the usefulness of this test for those who are not part of this linguistic field and yet are subjected to its normative 'technologies of power' (Foucault, 1980)? These are the kinds of questions we need to ask, this is the type of analysis that exposes the socio-cultural bias implicit in so many practices in the education system. Several other aspects of this bias are discussed widely in the literature by many of the sources cited in this chapter. However, the linguistic dimension of this bias is particularly problematic. Like many of the forms of cultural capital, language functions symbolically. To lose the battle for symbolic recognition is the greatest loss of all 'there is no worse dispossession, no worse privation, perhaps, than that of losers in the symbolic struggle for recognition' (Bourdieu, 2000, p. 241).

The central role language plays in the making of meaning (Willis, 1990), the construction of identity (Hall, 1998; Moore, 2001), the symbolic presentation of the self (Goffman, 1959) and the development of sense of self-efficacy (Layder, 1997) demands that schools take exceptional care in the language domain. 'Tread softly because you tread on my dreams' says W.B. Yeats in his poem, 'He Wishes for the Cloths of Heaven'. It is, after all, the language of the dreams of certain groups of children that is being negated. In choosing to test children on the dominant linguistic code, the test and the testing process negate a whole way of being, a complete and well-established way of making sense of the world by failing to validate the language variety used by specific groups to construct meaning. The meaning that is communicated to children in marginalised communities in relation to the lack of prestige and stigmatised nature of linguistic capital is overtly articulated in the practice of testing. The data reported here clearly expose the children's struggle to make sense of the language of the test. The attempts by the students to locate a resonance for the language register of the test in their linguistic repertoire is not acceptable practice in a school system that purports to enable the child 'to realise his or her potential as a unique individual' (Department of Education & Science, 1999, p. 7) which surely must involve validating the linguistic and cultural life world of each individual child.

ENDNOTES

1   Register refers to the way language can systematically vary according to the context in which it is used. Different registers can be characterised by their sentence structure, vocabulary and

pronunciation. There are three components to the linguistic register; *field* which refers to the subject matter, *tenor* which refers to the role being played by the speaker and the level of formality required and *mode* which refers to the medium of communication, e.g. speech or writing (Thomas et al., 2004).

2   'Functionalism' is one of a number of theoretical perspectives in sociology. It has its origins in the work of several European sociologists around the beginning of the 20th century and was developed by later sociologists in a number of countries, including the US, UK and Ireland. It is concerned with social structures and with processes at a macro level, such as the education system or the economy, and places particular emphasis on the functions of different social institutions in the maintenance (or otherwise) of social stability. The 'meritocratic' perspective has been a controversial one and refers to the assumption that, in education, the 'ideal' is that, through a combination of intelligence and effort, individuals are enabled to achieve the highest positions in society. Particular difficulties arise with regard to assumptions around the measurement of intelligence (see Drudy & Lynch, 1993, for an outline of the debates).

3   This research was funded by the Department of Education and Science in association with Leadership Development for Schools (LDS) and Clare Education Centre. This support is gratefully acknowledged.

4   The term 'habitus' is one particularly associated with the work of the French sociologist Pierre Bourdieu. It refers to the durable, transposable dispositions which people develop as a response to the different social structures and situations within which they find themselves (Bourdieu, 1977, p. 72).

9
THE ROLE OF MOTIVATION IN LEARNING AND USING IRISH AMONG PRIMARY AND SECOND-LEVEL STUDENTS: A REVIEW OF THE EVIDENCE

Lelia Murtagh

Motivation has been defined by Dörnyei (2001, p. 8) 'as the choice of a particular action, the persistence with it and the effort expended in it'. It is a complex and dynamic construct which plays an important role in determining learner success in educational achievement. Motivation is of particular relevance when talking about learning a second language (L2) because, as Dörnyei also points out (ibid., p. 46), mastery of a second language 'is not merely an educational issue, comparable to that of the mastery of other subject matters, but it is also a deeply social event that requires the incorporation of a wide range of elements in the L2 culture'. This chapter looks at the part motivation plays in relation to students learning Irish in the school system by reviewing studies which have tried to measure the strength of students' attitudes to learning Irish, the impact of socio-cultural and educational factors on motivation and associations between students' motivation and their achievement in Irish.

Irish may be considered differently from many second-language learning situations in that while it is an official language it is also a minority language and is taught to all children from when they enter the school system. Despite the high status attached to the language, it is spoken daily outside of the school situation, by only a small minority (approx. 3 per cent) of the population (Central Statistics Office, 2006). In spite of this, support for the preservation of Irish remains high among the adult population (Mac Gréil & Rhatigan, 2009) while 70 per cent believe it is important that their children grow up knowing Irish (Ó Riagáin, 2007, p. 386). In order to set the context for this review, it will be useful to trace the evolution of Irish teaching from the time the language was introduced as a mandatory school subject early in the life of the Irish Free State.

TEACHING IRISH IN SCHOOLS: FROM 1922 TO TODAY

In the constitution drawn up for the new Irish Free State in 1922, the Irish language was described as the national language and English as an equally recognised official language. Thus, a bilingual state was envisaged. The Irish education system was to be the main vehicle through which revival of Irish was to be achieved. All primary schools were instructed to teach Irish, or use it as a medium of instruction for at least a half an hour a day (INTO, 1941). It was also recommended that Irish be taught or used as a medium of instruction in all national schools that had a competent teacher with special training in Irish being provided for teachers. While primary education was compulsory for all young children (six-14 years) at this time, few continued to the post-primary level. Ó Buachalla (1988, p. 62) points out that in the period following independence 'access to education beyond the primary stage outside urban areas, was available only to about 8% of the age group'. In secondary schools, Irish and English were mandatory subjects from 1927. Irish was a compulsory subject for the two main examinations—the junior-level examination (Intermediate Certificate) and the terminal secondary-school examination (Leaving Certificate).

The new language policy was vigorously pursued through the 1930s and, by the early 1940s, 12 per cent of primary schools and 28 per cent of secondary schools in English-speaking areas were using Irish as a medium of instruction (Ó Buachalla, 1988, p. 65). However, there was growing unease among teachers and politicians regarding the suitability of Irish-medium education for infant classes in particular. Consequently, the rule was relaxed in the 1950s. The general public was also unhappy with other aspects of Irish language policy in the schools; particularly unpopular was the regulation whereby students who did not pass Irish in the two main state examinations (Intermediate and Leaving Certificates) would not be awarded a certificate, i.e. they were regarded as having failed the whole examination (see Ó Riagáin, 1997). As resistance to the compulsory aspect of Irish in state examinations mounted, the government finally capitulated and the rule was dropped in 1973, though Irish continued to be a compulsory subject, to be studied by all students until the end of second-level schooling. The 1970s was also marked by a growing dissatisfaction at official levels with the low return of the investment in teaching Irish. A report by Comhairle na Gaeilge (The Irish Language Council) published during this period, while acknowledging the high standards in some schools, asserted that 'in too many other schools, even after 12 years instruction, most pupils emerge unable to conduct a simple conversation in Irish' (Comhairle na Gaeilge, 1974, p. 3).

The introduction of free education and the establishment of comprehensive and community schools dramatically increased the participation rates in post-primary education between 1960 and 1970 (Clancy, 2001, p. 16; Ó Buachalla, 1988, p. 74). These increased demands on the state educational system together with the general dissatisfaction regarding certain aspects of Irish-language teaching policy, gradually led to a more pragmatic policy being adopted. A general shift took place from promoting bilingual or all-Irish programmes to concentrating resources on the teaching of Irish as a subject. While approximately 80 secondary schools were teaching through Irish in 1960, only one quarter of these was still operating by 1970 (Ó Buachalla, 1988, p. 67). There was an even greater decline at primary level in this 10-year period with the number of 'all-Irish' schools falling from 183 to 28 (Ó Riagáin, 1997, p. 201).

Alongside this change in official emphasis, there were indications of declining standards in Irish at primary and second level. Ó Riagáin (1997, p. 204) notes that from the early 1970s through the 1980s, there was an increase in the percentages of students not taking Irish in the two second-level state examinations, as well as growing percentages who failed Irish or who did not take the higher level paper in Irish in the Leaving Certificate examination. At primary level, various surveys of achievement during the 1970s and 1980s showed that only approximately one-third of children in English-medium schools were attaining mastery of the stated listening and speaking objectives of the audio-visual-based Irish courses which were in use at the time (Harris, 1984; Harris & Murtagh, 1988). In contrast, their counterparts in immersion schools (Gaelscoileanna—all-Irish-medium schools in English-speaking areas) and in schools in the Gaeltacht (Irish-speaking areas) were achieving mastery rates of between 70–80 per cent.

IRISH IN SCHOOLS TODAY

With a few minor exceptions,[1] all school-going children today study Irish as a subject from when they enter primary school until they complete their second-level education. Recent national education statistics (2005–2006) show that 7.6 per cent of primary schools use Irish as a medium of instruction (Department of Education & Science, 2009a). These include 106 (3.4 per cent) schools in the Gaeltacht, and 132 (4.2 per cent) immersion schools (Gaelscoileanna); the latter group has been growing steadily over the past two decades. There are proportionally fewer schools where Irish is the medium of instruction at second level (5.3 per cent) than at primary level. Full Irish-medium instruction at second level is offered in 20 Gaeltacht schools and in 19 Gaelscoileanna, while eight second-level schools have Irish-medium streams. There is evidence that pupils from Gaelscoileanna generally have much higher levels of achievement in Irish (Irish reading and spoken Irish) than those in mainstream (English-medium) primary schools (Cummins, 1982; Harris, 1984, Harris & Murtagh, 1988; Harris et al., 2006) and as high as their Gaeltacht peers (Harris & Murtagh, 1987).

New approaches to the teaching of Irish

Concerns about failure rates in Irish and the suitability of course content for all students prompted curriculum reform in Irish during the 1990s. In 1990, the Review Body on the Primary Curriculum recommended a new syllabus for Irish. The following year, a representative Curriculum Committee in the National Council for Curriculum and Assessment (NCCA) began work on the syllabus, completing their work in June 1998 (NCCA, 1999b). A new revised curriculum for Leaving Certificate Irish was already developed and published in 1995 (Department of Education, 1995a, 1995b). It was hoped that by adopting a new communicative approach (Canale & Swain, 1980; Hymes, 1972), as had already happened in the case of modern languages in post-primary schools (Sheils, 1988), Irish would become more accessible and relevant to all students (Ó Laoire, 2000). At primary level, it was argued that the discontinuity between the school and life outside it was at least partly due to the use of materials which were not considered by pupils to be modern or realistic (Harris & Murtagh, 1999).

Despite the changes instituted in the Irish curriculum and the development of new courses, the most recent survey of achievement in Irish shows a substantial decline in standards of both spoken Irish and Irish reading in ordinary level schools (Harris et al., 2006). In the case of key speaking objectives (vocabulary and verbs), Harris (2006, p. 162) states that 'the percentage failing now constitutes a majority'. He points to the need for pupils to achieve worthwhile levels of proficiency in Irish in order to maintain their motivation to learn the language and warns of the consequences of declining pupil and teacher motivation for the enterprise of teaching and learning Irish in primary schools (ibid., p. 165).

RELATIONSHIP BETWEEN USE AND ACHIEVEMENT IN IRISH

Studies over the years have shown the importance of Irish use in predicting levels of competence in Irish. The large-scale study of public attitudes, ability and use in relation to Irish (CILAR, 1975) found that the strongest correlate of ability (self-assessed) among the adult population was the amount of Irish used by the respondent during his/her primary and post-primary schooling combined. The second strongest correlate was the extent to which Irish was used by the respondent outside the classroom during these years. A survey of public use of, and attitudes to, Irish conducted in 1993 (Ó Riagáin & Ó Gliasáin, 1994) found higher levels of competence in Irish associated with those who had been taught through the medium of Irish. Various surveys (Harris & Murtagh, 1988, Harris et al., 2006) have confirmed the positive effect that even moderate home use of Irish can have on primary-school children's proficiency in Irish and on pupil attitude/motivation in Irish (Harris & Murtagh, 1999). In the recent Harris et al. (2006) survey, it was shown that parental ability to speak Irish and frequency of use of Irish with the child were strongly related to achievement in Irish, though less so in the case of children in Gaelscoileanna (ibid., p. 141). In relation to the latter finding, the authors concluded that parental ability and use are less powerfully related to the Irish-speaking proficiency achieved by English-speaking children generally where the exposure to Irish at school is extensive.

The general absence of a functional context for using Irish is disadvantageous for students not only in terms of limiting their chances of exposure to the naturalistic use of Irish but also because of the potentially negative effect on their motivation to learn the language. The remainder of this chapter reviews attempts to describe the various dimensions of student motivation in learning a second language such as Irish and assesses how these may impact on achievement, use and overall investment in Irish.

MEASURING ATTITUDE/MOTIVATION IN LEARNING A SECOND LANGUAGE

Gardner and Lambert (1959) were among the first to try to identify the major social and ability factors involved in second-language learning. Gardner (1985) went on to develop the Attitude Motivation Test Battery (AMTB), a series of measures designed with Canadian English-speaking children learning French in mind. Three attitude/motivational clusters—motivation, integrativeness and attitude towards the learning situation—were defined in terms of a conceptual analysis of the affective variables and their relation to second-language learning. The first component, *motivation,* refers to an individual who: (a) wants to achieve a particular goal; (b) devotes considerable effort to achieving this goal; and (c) experiences satisfaction in the activities associated with achieving the goal. The second cluster, *integrativeness,* refers to those learner attributes which reflect a positive outlook towards the target language group, or out-groups in general, or a desire to meet with and possibly associate with members of those groups. The third cluster, *attitudes to the learning situation,* refers to the learners' affective reactions to the learning situation, e.g. attitudes towards the teacher, the class, the textbooks, etc. Studies by Lalonde and Gardner (1985) found that of the three major components described above, motivation was the best predictor in the case of three different outcome measures—behavioural intention to study French, final French grades and a global measure of French achievement.

Attitude/Motivation in Irish primary schools

Harris and Murtagh (1999) used an adapted form of the Attitude Motivation Test Battery (AMTB) to assess pupil attitude/motivation in relation to learning Irish at primary school.[2] It was found that the sixth-grade pupils involved in the study (n=490) had quite positive *integrative* attitudes in relation to Irish, i.e. they were generally well-disposed towards the Irish language itself and towards the idea of integrating with the Irish-language speaking 'community' or 'group'. These integrative attitudes are important because they can help to maintain motivation during the long task of acquiring Irish. On the basis of this research, Harris and Murtagh (1999) concluded that the development of pupils' 'attitude to Irish speakers' and 'integrative orientation to Irish' are governed in part by home/social factors. One indication of this was the significant correlations between the various 'integrativeness' scales, on the one hand, and 'parental encouragement' (*r*s range from .34 to .53 and 'use of Irish at home' (*r*s range from .19 to .35) on the other.

The Harris and Murtagh (1999) study also showed that an overall measure of 'Irish attitude/motivation' (an AMTB-based index) was strongly related to the level of proficiency in Irish of pupils as measured by an objective test of spoken Irish (Harris & Murtagh, 1988). The strength of this relationship (*r*=.40) compared favourably with the corresponding correlations between the AMTB and French grades quoted by Gardner (1985). Regression analysis, however, indicated that the effect of 'Irish attitude/motivation' on achievement was small relative to other individual and socio-demographic factors (pupil's general academic ability, location and social class); the latter accounted for most (one-third) of the variance in pupil achievement in Irish. Two home factors, 'Use of Irish at home' and 'Parental encouragement', contributed an additional 3 per cent while the overall 'Irish attitude/motivation' index made a significant though not very large additional contribution (4 per cent) to the variance explained. Two specific components of the motivation factor—'Motivational intensity to learn Irish' and 'Attitude to learning Irish'—together with an aspect of the learning situation, 'Irish-lesson anxiety', were the most important correlates of achievement. Predictably, 'Irish-lesson anxiety' was negatively correlated with pupil achievement in Irish ($r=-.28$). In other words, pupils who experienced more anxiety during the Irish lesson tended to have lower levels of achievement in spoken Irish. Responses to items on this scale indicated that roughly one-third of pupils experienced lack of confidence or embarrassment about speaking Irish in class. An indication that anxiety can impact negatively on motivation was provided by the significant negative correlation between 'Irish-lesson anxiety' and the 'Motivation index' ($r=-.33$). A small but significant correlation was also found between 'Gender' and the 'Irish-lesson anxiety' scale ($r=.14$), with girls tending to be more anxious that boys.

In a small qualitative dimension of the Harris and Murtagh (1999) study, pupils' reactions to the Irish lesson, expressed in their own words, indicated that many found the materials and content of the course in use at the time to be boring, old-fashioned and repetitious. They expressed the desire for a course which was more modern, more fun and more realistic, with a greater emphasis on conversations and games, an objective which was to be given high priority in the design of the new Irish curriculum (Department of Education, 1999). General apathy/discouragement and unhappiness at not being able to understand the lesson or the teacher were themes which featured frequently in classes with low levels of achievement in Irish.

There has been no comparable research on pupil attitude/motivation on the scale of that described above, since the introduction of the new primary Irish curriculum. However, a small-scale study conducted by Fox (2007) involving focus-group interviews in five primary schools gives some interesting insights into fifth- and sixth-grade pupils' views on the new Irish course and on their motivation to learn the language. In general, the children interviewed were positive about the kind of language games and dramas in the course that made Irish more enjoyable and gave them the opportunity to practise their oral skills.

In particular, pupils were enthusiastic about opportunities to engage in real communication through the medium of Irish during the annual Irish week (*seachtain na Gaeilge*) in the school. However, there were several indications in the interview transcripts (see below) that children would like more freedom to speak during Irish class, to design their own dramas, spend less time learning scripts and, generally, to take more control of their learning.

> Niamh: It's like you are reading from the books and nobody knows half the words and nobody knows how to pronounce what they are saying and it just gets boring.
>
> Fox, 2007, p. 103

> Patrick: There is a lot of learning off and we don't have fun things. Like in Maths we might go outside measuring things and stuff and we never do anything like that in Irish. It's just learning the book.
>
> Fox, 2007, p. 109

> Caolan: It could be a lot better cause sometimes when they say, 'Oh, take out your *Bualadh Bos*' [textbook] and everyone says, 'Oh no', and if we did different stuff they would like it more.
>
> Fox, 2007, p. 113

A recent evaluation of the Irish curriculum in 40 primary schools and 159 classrooms by the inspectorate (Department of Education & Science, 2007a) concluded that children appear to enjoy the new curriculum. But concerns were expressed about the low standards of pupil-Irish observed, particularly in relation to Irish verbs and the absence of clearly defined learning objectives in the Irish lessons. Recommendations for improvement included the introduction of a graded teaching programme, greater use of the target language during class, more use of Irish outside the language lesson and among teachers themselves.

Irish attitude/Motivation in post-primary schools

In 2000, five years after the introduction of the new Irish-language curriculum at second level, and as part of a study of a longitudinal study of Irish proficiency and retention (Murtagh, 2003), a group of 240 Leaving Certificate students completed questionnaires which included items from adapted AMTB scales.[3] The students came from three types of instructional backgrounds ('instructional categories'—ICs), IC1: Leaving Certificate (LC) students studying the ordinary-level Irish course in mainstream (English-medium) schools; IC2: LC students studying the higher level Irish course in mainstream schools; and IC3: LC Irish-medium (Gaelscoileanna) students (all of whom studied higher level Irish). Mean item scores on attitude and motivation scales are shown in Table 9.1, set alongside comparable scores from Ó Fathaigh's (1991) second-level study and Harris and Murtagh's (1999) primary-school study.

In order to compare the results across studies, the mean ratings for the three IC groups were standardised on a scale of 1 to 5. Looking at the three motivation scales ('Desire to learn Irish', 'Motivational intensity' and 'Attitude to learning Irish'), it can be seen that mean item ratings for IC2 students (higher level Irish in mainstream schools) in the 2003 study fall almost midway within the scale. This suggests that, at best, these Leaving Certificate students are largely neutral about learning Irish and do not make any special effort in relation to learning it. IC1 (ordinary-level Irish in mainstream schools) students are, on average, negative in relation to learning Irish while IC3 ('all-Irish' school) students are generally positive and show that they make an effort in relation to learning the language.

It can also be seen that, on average, the ratings on scales in the Harris and Murtagh (1999) study of sixth-grade pupils in mainstream primary schools fall somewhere between ratings for these same scales for IC1 and IC2 students in the 2003 study. The mean ratings reported for the three equivalent scales in an earlier survey of junior secondary-school students' attitudes to Irish (Ó Fathaigh, 1991) are closer to that found among ordinary-level Irish students (IC1) in the present study. 'Irish-lesson anxiety' in the 1999 primary-school study is also similar to that found among IC1 students in the 2003 second-level study. Student reported 'parental encouragement', however, is generally higher in the primary-school study than in the case of students in mainstream second-level schools. Together, the comparisons indicate that motivation in the present study is as high, if not higher, than that found in late primary and early secondary but that parents may be less likely to encourage their children in relation to learning Irish at second level. It should be noted here that this comparison of mean ratings is useful only in indicating general trends; no firm conclusions can be drawn due to the different student populations, dates of studies and the changing socio-cultural and pedagogical contexts (new curricula) in the past two decades. In addition, cognisance must also be taken of the slightly different scoring formats and item wording used in the different studies.

Table 9.1: Comparing standardised* mean item ratings for comparable AMTB-based scales in various Irish studies

Attitude/Motivation Test Battery (AMTB)-based scales	Leaving Certificate students Murtagh (2003)				Other studies Mainstream schools	
	Instructional category (IC)**				6th grade primary pupils	2nd/3rd year secondary students
	IC1	IC2	IC3 (scale range 1–5)	Total	(Harris & Murtagh, 1999)	(Ó Fathaigh, 1991)
Desire to learn Irish (DTLI)	2.8	3.3	4.2	3.3	3.0	2.5
Motivational intensity (MI)	3.2	3.3	3.8	3.3	3.2	3.2
Attitude to learning Irish (ATLI)	2.7	3.5	4.6	3.5	3.3	3.2
Irish-lesson anxiety (ILA)	2.9	2.5	1.4	2.4	2.9	
Parental encouragement (PE)	2.6	3.1	3.8	3.1	3.5	

*Mean ratings were standardised on a scale of 1 to 5 to facilitate comparisons with the other studies which used a five-point rating scale for items instead of the seven-point one used in the original AMTB. **IC1=Mainstream: ordinary-level Irish students; IC2=Mainstream: higher level Irish students; IC3=Gaelscoil students.

Table 9.2: Leaving Certificate Students: Mean item ratings for AMTB-course evaluation scales by instructional category

Attitude/Motivation Test Battery (AMTB)-based scales	n items	(min, max)	Instructional category			eta	Total
			IC1	IC2	IC3		
Irish course: utility	5	(1, 7)	4.2	5.1	6.1	.45**	5.1
Irish course: evaluation	10	(1, 7)	3.9	4.5	5.6	.45**	4.5
Irish course: interest	5	(1, 7)	3.2	3.8	4.9	.44**	3.8
Irish course: difficulty	5	(1, 7)	4.8	5.0	2.9	.58**	4.5
Irish-lesson anxiety (ILA)	5	(1, 7)	4.0	3.5	1.9	.45**	3.3
Parental encouragement (PE)	10	(1, 7)	3.7	4.3	5.3	.45**	4.3

Note: eta is a correlation coefficient used when you cannot assume a linear relation between variables, such as between the categorical variable instructional category and AMTB scales.

A comparison of mean item ratings (range=1-7) on the three AMTB-based Irish course evaluation measures—utility, evaluation and interest (see Table 9.2)—shows that 'utility' rated highest for all Leaving Certificate students (5.1). This suggests that students valued the Leaving Certificate Irish course more for its practical or utilitarian value rather than for its inherent interest value. The ratings vary according to instructional category. Students in IC3 (Gaelscoileanna) are relatively positive, on average, about the Irish course and generally agree that it is very useful. Those in IC2 (higher level Irish in mainstream schools) also see it as useful but are less likely to see it as interesting. In general, IC1 (ordinary-level Irish in mainstream schools) students rated their course lowest in terms of interest, value it less than higher level Irish students and are largely neutral regarding its perceived utility. It is worth recalling that even though IC1 students follow a different and less demanding course than the other two groups, their course shares many common elements with the higher level course.

The data in Table 9.2 also indicates that mainstream students in IC1 and IC2 rate their respective courses as being above average in terms of difficulty. Gaelscoil (IC3) students, on the other hand, generally disagree that the higher level course is difficult. ANOVA statistics confirmed that the highest level of Irish-lesson anxiety was associated with students studying the ordinary-level Irish course and the lowest levels of anxiety with Gaelscoil students ($F(2,238)=29.47$; $p<.001$. Means: IC1=20.17; IC2=17.4; IC3=9.47). It is worth mentioning here that the effect was more evident among females in IC1; females scoring higher in terms of anxiety than males. Paradoxically, female students, in general, attained significantly higher proficiency scores compared to their male counterparts (Murtagh, 2003, p. 86; 2006, p. 55) across all three instructional categories.

Measures of association between achievement in Irish, and motivation and use scale scores in the Murtagh (2003) study are shown in Table 9.3. The two measures of achievement listed here are a general measure of proficiency in Irish (C-Test) and Irish grade in the Leaving Certificate Examination (see Murtagh, 2003 for a full description).

Table 9.3: Pearson Correlations: attitude/motivation, use of Irish outside school, with: (i) instructional category, gender; and (ii) measures of achievement in Irish

Student background variables	eta Instructional category (n=239-41)	Gender (n=239-241)	C-Test Score (n=211-213)	LC Irish grade (points) (n=187-189)
Desire to learn Irish (DTLI)	.58**	.06	.56**	.62**
Motivational intensity (MI)	.39**	.09	.39**	.44**
Attitude to learning Irish (ATLI)	.53**	.01	.52**	.58**
Motivation index (MI)	.55**	.03	.54**	.44**
Irish course evaluation total	.39**	.02	.40**	.44**
Irish lesson anxiety (ILA)	.45**	.23**	-.44**	-.45**
Parental encouragement (PE)	.45**	-.05	.31**	.43**
Use of Irish in home	.40**	-.03	.33**	.41**
Opportunity to speak Irish	.63**	-.08	.50**	.51**

Notes: eta is a correlation coefficient used when you cannot assume a linear relation between variables, such as between the categorical variable instructional category and AMTB scales. *Correlation is significant at the .05 level (2-tailed). ** Correlation is significant at the .01 level (2-tailed).

The table also includes correlations between scale scores and the two independent variables, gender and instructional category. It can be seen that students' scores on the Irish achievement measures have statistically significant correlations with all three motivation scales, as well as with the overall motivation. For the three AMTB-based scales, 'Desire to learn Irish', 'Motivational Intensity' and 'Attitude to learning Irish', the r values vary between .39 and .62. The highest correlations are found in the case of the 'Desire to learn Irish': r values for this scale with Irish C-Test score, and Leaving Certificate Irish grade are .56, and .62 respectively. High scores on items on this scale express a strong desire to learn and to speak Irish as much as possible. A variable measuring student 'Opportunity to speak Irish outside of school' was also strongly positively correlated with proficiency in Irish (r=.50) as was 'Use of Irish in the home', the latter to a lesser extent. Similar correlations for a subset of this sample have been reported for the same motivation and use variables with a measure of achievement in spoken Irish (see Murtagh, 2003, 2007).

DISCUSSION

The studies reviewed here show that Irish students are, by and large, positively disposed to the Irish language, though those with lower levels of ability in Irish are less so. At Leaving Certificate level, motivation to learn Irish is lowest for students studying the ordinary-level Irish course. The latter are less interested in the language, experience more anxiety in relation to learning it and see it as having less practical value to them than their peers studying the higher Irish level course. It seems that the utility factor remains the main motivating factor for higher level students in relation to learning Irish. Ó Riagain (1997, p. 275) has argued that 'it was the relationship between educational qualifications and the labour market—and not pedagogical factors *per se*—which is crucial to an understanding of the effectiveness of Irish language policies in schools'. Utilitarian motives for learning Irish and achieving high grades in the Leaving Certificate remain strong for those seeking access to many university courses. However, motivation such as this which is largely examination driven will not be enough to sustain the kind of individual investment needed to produce and sustain competent and committed speakers, who will, in turn, ensure the kind of intergenerational transmission needed for the creation of active and vibrant Irish-language speaking communities.

The evidence reviewed here suggests that changing methodologies alone are not enough to ensure that young learners engage in a personal way with the learning process and to attain the kinds of standards that are necessary to sustain their interest and ensure maintenance. While spoken Irish is clearly given a high level of priority in current Irish curricula at primary and second level, it would seem that learners are not being sufficiently challenged in their language production, i.e. they are not engaging actively in the type of negotiated interaction necessary to facilitate language development. Recent research (e.g. Swain, 1995, 2000) on second-language teaching emphasises the importance for learners to engage in different types of collaborative interaction in ways which will 'push' them in their output. Swain (2000) shows how such forms of language production can actually mediate the process of comprehension through reflection on performance and the construction of knowledge. Providing more opportunities for students to engage in collaborative dialogue and reflection may need to be applied across the school curriculum and not only in language teaching. A recent OECD teaching and learning international study (Shiel et al., 2009) has shown that Irish second-level teachers still hold stronger direct transmission beliefs about learning than constructivist beliefs, and favour more structuring teaching activities than student-orientated/mediated practices.

Given the decline in the amount of time spent teaching Irish in mainstream schools in the past two decades, it is essential to provide more focused opportunities for students to participate in the type of negotiated interaction which is routinely available to students in Irish-medium schools. Harris (2006) advocates the addition of Irish-speaking streams in mainstream (English-medium) primary schools in order to give children the opportunity to consolidate the communicative skills which are being taught in the new curriculum. The necessity for such expanded programmes has also been acknowledged by a recent departmental evaluation report on Irish in the primary school (Department of Education & Science, 2007a). But language policy needs to extend beyond the school, establishing links in the wider community if it is going to create the type of communities of practice that Irish learners need to help create and maintain their own linguistic identities. For the majority of mainstream students, the level of out-of-school contact with Irish is dictated by course/school expectations and access to school-related, Irish-speaking networks. After students complete their second-level schooling, an important utilitarian motive for learning and using Irish evaporates and their limited contact with communities of practice outside of school is further diminished. Accessing Irish-speaking networks outside of Gaeltacht regions is not easy. Even for all-Irish school students, there are concerns that the rapid expansion of Irish-medium schools may be advancing at a pace which is not being met by the kind of Irish-speaking community needed to sustain a high level of student proficiency in Irish. Ó Baoill (2007) recommends a period of consolidation for all-Irish schools in order to develop such speaking communities.

Finally, in order to give greater insights into the dynamic nature and effects of motivation, future research may need to focus on personal histories/narratives of language learners such as that advocated by Block (2003) and Pavlenko and Lantolf (2000). Such histories will help to facilitate an examination not only of the development of learners' proficiency but also to provide an account of the construction of learner identity and agency, and of learners' perceptions of themselves as members of the Irish-language-speaking community.

ENDNOTES

1   Children whose primary education up to 11 years was received outside the state and some
    categories of children with learning disabilities. (Department of Education, 1994, 1996).

2   It must be pointed out here, that this study was conducted before the introduction of the
    present new communicative curriculum for Irish.

3   More details on these scales may be found in Murtagh (2003, 2006).

Part 3
Teacher Education for Changing Times

10
RECRUITMENT TO PRIMARY TEACHING IN IRELAND: A NORTH/SOUTH COMPARATIVE ANALYSIS[1]

Sheelagh Drudy

INTRODUCTION

This chapter examines, compares and explains patterns of recruitment to primary teaching at the turn of the 21st century in the Republic of Ireland and in Northern Ireland. It puts a particular emphasis on a key dimension of entrance to primary teaching—that of gender. It draws on a comparative study using datasets from two studies of school leavers and of student primary teachers in both jurisdictions.

Analysis of trends from the mid-1990s to the mid-2000s in Ireland show that interest in becoming a primary teacher was high, and actually increased in the period, with many more applicants than there were places available (Drudy, 2006a). Analysis in Britain has also shown that, there also, there was no overall shortage of applicants to initial teacher education (White et al., 2006). However, studies in Ireland and Britain, and throughout many countries in Europe, North America, Australia and New Zealand, have shown that this interest is mainly on the part of women (Drudy, 2006a; Drudy et al., 2005).

This chapter focuses on recruitment to primary teaching. Comparable trends with regard to the representation of males in primary and post-primary teaching are to be found in both Northern Ireland and the Republic of Ireland. There has been a decrease in the percentage of males in the teaching force in both jurisdictions since the middle of the 20th century. This decrease has been particularly marked in the case of primary teaching.

THE BACKGROUND

Ireland is an interesting site in which to study patterns of entry to teaching for a number of reasons. It is a single geographical entity but political, cultural and national identities have been, and remain, highly contested. Different economic trajectories have also been characteristic of both parts of the island.

Initially, after independence in the 1920s, the Republic displayed economic features characteristic of many post-colonial societies. Nevertheless, the period from independence to the 1960s was characterised by high levels of economic stagnation and emigration. This was reversed by economic expansion in the 1960s and early 1970s, but again featured in the recessions of the late 1970s and 1980s. During the 1990s and the early 2000s, the Republic of Ireland experienced very rapid economic growth. Ireland became one of the new 'tiger' economies. Ireland became a 'showpiece of globalization, a prime example of how a region could turn around from economic laggard to tiger in just a few years, by integrating itself maximally into the global division of labour' (O'Hearn, 1999). At the beginning of the 21st century, Ireland was the most globally integrated country in the world due to its deep economic links and its high level of personal contact with the rest of the world as well as its technological/internet connectivity and its political engagement with international organisations (A.T. Kearney/Foreign Policy, 2004). However, before the end of the first decade of the new century, economic boom had turned to economic bust, as the economy proved vulnerable to the global financial crisis and the crash of Irish and international property markets.

Northern Ireland's economic trajectory has been rather different. At independence, the north-east of Ireland was a core industrial area of the British Empire. Belfast was a world leader in shipbuilding and linen manufacture and one of the main industrial areas of the United Kingdom, then the leading imperial power in the world. Northern Ireland was a net subscriber to the British exchequer and was expected to be financially self-sufficient (O'Dowd, 1995, pp. 132–3). De-industrialisation, the collapse of the linen and shipbuilding industries and the impact of the conflict led to a dramatic decline in the economic fortunes of Northern Ireland. It also led to increased dependency on the British exchequer. In effect, Northern Ireland became a dependent client of the British state (ibid.), with high levels of unemployment and migration. The impact of the economic decline varied according to gender and social class, but also according to ethno-national background (ibid.). From the establishment of the 'peace process', the consequent reduction in political violence and the growth of relative stability, economic investment and performance in Northern Ireland increased significantly. However, the economy of North was also adversely affected by the global economic downturn from 2008, though perhaps not as gravely as that in the Republic, due to its advantageous position with regard to sterling versus the euro.

With regard to education, after independence, the Republic of Ireland was faced with twin problems of political legitimacy and economic impoverishment. It succeeded in addressing many of the problems associated with this position through strong Church involvement in education. This resulted in both economic and ideological gains for the state (Drudy & Lynch, 1993, p. 74). It also resulted in high levels of Church control over entry to primary teaching, insofar as teacher education colleges were (and still are) organised along denominational lines. In the North, the educational system developed along ethno-national lines with the state sector (the controlled sector) largely attended and staffed by Protestant denominations, and with Catholics concentrated in the Catholic 'maintained' school sector (see http://www.onlineccms.com/ for further details). There is a small, but growing, (religiously) integrated sector in which pupils from different denominations attend (Cormack & Osborne, 1995; DENI, 2008). Primary teacher education colleges have also traditionally reflected ethno-national divisions in their intake patterns.

Ireland's rates of educational participation and generally good performance on international testing measures (e.g. Shiel et al., 2001; OECD, 2008a; Cormack & Osborne, 1995) proved attractive to foreign investors both North and South during the decade of rapid economic growth from 1997 to 2007.

INTERNATIONAL RESEARCH ON TEACHING

International research on teaching provides the context and the background to the surveys of school leavers and student teachers in the Republic of Ireland and in Northern Ireland.

Literature on the 'feminisation of teaching' refers to the processes by which teaching became a mostly female occupation. A number of factors contributing to this particular pattern of recruitment to primary teaching have been identified, namely, the economic policy of education administrators, beliefs about the nature of women and patriarchal control. These factors, though, have been less influential in rural areas than in industrialised, urban areas (Acker, 1994; Miller, 1996; Basten, 1997; Drudy et al., 2005).

The social construction of masculinity is another relevant factor. International research has suggested that the area of masculinity and education is a problematic one. First of all, the relation between the two is complex in that, although education systems have been subject to tight patriarchal control, there is a tendency for some masculine identities to be formed in varying degrees of opposition to that authority. Second, there may be conflict and struggle in the definitions of various masculinities, and a whole range of problems ensues from this divergence. There are obvious difficulties for those who do not identify with 'hegemonic' masculinity[2] (Mac an Ghaill, 1994; Connell, 1995). This would suggest that male entry into highly feminised occupations might be a difficult choice for young men (Drudy et al., 2005).

Research suggests that men's interest in female-dominated fields is, in general, less usual than women's interest in male-dominated fields. Although there are perceptible patterns, practices and ideologies in various careers, the structural configurations of gender differences vary from job to job, as do individual, subjective experiences of masculinity or femininity. The perception of particular occupations as female-dominated, and the associated perceptions (both negative and positive) of the minority of men who work in them, may have implications for school leavers' perceptions and decision-making (Jacobs, 1993; Williams, 1995; Connell & Messerschmidt, 2005). Studies on men in teaching have shown that there are conflicts and contradictions in their role (Lortie, 1975; Huberman et al., 1991). A considerable number of these contradictions are focused on being male in what is perceived to be a female profession.

The operation of difference is, to a large extent, mediated by wider socialising factors and by ideological constraints. The relative advantage that girls might have with regard to the entry requirements to primary colleges of education does not, in itself, explain why so few boys consider primary teaching as a career option.

The research question explored by this study is thus threefold:

- to identify similarities and differences in the patterns of recruitment to primary education in the Republic of Ireland and Northern Ireland;
- to examine gender differences in the perceptions and choice of primary teaching as a career in the two jurisdictions; and
- to locate the observed patterns within a social, economic and historical context.

RECRUITMENT TO PRIMARY TEACHING

As indicated above, the increases in entrants to primary teaching from the mid-1990s were accounted for mainly by females. The consequent decline in the proportion of males in teaching and the feminisation of the profession, especially at primary level, became the focus of frequent expressions of alarm by journalists and teacher union representatives alike (INTO, 2004). The position with regard to recruitment into primary teaching in the latter half of the first decade of the 21st century is illustrated in Table 10.1.

Table 10.1: Graduates with Bachelor of Education awards in the academic year 2006–2007 from higher education institutions (HEIs) in Northern Ireland and the Republic of Ireland

Gender	Northern Ireland HEIs %	Republic of Ireland HEIs %
Males	15.8	10.7
Females	84.2	89.3
Total	100.0	100.0
n	475	1,014

Sources: NI Department for Employment and Learning. Available at: http://www.delni.gov.uk/he_qual_0607 .pdf (accessed 05/06/2009). RoI Higher Education Authority. Available at: http://www.hea.ie/files/files/file /statistics/2008/Uni%2007-08/Awards%20UG%20Hons%20Bac%20Degree,FT,%200607%20academic% 20yr,%20Website%20Unis.xls (accessed 05/06/2009).

Table 10.1 presents the figures on those graduating with Bachelor of Education awards in the academic year 2006–2007 (the most recent year for which figures were available at the time of writing) from full-time programmes in higher education institutions in Northern Ireland and the Republic of Ireland. It does not include students from either Northern Ireland or from the Republic of Ireland who may have been graduating from courses in other jurisdictions or from postgraduate courses for primary teachers. Nevertheless, it illustrates the patterns of female dominance among entrants to primary teaching which have been well established in both jurisdictions (Johnston et al., 1998; Drudy et al., 2003; INTO, 2004; Drudy et al., 2005; Drudy, 2006a).

It also shows another persistent pattern—while female entrants dominate in both jurisdictions, the proportion of men recruited to primary teaching is somewhat higher in Northern Ireland (see also Johnston et al., 1998; Drudy et al., 2003; INTO, 2004). Given the political, cultural and economic specificities of the two parts of Ireland, and that there are also common cultural values as well as differences, comparative data from the two jurisdictions provides a unique and valuable opportunity to explore the dynamics of entrance to primary teaching.

METHODOLOGY

To explore perceptions of teaching and patterns of entry to the profession, this chapter draws on two surveys of school leavers and student teachers that were conducted in the Republic of Ireland and Northern Ireland over the period 1997–2001 (see Johnston et al., 1998; Drudy et al., 2003; Drudy, 2005). In both surveys, student teachers and pupils in their last year of second-level education were questioned on the motivational and attitudinal aspects of their career choices. In addition, issues relating to the possible structural and cultural links to gender and occupations were explored. There were a series of specific references to career values and perceptions with an emphasis on primary teaching.

In the case of both studies, the primary research instruments were two questionnaires—one for pupils in the senior cycle of second-level education, and one for primary student-teachers in the colleges of education. Although the questionnaires were developed independently, many common issues and attitudes were explored. The two studies of senior-cycle pupils (one in the Republic, one in Northern Ireland) and of student-teachers (in all of the primary education colleges, North and South) allowed for a number of very important comparisons to be made. These included the following: trends in the average female and male academic points at entry to primary teaching from the 1970s onwards; comparisons of girls' and boys' reasons for choosing primary teaching; gender differences in the perception of primary teaching and other selected careers; comparisons of the educational and career choices, attitudes, and decision-making processes of the two cohorts of school-leavers.

In the case of the Northern study, the questionnaire for senior-cycle pupils was administered to a total of 1,036 sixth-form students at eight schools.[3] The sample comprised 558 females (54 per cent) and 478 males (46 per cent). The student-teacher survey was completed by 334 second- and third-year BEd students in initial primary teacher training in the two university colleges of education, of whom 15 per cent were male and 85 per cent were female.

In the Republic of Ireland, the target population was school leavers who intended to apply to universities, colleges of education and other third-level institutions. A sample of 1,049 school leavers in 16 schools was surveyed, comprising 631 females (60 per cent) and 418 males (40 per cent). Questionnaires were also administered to all second-year students in each of the five primary education colleges in the state. The questionnaire was completed by a total of 457 (90 per cent female, 10 per cent male) student teachers.[4]

FINDINGS

Academic qualifications of entrants

During the last part of the 20th century and the beginning of the 21st, the quality of entrant to undergraduate, primary teacher training in the two primary education colleges in Northern Ireland consistently increased. Whereas in 1996–7 in England and Wales, the mean A-Level points total of entrants to undergraduate, primary teacher training was 12.9 for males and 14.0 for females (Johnston et al., 1998), in Northern Ireland the comparable means for entry to the two colleges were 21.3 for males and 21.5 for females. Arguably, explanations for this include the fact that numbers entering teacher training were tightly 'capped' by the Department of Education for Northern Ireland. Together with a strong regionality in terms of the high regard in which education is held in Northern Ireland, this operated to ensure that competition for restricted places was strong. In any case, these figures draw attention not only to the very high quality of entrants to primary teacher training in Northern Ireland relative to entrants in England and Wales, but also to the fact that, in Northern Ireland, a long-standing academic disparity between male and female entrants had all but disappeared.

In the Republic of Ireland, the academic requirements for entry to primary teaching have also been high for the past two decades or more. The minimum requirements are six Leaving Certificate subjects with three at Higher Level, to include Irish. At the time of the survey, the points level for entry were 420–475 depending on the college. This high points level attested to the continuing popularity of primary teaching as a career (Drudy, 2006a). However, this popularity was, and continues to be, chiefly among girls. Although girls in general are gradually moving into sectors previously associated with males (medicine, and law and commerce, in particular), there are still many who opt for traditional jobs such as nursing and teaching. Perhaps more significantly, there has been no corresponding move by boys into traditionally female employments. The CAO figures show a tendency for males to choose within a much smaller range of options (Drudy et al., 2005).

It is worth noting that, in the Republic, prior to colleges becoming co-educational at the beginning of the 1970s, there were separate male and female lists at entry. It was, therefore, possible for male applicants to gain places with lower Leaving Certificate achievements than their female counterparts. The change to common entry meant that the points level for entry to primary programmes became the same for males and females. Recent years in particular have seen significantly better performance in the Leaving Certificate Examination by females, leading to greater successes in gaining places (Department of Education & Science/O'Connor, 2007b). Another important factor in changing patterns was the opening up of university grants in 1969, which meant that, by the beginning of the 1980s, well-qualified students without means were less likely to opt for primary (national) teaching as the only way of getting a free, third-level education. A similar pattern emerged in Northern Ireland after the closure of a large men's college there (Johnston et al., 1998, p. 5).

With regard to the academic background of applicants (both male and female), the standard of entrant to the primary teaching profession has remained consistently high in both parts of Ireland. In Northern Ireland, the entry grades have traditionally been significantly higher than in England and Wales. In the Republic, the Leaving Certificate points average for entry to the colleges is competitive and is higher than that for many other degree courses. Indeed, the survey among student teachers in the Republic showed that almost 30 per cent of them had points above 500, and a third of those had sufficient points to be accepted on to the 'highest prestige' courses in the university system, had they expressed a first preference for them (Drudy et al., 2005).

Choice of primary teaching

Among the two school-leaver populations in both the Republic and Northern Ireland, post Leaving Certificate and A-level aspirations indicated a similar percentage choosing to pursue primary teaching (6 per cent). However, the proportion of males expressing this choice was approximately four times in the North than that in the Republic. This suggests that there was a substantial difference in the patterns of male choices of primary teaching in the two jurisdictions at the time of the surveys, which Table 10.1 shows continued into the mid-2000s. While males were in a minority of those selecting teaching on both sides of the border, Northern males were much more likely than males in the Republic to do so.

In both surveys, statistically significant gender differences were evident when school leavers specified which sector of teaching (primary or post-primary) was preferred. The proportions expressing a preference for primary teaching were almost identical in both jurisdictions. As observed above, a much higher proportion of males in Northern Ireland expressed a preference for primary teaching than in the Republic. The extent to which primary teaching is favoured by female respondents is evident from both sets of data. Post-primary teaching was a less popular choice in the Republic. In general, there were more positive perceptions of, and orientations towards teaching among males in Northern Ireland than in the Republic. This was evident both in relation to primary and to second-level teaching.

One possible factor which could be associated with this difference is career advice. Both surveys explored leavers' perceptions of the career advice they received. However, direct comparison between the Republic and Northern Ireland—of what are considered to be 'influential sources' of career advice—was not possible as the information was generated from both surveys in different formats. Nevertheless, it was clear that school guidance counsellors were important providers. Both surveys provided evidence that indicates that while careers teachers were generally well disposed to primary teaching as a career, some of them tended to steer high-achieving boys away from it. This suggests that the greater popularity of primary teaching among Northern male school-leavers was unlikely to be associated with differing attitudes to primary teaching (especially for high-achieving males) between careers teachers in both jurisdictions.

In both surveys, perceived job satisfaction was regarded as of major importance when choosing a career. The Northern Ireland data suggest that, in the formation of career preferences, males attached significantly greater importance than females to extrinsic factors, such as financial reward, the status perceived to be associated with their preferred occupation and peer reactions to their choice of career. It also revealed that males choosing teaching operate within the same value system when it comes to career choice, as did males not choosing teaching. They were guided by the same concerns and were much more concerned about the extrinsic aspects of being a teacher than were females. Likewise, females considering teaching displayed similar patterns of response to factors influencing choice as did females not considering teaching. It was therefore apparent that, regardless of whether or not teaching is chosen as a career, there are gender-specific value systems within which males and females make career choices.

In the Republic, males were also more concerned with the extrinsic aspects of a career than were females. Security of employment figured prominently in the Republic of Ireland among all respondents and among those who intended to follow a career in primary teaching. The degree to which those who aspire to teaching saw 'making a difference to others' as an important consideration, in comparison to the whole sample, suggested that prospective teachers attached high importance to altruistic (other-directed) values. Child-centred concerns were seen to be important among female school leavers in particular.

The patterns in male and female work-related attitudes in the Republic and the North were broadly comparable and provided valuable insights into gender differences in choice of teaching. However, they did not account for the higher proportion of males choosing primary teaching in Northern Ireland.

Respondents' perceptions of teaching in comparison to a number of other occupations were explored. When asked to rank teaching along a number of dimensions in relation to selected occupations in Northern Ireland, teaching was ranked second by both males and females with regard to its perceived value to society and its potential for job satisfaction. Neither gender ranked it quite so highly in terms of status and salary. In contrast to the Northern school leavers, leavers in the Republic tended to have less positive perceptions of teaching, tending to give lower ranking on factors such as value to society, job satisfaction and having high prestige/status. Both sets of school leavers ranked teaching poorly in terms of perceived salary potential. It may be that the generally lower perception of teaching in the Republic may have been associated with the lower proportion of males choosing teaching in the Republic, although this does not appear to affect females' disposition to teaching in the Republic.

Both studies explored respondents' perceptions of the likely responses/levels of support they would receive from a range of 'significant others' (e.g. parents, guidance counsellors, friends) if they chose primary teaching as a career. In both the Republic and Northern Ireland, males perceived proportionately much lower levels of support from each category. They perceived particularly negative responses from friends. The perceived perceptions of others showed the most marked gender differences of all, with a much greater proportion of males anticipating negative responses to their decision to become a primary teacher. Boys, therefore, undoubtedly perceived that there would be relatively less support for them from significant others for a decision to go into primary teaching. A young woman, by contrast, was likely to perceive herself as having the support of almost everybody. The perception of lack of support for a choice of primary teaching was evident among males on both sides of the border but could not serve to explain the more positive orientation to primary teaching among Northern males. The findings also indicated that respondents had internalised images and associations relating to the 'femaleness' of primary teaching and that these operated as a 'push' factor among males—for whom there was perhaps a socially determined wish not to pursue a 'female' career.

While the above factors provide an explanation of the gender differences at entry to primary teaching in both jurisdictions, they did not provide an explanation of the North–South differences among males. Two other factors may offer insights into this difference. One is area of rural–urban residence. The study in the Republic found a significant difference in relation to choice of teaching as one of pupils' college course preferences, where 26 per cent of rural and small to medium town school leavers, as against 17 per cent of urban school leavers, said that teaching was one of their preferred choices. The rural–urban breakdown of school leaver preferences was not possible in the Northern study. However, a rural–urban divide was evident from the Northern data on the distribution of males in the existing stock of teachers. When the distribution of males in primary teaching was compared across Education and Library Boards, in the most rural Library Board (NEELB) the percentage of males had actually increased in comparison to the other four where the proportion of males had decreased.

The second factor that may be of significance in the North (although it could not be explored in the South, given the small proportion of the population who are of the various Protestant denominations) may well relate to ethno-national differences in perceptions of the opportunities and appropriateness of different occupations by Catholic and other respondents, and to different ethno-national patterns of social mobility for males. The data provided in the Northern study showed that a relatively high percentage of males in the intake to BEd (Primary) in 1996–7, for example, was largely accounted for by an unusually high percentage of males in the 1996–7 intake to one of the university colleges where students were from mainly Catholic backgrounds, and by a corresponding *decrease* in the intake of males to BEd (Primary) in the other university college of education where students were mainly from other denominations. This is an issue worthy of further exploration in a largely (*de facto*) denominational system.

The very important issue of social-class background and choice of teaching was explored in the Republic, although not in the North. The research showed that pupils from the professional, employer and managerial social classes were a great deal more likely than others to have had grade-point averages in the highest achievement band, and were less likely to have scored in the two lowest bands. Farmers' children were also highly represented. While social-class background had an impact on academic performance, it had little direct impact on preference for teaching among the school leavers, or for selection of primary teaching at third level. The impact was indirect through its influence on academic achievement. However, when the question of the influence of having *teachers* within the family circle was specifically examined, it was found that school leavers who had teachers as family members were significantly more likely than others to have given some consideration to teaching as a career. Given the high points levels required for entry to primary teaching, there may be a form of 'double effect' at work here. Firstly, teachers as an occupational grouping fall within Social Classes 1 and 2 (the professional, employer and managerial grouping) which are more likely to achieve higher levels of academic performance in public examinations. They are thus more likely to be candidates for a third-level course in the first place. Secondly, exposure to teaching at home provides a positive orientation to the profession (Drudy et al., 2005, p. 83).

The two studies compared the perceptions of teaching, and rationale for choice of teaching among student teachers in the colleges of education. The main point of similarity in the reasons offered by student teachers in both surveys for the choice of primary teaching as a career was a focus on working with children. Student teachers saw primary teaching as offering job satisfaction, making a social contribution or as a worthwhile calling.

The results indicated that perceptions of teaching are differentiated by whether the context is the primary or the secondary setting. A general male bias towards females and against males as making 'better' primary-school teachers was evident and is suggestive of an association in the perceptions of males, between women and primary-school teaching. Insofar as this was the case, it may well have resonances which become expressed in the relatively smaller numbers of males entering primary-teacher training. This suggests a low association by them between teaching and masculinity. However, males in both surveys believed that it is important that males teach in primary schools and valued the contribution that teaching by males can make. In general, the data from both surveys indicated a relatively positive view of primary teaching among young people, although there was a strong perception that it is a profession particularly appropriate to females. In addition, the academic standard of entrants in both parts of the island had remained high.

CONCLUSIONS AND IMPLICATIONS

The comparison of patterns of entry to primary teaching in the two parts of Ireland allowed a number of interesting factors to emerge. Firstly, in spite differences in the pattern of economic development, in political structures and in the types of ethno-national differentiation, a common cultural phenomenon became evident in which there is still a very high interest in the teaching career in both jurisdictions. This is particularly evident in choice of primary teaching. Entry to primary teaching is very competitive in both jurisdictions and the academic credentials of candidates are comparatively high. In both parts of the island, as elsewhere, females predominate among entrants to teaching. However, Northern Ireland had a consistently higher proportion of males choosing primary teaching than the Republic (or, indeed, England and Wales). A higher rate of male entrance to teaching was associated with rural areas in both parts of the island. However, in the case of Northern Ireland there was some evidence that ethno-national differences played a part and that males from a Catholic/nationalist background were more oriented to teaching and used the educational system in a somewhat different way from other males, i.e. for the purposes of social mobility.

Arising from this study of the international research literature of school leavers and third-level students in the Republic of Ireland and Northern Ireland, a number of implications emerge. The findings clearly demonstrate the complexity of the problem of attracting more males into primary teaching. There are complex economic, historical, cultural and sociological factors at play. The changing patterns of entry to primary teaching are associated with changes in the economy, in the industrial structure and in the occupational structure. Since the mid-1990s, Ireland experienced processes that had been experienced in many other countries a decade, and in some instances a number of decades, ago. In addition, it may be argued that, to a significant degree, one is dealing not only with professional issues but with the social construction of masculinity and femininity. To some extent, attempts to change these processes could be described as attempts to change the course of history.

The analysis of both surveys implies that the feminisation of teaching is a historical and economic process as much as it is a social, psychological or educational one. Research on the history and sociology of teaching indicates that the gender composition of the teaching force at primary and at second level is influenced by: the level of economic development and degree of urbanisation of regions and countries; by the economic policies pursued by state administrators, especially educational administrators; by beliefs about the nature of women and men; and by patriarchal control (Drudy et al., 2005). Historical patterns identified, and contemporary figures on gender and teaching from around the world over the last quarter of the 20th century, in the survey in the Republic (ibid.), indicate that the proportion of women in teaching at primary and at second level could be used as a referent for the economic development and level of urbanisation of a society or region.

The findings on career orientations mirror findings of research conducted among established teachers in the US and elsewhere in Europe and in many parts of the Pacific rim. The patterns of differentiated gender socialisation outlined above result in different overall orientations to work and careers among boys and girls, and proved to be a differentiating factor between those school leavers who were seriously considering a teaching career versus those who were not. The majority of the school leavers and college students ranked intrinsic factors (such as job satisfaction) most highly when considering future careers. This was to be expected among this cohort as, by definition, they were either anticipating entry to higher education, or were already in it, and were thus contemplating middle-class careers where such rewards are available. In common with findings elsewhere, both girls in general, and those girls and boys considering teaching, were more oriented to caring and to service than were others. There are implications here for the socialisation of both girls and boys in the wider society and for their education in schools. In the Irish second-level school system which is still, in comparison to other countries, highly gender differentiated, there is evidence that girls' schools put a great deal more emphasis on caring than boys' schools (Lynch, 1989b). The implications of the research are that, if society wishes to substantially increase the proportions of young men entering primary teaching, schools, parents and all agencies of socialisation (including the media and the state) are going to have to place a very substantially greater emphasis on the centrality of caring as a core social value and one which is as relevant to men as it is to women.

Given the changes that have taken place in the Irish school system in recent times, especially with regard to the much more diverse pupil populations now to be found in Irish schools, two important variables—additional to gender—should be mentioned. These are the high proportion of teachers from rural and farming backgrounds still in the primary-school system and also the relatively strong influence of class (albeit indirect through examination performance levels in a highly competitive system) on entry to primary teaching. This presents a challenge to teacher education to prepare a fairly homogeneous body of student teachers to work with increasingly heterogeneous pupil populations. These issues are taken up in other chapters in this book which explore teacher education in relation to disability/special educational needs and ethnicity.

The findings in both jurisdictions imply that if Irish society, North and South, wishes to sustain the high calibre of, albeit mainly female, entrants to the profession that it has been able to take for granted until now, in order to support the move to a knowledge society, then a concerted effort will need to be made by the state and the education system. Internationally, the best evidence would suggest that policy makers should focus more on the quality of entrants to the profession rather than whether they are male or female. The policy goal should be to recruit effective, high-calibre teachers whatever their gender (Drudy, 2008b; Carrington et al., 2007).

ENDNOTES

1   This paper draws on analysis contained in a cross-border project funded by the Royal Irish Academy (Drudy et al., 2003). The support of the Royal Irish Academy for this project is gratefully acknowledged.

2   Hegemonic masculinity is the dominant form of masculinity and is distinguished from other masculinities, especially subordinated masculinities. It embodies the currently most honoured way of being a man and it requires all other men to position themselves in relation to it (Connell & Messerschmidt, 2005, p. 832).

3   Further details on the Northern Ireland methodology can be obtained in Johnston, McKeown, & McEwen (1998).

4   Further details on the Republic of Ireland methodology can be obtained in Drudy, Martin, Woods, & O'Flynn (2005).

11

CHOOSING POST-PRIMARY TEACHING AS A CAREER: PERSPECTIVES FROM THE REPUBLIC OF IRELAND[1]

Marie Clarke

INTRODUCTION

A substantial body of international research suggests that the characteristics, experiences, knowledge, dispositions, beliefs, attitudes and perceptions that pre-service teachers bring with them upon entering a teacher education programme substantially influence their subsequent development as students and, eventually, as teachers (Aksu et al., 2009; Minor et al., 2002; Witherell & Noddings, 1991). Lortie (1975, p. 65) argues that those planning to teach have already formed definite ideas about the nature of teaching. Goodson (2003) goes further and asserts that life experiences and background are key ingredients of the person, shaping practice within teaching. Yet, only a limited amount of research exists internationally concerning the background characteristics of the students who choose teaching as their future career (Aksu et al., 2009). Equally important for those involved in teacher education is the view that such programmes have varying degrees of success with regard to developing and changing the pre-existing pedagogical belief systems of student teachers (Gill et al., 2004; Wideen et al., 1998).

Little is known about those who enter second-level teacher education in the Republic of Ireland. This chapter argues that those involved in teacher education must identify, acknowledge and understand the experiences of those coming into teacher education and their reasons for choosing teaching as a career. Their prior experiences, socio-economic background, their diversity in terms of age and their reasons for wanting a teaching career contribute to their understandings about classroom contexts, reflective practice, approaches to teaching their subjects and their broader understandings about the profession of teaching. Teacher educators must consider these factors so that the needs and capacities of student teachers can be understood and developed.

A number of studies have focused on the socio-economic background of students entering teacher education programmes. In the United States Brookhart and Freeman (1992) found that student teachers came from a lower socio-economic background than their contemporaries pursuing other courses. Richardson and Watt (2006) reached the same conclusion in their survey of student teachers in Australian universities. In China, Su et al. (2001) reported that the majority of student teachers came from rural areas. It seems, therefore, in an international context that those pursuing teacher-education programmes come from backgrounds where socio-economic status is not as high as that of students pursuing other professional third-level courses.

The choice of teaching as a career has been explored in a number of international studies. Chuene, Luben and Newson (1999) investigated the views of student and novice Mathematics teachers in South Africa. Using qualitative analysis of semi-structured interview data, they identified that reasons for choosing teaching in rank order were: extrinsic; altruistic; intrinsic; and job related. In Slovenia, Kyriacou and Kobori (1998) analysed questionnaire data collected from student teachers of English and found that wanting to help children to succeed and enjoyment of the subject were two of the most frequently rated reasons that had motivated them to become teachers.

In the UK context, Huat See (2004, p. 214) suggests that, besides social determinants such as economic and social background, an individual's decision to become a teacher or not is also influenced by what they value in a job and their perceptions of teaching. In Huat See's study, it was found that those with, or expecting, a degree graded at 2:2 or below are more likely to become teachers than those with a 2:1 or above. This suggests that, in the UK context, it is generally the least qualified of those eligible who are most likely to be teachers. That study also revealed that those who had chosen teaching as a career appreciated the chance to share knowledge, enjoy job satisfaction, length of holidays and the opportunity to continue in the subject of interest, that a career in teaching offered (Huat See, 2004, p. 219). An examination of the international literature reveals that the commonly cited reasons for choosing teaching as a career include a perceived teaching ability and an appreciation of the intrinsic value of teaching. The literature also indicates that the desire to make a social contribution, to shape the future and work with children and to have a personal interest in the subject area are also important factors in career choice (Aksu et al., 2009; Richardson & Watt, 2006; Arends et al., 1998).

THE REPUBLIC OF IRELAND CONTEXT

The Republic of Ireland unlike many countries, has no difficulty in recruiting teacher education students at all levels of the education system. Student teachers in Ireland are academically high achievers, which is not typical internationally (Killeavy & O'Moore, 2001). Few studies in the Irish context have explored the demographic and biographical data of entrants to teacher education and their reasons for choosing teaching as a career in any detail. Some work has been completed about entrants to initial teacher education at primary level (Drudy et al., 2003; Drudy et al., 2005; Killeavy, 1998; Greaney et al., 1987; Kelly 1970; see also Chapter 10 in this book) where the majority of entrants come from professional, managerial and farming backgrounds (Drudy et al., 2005), and this has remained the situation over a 20-year period. The Drudy, Martin, Woods and Flynn (2005) study which focused on the gender imbalance in primary teaching, also found that the aspects of primary teaching identified by respondents as most attractive were extrinsic factors—the short day and good holidays, job security and availability and a respected position in the community (Drudy, Martin, Woods and Flynn 2005, p. 147).

In the post-primary sector, one study (Heinz, 2008) focuses on the selection process of entrants to the second-level teaching profession from the four NUI colleges in the period 1999–2005 through the Postgraduate Diploma in Education Applications Centre (PDEAC). The study revealed that: applications for places on the programme rose in that period; the number of mature students taking the programme had increased; applicants from the NUI pre-dominated, though there was a significant increase from those from Institutes of Technology; applicants to the Postgraduate Diploma in Education (PGDE) were of a very high academic calibre; and all of the applicants to the programme had prior teaching experience.

The findings reported in this chapter come from the first major study investigating this area and includes PGDE students from Trinity College Dublin in addition to the NUI colleges. The data that has emerged from this national study, explores, in a detailed way, the diversity that exists among students who participate on PGDE programmes, in terms of their socio-economic background, gender, age group and their reasons for choosing teaching as a career. The resultant picture is a complex one that raises many questions for those involved in teacher education who seek to understand the factors that impact upon the development of the emergent identity of their students. It also highlights the importance of establishing a research base which Coolahan (2003) suggests is necessary to inform the challenges that such diversity brings.

THE STUDY

This five-year study (2001–2006) has engaged with pre-service teachers across the five university Education departments in the Republic of Ireland in which the PGDE programme is offered. In the first year (2001–2002), a pilot study was completed with students from three universities—NUI Maynooth, NUI Dublin and Trinity College Dublin—providing an available sample of 490 respondents to which 275 student teachers responded yielding a response rate of 56 per cent. After resolving issues that arose with the survey from the pilot, the researchers broadened the study to include the other NUI universities, NUI Cork and NUI Galway. The study collected in-depth survey data from 2,348 PGDE students in order to identify patterns across the full sample, using a combination of closed-ended, rating-scale items and open-ended questions. Research instruments were informed by a systematic review of the literature in teacher education. Data was generated via a self-completion questionnaire. The instrument sought to collect:

- biographical and demographic data about the students; and
- attitudinal data towards agreement or disagreement with a number of propositions dealing with their reasons for choosing teaching as a career option.

A total of 3,720 PGDE students who had participated in all five universities (NUI Cork, NUI Dublin, NUI Galway, NUI Maynooth and Trinity College Dublin) in the Republic of Ireland offering the PGDE during the period 2002–2006 were identified in the sampling frame and surveyed; 2,348 responded, giving a response rate of 63 per cent. In total, 2,244 usable responses for analysis were received in the returned questionnaires.

Permission to reproduce and use the questionnaire was granted by each of the Education departments in the universities. Ethical approval was received from each of the five universities participating in the study. Due to the procedures adopted by the universities in this study, direct access was not permitted to student contact and record details, thereby ensuring respondent anonymity. Consent to participate was indicated on the questionnaire, which allowed each respondent to indicate their agreement as participants in the study. Data obtained was analysed using the Statistical Package for the Social Sciences (SPSS version 15.0). Both descriptive and inferential statistics were used in the description and analysis of the data set. Descriptive statistics were used to summarise demographic data and the results from the questionnaire. Correspondence analysis, which can be used with frequency data, with percentages, with data in the form of ratings and with heterogeneous data sets, was used to establish the profiles and was selected due to its versatility (Greenacre, 1993). Factor analysis was used to identify scales; reliability analysis was undertaken using an internal consistency measure Cronbach's Alpha (see Cronbach, 1951); and a two-way analysis of variance was conducted to explore the impact of gender and age in relation to the scales identified.

Section 1 Biographical and demographic characteristics of student teachers

The age group and profiles of the graduates who were surveyed are outlined in Table 11.1.

Table 11.1: Gender and age-group profiles of respondents

Characteristic		
Age Groups	**%**	**(n)**
Under 25	63	1,275
25, but under 30	21	435
30, but under 40	11	228
40 and over	5	91
		Total n=2,029
Gender	**%**	**(n)**
Female	74	1,553
Male	26	482
		Total n=2,035

Note: Missing responses excluded from distribution.

The majority of respondents were under 25 years and were female. This is not surprising as most graduates entering the consecutive model of teacher-education programmes do so immediately, or soon after, their graduation. The gender balance of the cohort is consistent throughout the universities in question and is also similar to the trend internationally. The occupational profiles of respondents' parents are presented in Table 11.2. The categories used to establish socio-economic background were 10 specific socio-economic groups (introduced in 1996) by the Central Statistics Office (CSO) (see Table 11.2). These categories, used by the CSO, are based on the UK Standard Occupational Classification, with modifications to reflect Irish labour market conditions.

Table 11.2: Occupational profiles of respondents' parents

Characteristic	Father	Mother
Social Class	%	%
Farmers, farmers' relatives and farm managers	16.4	1.7
Other agricultural occupations and fishermen	1.3	0.3
Higher professional	7.2	1.7
Lower professional	13.4	28.5
Employers and managers	13.8	6.3
Salaried employees	7.4	5.3
Intermediate non-manual workers	5.3	20.4
Other non-manual workers	4	0.3
Other in receipt of social welfare, loans or dependent	17.1	8.6
Manual workers: tradesmen, contractors, labourers, factory workers	11.1	0.7
Miscellaneous (printer, home-help assistant, study supervisor)	3	3.6
Stay-at-home parent	0	22.8
		Total n=846

Note: Missing responses excluded from distribution.

Of the 2,244 respondents, only 38 per cent (846) answered the question concerning parental occupations. It is not possible to establish the cause of respondents' reluctance to answer this particular question. However, it means that any interpretation of the figures must be careful. Further, it means that a comparison with the participation ratio in terms of the population nationally must also be undertaken with care.

There are some aspects of the data that require mention. The category of respondents' fathers with the highest representation was that of recipients of social welfare and this was followed by farmers, employers and managers. While the percentage of fathers in receipt of social welfare is high, it is not possible to provide meaningful interpretations of this area due to the varied forms that social-welfare payments may take and they contain many financial supports apart from unemployment payments and assistance. Farmers, with the second highest representation in the cohort, have a participation ratio of 1.56. This indicates that post-primary teaching is an attractive profession for students from the farming community. This profile in post-primary teaching represents a much broader spread of socio-economic background than that of the primary sector in which the representation of farmers predominates, with a participation ratio of 2.08 (Killeavy, 1998). Similar findings are reported by Drudy et al. (2005) who found that the professional, managerial and farming backgrounds predominated among entrants to primary teaching.

Respondents were next asked to indicate the type of degree that they had prior to entering the PGDE. More than half of the respondents who answered this question had a Bachelor of Arts degree, followed by Commerce/Business degrees and Science degrees. Nine per cent indicated that they held other degrees but did not indicate what they were. Table 11.3 illustrates the data on gender and age of respondents.

Data on respondents' fathers' occupational category is not included in this table but has been outlined in Table 11.2. The majority of those who held an Arts degree came from intermediate non-manual workers category (66 per cent), followed by those from a lower professional background (62 per cent) and employers category (61 per cent). Those with Science degrees had the highest representation in the higher professional category (26 per cent); 15 per cent came from the manual-workers category and 13 per cent came from farming backgrounds. Those with Commerce/Business degrees had the highest representation from the farming sector (24 per cent), followed by those from the salaried-employees category (23 per cent) and the intermediate non-manual workers category (20 per cent). There was no significant association between fathers' occupation and type of degree held by respondents ($x^2$133.330, df-143, p=.707). There was an equal split between males and females with an Arts degree and there was a significant association between gender and type of degree, (x^2=32.998, df-13, p=.002). More males than females had science degrees and more females than males had Commerce/Business degrees.

There was also a significant association between age range and type of degree (x^2=71.995, df-39, p=.001). Group 4 (those 40 years and over) had the highest percentage of respondents who had Arts degrees. Group 1 (those under 25 years) had the highest percentage of respondents with Business-related degrees. Group 2 (those aged between 25 and 30 years) had the highest percentage of respondents with Science degrees. This data is interesting because it suggests that those with Science degrees who chose teaching were males who were mature students, they had either continued with other postgraduate degrees or had worked before making a decision to opt for teaching as a career.

Table 11.3 Degree profiles of respondents to this question

Characteristic				
Type of degree	**Gender representation by degree**	**%**	**Age representation by degree**	**%**
Arts 55%	Males	54	Under 25	52.9
(n=656)	Females	54	25, but under 30	52
			30, but under 40	52.6
			40 and over	69.6
Commerce/Business	Males	17.2	Under 25	14.7
18% (n=223)	Females	19.2	25, but under 30	22.5
	Under 25		30, but under 40	23.7
			40 and over	5.4
Science 18%	males	18.8	Under 25	14.7
(n=213)	Females	17.2	25, but under 30	25.5
			30, but under 40	23.7
			40 and over	5.4
Other 9%				
(n=110)				

Note: Missing responses excluded from distribution.

Respondents were asked to indicate the type of third-level institution that they had attended prior to coming on to the PGDE. Table 11.4 illustrates the data on gender and age of respondents.

Table 11.4: Type of third-level institution attended of respondents to this question

Characteristic		%		%
University 75% (n=913)	Males	26	Under 25	59
	Females	74	25, but under 30	23
			30, but under 40	14
			40 and over	4
Institute of technology 22% (n=262)	Males	23	Under 25	74
	Females	77	25, but under 30	18
			30, but under 40	5
			40 and over	3
Primary teaching training college 2% (n=20)				
Institution in another jurisdiction 1% (n=12)				

Note: Missing responses excluded from distribution.

The majority of respondents had attended university (75 per cent), with 22 per cent indicating that they had attended an Institute of Technology. These figures are broadly in line with data from Heinz (2008). Those whose fathers' occupation was in the higher professional category had the highest representation among those who had attended university, at 90 per cent; followed by 82 per cent representation from the lower professional category and 78 per cent from salaried employees. Those who attended the Institute of Technology sector were from the other non-manual category (46 per cent), followed by those from farming backgrounds (32 per cent) and miscellaneous category (printer, home-help assistant, study supervisor) (29 per cent). There was no significant relationship between fathers' occupation and type of third-level institution attended (x^2=51.226, df-44, p=.211) and there was no significant association between gender and type of third-level institution attended (x^2=1.396, df-4, p=.845). There was a significant association between age range and type of third-level institution attended (x^2=45.561, df-12, p=.000). Group 1 (those under 25 years) had the highest percentage who had attended Institutes of Technology. The level of respondents' degree is illustrated in Table 11.5.

Table 11.5: Academic profile of respondents to this question

Characteristic	Gender representation by award	%	Age representation by award	%
1st Honours 23% (n=277)	Males	22	Under 25	22.9
	Females	23	25, but under 30	21.8
			30, but under 40	20.8
			40 and over	27.3
2nd Honours 73% (n=889)	Males	70.5	Under 25	74
	Females	73.5	25, but under 30	70.8
			30, but under 40	71.1
			40 and over	69.1
3rd Honours 1% (n=19)				
Pass 3% (n=37)				

Note: Missing responses excluded from distribution.

The majority of respondents (73 per cent) held second-class honours degrees with over one fifth achieving first-class honours degrees. There was no significant association between fathers' occupational background and degree result attained (x^2=19.16, df-44, p=1.0). There was a significant association between age range and standard of grade achieved (x^2=23.781, df-12, p=.02). Group 4 (those aged 40 years and over) had the highest percentage of first-class honours degrees when compared to other age groups.

Previous teaching experience

Applicants for PGDE programmes in the NUI colleges are awarded points as part of the selection process through the PDEAC system (Heinz, 2008). Respondents were asked to indicate the nature and type of teaching, other education and other work experience that they had engaged in prior to undertaking the programme.

Fifty-seven per cent of the sample indicated that they had secured teaching experience prior to coming onto the PGDE. The levels of teaching experience secured by applicants was interesting and diverse as illustrated in Table 11.6.

Table 11.6: Type of teaching experience of respondents to this question

	Percentage with teaching experience
Pre-primary (Total n*=609)	7.6 n=46
Primary (Total n=810)	55 n=446
Post-primary (Total n=1051)	78 n=823
Third level (Total n=687)	23 n=161
Adult education (Total n=707)	31 n=219
TEFL (Total n=745)	38.7 n=288

* The total n in each case represents the number of respondents who answered this section of the question. Missing responses excluded from distribution.[end note text]

It is important to note that some respondents had secured teaching experience in a number of settings, which is obvious from the numbers which are expressed as percentages in Table 11.6, 43 per cent had no teaching experience at all. The majority of respondents had secured teaching experience in the post-primary sector, followed by the primary sector and TEFL. There was a significant association between age range and having had teaching experience (x^2=93.677, df-3, p=.000). Group 3 (those aged between 30 and 40 years) had the highest levels of teaching experience prior to undertaking the programme at 72 per cent. There was no significant association between gender and having prior teaching experience but there was a significant association between gender and primary-school teaching experience (x^2=7.844, df-1, p=.005). More females (61.8 per cent) had had primary-school teaching experience than males at (49 per cent). There was no significant association between age range and pre-primary, primary and post-primary teaching experience.

Table 11.7: Type of teaching experience (other than school) of respondents to this question

Characteristic				
	Gender representation by experience type	**%**	**Age representation by experience type**	**%**
Teaching experience in TEFL (n=288)	Males	51.3	Under 25	37.7
	Females	39.1	25, but under 30	47.2
			30, but under 40	52.8
			40 and over	26.7
Third-level teaching experience (n=161)	Males	32.6	Under 25	18
	Females	24.1	25, but under 30	29.9
			30, but under 40	44.2
			40 and over	41.2
Teaching experience in adult education (n=219)	Males	35.2	Under 25	28.4
	Females	34	25, but under 30	31.3
			30, but under 40	27.4
			40 and over	12.9

Note: Missing responses excluded from distribution.

In relation to TEFL teaching, there was a significant association with gender (x^2=7.037, df-1, p=.008). More males (51 per cent) than females (39 per cent) had previous TEFL teaching experience. There was a significant association between age range and having TEFL teaching experience (x^2=11.641, df-3, p=.000). Group 3 (those aged between 30 and 40 years) had the highest percentage of TEFL teaching experience at 53 per cent. There was a significant association between gender and having teaching experience at third level, (x^2=4.094, df-1, p=.043). More males (32.6 per cent) had third-level teaching experience than females (24.1 per cent). There was also a significant association between age range and having teaching experience at third level (x^2=27.984, df-3,p=.000). Group 3 (those aged between 30 and 40 years) had the highest percentage of teaching experience in third-level education at 44 per cent. A significant association emerged between age range and teaching experience in adult education (x^2=78.865, df-3, p=.000). Group 2 (those aged between 25 and 30 years) had the highest levels of teaching experience in adult education at 31 per cent. The level and diversity of teaching experience and other educational work was striking. Teaching experience is awarded points as part of the selection process for a place on the PGDE through the PDEAC. Fifty-seven per cent of respondents to this question in this study had secured teaching experience prior to coming onto the programme. Post-primary and primary teaching experience predominated, followed by TEFL and teaching experience in adult education. Females tended to have more teaching experience in the primary sector and males tended to have more teaching experience in third level and TEFL. In terms of teaching experience according to age range, a number of interesting findings emerged, those aged between 30 and 40 years had the highest level of teaching experience at third level and in TEFL. Those aged between 25 and 30 years had more teaching experience in adult education than those in the other age groups. It is clear that respondents had secured a range of teaching experiences prior to coming onto the PGDE programme. In the context of teacher education these areas are very different from both theoretical and praxis perspectives. It is noteworthy that a range of sectors in the Irish education system allowed such a high percentage of unqualified people to engage actively in teaching roles. Section 30 of the Teaching Council Act (2001) when implemented will prohibit the employment of non-qualified teachers by recognised Irish schools, so this situation will be addressed, however, students will still bring with them a range of experience from educational areas other than teaching which need to be considered within their teacher education context.

Other educational work

Respondents were asked to indicate if they had been involved in educational work other than teaching prior to coming on to the PGDE. The diversity of other educational work involvement is also very interesting. Forty-eight per cent of the sample had other educational work experience prior to undertaking the PGDE programme.

Some respondents had secured experience in other educational work in a variety of settings. The majority of respondents had experience of giving grinds and tutoring. There was no significant association between gender and other educational work experience and there was no significant association between age group, tutoring, giving grinds, mentoring, working in homework clubs and drama and music teaching.

A significant association did emerge between age range and having worked in the literacy area (x^2=38.916, df-3, p=.000). Group 4 (those aged 40 years and over) had more experience in this area than those in the other age groups at 39 per cent.

Table 11.8: Type of other educational work of respondents to this question

	Percentage with teaching experience
Tutoring (Total n*=661)	44 n=291
Giving grinds (Total n=864)	81 n=702
Mentoring (Total n=529)	11.5 n=61
Homework club (Total n=567)	22.9 n=130
Literacy training (Total n=527)	12.5 n=66
Drama/Music teaching (Total n=579)	29.9 n=173

*The total n in each case represents the number of respondents who answered this section of the question. Missing responses excluded from distribution.

Table 11.9: Experience in literacy training of respondents to this question (n=527)

Characteristic	Percentage with literacy training experience
Males	15.5
Females	13.5
Under 25	6.6
25, but under 30	15.5
30, but under 40	30.8
40 and over	39.3

Non-educational work

Respondents were also asked to indicate the range of previous non-educational work that they had engaged in prior to pursuing a teacher education programme.

Fifty per cent of the sample indicated that they had been involved in a range of non-educational work.

Table 11.10: Non-educational work of respondents to this question

	Percentage with non-educational work
Sports (Total n*=828)	63.8 n=528
Religious groups (Total n=604)	19.2 n=116
Youth/Children's clubs (Total n=734)	51.2 n=376
Work with disabled young people (Total n=631)	27.4 n=173
Drama/Music/Arts groups (Total n=691)	36 n=249

*The total n in each case represents the number of respondents who answered this section of the question. Missing responses excluded from distribution.

Some respondents had secured experience in a variety of non-educational settings. The majority of respondents had previous experience in the areas of sport, working in youth and children's clubs, and drama, music and arts clubs. There was no significant association between gender and having worked in youth or children's clubs, having worked with disabled young people or having worked in Drama/Music/Arts groups and there was no significant association between age range and having worked with these groups. There was a significant association between gender and sports (x^2=31.366, df-4, p=.000). More males (81 per cent) than females (58 per cent) had worked in this area. There was no significant association between age group and involvement in sports (x^2=4.739, df-16, p=.997). There was a significant association between gender and having worked with religious groups (x^2=8.212, df-1, p=.004). More males (30.3 per cent) than females (15 per cent) had experience in this area. A significant association emerged between age range and having worked in a religious group (x^2=19.204, df-3, p=.000). Group 3 (those aged between 30 and 40 years) had the highest percentage in this area at 40 per cent.

Section 2 Choosing teaching as a career option

The demographic and biographical backgrounds of respondents set the context against which their motivation to choose second-level teaching as a career was examined. Table 11.11 illustrates this data.

Table 11.11: Participants' reasons for opting for a teaching career

Rank	Reason	Item Mean	Scores SD	Percentage Agreement %
1	Job satisfaction	3.73	0.498	97.3
2	Interest in working with young people	3.62	0.554	95.5
3	Love of subject(s)	3.57	0.597	95.2
4	Variety of possible activities in teaching	3.44	0.673	89.3
5	Making a worthwhile contribution to society	3.40	0.669	89.5
6	Holidays and free time	3.10	0.821	78.5
7	Availability of permanent posts	2.71	0.875	60.0
8	Levels of pay	2.68	0.834	61.4
9	Pension rights	2.57	0.891	51.5
10	Social status of teaching	2.28	0.841	36.0
11	Possibilities for promotion	2.28	0.818	34.4
			Total n=(2,233)	

Note: Missing responses excluded from distribution.

'Job satisfaction' (97 per cent) was rated as being most important for the majority of respondents, followed by an interest in working with young people (96 per cent) and love of subject (95 per cent). 'Making a worthwhile contribution to society' (90 per cent) and the variety of possibilities activities in teaching (89 per cent) also yielded high levels of agreement. In relation to 'job satisfaction', those who came from farming and employer backgrounds had the highest levels of agreement with this item (99 per cent), followed by those who came from higher professional backgrounds (97 per cent). There was no significant association between fathers' occupation and job satisfaction (x^2=38.517, df-44, p=.705).There was a significant association between gender and 'job satisfaction' as a motivating factor for choosing teaching as a career (x^2=22.373, df-4, p=.000). Females (98 per cent) considered this a more important factor than males (96 per cent). There was also a significant association between age and job satisfaction, (x^2=30.860, df-16, p=.014). Group 3 (those aged between 30 and 40 years) rated job satisfaction more highly than those in the age categories (99 per cent).

The highest level of agreement with the reason for the career choice 'working with young people' at 96 per cent came from those whose fathers were in receipt of social welfare or members of the farming community. It should be noted that social welfare here includes any of the diverse social welfare payments available in the state. This was followed by those who came from the lower professional category (28 per cent). There was no significant association between fathers' occupation and an 'interest in working with young people' as a career motivator (x^2=38.517, df-44, p=.705). There was a significant association between gender and choosing a teaching career due to an interest in 'working with young people' (x^2=54.856, df-3, p=.000). More females (98 per cent) than males (93 per cent) cited this as a reason. A significant association also emerged between age range and being interested in working with young people (x^2=20.069, df-9, p=.017). Those under 25 years (97 per cent) considered it more important than those in other age groups. Table 11.12 illustrates the data.

Table 11.12: Working with young people

Characteristic	Percentage agreemant
Male	93
Female	98
Under 25	97
25, but under 30 years	96
30, but under 40 years	96
40 and over	94
Total n=2225	

Note: Missing responses excluded from distribution.

In relation to 'love of subject' those from the higher professional group rated this very highly (99 per cent) followed by those from employers and farming backgrounds (98 per cent). There was no significant association between fathers' occupation and love of subject.

A significant association emerged between gender and 'love of subject' as a reason for choosing teaching as a career (x^2=30.255, df-3, p=.000). More females (97 per cent) than males (93 per cent) cited this as reason for wanting to have a teaching career. However, this association between age range and 'love of subject' was not significant (x^2=20.789, df-16, p=.187).

There was no significant association between fathers' occupation and 'making a worthwhile contribution to society' (x^2=43.489, df-44, p=.497). There was no significant association between gender and 'making a worthwhile contribution to society' (x^2=2.384, df-4, p=.666). Making a worthwhile contribution to society as a reason for choosing teaching as a career was significantly associated with age range (x^2=35.862, df-9, p=.000). Those aged between 30 and 40 years (97 per cent) and those aged 40 years and over (97 per cent) considered this to be more important than members of the other age groups. Table 11.13 illustrates the data.

Table 11.13: Making a worthwhile contribution to society

Characteristic	Percentage agreement
Male	92
Female	92
Under 25	90
25, but under 30 years	94
30, but under 40 years	97
40 and over	97
Total n=2234	

Note: Missing responses excluded from distribution.

The items were subjected to principal component analysis using SPSS (see Velleman & Wilkinson, 1993, for a discussion on appropriate procedures for scaled data). Inspection of the correlation matrix revealed the presence of many coefficients of 0.3 and above. The Kaiser-Meyer-Oklin value was 0.71, exceeding the recommended value of 0.6 (Kaiser, 1970, 1974) and the Barlett's Test of

Sphericity (Bartlett, 1954) reached statistical significance, supporting the factorability of the correlation matrix.

Principal components analysis revealed the presence of two components with eigenvalues exceeding 1. To aid in interpretation of these components, Varimax rotation was performed. The rotated solution (presented in Table 11.14) revealed the presence of a simple structure (Thurstone, 1947) with both components showing a number of strong loadings. The two-factor solution explained a total variance of 49 per cent, with Component 1 (extrinsic motivating factors) contributing 29 per cent and Component 2 (intrinsic motivating factors) contributing 20 per cent. The extrinsic motivating factors were identified as: levels of pay; pension rights; availability of permanent posts; possibilities for promotion; the social status of teaching; and holidays and free time. The intrinsic motivating factors were identified as: interest in working with young people; job satisfaction; variety of possible activities in teaching; making a worthwhile contribution to society; and love of subject.

Table 11.14: Varimax Rotation of two factor solution for questionnaire items

| | | Component | |
		1	2
Item Variables			
3	Levels of pay	0.765	
2	Pension rights	0.746	
1	Availability of permanent posts	0.709	
5	Possibilities for promotion	0.642	
4	Social status of teaching	0.598	
6	Holidays and free time	0.496	
8	Interest in working with young people		0.706
11	Job satisfaction		0.681
10	Variety of possible activities in teaching		0.675
9	Making worthwhile contribution to society		0.668
7	Love of subject(s)		0.464
	% of variance explained	29%	20%

Note: Only loadings above 0.3 are displayed.

When the two scales were identified, reliability analysis was undertaken using the internal consistency measure, Cronbach's Alpha. Of the two scales identified, on the first scale extrinsic motivating factors had a value of 0.817 and the intrinsic motivating factors scale had a value of 0.660. As the scales were within the recommended values of 0.70 for reliability (Nunnally & Bernstein 1994), they were included.

Table 11.15: Reliability estimates of scales

Scale Name	Number of Items	Cronbach's Alpha
Extrinsic motivating factors	6	0.817
Intrinsic motivating factors	5	0.660

A two-way, between-groups analysis of variance was conducted to explore the impact of gender and age in relation to the two scales identified; extrinsic motivating factors and intrinsic motivating factors. Respondents were divided into four ranges according to their age (Group 1: Under 25 years; Group 2: 25 but under 30; Group 3: 30 but under 40 and Group 4: 40 years and over).

Extrinsic motivating factors

In relation to extrinsic motivating factors the main effect for gender [$F(1, 1866)=6.28$, $p=.01$] was statistically significant, however the effect size was small (eta squared=.004). The mean score for females (M=15.57, SD=3.67) indicated that females were less motivated by extrinsic factors than males (M=15.67, SD=3.66). The main effect for age [$F(3, 1866)=3.85$, $p=.009$] was statistically significant, however, the effect size was small (eta squared=.007). Post-hoc comparisons using the Tukey HSD test indicated that the mean score for Group 1 (those under 25 years) (M=15.82, SD=3.57) was statistically significantly different from Group 3 (those aged between 30 and 40 years) (M=15.00, SD=3.96) and Group 4 (those aged 40 years and over) (M=14.07, SD=3.67). The mean score for Group 2 (those aged between 25 and 30) (M=15.58, SD=3.69) was statistically significantly different from Group 4 (those aged 40 years and over) (M=14.07, SD=3.67). The mean score for Group 4 (those aged 40 years and over) (M=14.07, SD=3.67) was statistically different from Group 1 (those under 25 years) (M=15.82, SD=3.57) and Group 2 (those aged between 25 and 30 years) (M=15.58, SD=3.69). Those 40 years and over were less motivated by extrinsic factors than their colleagues in the other age groups.

The interaction effect between gender and age range [F(3, 1866)=2.83, p=.04] was significant. Males in each age range had higher levels of extrinsic motivating factors for going into teaching except in Group 1 (those under 25 years), where females (M=15.88, SD=3.55) had higher extrinsic motivating factors than males (M=15.57, SD=3.66). Males in each of the remaining groups—Group 2 (those between 25 and 30 years) (M=15.98, SD=3.66); Group 3 (those aged between 30 and 40 years) (M=15.63, SD=3.76) and Group 4 (those aged 40 years and over) (M=15.17, SD=3.38)—were more motivated to choose teaching due to extrinsic factors than their female counterparts in these age groups—Group 2 (those aged between 25 and 30 years) (M=15.41, SD=3.70); Group 3 (those aged between 30 and 40 years) (M=14.60, SD=4.04) and Group 4 (those aged 40 years and over) (M=13.54, SD=3.72).

Intrinsic motivating factors

In relation to intrinsic motivating factors, the main effect for gender [F(1, 1866)=20.96, p=.000] was statistically significant, however the effect size was small (eta squared=.011). The mean score for females (M=17.91, SD=1.86) indicated higher intrinsic motivating factors than males (M= 17.32, SD=2.17). The main effect for age [F (3, 1687)=.3.42, p=.02] was also statistically significant, however, the effect size was small (eta squared=.005). Post-hoc comparisons using the Tukey HSD test indicated that the mean score for Group 3 (those aged between 30 and 40 years) (M=18.03, SD=1.78) was significantly different from Group 1 (those under 25 years) (M=17.72, SD=1.99). Group 3 (those aged between 30 and 40 years) had higher levels of intrinsic motivating factors for going into teaching. Group 2 (those aged between 25 and 30 years) (M=17.77, SD=1.93) and Group 4 (those aged 40 years and over) (M=17.97, SD=1.77) did not differ significantly from the other groups in relation to intrinsic motivating factors.

CONCLUSION

It is argued in this chapter that teacher educators should be aware of and understand the backgrounds from which their students come, the prior experiences that they bring with them to teacher education and their reasons for choosing teaching as a career. The socio-economic background of entrants to post-primary teaching in Ireland has not been investigated in this manner and on this scale before. Neither have patterns of relationship and association between socio-economic and other demographic factors with career choice been studied in-depth. While it is too early to present broad-ranging conclusions from the study, some factors not commented on until now deserve mention. Further, some factors differentiating Irish post-primary teacher education students from their peers in Europe and the United States have emerged from the study. In other respects, data collected from this sample is broadly similar to that reported in international research studies undertaken in the United States, the United Kingdom and China.

A broader socio-economic profile among entrants to post-primary teaching than among the entrants to primary teaching in the Republic of Ireland emerged from this study. This is a significant finding for those involved in teacher education and programmes should reflect the experiences of a diverse group of entrants. The background characteristics of entrants to teacher education programmes were broader in socio-economic terms than was often assumed to be the case. Caution, therefore, must be used when interpreting the data in this area as no significant relationship emerged between their socio-economic backgrounds and their academic profiles, the type of institutions that they had attended prior to taking a teacher education programme and their motivations for opting for a teaching career.

The high level of academic attainment of those entering teacher education in Ireland was borne out by the findings. Approximately, one fifth of the cohort had secured a first-class honours degree and over 70 per cent had been awarded second-class honours in their primary degree. This is in marked contrast to the findings of the Huat See (2004) in the United Kingdom, which reports that it is generally the least qualified of those who are eligible that enter teacher education.

The predominance of males and mature students entering teacher education with Science degrees is also an important finding, and is an area that requires further investigation in view of the current shortage of science teachers in the Irish education system. This raises major issues concerning the selection process for entrance to post-primary teacher courses and poses questions about whether or not the teaching subject requirements of the education system are being met currently.

The growing diversity in the backgrounds of entrants to the profession, which is highlighted in the data, must be taken into account in future planning. A particular factor here is the growing number of students who come from Institutes of Technology. This group tends to be younger with 74 per cent of students under 25 years, than those from university backgrounds where 59 per cent are under 25 years. These younger students bring with them different experiences of third-level education than their university counterparts and this factor must be taken into account by those involved in teacher education where such programmes have traditionally adopted university practices and norms.

One of the most striking aspects of the data is both the extent and the wide range of previous teaching experience those entrants to post-primary teacher education brought with them to their teaching education programme. The actual breadth of experience across different sectors, primary, post-primary, TEFL, third level and adult education raises, if tangentially, a serious question as to the extent to which unqualified teachers are working within the Irish education system generally. It also raises questions about the allocation of points for such experience as part of the selection process for entry to the PGDE (Heinz, 2008). The value of this, often unsupported, unqualified experience as a factor in the selection process requires investigation. More concerning, however, are the effects of the experience of unqualified teaching on potential entrants to teacher education and the problems which may ensue in terms of the professional development and socialisation of those future teachers. Such experience has been found to have a big impact on students' pedagogical beliefs and can be difficult to change (Gill et al., 2004; Wideen et al., 1998). Given the current situation, it is crucial that teacher educators are aware of students' unqualified teaching experience. This is necessary if these students' pedagogical approaches and teaching skills and their capacities to engage in reflective practice, which may have been formed without guidance or knowledge, are to be developed.

The range of prior experience involvement in non-specific teaching activities represented in the cohort is also of interest. This includes their voluntary work with youth and children's groups, with disabled young people, and their involvement with religious and drama, arts and music activities. Undoubtedly, such involvement provides teacher educators with a rich source of experience to explore a range of educational issues with their students. It is not surprising that these involvements were reflected in their reasons for choosing teaching as a career. Similar patterns of involvement are reported in international studies in which job satisfaction, working with young people, love of subject and making a worthwhile contribution to society are among the major reasons for choice of teaching as a career (Aksu et al., 2009; Richardson & Watt, 2006; Arends et al., 1998).

The findings presented in this chapter also necessitates some commentary on gender balance, which is an important issue for those involved in teacher education, is indicated. In overall terms, the gender balance of the cohort is similar to what pertains internationally (Drudy et al., 2005). An examination of gender differences within the cohort itself revealed that more males had university degrees and a higher percentage of men had degrees in science. Men also tended to have more teaching experience at third level, in adult education and in TEFL teaching. They also had more experience than females in tutoring, giving grinds, mentoring and literacy. Women, on the other hand, had more teaching experience in the pre-primary and primary sectors. It seems, then, that women had more experience than their male peers in classroom teaching in school settings and at lower educational levels.

The prior experience of the cohort apart from teaching and involvement in education related areas, revealed that men had more experience working in sports and with religious groups but not with other groups. Women had more experience than males working in homework clubs and in the areas of drama and music. They also had more experience working in youth and children's clubs and with disabled young people than their male colleagues.

Significant gender-related motivations for choosing teaching as a career were identified in the study. Females who were motivated by intrinsic factors in choosing teaching as a career, rated job satisfaction, working with young people and love of subject more highly than males. Males, for the most part, were more motivated by extrinsic factors in choosing teaching as a career than females. One exception to this pattern related to those under 25 years where females were more motivated by extrinsic factors than males. It is clear from these findings that women and men bring a varied range of prior experiences with them to their teacher education, some of which are likely to impact on their future professional development. Further, the central focus of their motivation for choosing teaching as a career, revealed in this study, although similar in certain ways differs in fundamental respects.

This study indicates that the age profile of entrants to post-primary teacher education is wide and in line with national trends (Heinz, 2008). Apart from this general trend, some patterns of difference also occurred within the various age groups examined in the study. The mature students who featured prominently in the cohort had, for the most part, become dissatisfied with their existing careers in preference for teaching. This choice had been made despite the financial burden this step entailed. This group aged 40 and over, had the highest percentage of Arts degrees and degrees awarded with first-class honours. The extent of prior teaching experience among the different age ranges was also an interesting finding. Those mature students, aged between 31 and 40, had the highest levels of teaching experience. Their experience, however, had been gained primarily in such areas as TEFL and in third-level institutions, contexts very different from post-primary teaching. This particular group rated job satisfaction more highly as a motivating factor for choosing teaching as a career than any of the other groups. Those members of the cohort who were under 25 years of age were most representative of the Institute of Technology sector, members of this group considered working with young people to be a more important career motivating factor than their colleagues in other age groups.

The issues that have emerged in this study are very important for all involved in the provision of teacher education programmes for the post-primary sector. Using knowledge about students' prior experiences, their socio-economic backgrounds, their diversity in terms of age and their reasons for wanting a teaching career should enable teacher educators to explore more deeply with student teachers their understandings about classroom teaching. It should enable teacher educators to guide students towards meaningful reflective practice, facilitate their development away from pre-existing pedagogical beliefs and understand the difficulties that they encounter while trying to bridge the theory–practice divide.

ENDNOTES

1   This chapter is from an ongoing major research study by Marie Clarke, Anne Lodge and Michael Shevlin entitled 'The Future of Consecutive Post-Primary Teacher Education: An Assessment of the Needs of Pre-Service and Newly Qualified Teachers and the Changing Contexts of the Post-Primary Sector'.

12

THE ROLE OF INDUCTION AND MENTORS IN SUPPORTING NEWLY QUALIFIED TEACHERS[1]

Maureen Killeavy and Anne Moloney

INTRODUCTION

> There is no ... single story of learning to teach. There are, however, some shared persistent dilemmas, contradictory realities and common narratives that the newly arrived personally confront and internalize as their own.
>
> Britzman, 2003, p. 6

Social, demographic, technological and other changes in recent decades have placed new demands on the teaching profession. Increasingly, across Europe, teachers teach in more diverse, multicultural classrooms than heretofore. Teachers are expected to prepare students to develop flexible approaches to learning, to be independent learners yet able to collaborate and work in teams, and to use technology to support and enhance learning. Such a broad range of requirements demands that teachers engage in continuing professional development to update and develop their professional skills to better meet the needs of learners in this 'knowledge society'. In Ireland, these societal changes have become more apparent due to the enlargement of the European Union and a growth in economic prosperity in the first decade of the 21st century, resulting in increased inward migration, increased participation of women in the workforce and dispersed populations.

Initial teacher education has changed in recent decades in response to these changing societal needs. Each year, approximately 1,800 students in Ireland obtain a postgraduate teaching qualification, allowing them to teach in second-level schools (Higher Education Authority, 2009). A similar number of teacher education students, 1,800 approximately, gain a BEd degree each year, qualifying them to teach in the primary-school system. However, the complexity of teaching today means that beginning teachers need further systematic support and professional development in order to navigate the complex landscapes of teaching. Attrition from the profession, which is an issue for many developed countries, is not yet perceived as such in Ireland. This is perhaps for a number of reasons. There is intense competition for places on teacher education programmes with the number of applicants continuing to far outstrip available places. Teaching in Ireland continues to hold some of its 'legendary high status' in comparison to other developed countries (Coolahan, 2003; see also chapters 10 and 11 in this book). In the United States, the National Commission on Teaching and America's Future (NCTAF) stresses the importance of teacher preparation programmes that develop teachers' abilities to manage in increasingly complex classrooms (NCTAF, 2003). In addition, comparative studies suggest that attractiveness of salary can be a determinant of reasons for teachers to stay or leave. These and other factors account for the different situation in Ireland.

Unlike their peers in other countries, newly qualified teachers in Ireland face particular difficulties in securing employment. The Organisation for Economic Co-operation and Development's (OECD) background report on Ireland (part of a major study of entry to teaching in OECD countries) details this and reports that newly qualified teachers 'commonly spend their early years of teaching in a series of temporary positions, in a variety of schools' (OECD, 2005, p. 117). The report goes on to say that such beginning teachers:

> ... do not have the benefit of a time period to establish themselves in a stable school context, to get to know the school climate and dynamics, and to establish supportive professional relationships with fellow staff members. To the apprehensions and difficulties of finding one's 'professional feet' is added the insecurity of employment patterns and the lack of continuity of professional context.
>
> OECD, 2005, p. 117

Yet, unlike other professions, such as medicine and law, newly qualified teachers are required to assume full professional responsibilities from the first day they enter a classroom (Killeavy, 2006).

These and other challenges facing new teachers are documented in a number of reports that describe how the profession of teaching is becoming more and more complex, with increasing demands placed upon teachers in more and more challenging work environments (Commission of the European Communities,

2007). Recommendations from international research, and transnational bodies such as the OECD, stress the need to view teaching as a continuum, from initial education to ongoing professional development, emphasising induction as a vital stage in professional formation.

This chapter presents an overview of the work of the National Pilot Project on Teacher Induction Post-Primary. It describes the background to the programme in the context of teacher education in Ireland, and presents some pertinent findings from initial and ongoing research in the programme in relation to the supports and challenges for newly qualified teachers in Ireland.

INDUCTION

A growing body of research in recent decades, and in particular since the 1990s, has advocated the need for quality induction programmes as a pivotal and valuable stage in the continuum of teacher lifelong learning (Darling-Hammond, 1995). Induction refers to the transition into teaching, usually the first year following a teacher education programme. In Ireland, as elsewhere, teacher education is recognised as comprising three phases: initial teacher education; induction; and in-service education (sometimes called continuing professional development).

Induction programmes are recommended for a number of reasons, including their role in the retention of new teachers in the profession. Halting attrition from the profession is now a major goal in many developed Western countries and the provision of induction support for beginning teachers in the early stages of their careers is considered the most effective method of preventing this attrition. The OECD suggests that the 'quality of the professional experience in the early years of teaching ... is now seen as a crucial influence on the likelihood of leaving the teaching profession' (OECD, 2005, p. 135). Strong induction programmes are advocated as key pillars in supporting teachers in managing the difficult transition from 'novice' to 'expert' practitioner and are credited with beneficial effects for the professional competence of newly qualified teachers (NQTs) and mentors (Cochran-Smith, 2004b; Darling-Hammond & Bransford, 2005; Totterdell et al., 2004; Cameron, 2007). Cameron (2007) describes other benefits, including the provision of emotional support, while Totterdell et al. (2004, pp. 43–4) go further and suggest that induction is a central element in the fostering of innovation and changing the cultures of schools. Induction programmes for new teachers in the first year are now standard throughout the developed world. For example, in Scotland, induction is mandatory and supported for all teachers in their first year (GTCS, 2002) while a structured support and training programme for all new teachers has been ensured on a statutory basis in England since 1999.

Background

The OECD 1991 *Review of National Policies for Education* was influential in placing the spotlight on induction as a critical element in teacher education policy, citing it as an 'essential component of a policy for maintaining the quality of schooling and of teachers' (OECD, 1991, p. 101). The Green Paper on Education (Government of Ireland, 1992) and the White Paper on Education (Government of Ireland, 1995) echoed this policy, highlighting the importance of induction in the professional formation of teachers. Throughout the 1990s, the voices of teacher educators, the teacher unions and the wider education community in Ireland were added to the debate, all expressing growing concerns about the challenges facing newly qualified teachers and the need for appropriate support structures in the initial stages of their professional life to enable them to face these challenges. This discourse emerged in the light of international best practice in teacher education which emphasises the importance of an induction year for NQTs in which partnerships between schools and teacher education institutions are promoted (Totterdell et al., 2004). A decision emerged at ministry level to establish a pilot programme to develop models of induction and identify best practice as a basis for a future national policy on induction in Ireland.

The National Pilot Project on Teacher Induction

The National Pilot Project on Teacher Induction (NPPTI) was established in 2002 by the Department of Education and Science (DES) and funded through its In-career Development Unit. The NPPTI, which is still ongoing, is based on a partnership initiative including the DES, the three teacher unions in Ireland— the Association of Secondary Teachers of Ireland (ASTI), the Teachers' Union of Ireland (TUI) and the Irish National Teachers' Organisation (INTO)—the university Education departments, partner schools and education centres. The project has two self-contained pillars: the School of Education, University College Dublin (UCD) is responsible for the operation of and researching induction models for second-level schools in the post-primary pillar, while St Patrick's College, Drumcondra, is responsible for the primary pillar.

The principal aim of the NPPTI is to develop proposals and identify models of induction for an effective national programme for newly qualified teachers based on research within the Irish context and international studies on the area. The post-primary pillar of the project provides ongoing research on the support needs of beginning teachers together with the continuing professional development requirements of mentors who support these beginning teachers in their schools. Research is one of the major remits of the project and it serves to ensure that the supports provided for both mentors and their mentees are appropriate to meet the current and emerging needs of the teaching profession at post-primary level in Ireland.

Research in the project is carried out in the context of international research in the area of induction and mentoring, and includes initial and ongoing investigation of current models of induction internationally. Given that there is no single 'definitive model of induction' (Totterdell et al., 2004), these processes were designed to provide a theoretical and research basis for the development of a national induction policy for all members of the teaching profession in Ireland. In addition, an action research developmental model, that is essentially a knowledge-generation process, seeks to produce insights for teachers, researchers and policy makers on induction and mentoring in the context of Irish schools.

Research within the NPPTI

While evidence from international induction programmes was useful in providing signposts for the project, research on the specific needs of newly qualified teachers in Ireland was deemed necessary because of the particular contextualised nature of the local education system. A countrywide needs analysis involving all post-primary school principals and all new teachers who began their career in 2002 was carried out to establish the priorities in professional support provision in teacher induction. It was considered that the work of the project should be based on a nationally based perspective of insiders in schools and of the teachers themselves, during the initial stages of the project. An almost 70 per cent response to the anonymous questionnaire, which formed part of the study, was an indication of the importance of the area from both the point of view of school principals and new teachers. The high response rate provided a confidence level to the data which emerged from the study. Findings, which are available in the NPPTI report (Killeavy & Murphy, 2006), indicate that induction support involving mentoring and other support provision is regarded as essential by virtually all post-primary school principals and beginning teachers.

The next section presents some of the main findings of this initial survey, and places them in the context of ongoing work and development in the project.

INITIAL RESEARCH: THE SUPPORT NEEDS OF NEW TEACHERS

Analysis of the responses of principals and NQTs to the survey reveals similar concerns from both groups with some variations in relation to priorities. The three main aspects of teaching in which new teachers face particular challenges, according to principals, involve pedagogical concerns, professional issues, and interpersonal and communication skills. Each of these areas is presented here in greater depth.

Pedagogical areas

The pedagogical areas of concern identified by principals in which new teachers need induction support include discipline and classroom management, preparation, methodology and assessment, special educational needs (SEN) and mixed-ability teaching. While these areas are mainstreamed within all teacher education courses in Ireland, principals suggest that these areas should be further developed in support seminars, then put into practice by NQTs and later discussed with their mentors.

The concerns of new teachers and principals are, for the most part, in broad agreement in relation to pedagogical issues. New teachers considered teaching special needs students in the mainstream classroom to be the number one priority in terms of support requirements, while principals viewed discipline and the management of disruptive behaviour as the area in which new teachers required most support. Classroom management and discipline and student behaviour issues are considered to be the second most important in terms of support requirements by beginning teachers themselves. These findings remained stable in all subsequent replications of the questionnaire although some small variations occurred which may be attributable to particular local circumstances. For example, while teaching multicultural students was identified as low in the order of importance in the initial survey, particularly with principals who rated it as 17th in importance in 2001, this aspect emerged as an increased support need in subsequent surveys with NQTs. This may reflect the increased immigration into Ireland in latter years, particularly since the accession of additional countries to the European Union in 2004. In addition, there was evidence of some 'clustering' of responses, due to uneven demographic patterns as a result of the clustering of immigrant populations in certain regions or towns related to local employment availability.

Professional competences

Professional competence comprising awareness of school policy and ethos, professionalism, willingness to be involved in extra-curricular activities, and classroom observation, are considered to be very important by principals. These perceptions and awareness of the professional role of the teacher are viewed as essential attributes for future employment and career advancement. In this instance, the views of beginning teachers are not at one with those of principals. New teachers' concern about the professional aspects of the teacher's role was not nearly as serious as that of the school principals.

Interpersonal and communication skills

Principals placed a strong emphasis on interpersonal and communication skills for NQTs. These skills do not form as major a part of the courses of teacher preparation as pedagogical issues, partly because it is expected that teacher education students acquire such skills both indirectly and through their teaching practice. In addition, a number of the courses which form part of teacher education programmes, in particular psychology, are concerned with these areas. Some of the skills mentioned by principals such as dealing with students' problems, conflict resolution and stress management are indicative of the changing complexities and challenges of the teacher's role. Nevertheless, NQTs focus on the need for support in areas which require the ability to work effectively with students, colleagues and parents, including: student motivation; classroom management and organisation; working with parents; and the preparation of tests and assessment. Findings suggest that teachers' concerns cluster largely on aspects of teaching common to all subjects, rather than on pedagogical matters related to the teaching of particular subjects.

Findings from the initial survey served as the basis for the development of the key elements of the mentoring and induction programme for NQTs and mentors. Certain elements of the NPPTI research findings offer potential for follow-up research. The support needs identified by NQTs has led to an exploration of their perceptions of their levels of preparedness for certain aspects of the teacher's role following their pre-service preparation.

ONGOING RESEARCH WITH BEGINNING TEACHERS

NQTs: level of preparedness for their future career

An ongoing investigation of beginning teachers' perceptions of the level of their preparation has been undertaken as part of the assessment of their induction needs. What emerges strongly from this study is the sense that NQTs, in the main, feel unprepared for all the practical application elements of their professional role as full-time teachers. A more in-depth analysis reveals that this expressed need is not an indication that teacher's pre-service courses lack sufficient attention to such areas. In the main, new teachers view their theoretical courses favourably, however, they are strongly of the view that many of the practical aspects of teaching cannot be adequately covered within a pre-service course and should take place later. NQTs report that although they have a sound theoretical knowledge of areas such as dealing with discipline problems and teaching special needs students in the inclusive classroom, it is very difficult to put this knowledge into practice when they have the responsibilities of full-time professional employment. The teaching-practice component of their professional preparation usually provided some practical experience in these areas of particular challenge. However, the limited class time interaction during the school day and the fact that the class teacher was the one with ultimate responsibility meant that support was always on hand. Beginning teachers identify other aspects of teaching, such as parent–teacher relationships, for which the theoretical preparation could take place at pre-service level but for which practical guided learning experiences are more suitably provided during induction. These views expressed by beginning teachers seem in line with the internship model of teacher support which is practised in some US states and is similar to models of preparation in other professions.

While the NPPTI programme looks at particular areas of pre-service in this research area, the focus is to gain insights to enable the programme to better align the induction programme with the expressed practical needs of NQTs. The information gathered is used to explore how this practical 'applied in the field' type of support might best be provided within partner schools in the programme. International practice to alleviate this division between theory and practice includes the provision of opportunities for NQTs to observe experienced teachers within the school (Wong et al., 2005). Structured observation is advocated within the NPPTI programme of support, and training is provided for mentors and NQTs in observation methods. Engaging in observation has emerged as a challenge for many teachers due in large part to the critical element of time. The NPPTI sought to gain a deeper understanding of the concerns expressed by teachers in relation to time for induction activities.

NQTs: the crucial element of time

Ongoing work with teachers in the project indicated that the transition from teacher education student to classroom teacher is a major change involving unexpected effort and fatigue. Further, NQTs report that time management is a constant and unexpected problem, particularly for those who are teaching full-time hours, given the additional work load in planning, developing new courses and materials, marking, and other tasks. Time is also a challenge for mentors. There is a sense of time for mentoring support being snatched during the school day rather than being formally timetabled, as recommended in the guidelines for good mentoring practice.

Induction programmes in many countries include a recognition of the challenges for NQTs in adapting to the increased work load of a full timetable in their first job. Teachers require time and space to plan, to learn, to reflect on their practice and to consult their mentors and experienced colleagues. In Scotland, newly qualified teachers are guaranteed a teaching post for their induction year, which includes a 70 per cent teaching load, along with a 30 per cent commitment for Continuing Professional Development (CPD) (O'Brien & Christie, 2005). In addition, each NQT has a mentor with 10 per cent in-school time allocation to the role. This time allocation is not unusual and is reflected in practice in most European countries, in Australia, New Zealand, the United States and Canada where beginning teachers are provided with between 10 per cent and 30 per cent of time within their teaching week to take part in induction activities.

In Ireland, the report of the NPPTI (phases 1 and 2) (Killeavy & Murphy, 2006) recommends that induction and mentoring activities should be timetabled in scheduled meetings within the school day. However, this is not to suggest that less formal mentoring activities cannot have very beneficial effects. Our research has found that successful mentors are those who are approachable and who are willing to provide on the spot advice to deal with contingencies. What is required is a balance between the more formal aspects of mentoring which are important and the establishment of a helping professional relationship in which the beginning teacher can approach their mentor for a quick word of advice in the course of the school day. Effective induction programmes include the development of the professional learning skills and attitudes of the NQT. Within the NPPTI, strategies are embedded to support the development of these crucial skills and attitudes in the seminar workshop programme in which all mentors and beginning teachers take part.

NQTs: supporting reflective practice

Reflection is recommended as an essential part of the repertoire of teachers both in initial pre-service education and in continuing professional development (Harris & Johnson, 1998). Calderhead (1989) claims that teachers can improve their effectiveness in the classroom by gaining a better understanding of their own individual teaching styles achieved through reflection on practice. However, beginning teachers report that the demands of a busy, full-time schedule of classroom teaching and the challenges of coming to terms with their full professional role are extremely time consuming and leave little room for reflection. A NPPTI research initiative to encourage NQTs' involvement in reflective practice was set within the framework of a support network using ICT. This study involved two groups of NQTs in different centres using web logs (blogs) as an electronic personal journal to document their experiences and views on their ongoing professional development. These NQTs were also encouraged to use the blog as a communication tool with the other new teachers in their group. The mixed methods design of the study involved documentary analysis, focus group interviews and quantitative analysis. Analysis of findings revealed reluctance on the part of these teachers to use blogs as a means of documenting and sharing their reflections. A possible reason for this is NQTs' lack of early experience in this method of communication. The lack of a pre-existing learning community may also have contributed to the low level of use of blogging as a reflective and communication tool by NQTs within the groups. This latter explanation lends support to findings by Preece (2000) who suggested that in order to engage in a community, members need to have a shared purpose, be with compatible people and agree on group policies.

Given that reflection is advocated as a powerful tool in the arsenal of the professional practitioner, the outcomes from this study suggest that pursuit of the goal of promoting reflection on practice warrants exploration using other tools which may prove more amenable to NQTs. A development to this end in the project involves the use of a private social networking site for NQTs affording them opportunities to record personal concerns, while sharing resources and supports with peers.

NQTs: diversity

Social change in Ireland in recent decades has been apparent in many areas of endeavour including increased female participation in the workforce, increased inward migration and the dispersal of families to new suburbs frequently far removed from supports of wider family and friends. These demographic changes have accelerated since the 1990s. Further, the Education for Persons with Special Educational Needs Act (Government of Ireland, 2004a) providing for education in an inclusive setting has led to a change in the student cohort in second-level schools with the integration of students with SEN in mainstream classes. Social and demographic changes have led to a need for support for NQTs in relation to working with students with disabilities and special educational needs, students from different ethnic backgrounds, and students from disadvantaged backgrounds. While initial teacher education covers these and other areas, they are complex areas and require further continuing professional development in response to ongoing changing needs. Diversity and inclusion now form a central part of the professional development support for NQTs and mentors within the NPPTI. A recent report on a survey of teachers across 23 OECD countries presents some interesting findings in relation to the importance of these areas for teachers, citing teaching special educational needs students 'as the single most important aspect of their work in which they require support' (OECD, 2009b, p. 77). In Ireland, 38 per cent of teachers report that teaching students with special learning needs is their area of greatest development need. Other areas of need reported by teachers in Ireland include teaching in a multicultural setting and student counselling, as well as ICT teaching skills (ibid.).

Taking note of these changes, research in the NPPTI sought to examine mentors' perceptions of the changing nature of the relationship between parents and teachers in the context of the challenges and opportunities of current cultural and societal norms. Following changes in legislation, such as the Education Act in 1998, parents are partners in the education process and adopt a consultative role in the education of their children. This development has had an impact on the work lives of teachers and has important implications for new entrants to the profession, requiring NQTs to develop skills in working as partners with parents. These changing aspects of teachers' professional roles are relevant and must be taken into account in an induction support programme given that the new teacher's relationship with parents is fundamental in their development as professionals.

ONGOING RESEARCH WITH MENTORS

Induction programmes are credited with a number of benefits for NQTs as described above. They also benefit mentors by developing their skills, efficacy and professional practice. Mentoring is not merely the provision of a 'buddy' system, a wise and experienced colleague who can pass on tips of the trade to the novice teacher. According to a recent Organisation Economic Co-operation and Development (OECD) report:

> Mentors must have a level of professional expertise that goes beyond being a source of emotional support and practical information. They should be able to provide not only a good role model, but also offer the help necessary to establish the beginners as competent professionals.
>
> OECD, 2005, p. 121

Thus, a commitment to mentoring requires that mentors be trained and supported for their roles. Within the NPPTI, the training of mentors has emerged as a key strategy in the development of the induction programme. The professional development needs of mentors are more than a battery of skills and information giving practices. Research within the NPPTI has sought to clarify needs and embed practices that support successful mentors.

Mentors: the role of professional experience in supporting beginning teachers

According to Hargreaves and Fullan (2000), the role of the mentor is a multifaceted one, requiring skills in communication, observation, negotiation, and providing feedback and support. Chief among the tasks of the mentor is to smooth the transition for the beginning teacher between the university pre-service course and the realities of teaching in the classroom. Thus, the mentor's role requires not only an understanding of the practical knowledge of teaching, and the contexts and cultures of teaching, but also the ability to make links between these realities and the theory-based learning of the beginning teacher

(Feiman-Nemser & Remillard, 1996). Mentors also need an awareness of their own beliefs and values about teaching (Zanting et al., 1998) and the ability to articulate these (Bradbury & Kobala, 2008). Exploring the origins of their own professional knowledge then becomes a crucial exercise for the mentor.

Within the context of the NPPTI programme, research was undertaken with two groups of mentors to explore this particular element of the mentoring relationship. The understanding and conscious awareness of the processes involved are critical factors in helping mentors facilitate the induction and professional development of new teachers. Mixed methods research (utilising both qualitative and quantitative research) was used to investigate mentors' views of their professional experience and its contribution to their professional repertoire. The findings indicate that the process of self-scrutiny is not easy for mentors. It requires openness to different points of view and a willingness to question strongly held beliefs and honesty. Mentors who approached the process with an open mind and who were willing to explore the nature of their own professional learning found the process rewarding both professionally and personally. By facilitating mentors in understanding their experience and giving them their own unique voice, the insights gained enhanced not only their own but also their 'mentees' professional development.

Mentors: reflection and explorations

A further study on the support needs of mentors sought to facilitate mentors in examining and reflecting on their own professional expertise in preparation for their roles as mentors to beginning teachers in schools. The impetus for this investigation stemmed from difficulties experienced by mentors within the programme in critically interrogating, assessing and discussing teaching in theoretical terms in order to justify their own recommendations on classroom matters to their mentees. A small research study focused on examining the extent to which mentor teachers considered their expertise to derive from their professional education, their classroom teaching experience, their personal value system, their involvement in in-career professional support, and on other factors. Participation in the study resulted in teachers articulating a growing awareness of the need to reflect on and challenge the assumptions underlying their current practice. These experienced teachers report an increase in self-confidence as they worked through a process of reflection, although this often meant that they had to challenge accepted wisdom and deeply held beliefs and values. Most importantly, they found the process to be very rewarding and a source of reaffirmation and professional growth.

CONCLUSION

Within the ambit of the NPPTI, a number of crucial factors emerge concerning the professional support needs of mentors and NQTs. As elsewhere, it appears that the needs of NQTs are various, multifaceted and context dependent. Support needs are not only concerned with the professional development of teachers in its strict sense, they also involve the personal, social and emotional aspects of the teacher's role. A 'one size fits all' approach is therefore contra-indicated and will not suffice. The findings of the report on phases 1 and 2 of the project (Killeavy & Murphy, 2006) have been borne out in subsequent research. NQTs require a balanced mix of supports and resources including in-school support and mentoring, professional development seminars led by teacher education institutions and collaboration with peers, in addition to support in the development of a personal reflective stance as a teacher. Mentors too require adequate training and time in order to enhance their own professional development and to develop their skills as a mentor, a role which can be challenging both personally and professionally. Adequate resource provision to meet these challenges remains a key factor in the provision of mentoring and induction.

International research suggests that induction should be an integral stage in a continuum of teacher development, in which NQTs are supported in their entry to a professional community (NCTAF, 2005; Totterdell et al., 2004). Successful induction programmes require commitment and leadership at all levels within schools and in the education system generally. Ongoing work on the NPPTI in Ireland has reflected international findings concerning the support needs of beginning teachers. Investment in the professional development of teachers has been identified by international bodies, such as the OECD and the EU, as important in developing the quality of the teaching profession as a whole.

The precarious nature of employment, including part-time and temporary contracts for many beginning teachers in Ireland, remains a problem which has far-reaching effects for classroom discipline and for teachers themselves. The recent international OECD TALIS report found that teachers employed on a permanent contract and those who were full-time were more likely to have a positive classroom discipline climate and to report a positive sense of self-efficacy

(OECD, 2009b, p. 228). The areas highlighted for professional development support within the NPPTI are remarkably similar to those outlined in the findings of the recent TALIS survey from OECD. The five most requested areas for support by Irish teachers surveyed for this OECD report were: teaching special educational needs students; ICT teaching skills; student counselling; teaching in multicultural settings; and student discipline and behaviour problems (ibid., p. 84). These findings lend support to the emerging notion, as the NPPTI has developed, that induction needs to be viewed as an essential component of the preparation of teachers and that induction is the foundation for the continuum of professional development to meet the challenging complexities of the teachers' role in a changing society.

ENDNOTES

1   This project has been supported by the Teacher Education Section of the Department of Education and Science. This support is gratefully acknowledged.

13
PROGRESSING TOWARDS INCLUSION IN IRELAND: PROFESSIONAL DEVELOPMENT FOR LEARNING SUPPORT/RESOURCE TEACHERS[1]

Elizabeth O'Gorman

Inclusive education espouses educational values of diversity, equity and social justice. It is about the entitlement of all children to a quality education irrespective of their differences (Booth et al., 2000; Thomas & Vaughan, 2004; Moran, 2007). The legislative and moral imperative to provide inclusive education for students with special educational needs (SEN)/disabilities is underpinned by the 1998 Education Act, the 2000 Education (Welfare) Act, the 2000 & 2004 Equal Status Acts, the 2004 Education for Persons with Special Educational Needs Act and the 2005 Disability Act (Government of Ireland, 1998b, 2000a, 2000b, 2000–2004, 2004a, 2005). However, simply providing access to regular, mainstream education is not inclusion (Ferguson, 2008). Students must benefit from and actively participate in their educational experience. Providing for inclusive education in the context of the regular mainstream school is a major challenge which requires unsettling the previous default mode of schooling where segregation and exclusion were the norm (Norwich, 2008; Barton & Slee, 1999; Dyson, 2001).

In the past decade, an increasing number of students in mainstream schools in Ireland have been identified as having special educational needs. This appears to be due to two trends, namely the placement in mainstream schools of students with SEN who previously might have attended special schools and the increased use of assessment procedures to identify special educational needs. In responding to the upsurge in students identified with SEN in mainstream schools, there has been a substantial increase in the numbers of teachers appointed to teach these students. At primary level, SEN-related posts increased from 1,500 in 1998 to almost 5,000 in 2005—one out of every five teachers. At second level, the increase was from 200 resource teachers in 1998 to 1,600 whole-time equivalent resource teachers by 2005 (Department of Education & Science, 2006).

As international experience had shown, simply providing additional teachers to work specifically with students with SEN does not guarantee inclusive educational practices. Indeed, unsupported teacher provision may have the unintended effect of ghettoising SEN within a mainstream school (Vlachou, 2006; Imants et al., 2001; Pijl et al., 1997). Teachers appointed to this position require access to professional development that enables them to develop an understanding of the role they are to undertake and the significance of that role in progressing towards a goal of inclusive education. Without professional development which seeks to challenge the status quo, teachers may simply locate their role within a 'medical model' where the focus is on assessing student deficits and devising remediating approaches to learning support/resource outside the regular classroom setting. The danger of transplanting special education 'exclusionary' thinking and practice into mainstream contexts is ever present (Ainscow, 2007).

An alternative role for the learning support/resource specialist is to support the transformation of mainstream classroom practice. This is rooted in an inclusive role which contests current practices, queries why it is that schools fail so many children and strives for change (Dyson & Millward 2000; Slee 2006). In effect, the learning support/resource specialist must adopt a revolutionary role which is founded on a broad and deep reading of issues pertaining to inclusion, instigated by and supported through apposite, professional-development programmes.

TEACHER EDUCATION: RATIONALE AND EFFECTIVENESS

The benefit of investing in teacher education has been attested to by a number of international research reports. In New Zealand, a recent synthesis of research on educational practice demonstrated that the quality of teaching has an impact on student learning outcomes (Timperly et al., 2007). Furthermore, there is evidence from the United States that teacher preparation contributes significantly to teacher quality and effectiveness (Darling-Hammond et al., 2005). Similar findings underscore the importance of teacher education in effecting change and moving to more inclusive systems (Howes et al., 2005).

The type of professional development provided to teachers has been the subject of much debate. Previous research showed that professional development which was longer in duration, regular, structured, collaborative and embedded in practice was more effective in impacting on teacher practice (Joyce et al., 1987;

Cochran-Smith, 2004a; Darling-Hammond et al., 2005; Meiers & Ingvarson 2005). Similarly, in a survey of teacher attitudes towards inclusion in Greece, researchers found that in-service training that was substantial in nature was key to the formation of positive teacher attitude and stated that low-level 'technical' courses, focusing on specific needs or on syndromes, tended to reinforce special education as being problematic within mainstream structures (Avramidis & Kalyva, 2007). The greater impact of substantial programmes was also noted in professional development for SEN co-ordinators (SENCos) in England which found that professional development, which was thorough and longer in duration, resulted in more competent SENCos and noted that taking part in the longer courses enhanced confidence, skills and knowledge (Cowne, 2005; Wearmouth et al., 2004). Thus, teacher education and professional development programmes which are substantial and intensive are at the core of the development of more inclusive educational systems.

THE SPECIFIC NEED FOR PROFESSIONAL DEVELOPMENT FOR LEARNING SUPPORT/RESOURCE TEACHERS

As stated, access to mainstream education is insufficient in itself to ensure equity in the educational experience offered to students identified with SEN. While, ideally, all teachers should willingly take on responsibility for all students in their care, the historical emphasis on a distinctive and separate educational setting for students with SEN may instil fear and assumptions of ineffectiveness in many teachers. A mistaken presumption here is that competence in SEN should precede practice whereas in fact competence is more likely to be achieved through practice.

In response to the inclusion of students with SEN in the mainstream school, additional posts of learning support/resource teachers have been allocated to schools. As Wedell (2008) articulates, there is a dilemma about designating a post to address special educational needs, since this risks a 'separation' from the mainstream. However, he resolves this dilemma by suggesting that moves towards a flexible response to SEN points to ways of increasing the flexibility of the school system as a whole. Thus, the role of a learning support/resource teacher can be directed towards system change rather than shoring up existing exclusionary practices. In order to effect this change, professional-development courses in special education must incorporate critical discussions of the concept of inclusion. (Avramidis & Kalyva, 2007).

RESEARCH QUESTION

The review of the literature attests to the need for professional development for learning support/resource teachers in progressing towards inclusion. In the field of education, professional development is generally associated with the perceived demands of current and future work-related tasks. These aspects of professional development were considered worthy of investigation in the Irish context and a large-scale research project was undertaken. Both qualitative and quantitative data were gathered on various aspects of this topic in order to explore the parameters of the types of professional development teachers in Ireland considered best suited to their requirements, however, for this discussion, two core areas were highlighted for consideration.

The key research question identified for deliberation in this study was as follows:

1. What do learning support/resource teachers in Ireland perceive as their main roles and responsibilities?

The second research question focused directly on the professional development requested by learning support/resource teachers:

2. What are the professional development elements requested by learning support/resource teachers?

A further area explored was the relationship between professional development and the roles of the learning support/resource teachers. Consideration was given to whether the roles determined the professional development requested or whether the professional development undertaken determined the roles adopted.

METHODOLOGY

Both quantitative and qualitative data were sought for this research. A postal survey questionnaire, focus groups and individual interviews were the main sources of data. One questionnaire was sent to each of the 732 post-primary schools and to a random sample[2] of 760 primary schools. Responses were received from 399 (55.2 per cent) post-primary and 417 (54.8 per cent) primary learning support/resource teachers, yielding information on 816 schools. These schools represented almost 250,000 pupils.

The qualitative data emerged from open questions in the questionnaire, from 10 focus groups and from telephone and face-to-face interviews which were held with a sub-sample of 22 responding teachers. The groups contributing to the interviews were self-selecting as were the respondents to the questionnaire. Those participating in the research were motivated by interest in the area and thus may not be representative of the full range of opinion. However, as there was a 55 per cent response rate, which included responses from schools in every county in the Republic of Ireland and from the different types of school, inferential statistics suggest that the questionnaire sample is broadly representative of the school population (Cohen, et al., 2007).

Analysis of the data was conducted using both traditional manual analysis and computer software packages. Excel and SPSS were used for the quantitative data while Word, Excel and MAXQDA were used for the qualitative data.

FINDINGS

The research recounted here was part of a large-scale project. The focus in this chapter is on two of the key areas, namely the roles of learning support/resource teachers and the professional development associated with these roles that is sought by the learning support/resource teachers.

Roles and Responsibilities

Learning support/resource teachers' roles and responsibilities were explored through questionnaire survey, focus groups and interviews. This gave rise to both quantitative and qualitative data.

In the questionnaire, respondents were asked to rate the importance of a series of possible roles and in the focus groups and interviews teachers were asked what areas they regarded as being their main roles and responsibilities. The list of potential roles used in the questionnaire was developed over a three-year period in consultation with practising teachers (see O'Gorman & Drudy, 2009 for further details). The information emerging from this aspect of the research offered us an insight into the responsibilities deemed part of the learning support/resource teacher's role. The range of responsibilities undertaken was very broad. This was true for both primary and post-primary teachers. The majority of teachers rated the withdrawal of students in small groups as being the most significant aspect of their role. There were slight differences between primary and post-primary teachers in the ratings of some aspects of their roles. The other top areas rated as important included: individual withdrawal; the identification of students with SEN; the administration of screening tests; the monitoring of student progress; tasks relating to Individual Education Plans (IEPs); and undertaking administrative duties (see Table 13.1).

Table 13.1: Roles rated as important (lower mean=greater importance)

Role (descending importance)	Number responding to item	Mean level of importance attached
Withdrawal for small group instruction	756	1.70
Identifying students with SEN	736	1.85
Withdrawal for individual instruction	729	1.93
Screening/diagnostic tests	737	2.04
Monitoring student progress	732	2.13
Record keeping	752	2.20
Timetabling additional support	707	2.25
Liaison with principal	743	2.32
Preparation individualised teaching	731	2.35
Reassessing student progress	712	2.38
Collaborating with other teachers	761	2.41
Liaison with parents	757	2.41
Implementing IEPs	692	2.50
Formulating IEPs	695	2.54

Among questionnaire respondents, collaborative aspects of the role and areas which highlighted a proactive, inclusion focus received poor ratings (see Table 13.2). Differences between primary and post-primary teachers emerged in that post-primary teachers were more likely to rate collaborative and liaison responsibilities as more important than their primary counterparts. This may be due, in part, to the organisational structure of the post-primary school where each student has many different subject teachers.

While the information obtained through the questionnaire is interesting in the factual evidence it provides of the work of the learning support/resource teacher, the fine detail of how these roles are played out can be best garnered through the descriptions of the lived lives of teachers as recounted in the interviews and focus groups.

Table 13.2: Roles rated least important (lower mean=greater importance)

Role (descending importance)	Number responding to item	Mean level of importance attached
Co-ordinating IEP meetings	683	3.05
Liaison feeder/follow-on schools	684	3.09
Preparation of differentiated teaching materials	719	3.13
Coordinating/allocating SNA duties	650	3.17
Team-teaching for SEN students	665	3.46
Staff development/in-service training	686	3.50
Providing substitute cover	655	3.65
Liaison Special Education Inspectorate	663	3.86

The findings from the qualitative data supported the quantitative data overall, although some differences emerged. When asked to reflect on their main roles and responsibilities teachers listed a wide range of roles which encompassed individual teaching, individual and group assessment and administration:

> I'd say, you know, like, open any of those books, and there's a list a mile long of the roles and responsibilities … teachers are, you know, to a greater or lesser extent, trying to achieve all of those things, there's so many different aspects to the job …
>
> Interview, post-primary teacher, PPT4 260

The role seemed to encompass a broad range of responsibilities and, in the main, teachers reported being overburdened in their role. This was noted by both primary and post-primary teachers. There was a sense that the demands on learning/support resource teachers were continually expanding and that in both sectors, boundaries to the remit of their roles needed stronger definition:

> Any problem that any student seems to have is brought to me, whether or not it might be say a literacy problem or numeracy problem or a behavioural problem or even if they are, well, I suppose, all problems fall under those, they are all in my remit but even if, say, the child gets distracted easily and

ends up staring out the window most classes, this is brought to me so that I can see what we can do about it.

Interview, post-primary teacher, PPT3: 99

The administrative aspects of the role were considered to take away from the professional teaching focus.

I just feel the actual paperwork and administration and all the filing and all that is taking up too much time. And actually cutting into the time I have to work with students. And I'd love to get rid of that.

Interview, post-primary teacher, PPT 7: 106

I would feel that for resource teachers, the amount of paperwork [is overwhelming]. Between planning and [individual] plans ... the paperwork takes away from the teaching time.

Focus group, primary teacher, B PT2: 3

The finding that the roles undertaken by learning support/resource teachers were wide ranging and were considered onerous is mirrored by research in other countries (Pearson, 2008; Mackenzie, 2007; Cowne, 2005; Kearns, 2005; Forlin, 2001b). Teachers in some countries also shared the Irish learning support/resource teachers conceptualisation of their role as being primarily one of withdrawing students from regular classroom settings (Vlachou, 2006).

Within the Irish research, an interesting divergence emerged between the quantitative and qualitative data. In contrast to the results from the analysis of roles in the questionnaire, 'liaison' and 'collaboration with colleagues and parents' were given greater importance in the interviews. This may have been due to the fact that more experienced, competent and confident teachers were more likely to self-select for interview. It would appear that these teachers, almost all of whom had specialist qualifications in SEN, were more willing to undertake proactive, inclusion-focused roles.

This aspect of the research, the roles and responsibilities of learning support/resource teachers, is investigated in greater depth in an extended report on the research project (O'Gorman & Drudy, 2009).

The Professional Development Requirements of learning support/resource teachers

The area of the learning support/resource teachers' professional-development requirements was also explored in both the questionnaire and the interviews. Again, this resulted in both quantitative and qualitative data. In the questionnaire, respondents were asked an open question on their professional development needs (see Table 13.3) and were subsequently asked to rank potential components of a programme of professional development for learning support/resource specialists in relation to their own needs (see Table 13.4). These questions also formed the basis of questions in the interview.

Table 13.3: Teachers' professional-development requests, open question (n=642)

Area requested for professional development	Frequency	%
IEPs	128	19.9
General courses/In-service to upskill	104	16.2
Information on various disabilities	72	11.2
Time management (timetables, co-ordination, admin.)	42	6.5
Testing: diagnosis and assessment	38	5.9
Teaching methodologies relevant to SEN	33	5.1
Contact with others, etc.	29	4.5
IT skills/assistive technology	27	4.2
Dealing with emotional and behavioural issues	24	3.7
Whole school approach to SEN	24	3.7
Speech and language supports	21	3.3
Resources: sourcing, using	21	3.3
Understanding psychological assessments	18	2.8
Policy and law	12	1.9
Mathematics support	12	1.9

Here we can see that individual education plans (IEPs) dominate the list of learning support/resource teachers' professional-development requirements. Other areas that featured strongly were: knowledge of specific disabilities; administrative skills; testing diagnosis and assessment; teaching methodologies relevant to SEN; and contact with experienced teachers. There was high frequency of requests for general 'up-skilling' and unspecified courses and in-service.

These findings from the open question were supported by the answers from a ranking question on potential course components. Although the relative importance accorded to the course elements varied slightly with those from the open question, the areas considered important reappeared in the learning support/resource teachers' top rankings.

Table 13.4: Teachers' ranking of the top 10 course components for a professional-development programme in SEN

Combined primary & post-primary responses		N	%
1	Types of learning difficulties	125	21.9
2	Assessment of learning difficulties	79	13.8
3	Teaching strategies	74	12.9
4	Developing IEPs/education plans	38	6.6
5	Language and literacy	36	6.3
6	School policy and planning	30	5.2
7	Developing alternative curriculum	25	4.4
8	Psychological development in childhood	21	3.7
9	Psychological development in adolescence	18	3.1
10	Interpreting psychological assessments	17	3.0

Student-focused items and curriculum-related items dominated the top 10 priorities of the learning support/resource teachers in terms of course content. It might have been expected that collaboration would be represented in their professional-development priorities—especially in the case of the post-primary teachers who had valued collaboration more highly than their primary counterparts. However, just one collaborative activity (school policy and planning) was in their top 10 priority rankings. Courses which explore and critique the theory and practice of inclusion and special education, such as sociology and philosophy, also received low rankings. Conducting research into special education ranked marginally higher than the critical reflective courses of philosophy and sociology which were bottom of the list of first preferences. Nor was their any evidence of a desire for professional development in leadership skills in the responses to the open-ended questions. In view of the international emphasis on the importance of research/evidence-based teaching and its importance to high-quality teaching and learning, of the need for leadership qualities in the SEN role, and of the need for a critical and reflective profession, the evident absence of such awareness among such a large cohort of learning support/resource teachers with the main responsibilities for SEN in their schools is a matter of concern and points to the need for these elements to be included in learning support/resource teachers professional development as a matter of urgency.

In the interview data, the need for professional development for newly appointed learning support/resource teachers was highlighted.

> You're a mainstream teacher on Monday and when you take up resource or whatever you take up, the next day you're labelled resource teacher and you're automatically expected to know how to deal with everybody.
>
> Focus group, primary teachers, GPT 2: 168

Such teachers, appointed to specialist positions, require professional development to explore the parameters of their role, and to counteract the danger of mere segregation within a mainstream setting being adopted as the automatic response to increased diversity in the student population. In order to undertake their role effectively learning support/resource teachers must broaden their awareness of the full gamut of possibilities of inclusive education.

In relation to professional development sought, again there was a slight difference between the questionnaire data and the interview data. The interview data supported the questionnaire findings of requests for a wide range of course components in professional development programmes, but there was also an awareness of the need to develop system capacity at school level. A tension emerged here between the need for individual expertise in the area of special education and the need for distributed expertise among the whole school staff.

> [Professional development] is a thing that management has to look at, and has to maybe organise on a whole staff level. I can go off and I can do my course maybe, as I said, at a weekend or whatever, you know, but ... there needs to be more whole-school development, or in-service and that, and training, you know.
>
> Interview, primary teacher, PT 9:191

I think I would very definitely like to see in-school development, as a whole staff, you know, help teachers to become more comfortable with the idea that they actually are teaching them [students with SEN] ... they actually are doing the work, you know, but maybe help them to develop their skills.

Interview, post-primary teacher, PPT4 22-26

Overall, the findings indicate that the questionnaire data highlighted the desire for professional development which was student-deficit focused (such as information on different syndromes and assessment procedures) whereas the requests for professional development from the interview data were broader in nature and tended to be less student-deficit oriented. The interviews with the teachers offered glimpses of alternative approaches to the challenge of embracing all students within the school community and opened a vista of the potential for the role to become more proactive in promoting whole-staff responsibility for including students with SEN in regular classrooms. This difference between the questionnaire data and the interview data again might be attributable to the fact that the teachers self-selecting for interview may have been more confident, experienced teachers.

There was a strong indication that all teachers on a school's staff were in need of professional development in SEN. Similarly, Abbott (2006) in a survey of head teachers found that a need for in-service for all staff members on aspects inclusion was articulated by the research participants. In this current research, the suggestion that this training be given by the learning support/resource teacher was proffered by a minority of interviewees.

I think that we could have, at least two approaches to it [professional development] which might help, one would be to train us as teachers [of students and] as team developers. You know that we are not just teachers. If we're working with a team of teachers and if we could be helped to train us to be able to facilitate our colleagues.

Focus group, primary and post-primary mixed, D PPT&PT 1: 97

I would love to come in to classrooms with new members of staff, who haven't been in this school before, are only new in the school, and equip them with the skills that they need to, and work with them, to accommodate the students with special needs in the school.

Interview, post-primary teacher, PPT8:192

The proposition that schools take on responsibility for developing staff capacity for promoting inclusive practices is a welcome indication of a deepening awareness of the complexity of professional development. Such initiatives are steps on the pathway to ensuring that all teachers engage in self-reflexive professional learning and ensure more responsive schools in the quest to accommodate the needs of all learners.

DISCUSSION—IMPLICATIONS OF FINDINGS

The findings from this research suggest that despite a desire to include students with special educational needs in regular schools, the education system in Ireland remains exclusionary in nature. The roles undertaken by learning support/resource teachers promote practices which withdraw students from the regular education system. The professional development requested by the learning support/resource teachers focuses on developing skills for identifying student deficits, for developing individual plans for students and developing techniques for remediating students outside the regular class. In general, there is evidence in this research of training teachers to respond to their current, specific situation and insufficient attention paid to developing teachers' capabilities in researching, implementing and evaluating effective teaching and learning strategies for supporting the whole school to provide education for a diversity of learners.

This focus on the assessment, identification and withdrawal role of the learning support/resource teacher has given rise to an expanding role for the learning support/resource sector in Ireland. A spiralling process has commenced. Following assessment, students identified as not benefiting from the regular class education are offered additional support and if the withdrawal model is favoured, are supported outside the classroom. In due course, the next lowest achieving cohort are assessed and then added to a group receiving support from the learning support/resource teacher outside the regular classroom. Thus, the learning support/resource teacher's workload increases. This inflationary model of the role has been noted in other jurisdictions (Emanuelsson, 2001; Forlin, 2001a; Arnaiz & Castejon, 2001).

The current structures which place responsibility for students with SEN firmly within the remit of the learning support/resource teacher, is a process which emphasises an expanding need for additional teacher time to deal with the individual pupil's difficulties. The process does not, as might be reasonably expected of a system which purports to support inclusive education, demand the adjustment of class teachers' practices which are creating the student failure. Perhaps, instead of investigating the problems deemed to lie within the individual student, we need to ask why is it that more and more students are perceived to be failing. Vlachou (2006) similarly found that, in Greece, teachers located students' learning difficulties within the child or home circumstances rather than associating them with teacher or school practices.

Professional development which responds directly to the current role requirement of the learning support/resource teachers will revolve around the use of tests and individualised programmes. These skills in assessment and individualised programmes then become the learning support/resource teacher's modus operandi and they enter a cycle where their role is primarily conceived of as that of assessing students and withdrawal for segregated teaching. In this situation, both the role and the professional development inflate each other. Moreover, the focus on individual student deficit is further reinforced where access to additional resources (most often perceived as teaching hours for withdrawal) is linked to assessment by educational psychologists. Both the evidence required to support a request for an assessment and the psychologists' assessment itself are mainly based on the individualised diagnosis of the student's deficits. Less attention is paid to the teaching and learning environment within which the students receive their education. If learning support/resource teachers and psychologists have training primarily based on knowledge of a battery of tests, utilising their hard-earned skills of assessment may become the main focus of their role. Perhaps the roles of both the learning support/resource teachers and educational psychologists should be reconfigured to incorporate an analysis of teaching and learning environment and the dominant pedagogy in use. Such refocusing of learning support/resource teachers' roles should be embraced within their professional development. In adopting a proactive stance to exploring new ways of addressing the needs of all learners in the progress towards inclusion, the learning support/resource teacher must become an agent of change within the school community (Tangen, 2005). This facet of the role must be incorporated in the professional-development programmes on offer.

There is a need to divorce the concept of inclusion from its operationalisation as 'withdrawal', as found in this research and elsewhere (Kearns, 2005; Vlachou, 2006; Arnaiz & Castejon, 2001). The link equating special educational needs with special provision and withdrawal needs to be broken. The focus on extraction from the mainstream helps students work well in excluded setting but does little to prepare them to return to the mainstream setting where they will be for the majority of their school experience (Thomas & Loxley, 2007). Current research has indicated that there is little that is 'special' about special education (Davies & Florian, 2004; Lewis & Norwich, 2001, 2004) and that strategies that are particularly beneficial for students with SEN are also appropriate for the majority of students. Inclusive pedagogy, therefore, is best characterised as a cyclical process where mainstream, regular class teachers adopt a problem-solving approach to teaching the full cohort of student diversity, seeking best practice to the challenges of including all students and supported in this endeavour by the extended school community and education system.

Introducing a new element to schools, such as the inclusion of students with special educational needs, introduces change. Adapting to this change requires all teachers to engage in a professional learning process, not just the learning support/resource teachers. Ideally, this new learning will 'disrupt the default mode of schooling' (Johnston & Hayes, 2007) and will expand the school's capacity to include the diverse population that comprise society's citizens. The re-conceptualisation of the roles of both the general and learning support/resource teacher envisaged in an inclusive school will require considerable support from all levels of the education system. For mainstream teachers, this change will require them to undertake responsibility for all students in their classroom and, consequently, to adopt a more inclusive approach to pedagogy, engaging in a cyclical process of action research to adapt the curriculum to benefit all learners.

For learning support/resource specialist teachers, this change will require a revision of their role to undertake more collaborative and advisory functions and to develop new skills in leadership, teamwork, expertise in a range of pedagogical options and research skills to evaluate the effectiveness of innovations. This reconfigured remit of the learning support/resource teacher emphasises a liaison and advisory role which will reposition the teacher within the core school-management team.

This change in role will be both instigated and supported by a concomitant change in the professional development provided for learning support/resource teachers. The change will be from professional development which focuses primarily on developing expert learning support/resource teachers to professional development which includes the development of advisory skills, team building and managerial skills and will be linked with instructional pedagogy and developing research skills in collaborative enquiry.

RECOMMENDATIONS

In England, the SENCo role was envisaged as a pivotal post in the *National Standards for SENCos* (TTA, 1998) and in the *Revised Code of Practice on the Identification and Assessment of SEN* (DfES, 2001) with responsibility for the strategic direction and development of inclusive provision in the school and with implicit managerial and leadership functions. However, the potential of the role as an agent of change has been diminished in cases where the administrative and individualised aspects have taken precedence over the strategic dimensions of the role (Mackenzie, 2007) and the lack of progress towards a more inclusive education system has been disappointing.

Avoiding the setbacks experienced by our neighbouring jurisdiction should be a key target for professional development in SEN in Ireland. We are fortunate in Ireland to have substantial Department of Education and Science funded professional development postgraduate programmes for learning support/resource teachers. Programmes aimed at enhancing the skills, knowledge and confidence of the learning support/resource teachers should ensure that all facets of the *strategic* aspects should be included along with traditional elements of such courses. Learning support/resource teachers need to expand their experiential learning beyond the confines of individual focused, selective school functions, and plan their exposure to school leadership in all its forms (Kearns, 2005). To do this, they will need continual, external support and assistance in undertaking a programme of action research to assess the success and adaptations needed of new initiatives. Hence, leadership, managerial and team-building skills should be given equal emphasis to teaching, assessment and IEP-related skills. Furthermore, the continuing change inherent in the move towards inclusion should be reflected in a research-based approach to implementing inclusive practices and, consequently, skills in this area should become part of the learning support/resource teacher's repertoire through their engagement in professional development for SEN.

An interesting study by Clark, Dyson, Millward and Skidmore (1997) described distinct stages in the evolution of the SENCo role in England from one where the SENCo was responsible for all aspects of students with SEN to one where the responsibility is shared among the whole school staff. They posited that the SENCo role should progress towards self-obliteration as the ultimate goal. Smith and Barr (2008) developed this concept of the self-eliminating SENCo role further and this was expanded by O'Gorman, Drudy, Winter,

Smith and Barry (2009) to describe contrasts between the SENCo and learning support/resource teachers roles in the North and South of Ireland. Indeed, this notion of built-in obsolescence in the learning support/resource role as currently configured, has much to offer as an indicator of the inclusivity of a school. Professional development for learning support/resource teachers is the key to effecting this change of role. Without external guidance, there is a danger that the role would become self-perpetuating and stagnate in concept at a point where the learning support/resource teacher retains sole responsibility for the educational outcomes of all students identified with SEN.

A student-deficit-led model underpins the current structures of student support with withdrawal from the mainstream class or school being the preferred modus operandi. This has the outcome of attempting to assist students to jump over the barriers they face rather than breaking down these barriers to achievement, which is what true inclusion would entail (Lloyd, 2008). Professional development which is based solely on learning support/resource teachers' current requests for information on syndromes, student assessment and individualised planning will hamper the progress towards more inclusive systems. There is an urgent requirement to develop a more proactive approach to including students with SEN within the mainstream class and avoid an escalation of increased withdrawal and increased deployment of additional teaching resources to support exclusionary practices. Perhaps now that the monetary supports are no longer available to finance the incremental spiral of withdrawal, more revolutionary processes which reconstruct the regular classroom to provide education for all members of the nation's children will be initiated.

CONCLUSION

The findings from this research project help identify the professional development requirements of the mainstream learning support/resource primary and post-primary teachers who are responsible for an increasingly diverse range of students identified as having special educational needs. Current policy in SEN tends to focus on compensating for difficulties and enabling students to overcome barriers rather than dismantling the barriers they face (Lloyd, 2008). This is symptomatic of the failure to critique and challenge assumptions underlying SEN which consequently prevents change and enables dominant deficit discourses to prevail (Skrtic, 1991).

The move towards inclusive education is a moral and legislative responsibility and is currently espoused by Irish education policy. The adoption of inclusive education will not occur without professional development for teachers who have been familiar with segregated education provision. This professional development must be systematic, long-term and include critical reflection to induce the required change. The support of agencies both within and external to the school is essential to the development of an education system which welcomes and values diversity. The appointment of learning support/resource teachers to oversee the education of students identified with special needs must be accompanied by professional development to ensure that the role undertaken is one which de-emphasises withdrawal as the default mode of instruction and instead takes on a proactive role in supporting colleagues to adopt transformative practices in a bid to expand regular education. Thus, the professional development required by learning support/resource teachers emphasises the skills of collaborative enquiry, team building and leadership along with the traditional exploratory pedagogy and assessment aspects of the role. This professional development will enable the learning support/resource teacher contribute to the expertise of the school-management team in developing flexible approaches to general regular education for the benefit of all of our nation's children.

ENDNOTES

1   The chapter draws from an account of a large-scale research project that was conducted to explore the work of learning support and resource teachers in Ireland, part-funded by the National Council for Special Education (see O'Gorman & Drudy, 2009). The support of the NCSE for this study is gratefully acknowledged.

2   In order to obtain a probability sample with a 95 per cent confidence level and 5 per cent confidence interval, the random sample size for 3,290 schools was calculated at 344 using a computer software package. As a response rate of 45 per cent had been achieved in previous research, through sending 760 questionnaires it was anticipated that the target of 344 would be achieved. The 760 schools were selected through applying a computer-generated, random-number selection process to the Department of Education and Science database of primary schools.

14

PEDAGOGIES OF PRIVILEGE: RETHINKING INTERCULTURALISM AND ANTI-RACISM IN EDUCATION[1]

Audrey Bryan

This chapter draws on recent research examining teachers' understandings of diversity and racism and their experiences of teaching within ethnically and racially diverse settings. It considers the question of how teacher educators can prepare their students to understand and address issues of racism, inequality and discrimination in their own classrooms, and to work with culturally diverse student groups. The research is contextualised within a broader critique of intercultural educational approaches to diversity in education. The stated aim of intercultural education in Ireland is to contribute to the development of Ireland as an intercultural society (NCCA, 2006). The guidelines on interculturalism are premised on the notion of respecting and celebrating diversity, and developing empathy with those who are discriminated against. There is obviously a great deal to commend in such approaches. However, the approach adopted in this chapter seeks to develop an additional dimension: that of exploring a range of theoretical and pedagogical approaches which utilise 'whiteness' as an analytic tool to explore racism, anti-racism and diversity within teacher education. This alternative perspective conceptualises whiteness as a system of power relations which grants advantages or privileges to those racialised as white, while simultaneously disprivileging those who are racialised as black, Asian, and so on (Garner, 2007a).[2]

The immigration that accompanied the economic boom years of the Celtic Tiger era resulted in a newfound emphasis on interculturalism and anti-racism at multiple levels of Irish society, including schools. Interculturalism has also become the dominant paradigm where the education of indigenous minorities within Irish society are concerned, with guidelines on Traveller education, for example, stressing the need for an intercultural approach that 'validat[es] Traveller culture within the curriculum' (Department of Education & Science, 2002c, p. 39). Irish classrooms have become increasingly ethnically diverse:

about 10 per cent of all primary students, and 7 per cent of post-primary students from 160 countries are classified as 'migrant students' (Department of Education & Science, 2008b), and over 10,000 Traveller children are enrolled in school (Department of Education & Science, 2008c, p. 39). However, this ethnic diversity is not mirrored in the teaching profession or in the profile of teacher candidates (Gannon, 2009). This asymmetry raises important questions about what it means to be a white, settled teacher in classrooms which are increasingly ethnically and/or racially diverse. The chapter makes the case for anti-racist approaches within teacher education which provide spaces for teacher candidates to interrogate their own racial-ethnic identities, as well as their pre-existing assumptions, beliefs and knowledge regarding 'race', racism and racialised minority students (Soloman et al., 2005).

The chapter is organised as follows. I begin by offering a brief outline of some of the main features of the whiteness perspective which serves as the analytic framework for the chapter as a whole, and providing an overview of recent educational responses to the increasingly ethnically diverse nature of Irish schools and society. Next, I present a critique of recent state-sanctioned models of intercultural education that are advanced as a means of alleviating racism, and present key findings from recent research examining teachers' understandings of diversity and racism and their experiences of teaching within ethnically and racially diverse settings. I argue that the combined emphasis on celebrating diversity and enabling individuals to develop empathy with those who are discriminated against within the intercultural education paradigm does not lend itself to an interrogation of the ways in which celebrating and empathetic subjects benefit from, and are themselves implicated in, reproducing patterns of racial inequality. In other words, intercultural education privileges an understanding of racism as a problem affecting racialised minorities that can be reduced through increased contact and empathy with, and celebration of, Others. However, an examination of the privileges whiteness bestows upon whites themselves, and how it impacts negatively on those who are racialised, is obscured by this celebratory/empathising approach (Garner, 2007a; McIntosh, 1990). The analysis highlights the need for critical engagement with the racialised dynamics of power and privilege within teacher-education programmes in Ireland. The chapter concludes with implications and specific pedagogical strategies for teacher educators who seek to cultivate in their students and themselves the skills to critically reflect upon their assumptions, beliefs and knowledge about 'race,' racism and racialised minorities in schools and society.

THE WHITENESS PARADIGM

Recent years have witnessed increased prioritisation of, as well as financial support for, a host of interrelated 'adjectival educations' within teacher education, including inclusive education, human-rights education, citizenship education and development education. These initiatives, which are sanctioned by government bodies, such as Irish Aid and the Department of Education and Science (DES), provide opportunities for teacher educators to engage students with issues of diversity, anti-racism, equity and inclusion.

Existing research carried out in geographical contexts with much longer histories of multicultural education, such as the United States, suggests that student teachers tend to experience high levels of discomfort when discussions of oppression, marginalisation, colonisation, racism and alternative ideologies, etc. are initiated (Solomon et al., 2005). Such discomfort stems from the fact that student teachers are typically members of dominant cultural groups (e.g. in an Irish context, white, Irish, settled, Catholic), and this information presents an inevitable challenge to their reality system and knowledge base, resulting in feelings of vulnerability, guilt, indignation, uncertainty, anger and paralysis. Solomon et al. (2005) stress that in preparing teachers to work in multicultural classrooms and against racism, teacher educators must work with students to understand their own racial identity formation and provide the learning space to work with the range of emotions and feelings that may evolve from exposure to 'thorny' ideas like white privilege. Although much of the existing whiteness literature has focused on the dynamics of racism in North America, the relevance of, and growth of interest in, whiteness within Europe, and the Irish context more specifically, has recently been demonstrated (e.g. Garner, 2007a, 2007b).

The concept of 'white privilege' focuses on the historical construction of whiteness as the dominant and unquestionable centre and invisible norm in society, and an associated set of unearned assets or social advantages which benefit whites in their daily lives but to which they remain largely oblivious. Peggy McIntosh (1990), one of the architects of the concept of white privilege, argues:

> As a white person, I realised I had been taught about racism as something that puts others at a disadvantage, but had been taught not to see one of its corollary aspects, white privilege, which puts me at an advantage. I think

whites are carefully taught not to recognise white privilege, as males are taught not to recognise male privilege.

McIntosh, 1990, p. 1

The need to engage with issues of whiteness and its associated privileges within the context of teacher education poses significant challenges for teacher educators who wish to engage their students with issues of racial inequality, particularly within the context of initial teacher-education programmes where an already 'overcrowded' curriculum means that opportunities to engage with anti-racism issues in a sustained and meaningful way are limited. Nevertheless, teacher education constitutes an important site for engaging with notions of white privilege and its detrimental effects on racialised Others.

RACISM IN THE IRISH CONTEXT

The need to carve out effective spaces for teaching against racism within teacher education, and schools more generally, is all the more pertinent when one considers the available evidence about rising levels of racial hostility that have occurred in Irish society in recent years. As the Irish population rapidly became more ethnically diverse in the late 1990s and 2000s, evidence of growing anti-immigrant sentiment became apparent, exemplified by sensationalist media reports which depicted immigrants, refugees and asylum seekers in a predominantly negative and stereotypical light (e.g. Devereux, et al., 2005). Eurobarometer polls designed to measure levels of racism and xenophobia in European member states were carried out in 1997 and 2000 and provide evidence of rising levels of hostility towards minority groups during the Celtic Tiger era. Whereas in 1997, 16 per cent of Irish respondents agreed that the presence of people from minority groups offered grounds for insecurity, three years later, the percentage of those who agreed with that view had increased to 42 per cent (Thalhammer et al., 2001). Moreover, the proportion agreeing that it is a good thing for society to be made up of people from different 'races', religions and cultures fell from 76 per cent in 1997 to 61 per cent in 2000 (ibid.). While the results of the 2000 study showed that, on the whole, Irish respondents were similar to other Europeans in their attitudes to minorities, there were a number of responses indicative of more negative perceptions. For example, on the question of whether minority groups receive preferential treatment by the authorities, this perception was most widespread in Ireland (48 per cent), compared with a European average of 33 per cent. Meanwhile, only 32 per cent of the Irish sample thought that minority groups enriched cultural life in Ireland, against a European average of 50 per cent.

Against this backdrop, the education system—and intercultural education in particular—has come to be viewed as 'one of the key responses to the changing shape of Irish society and to the existence of racism and discriminatory attitudes in Ireland' (NCCA, 2005, p. 17). A host of educational materials and guidelines has been produced by various statutory and non-statutory agencies in recent years, focused on opportunities for the inclusion of intercultural applications in classroom contexts. Most notably, perhaps, the National Council for Curriculum and Assessment (NCCA) published intercultural guidelines for both primary and secondary schools, which focus on 'mediat[ing] and adapt[ing] the existing curricula to reflect the emergence of a more culturally diverse society in Ireland' (Department of Justice, Equality & Law Reform, 2005, p. 110). These guidelines promote intercultural education as a means of underscoring '… the normality of diversity in all parts of human life' (NCCA, 2006, p. i). Intercultural education is believed to 'help prevent racism' by enabling students to 'develop positive emotional responses to diversity and an empathy with those discriminated against' as well as enabling them to 'recognise and challenge discrimination and prejudice' (NCCA, 2005, p. 21). As such, intercultural education is deemed 'one of the key responses to the changing shape of Irish society and to the existence of racism and discriminatory attitudes in Ireland' (ibid., p. 17).

The remainder of this chapter offers a critical analysis of state-sanctioned approaches to the alleviation of racism, and draws on discrete, yet related, research projects that offer insights into both in-career and novice teachers' understandings of diversity and racism and their experiences of teaching within ethnically and racially diverse settings.

METHODOLOGY

The findings on in-career teachers' understandings and experiences of teaching in ethnically diverse settings presented below are drawn from a larger study combining discourse analysis and ethnographic methods to link micro-events at the level of the school with the broader macro-structural context of racism and anti-racism in Ireland. Methodologically, the study combined a critical discourse analysis of policy documents and curriculum materials, as well as observations of classroom and school events and in-depth interviews over a 12-month period at a large, co-educational, ethnically diverse school located in a middle-class suburb of Dublin, which I have called Blossom Hill College (BHC). Adopting a policy of 'positive interculturalism', BHC has been identified as a model of 'best practice' in 'promoting inclusivity, interculturalism and equality', and approximately 10 per cent of its student body is 'international'.[3] To elucidate the perspective of those in initial teacher education, the study also draws on more recent qualitative and quantitative research exploring teachers' perceptions and understandings of diversity, social justice and international development (Bryan et al., 2009).

'Do I just read the novel?'

Existing research on immigration and education carried out during the Celtic Tiger era suggests that teachers experienced uncertainty and anxiety about how to cope with the additional demands placed upon them as a result of rapid immigration during this period (Devine, 2005). At BHC, some teachers expressed similar levels of discomfort and uncertainty about how best to address issues of 'race' and racism in their classrooms, as well as concern about the negative impact this might be having on their students. Miss Kearns[4] described the uneasiness she felt during English lessons when working with students on a prescribed text that explicitly addressed the theme of racism:

> I am in there as their [the students'] English teacher, and there are some children that are black, if you are from Africa, but the word 'nigger' is used in the novel [*Roll of Thunder, Hear my Cry*]. And I often say to myself, 'Do I stand here for 10 minutes talking about, you know, that this is a time and a place outside of Ireland and we must respect one another and [protect] human rights and so forth, or do I just take the novel and read the novel?

Miss Kearns expressed her uncertainty and discomfort as part of a broader concern about the lack of 'multicultural training' she had received as a teacher working in a multicultural school; in particular, she was critical of the English Department's failure to engage teaching staff in dialogue about how best to handle the presence of racist terminology and racism themes in prescribed texts from the English syllabus, despite the presence of racialised minority students in the school.

But you have got children who are part of that race, of that ethnic group and you can often feel uncomfortable with it, and I feel as the English Department, we have never addressed that issue. Each year we pick up the novel, we go into class, prepare the students, the students do really well in the exam, next year a new class come into us, we regurgitate our notes. And I was talking about this with a colleague of mine about a month ago, and I was just saying how uneasy I feel about that. I haven't had training, and I don't know how uneasy the children feel about it, or if it is influencing the children, and it is just very, very dangerous.

Comments like these underscore the need for pedagogical interventions that can equip teachers with the tools and vocabulary to enable them to address and engage with issues of racism in their classrooms. If teachers feel ill-prepared in such contexts, they may be reluctant to tackle, or they may avoid discussion about, racist discourse and practices, and/or, may engage in teaching practices that are damaging for minority students (Picower, 2009).

'Culture shock'

Miss Kearns' feelings of uncertainly and discomfort stemmed in part from the fact that the presence of racialised minorities at BHC posed a significant challenge to her prior experience and understanding of Irish classrooms as spaces occupied by white (non-Muslim) students.

> I have to be honest … I came here [to BHC] in the year 2000. I had never taught a black child, I had never taught a Muslim. I had only ever taught Irish [sic] children, and maybe American children, and I walked into this school and I was just spellbound, trying to get used to [the idea of] what does that mean to teach a Muslim with … Ramadan and things like that … and it was a culture shock to me.

Miss Kearns' account of the culture shock she experienced when she first began teaching at BHC is noteworthy in terms of its implication that white (non-Muslim) students represent the norm in Irish classrooms, and the extent to which the presence of 'black' and/or 'Muslim' children disrupts the perceived normality of these previously 'white' spaces. Devine (2005) argues that teacher attitudes towards immigrant children in an Irish context are underpinned by a particular conceptualisation of Irish and national identity which positions minority-ethnic groups as Other. The statement 'I had never taught a black child, I had never taught a Muslim. I had only ever taught Irish children', is indicative of how whiteness serves as the unconsciousness benchmark from which other identities are constructed as deviant. The conflation of an unmarked whiteness (not being black) with Irishness (or Americanness), in this instance, implicitly positions black and/or Muslim children as not Irish, and hence, Other in Irish schools.

Contrary to the ways in which racial-ethnic minority students are portrayed as Other within teacher discourses, recognising 'the normality of diversity in all parts of human life', and reconfiguring Irish national identity around a *civic*, rather than an *ethnic*, ideal are two of the central tenets of the intercultural project in education (NCCA, 2006, p. 1). Intercultural education is thus geared towards fostering more inclusive (civic as opposed to ethnically nationalist) versions of Irish identity and the normalisation and celebration of diversity, but this goal is compromised and complicated for a host of reasons, not least of which is that the intercultural educational dimensions of the curriculum are essentially an 'add-and-stir' approach that seek to accommodate change without altering the existing curriculum to any significant extent (Bryan, 2008). Drawing on a corpus of recently published policy documents, and curriculum materials currently being used in Irish secondary schools, I examined the ways in which instructional materials problematically, if unwittingly, abnormalise diversity in Irish society and actually re-inscribe narrow and restrictive, ethnically nationalist versions of Irishness (ibid.). This suggests that a radical revision of the existing curriculum is necessary if the intercultural goal of viewing diversity as normal is to be realised, and highlights the need for pedagogies that critically interrogate whiteness as the 'natural, inevitable ordinary way of being human' (Dyer, 1988, p. 44).

'Celebrating diversity'

Another dimension of the intercultural project which warrants critical scrutiny, given its increasing centrality within educational discourse, is how the celebration of diversity is practised in schools. Efforts to celebrate cultural diversity, such as 'world food days' and 'variety show' performances of music, song, dance, costumes and so on from around the world, have become commonplace in schools in an Irish context as a means of embracing and enacting intercultural principles, as the following quotation from a student teacher reveals.

Shortly after St Patrick's Day last year, the school principal decided to hold an intercultural week in the school to celebrate the cultures and countries where the non-national [sic] children were inherited from. This was an excellent example of good practice that I have experienced in my career to date. The whole week was a success with teachers preparing lessons about different cultures and traditions around the world.

While this novice teacher viewed this intercultural celebration as an effective way of building cultural awareness, once again, it reveals a tendency amongst teachers to rhetorically and/or symbolically position minority students as Other. The intercultural event in question pertained exclusively to the celebration of the 'cultures and countries' of 'non-national' students, which has the effect of inscribing an 'us'/'them' dichotomy, wherein 'their' nationalities and cultures are marked separately from St Patrick's Day, i.e. separately from the celebration of the Irish 'nation'. When special intercultural events of this nature fall outside the core of school practice and curriculum, they can be seen to reproduce the very marginality they are designed to overcome (Perry, 2002). Furthermore, the term 'non-national[s]' (prevalent within Irish political and educational discourse) casts racialised minorities as territorial Others and rhetorically excludes them from any sense of belonging, or being part of, the Irish nation.

The intercultural educational guidelines produced by the NCCA do highlight the need to ensure 'that representations of minority groups do not focus on the spectacular or colourful events, as this may lead to stereotyping and may counteract the desire to represent diversity as normal' (NCCA, 2006, p. 29). Nevertheless, they encourage schools to put on 'special event[s] or awareness day[s] to celebrate diversity in the school' (ibid., p. 64) and activities to mark 'the calendars of a diversity of cultures' (ibid., p. 27). It is difficult to see how 'colourful' displays of minority culture are to be avoided at such events, wherein complex histories and cultural traditions are reduced to 'special' days, while white, Irish, settled culture and history remain the dominant and unmarked features of the curriculum.

More fundamentally, the very discourse of 'respecting,' 'celebrating,' 'valuing' and 'appreciating' diversity is problematic because it has the effect of denying the possibility of a national 'we', which is, itself, diverse (see Ang, 1996; Bryan, 2009; Hage, 1998). In this vein, Hage (2008) offers a useful critique of the equality of recognition paradigm which forms the philosophical backdrop to dominant models of multiculturalism. He argues that to the extent that recognition always involves a recognis*er* and a recognis*ed*—i.e. a 'subject' who does the recognising and an 'object' who is recognised—true equality cannot be achieved. Rather than promoting equality, then, celebratory interculturalism and models of inclusion based on recognition reinforce the privileged status of culturally dominant groups within society by positioning them as the 'embracer' or 'recogniser' of difference, who get to decree the acceptability (or otherwise) of the ethnic Other.

'Building awareness of other cultures' and 'getting to know each other'

The research also revealed a widespread belief amongst novice and in-career teachers that celebratory events that involved people from different ethnic backgrounds coming together to learn about each other's cultures had an important role to play in combating racism. As one student teacher explained, the school where she taught hosted celebratory events to raise 'awareness of other cultures' in an effort to combat racism.

> Teachers in my … school celebrated ethnic differences … by hosting a trip around the world week at the beginning of the school year. … Racism is often built on assumptions and this was a way of building awareness of other cultures, through which [the school] hoped to dispel any myths.

Activities and events to recognise and celebrate cultural diversity were also commonplace at BHC. Some teachers and administrators perceived these celebratory interventions as crucial to the school's anti-racist efforts. Miss Jones, the teacher with responsibility for co-ordinating the school's intercultural programme, explained that contact between members of different groups had the potential to change racist attitudes and beliefs.

> I think the only way that we are possibly going to change [racist attitudes] is by having people together, getting people together. So, for instance, we are organising an Afro-Caribbean evening. … So I think in ways like that, we get to know each other.

While interpersonal relations may indeed have the potential to reduce racist attitudes and behaviours, in the absence of any consideration of the broader social processes, institutions and structures that help to create and sustain racial oppression, the 'contact hypothesis' (Allport, 1954) restricts the nature and causes of racism to the realm of individual ignorance and misunderstanding that can be combated through greater 'contact' with the Other (Connolly, 2000).

Results from a quantitative survey of student teachers' attitudes towards, and understandings of, diversity and social justice indicated that over 80 per cent 'strongly agreed' or 'agreed' that racism is primarily the result of ignorance and a lack of understanding of other cultures (Bryan et al., 2009). The belief that racism is primarily a question of individual ignorance and lack of understanding implies a failure to recognise whiteness as a privileged social location and precludes analysis of issues of power, dominance and oppression. As Garner (2007a) maintains: 'understanding how [whiteness as a system of privilege] works, not just to disadvantage people who are not white, but to benefit those who are, requires thinking beyond individual opinions and into the realm of institutionalised, patterned and structural inequality' (ibid., p. 39).

Nor does the 'feel good' factor associated with recognising, respecting and celebrating diversity lend itself to a consideration of the dynamics of power and privilege that are central to racism, or the ways in which cultural dominants are favoured by, and implicated in, reproducing these dynamics (Solomon et al., 2005). The existing intercultural framework, to the extent that it focuses on the celebration of difference, and is firmly rooted in a focus on 'other' cultures, does not lend itself to a consideration of what privileges whiteness bestows upon whites themselves, and how it impacts negatively on those who are racialised as other than white (Garner, 2007a; McIntosh, 1990).

'Empathy with those who are discriminated against'

Helping students to develop empathy with those who are discriminated against is another major feature of intercultural education and is viewed as one of the key means by which intercultural education can 'help [to] alleviate racism' (NCCA, 2006). One of the difficulties with this approach to anti-racism is that it ensures that cultural dominants' awareness of inequality is grounded in Others' experiences of discrimination and not their own experiences of privilege, thereby reinforcing the view of racism as a problem affecting Others and not as something which is tied to whiteness itself (Pence & Fields, 1999). The focus on empathy within intercultural education is, therefore, a weak basis for anti-racism because, unless it becomes a step towards confronting injustice, it does not adequately address how the empathetic subject is implicated in another's oppression. Rather, it constructs the Other as an object of benevolence (Jefferes, 2008), thereby serving a redemptive function for the empathiser who comes to identify with the racialised Other and his or her experiences of discrimination (Roman, 1997).

IMPLICATIONS FOR ANTI-RACIST TEACHER EDUCATION

The foregoing analysis suggests that interculturalism's combined focus on respecting and celebrating diversity and helping students to develop empathy with those who experience discrimination and prejudice needs to be augmented by critical reflection on the unearned benefits and advantages associated with whiteness or to deep understanding of the destructive impact of white privilege on those who lack these 'naturalised entitlements' (Shore & Halliday-Wynes, 2006, p. 2). The focus on Others ensures that cultural dominants' awareness of inequality is grounded in *their* experiences of discrimination and not in one's own experiences of privilege (Pence & Fields, 1999). This failure to engage with privileged groups' own complicity in perpetuating racial inequality is reflective of a broader tendency within teacher education to avoid especially 'controversial' subjects, or to embrace 'soft' as opposed to more critical versions of social justice, for fear of alienating, disengaging or paralysing students from taking action (Andreotti, 2006). Indeed, some educators have identified a tendency for white students to 'resist' whiteness pedagogy, i.e. to deflect or distance themselves from critical engagement with systems of racial privilege (e.g. Hytten & Warren, 2003; Picower, 2009; Solomon et al., 2005). These tendencies highlight the complexities associated with 'doing' critical anti-racist work, challenges which are compounded by the overloaded nature of the curriculum.

While some degree of resistance to more critical versions of anti-racism may be unavoidable, the danger of adopting 'softer', more sanitised versions of anti-racism is that teachers are likely to emerge from their teacher preparation or professional-development programmes with superficial understandings of racism and to embrace pedagogical approaches that reinforce, rather than challenge, the privileged status of culturally dominant groups within society. Instead, teacher education needs to expose students to a range of alternative critical theoretical perspectives and pedagogical strategies that will enable them to interrogate their own positionality as a function of historical and contemporary inequalities (Heyer, den, 2009). This kind of identity work cannot be achieved through isolated, one-off, 'add-and-stir'-type lectures and seminars on 'race' and ethnicity, but rather demands the forging of curricular and pedagogical spaces that enable sustained and critical interrogation of constructs like whiteness, privilege and the socially constructed nature of 'race', as well as an exploration of the ideologies with which student teachers enter the classroom, and how these ideologies impact on their teaching practices and their interactions with students (Solomon et al., 2005, p. 149).

Theoretical perspectives which lend themselves to a consideration of more critical versions of anti-racism include, but are not limited to: whiteness studies; cultural studies; critical race theory (CRT); post-structural theory; post-colonial theory; and critical pedagogy. While space considerations do not permit elaboration of these discrete, yet at times overlapping frameworks, collectively they can be said to examine the larger socio-historical contexts that cause injustices like racism and theorise whiteness not as a racial category but rather as a socially constructed ideology that has been used to legitimise historical injustices like colonialism and slavery, as well as contemporary forms of racial inequality and exploitation.

Pedagogically speaking, Solomon et al. (2005) identify a range of areas that should be addressed in the education of white teachers in preparing them to work with diverse student groups, as well as addressing issues of racism, inequality and discrimination. These include the importance of prior knowledge of the teacher candidates, providing spaces within the programme wherein which they can address their questions and concerns, preparing them for the range of emotions they may experience, and providing concrete strategies for including anti-discrimination practices in their classrooms.

Within the 'confined spaces' of programmes in initial teacher education, Peggy McIntosh's article 'White Privilege: Unpacking the Invisible Knapsack' (McIntosh, 1990) can be used as an entry point for conversations about white privilege and the ways in which racism is embedded within routine experiences that make up our daily lives (Shore & Halliday-Wynes, 2006). Whiteness can also be introduced as one of a number of interlocking social identities, or *systems of privilege* (Garner, 2007a)—including gender, ethnicity, sexual orientation, social class, dis/abilty, etc.—which are often covered in some depth within sociology of education and inclusive education modules within teacher-education programmes.

Analysing racism through the lens of white privilege is a useful tool to explore both the personal as well as the structural dimensions of racism. At the systemic or structural level, the privilege paradigm seeks to promote deeper understanding of the historical, economic and cultural processes through which whiteness is forged, and of the destructive impact of privilege on those who are not racialised as white. At the level of the individual, the utility of whiteness as an analytic tool lies not in its capacity to encourage or indeed ultimately alleviate 'white guilt' among teachers, but rather in its potential to provide a foundation for more informed classroom practice by promoting critical reflection on how this practice is influenced—often unconsciously—by our expectations, assumptions and unexplored biases regarding racialised majority as well as minority students.

One pedagogical device that has been identified as both an engaging and productive means of examining the impact of these ideologies on classroom practice is the analysis of popular representations of 'race' and racism in contemporary popular culture (see e.g. Giroux, 1997; Trier, 2005). Working with film and related media provides a creative space within which to explore the extent to which our understandings of what it means to be white, black, Asian, etc. are replete with assumptions and how these assumptions might impact on our interactions with students who belong to these racially ascribed categories (Solomon et al., 2005). Popular films, such as *Crash, Freedom Writers, Dangerous Minds* and *Bend it like Beckham,* which invoke 'race' and ethnicity, have been used as a basis for interrogating how students see themselves, Others and the larger society they inhabit (Giroux, 1997). Recently released European 'school films', such as *The Class*, which focuses on teacher–student interactions in a multi-ethnic Parisian secondary school, or scenes from Season 4 of *The Wire,* which focuses on the Baltimore city public-school system in the United States, could also be used as stimuli with both pre- and in-service teachers to interrogate such themes as power, discipline and teacher/societal expectations about racialised minority/immigrant youth.

Trier (2003, 2005) documents strategies for engaging pre-service teachers in theoretical explorations of issues related to 'race' and power that involve reading academic and popular culture texts simultaneously. Viewing films through the lens of the theoretical constructs explained in academic texts enables students to derive multiple interpretations of the information and messages on the screen or indeed to develop 'oppositional readings' that resist the problematic representations that many of these Hollywood or related productions promote (Trier, 2005, p. 184).

These theoretical and pedagogical approaches to teaching against 'race' and racism within the context of teacher education are by no means a panacea to the ongoing problem of racism in Irish schools and society. However, they do serve as an important corrective to versions of interculturalism which mute genuine possibilities for transformation and ensure that existing racialised patterns of domination and exclusion remain intact.

ENDNOTES

1   I would like to acknowledge the generous support of a President's Grant for Student Research in Diversity and a Dean's Grant for Student Research, from Teachers College, Columbia University, a Spencer Foundation Research Training Grant, an Interdisciplinary PhD Conflict Resolution Research Award, from Columbia University, and an Ubuntu project (Teacher Education for Sustainable Development) Action Research award, in facilitating the conduct of this research. I would also like to thank Melíosa Bracken, Sheelagh Drudy, Andy Storey and an anonymous reviewer for their helpful comments on an earlier version of this chapter.

2   I use the term 'racialised' when referring to minority groups, to denote that 'race' is a social construction, namely that 'races' do not naturally exist, but rather become real only as a result of human beliefs and practices (Montgomery, 2005).

3   The source of this quotation is not provided to protect the identity of the school. The term 'international students' was typically applied to ethnic and/or linguistic minority students at BHC, irrespective of how long they had lived in Ireland or whether or not they had Irish citizenship.

4   The names of all those who took part in the research are pseudonyms.

15

CONSTRUCTIVISM AND THE TEACHING OF SCIENCE EDUCATORS

Paul McElwee

INTRODUCTION

Ireland has recognised the need for developing a knowledge-based economy (Government of Ireland, 2006). Scientific knowledge is seen as an essential ingredient in order to sustain continuing development. In international comparisons of scientific literacy, Ireland ranks average in relation to other OECD (Organisation for Economic Co-operation and Development) countries (OECD, 2007b). While such comparisons can be made easily, they often fail to take into account the many variables that can give rise to such differences. These variables can include the types of school provided in each country, the type of curriculum, the education of teachers and the continuing professional development of teachers. One aspect of note that has emerged from an analysis of one of the highest scorers in scientific literacy (Finland) is that its teacher education is based on the cognitive sciences and is underpinned by research into teaching and learning (Pehkonen et al., 2007). Schoen and Fusarelli (2008) have argued that an information-based society requires teachers to be able to employ constructivism[1] and teach students to use their minds. While there are arguments for and against such an approach, it will be considered here that adoption of a constructivist approach satisfies certain criteria in relation to the teaching of science.

Constructivism reflects the human and contextual dimensions of scientific discovery identified through an analysis of the history of science; it addresses the claim that students often get through science courses without a proper understanding of fundamental concepts. Despite epistemological arguments against it, constructivism reflects the nature of the process of scientific discovery and, lastly, it engages students in an active way that motivates them to become scientifically literate. Empirical research needs to be carried out on the validity of such claims particularly in relation to the transformation of a constructivist theory of learning to a constructivist pedagogy and research findings need to be incorporated into teacher-education courses.

TYPES OF KNOWLEDGE FOR THE KNOWLEDGE ECONOMY

To many scientists and science educators, constructivism is anathema while, to others, it is the most influential theory of learning in science (Fensham, 1994; Bentley, 1998). Those who object to constructivism (Solomon, 1994) often do so because of the relativistic view it places on scientific knowledge which contrasts with the realist view of an objective reality to be uncovered by the scientific enterprise (Osborne, 1996). For some, scientific knowledge consists of the accumulated objective knowledge derived by the constant testing of theories against the reality of nature. Then, when hypotheses are proven (or not), another nugget is added to the cumulative store. This is reflected in the textbooks that make up the testimony of the various disciplines. Such an epistemology has a certain consequence for the teaching of science: namely, that an emphasis is placed on knowledge content alone (often referred to as 'product') to the detriment of knowledge as the 'process' of science, e.g. how hypotheses can be generated and tested in valid ways.

The Programme for International Student Assessment (PISA) is a triennial survey of the knowledge and skills of 15-year-old students and is organised with participating countries through the OECD. The 2006 PISA study of scientific literacy across 57 countries makes a similar argument for regarding scientific knowledge as both product and process.

> Knowledge of science. This entailed an understanding of fundamental concepts and theories in core scientific areas. [...]
>
> Knowledge about science. This included understanding the purposes and nature of scientific enquiry and understanding scientific explanations, which are the results of scientific enquiry.
>
> OECD, 2007, p. 12

Any argument put forward for the development of a knowledge economy must take into account the different forms of scientific knowledge. The 2006 government report *Strategy for Science, Technology and Innovation 2006–2013* (Government of Ireland, 2006) suggests that if Ireland aspires to build a sustainable knowledge economy, then strong foundations must be laid in primary and second-level science education. In recognising this, it suggests (Chapter 5) that there needs to be a rebalancing of the science curriculum in the direction of problem solving, i.e. rebalancing product and process in science. This has also been emphasised by Schoen and Fusarelli (2008) in their argument for change in content, curriculum and instruction for the 21st century. A consequence of this is that this view of knowledge as both product and process will require transformation into a pedagogy that reflects it. The report, therefore, proposes investment in continuous professional development and networks for teachers. Putting new wine into old skins is not the way forward for teacher education because, as Prawat (1992) points out, the beliefs teachers hold about the teaching process are hard to change. Critical reflection is necessary for any proposed theories, including constructivism.

CONSTRUCTIVISM AND SCIENCE

One of the difficulties of defining constructivism lies in the fact that it means different things to different people. Larochelle, Bednarz and Garrison (1998) describe constructivism as an umbrella term for a variety of approaches to learning. Mistakenly, some commentators (Matthews, 1998; Osborne, 1996) describe constructivism as an epistemology rather than a theory of learning whose roots lie in cognitive psychology. Others use constructivism to refer to methods of teaching, but a difficulty with this is that a theory of learning does not automatically describe a theory of teaching (Jenkins, 2000). Essentially, constructivism means that learners approach any new learning task not with an empty mind but with a mind already populated with theories, ideas, beliefs and wild guesses (constructs) about the way things happen and events unfold. Failure to recognise this from a teaching viewpoint, according to constructivists, will result in a failure on the part of the learner to understand fully, resulting in the many reported misconceptions in science (see below). A constructivist view of learning sees the learner building understanding by imposing meaning on the world. Constructivism is concerned with the way someone makes sense of things and attempts to foster a deeper understanding. Margaret Donaldson in her book *Children's Minds* (1978) refers to the personal constructs held by the learner as akin to having a model or map of the world by which one steers a course through life.

In this way we build up a model of the world—a kind of system of inner representations the value of which is to help us to anticipate events and be ready to deal with them.

Donaldson, 1978, p. 68

Understanding of reality is, in the first instance, personal and contextual (Burns et al., 1991). Failure to understand this from a teaching point of view is to miss the opportunity of building on a rich tapestry of personal meaning through elaboration and exploration. This is a point also made by Nickerson (1985) when he argues that students often manage to successfully get through science courses without a full understanding of some of the fundamental concepts that go to make up the science subjects.

One of the difficulties in applying a constructivist approach in the classroom is the difficulty in identifying children's constructs of the world. The time necessary to do this is considered an impediment when teachers are faced with teaching a fixed curriculum (Millar, 1989). Jenkins (2000) has suggested that constructivism is best suited to teaching science at primary level. One approach that enables the teacher to identify students' constructs is to allow them to predict what is going to happen in an experiment or demonstration.

The cognitive foundations to this can be traced to the work of George Kelly (1955) who put forward the idea of Personal Construct Psychology (PCP) where he asserts that a person's cognitive processes are psychologically directed (he uses the word 'channelized') by the ways he anticipates events (Bannister & Fransella, 1993). In other words, we bring to every learning situation personal and contextual ideas or constructs that enable us to anticipate what will occur. The idea of anticipation and prediction is also contained in Bruner's idea of 'surprise'. Surprise occurs when the unexpected happens. A phenomenon or event is unexpected when the model used to interpret the world fails because it does not predict accurately. The element of surprise enables us to '… probe what people take for granted. It provides a window on presupposition: surprise is a response to violated presupposition' (Bruner, 1986, p. 46).

Piaget was the original personal constructivist. A Piagetian view (Bliss, 1993) sees constructivism as a result of the process of adaptation caused by disequilibrium between schemata and discrepant sensory information. Disequilibrium is the surprise experienced by learners when something unexpected happens and can be harnessed to motivate students. The pedagogical transformation of this idea is 'cognitive-conflict'. This latter aspect has been adopted by some researchers as a crucial aspect of any attempt to make constructivism a useful pedagogical tool for science educators (Baviskar et al., 2009).

Von Glasersfeld (1996) has been a seminal theorist in advocating constructivism in science education. He has promoted a radical constructivism that ascribes a validity to personal constructs because of their viability in terms of understanding and navigating in the world. This emphasis on multiple viable personal realities runs contrary to those who hold that there are such things as 'truth' and 'objective reality' in science. Such realists, who include Suchting (1992), Osborne (1996) and Matthews (1998), argue against the relativistic position of constructivism in science education because science does produce laws which can be proven. Thus Newton's idea of F=ma (the force on an object is proportional to its mass and acceleration) is independent of the personal views of the observer. According to Bruner (1986), science attempts to make a world that remains invariant across human intentions and human plights. Galileo's view is that the book of nature is written in the language of mathematics. Thus, epistemologically, constructivism is considered by some to be unsound and is based on the philosophico-pathology of relativism (Grandy, 1998). Radical constructivists do not see this as a problem because all constructs, be they personal or scientific, have a validity within the context of a given situation. That science actually consistently works in our present society of mobile phones and computers is proof enough of its objectivity and freedom from personal constructions. Science looks for the rules that underpin the universe and should, according to Matthews (1998), not be distracted by constructivist views. This is a point addressed by Jenkins (2000) when he queries whether constructivism in science education is a most dangerous intellectual tendency. He makes the point that 'the notion of the mind actively constructing knowledge does not, for example, lead in any logical way to a rejection of the world as an external reality' (Jenkins, 2000, p. 601).

As already stated, constructivism is a theory of learning which has developed with advances in cognitive psychology particularly the importance of knowledge structures in the process of learning (Vosniadou, 1996). It does not lay claim to an epistemology although its origins can be traced to Immanuel Kant (1724–1804) who put forward in his critique of pure reason (as separate from knowledge derived from the senses) the idea the mind imposes spatial, temporal and causal order on the world in order to bring coherence and structure to thought and action. 'Space and time are modifications of our sensibility; forms which we project upon the world; forms according to which our minds construct the world' (Wilkerson, 1976, p. 28). Kant's work (Kant, translated by Kemp-Smith, 1929) is crucial in marrying the contrasting epistemologies of rationalism and empiricism in science and in linking the ideas that knowledge can be derived solely by collecting data from nature or by imposing ideas on nature without recourse to empirical testing (Brittan, 1978).

According to Kant, we anticipate nature. This idea of anticipation could be considered a psychological argument rather than an epistemological one, just as Hume's argument against induction could also be considered as psychological, and frees us, as science educators, to validly consider constructivism as a useful tool in learning while allowing at the same time an objective realist view of the world. Popper (1972) said that Kant was right when he said that our intellect imposes its laws on nature, except that he did not notice how often our intellect fails in the attempt. Nola (1998) argues that while the regularities imposed may be psychologically 'a priori',[2] there is no reason to suppose that they are, in fact, a priori valid from a realist viewpoint. However, the history of scientific discoveries shows how science attempts to make psychological a priori constructs a priori from a realist viewpoint.

PERSONAL AND OBJECTIVE KNOWLEDGE: HISTORY OF SCIENCE

Carey (1985) has argued that the change from personal to scientific in a learner is mirrored in this process where historically one scientific concept is replaced by another which better explains and predicts the natural world. This is not a simple process and just as there may be difficulties in changing concepts in science, despite empirical evidence, there is a similar reluctance in learners to change from the useful constructs developed by them to explain and predict the world they live in. This point was put by Thomas Kuhn in his book *The Structure of Scientific Revolutions* (1962) where he argued that anomalies to an existing paradigm or set of constructs are often ignored so that the paradigm, to which scientists have committed themselves, is preserved.

How, then, do the personal constructs of scientists become the objective knowledge of science? Turning to the history of science, such as outlined by James Conant in his *Harvard Case Histories of Experimental Science* (1957), it is possible to elucidate a connection between personal and objective knowledge.

Phlogiston was a construct of 18th-century science that was evoked to explain the burning of substances in chemistry. As a construct, it had its origins in Aristotle's idea that all substances were made of the elements earth, wind, fire and water. Phlogiston was a modern—18th century—equivalent of fire. Thus when a substance burned, it was because it contained phlogiston. Substances not containing phlogiston did not burn. When a metal, such as mercury, burns it produces a substance which Ernest Stahl, in 18th-century Germany, called a 'calyx' and phlogiston was removed. Accordingly, one would expect (prediction or hypothesis) that the calyx would weigh less than the metal. In France, using very precise balances, Anton-Laurent Lavoisier (1743–1794) showed, in fact, that the calyx weighed more when the metal had been burned in an open container. Despite this refutation of the construct of phlogiston, eminent scientists, such as Cavendish and Priestley, continued to believe in phlogiston as an explanation of burning until their deaths. The point made here is that when the construct of phlogiston is tested against reality, it failed to account for what was happening. This experimental testing of a hypothesis could be likened to the testing of personal constructs in their predictive ability to explain the personal world of the learner. What happened in the case of phlogiston was that a new construct of 'oxidation' was used to explain what was happening and this did accord with the experimental evidence. As is the case in all areas of scientific research, the concept of oxidation has been further refined and can now be explained in terms of the removal of electrons from a substance. In a similar way, the Irish scientist Boyle considered heat as a material substance rather than the modern idea of heat as a form of energy. Consequently, it could be argued that if something was heated in a hermetically sealed container, then the container should weigh more after heating than before, because of the addition of the substance of heat. But this was not the case and allowed the evolution of a different concept of heat. Concepts in science are not, therefore, constant objective truths but are always open to elaboration and redefinition.

Evidence for this at the personal level of learners in the classroom has been found in the misconceptions that students bring to the science classroom (Driver, 1983) and which often persist through both secondary and tertiary science education. Student science teachers can often demonstrate that, despite being successful in passing their science courses, deep-seated personal constructs which are contrary to science persist because they have never been challenged at a level that had meaning to them (McElwee, 1993).

One other aspect which can be taken from an analysis of the way scientific discoveries are made is that, besides coming up with a more accurate scientific theory, the way discoveries are made can be equated with a constructivist view of learning in the classroom. Just as a scientist can propose a hypothesis based on intuition (rationalist) or on observations (empiricist) so, too, can a student in the classroom propose a guess based on his/her construction of the world and then test in a valid way the truth or otherwise of such a construction. Lawson (1995) proposed a similar approach to develop the thinking of science students.

That students often have misconceptions in science which are at variance to science has been well documented in the literature (Pfundt & Duit, 1994). Both physics and chemistry have been rich sources of misconceptions including conceptions of matter as well as changes in state (Andersson, 1980, 1990; Osborne & Cosgrove, 1983; Renstrom et al., 1990; Bar & Travis, 1991; Stavy, 1990; McElwee, 1991; Lee et al., 1993; Bar & Galili, 1994; Clough & Driver, 1985; Johnson, 1998; Tytler, 2000; Tytler & Peterson, 2000; Selley, 2000). In biology, too, the concept that the material that makes up the substance of wood in trees is mainly derived from air and not soil is sufficient to throw many a biology graduate into what psychologists call 'cognitive dissonance'. It is this dissonance or 'cognitive conflict' that often acts as the trigger for the exploration of a science topic using a constructivist approach (Champagne et al., 1985).

INTERNATIONAL COMPARISONS

While, in 2006, the focus of the PISA study was mainly on science, it also included reading and Mathematics. Students were assessed in relation to science competencies, such as being able to identify scientific issues, explaining phenomena scientifically and using scientific evidence to draw conclusions, which contribute to scientific literacy. In addition to these competencies, students' scientific knowledge, as outlined above, was measured. Finland with an average score of 563 points was the highest performing country. Among the countries that scored higher than the OECD average of 500 points were Canada, Japan, New Zealand, Estonia, Australia, The Netherlands, Korea, Germany, the United Kingdom, the Czech Republic, Switzerland, Austria, Belgium and Ireland, with 508 points. The United States, which has poured millions of dollars into science education, scored 489 points, and this will be considered below. What is of interest to a future knowledge economy is the number of students who displayed proficiency at the highest levels. These are: Level 6, where students can consistently identify, explain and apply scientific knowledge; and Level 5, where students can identify the scientific components of many complex life situations. The average percentage of students who scored at levels 5/6 across the OECD countries was 9 per cent. Finland had 20.9 per cent, New Zealand 17.6 per cent, the United Kingdom 13.8 per cent and Ireland 9.4 per cent.

While it could be argued that these higher skills are essential for future scientists, it should also be considered that all students need to be scientifically literate in an increasingly scientific age. This could be one of the 'strong foundations' identified in the 2006 government report *Strategy for Science, Technology and Innovation 2006–2013* (Government of Ireland, 2006) and is the core of Schoen and Fusarelli's (2008) argument for schools of the 21st century.

As a result of the success of Finland in these scientific literacy stakes, there has been an analysis of how this was achieved. Among a number of variables identified, it was suggested that one of the main factors was a research-based, teacher-education system (Pehkonen et al., 2007). Schoen and Fusarelli (2008), while acknowledging that a number of interrelated factors contributed to Finland's success, noted that a strong background in cognitive psychology was required for all pre-service teachers and that there was a shift towards less structured curricula and the inclusion of active (constructivist) learning methods. They argue that the demands for the 21st century do not warrant having students acquire a static body of knowledge but require 'individuals with technological savvy, keen communication and observation skills, who possess an attitude of informed adaptability and analytical ability' (Schoen & Fusarelli, 2008, p. 186). They argue that the low results achieved by the United States in the PISA are a result of the standardised testing made necessary for the implementation of the 2001 No Child Left Behind Act (NCLB) (United States, 2001), because curricula content becomes very important in comparisons within and between schools at the expense of curricula that emphasise thinking skills. In the United States, the National Research Council (NRC), in its publication *America's Lab Report* (National Research Council, 2006), endorses the aim of providing scientific literacy for all in order to prepare students for further study, work and citizenship. However, the council also points to the fact that educators do not agree on the role of laboratory work in the high-school curriculum.

CONSTRUCTIVISM AND SCIENCE TEACHER EDUCATION

Science teachers being prepared for the 21st century require not a prescriptive approach to teaching but one based on an understanding of the many methods of teaching science and the ability to critically reflect on them to achieve definable learning outcomes for students. In the past, there was an undue emphasis on 'knowledge as content' rather than 'knowledge as a set of thinking skills'. The introduction of new curricula, such as the Junior Certificate Science with its emphasis on 'enquiry', attempted to address this issue. However, while the curriculum changed, there is concern that the newer teaching methods required were not adopted by all teachers. In a recent report by the science inspectors of the DES (Government of Ireland, 2008b), a number of issues relating to both good practice and concerns about the teaching of science were noted. They commented that some teachers fostered participation in science through problem-solving approaches which encouraged independent thinking and the development of problem-solving skills (process). This, they suggested, produced a deeper understanding of science (product). While constructivism was not specifically identified in this report an examination of material supplied by the Second Level Support Service (2009) shows that students are often asked to 'predict' what is to happen in an experiment or demonstration. This indicates an attempt to incorporate pupils' thoughts into the scientific enterprise both in order to clarify misconceptions and to involve them in a problem-solving exercise.

What was of concern to the inspectorate was a teacher-centred rather than a student-centred approach to teaching. This had also been noted by the Task Force on the Physical Sciences in 2002 (Government of Ireland, 2002). This task force addressed the issue of falling numbers in the physical sciences and the implication of this for the economy. While the task force lamented the lack of data on methods used by science teachers, they did report from a student survey that the most frequent activities in science were teachers explaining to class, students writing in notebooks and students reading science textbooks (p. 53). About 50 per cent of students do 'experiments in the classroom' on a weekly basis which, according to the report, they enjoyed more than anything else. There was, however, no indication of how such experiments were carried out. For example, experiments may 'prove' some theory already explained in class or may be part of a problem-solving exercise or part of a 'enquiry' or a constructivist approach.

One of the factors influencing student subject choice, which the task force identified, was that of a positive experience of science at junior cycle. From a survey carried out, by the task force, it appears that there is a decline in interest in science during the course at junior cycle (a drop from 83 per cent to 39 per cent of students who say that they will continue to study science). This was in 2002, one year prior to the introduction of the revised Junior Certificate programme in science. Not all schools adopted the new programme but did in subsequent years. This programme was first examined in 2006 which was the year of the PISA survey but because the PISA survey was on students between 15 years and three months and 16 years and two months, these Junior Certificate students were probably not included. However, introduction of a new programme does not of itself guarantee changes in teaching methodology. Research has shown that when new curricula are introduced, classroom observation of teaching often shows an incongruence between the intentions of the curriculum planners and the minds of the teachers to the extent that teachers did the exact opposite of what the new scheme required (Hamilton, 1975).

The question of what methods teachers are using in their classrooms is not restricted to Ireland. It is a major concern in countries such as the United States and Australia. A study on the status and quality of teaching in Australian schools (Australia, 2001) reports that disenchantment with science is reflected in the declining numbers of students who take science subjects in the post-compulsory years of schooling. In describing the actual picture of teaching in high schools, the authors report that many students experience disappointment because the science they are taught is neither relevant nor engaging and does not connect with their interests and experiences. The teaching methods used are traditional chalk-and-talk, copying notes and what are described as 'cookbook' practical lessons, which offer little challenge or excitement to students. One of the solutions favoured in some states is the adoption of constructivist approaches to teaching science.

In the United States, a similar concern with teaching methods has been expressed by Bentley (1998) who reported that the textbook was often the sole source of the curriculum and 'stand-and-deliver' teaching methods eclipsed all else in classroom practice. This is little different to that reported 15 years earlier when Yager and Penick (1983) were able to say that, despite considerable investment in curriculum reform, in the science classroom the textbook was still supreme being, used by 90 per cent of teachers 90 per cent of the time. Thus, failure to address changing teaching methods may also be a factor in the below-average score of the United States in the 2006 PISA report.

An examination of the data from the PISA report shows that, in countries such as New Zealand and, to some extent, Australia as well as Finland and the United Kingdom where constructivist practices have been adopted, there is a high level of students operating at the higher scientific levels of 5/6. This is not necessarily cause and effect as many other variables are involved but what is indicated is that research needs to be carried out to determine the precise learning outcomes of constructivist learning. One example of this carried out in Ireland indicated that third-level students, despite successfully completing science at second level, had a variety of misconceptions about fundamental scientific ideas but that, when these ideas were challenged using a cognitive conflict approach (Predict/Observe/Explain), concepts were changed and remained changed after three months (McElwee, 1993). This POE approach (Gunstone, 1995) is but one of many pedagogies developed in science education and aspects of these pedagogies need further research for them to be used. One issue is the problem of teaching abstract ideas in science, such as the particulate theory of matter (Millar, 1990), that may have no real correspondence or context for learners. While there has been a plethora of research in science education, there has been little transfer to the real teaching situation (McElwee, 2005). It is unfortunate that the many excellent recommendations of the Task Force on the Physical Sciences (Government of Ireland, 2002) have never been implemented; this at a time, when the demands on the knowledge economy have never been greater.

Osborne and Dillon (2008), in a report to the Nuffield Foundation on the future of science education in Europe, have argued that European Union countries should ensure that teachers of science of the highest quality are provided for students in primary and lower secondary. This accords with the observation by the Task Force on the Physical Sciences that students develop or lose their interest in science during these early years of secondary education. Osborne and Dillon (2008) also argue for developing and extending the way science is taught and that transforming teacher practice across the European Union is a long-term project.

The days of a prescriptive approach to the training of science teachers are over and what has taken its place is an approach based on reflective practice where student teachers are exposed to methods of teaching, not previously encountered by them as students, and where they are encouraged to try such methods under the tutelage of supervisors and mentors. Evaluation of learning outcomes might result in the questioning of the constructs of teachers about the process of teaching and learning which inhibit the introduction of methods such as constructivism (Aubusson, 2002). Such an approach may go some way to producing the scientifically literate citizens demanded of the 21st century.

ENDNOTES

1   See below for a definition.

2   Here, 'a priori' is used to mean prior or before-sense experiences.

16

A RESEARCH-BASED PROFESSION: THE IMPORTANCE OF ACTION RESEARCH IN TEACHER EDUCATION

Bernard McGettrick

INTRODUCTION

The decade of the 1990s and the early years of this century was a period of unprecedented change in education both in Ireland and internationally. The social, economic, policy, legislative, cultural and religious changes that have taken place must be integrated into the content and process of teacher education in the 21st century. Drudy (2006b, p. 5) has argued that the changes in the economy, society and education and the increasing propensity of society to look to schools and the teaching profession to address social problems, confirm the complexity of the teacher's role. These changes also have implications for teacher education in many different respects. In a review of post-primary teacher education in 2002, the Advisory Group on Post-Primary Teacher Education placed a strong emphasis on the value of enquiry-based models of teacher education (Advisory Group on Post-Primary Teacher Education, 2002).

Internationally, there is a growing emphasis on the concept of teacher education as a continuous and ongoing process. The European Commission, for example, has asserted that teaching should be a profession of lifelong learning and articulates a vision that:

> Teachers are supported to continue their professional development throughout their careers. They and their employers recognise the importance of acquiring new knowledge, and are able to innovate and use new knowledge to inform their work.
>
> Commission of the European Communities, 2007, p. 12

The commission also emphasises the necessity of teachers taking responsibility for mapping their own learning (Commission of the European Communities, 2007, p. 12) and their responsibility to develop new knowledge to inform their work. In the context of autonomous lifelong learning, the commission articulates a vision in which teachers would: continue to reflect on their practice in a systematic way; undertake classroom research; incorporate into their teaching the results of classroom and academic research; evaluate the effectiveness of their teaching strategies and amend them accordingly (ibid., p. 14).

Drawing on the Finnish experience, Niemi (2008, p. 183) makes the point that 'in knowledge based societies, policies and practice based on research and evidence have become an urgent requirement'. She provides ideas on how in-service training should be closely connected to research and should support teachers' professional practice and argues for research studies to be an integral part of initial and continuing teacher education. This chapter suggests that training in action research has the potential to facilitate teachers in working effectively in periods of change and development in education.

THE IMPORTANCE OF ACTION RESEARCH

The importance of action research is based on an appreciation that models of professional development which adopt a directive approach to specifying the knowledge and skills required for any profession not only date quickly but give the impression of fixity and permanence, and that the capabilities that are most useful are those that enable the practitioner to adopt a self-aware, critically reflective stance in relation to one's own professional activity and changing circumstances, policies and practices. With respect to teaching, Koshy (2005) makes the point that the quality of educational experiences provided for children will depend on the ability of teachers to question and reflect on their own experience and continually strive to improve it. In relation to curriculum development, Stenhouse (1993) suggests that effective curriculum development depends on the capacity of professionals to take a research stance in relation to their own practice. These functions, questioning and reflecting, and taking a research stance in relation to practice, are central to action research. Action research can be identified with practitioner-based research, self-reflective practice, participatory research and emancipatory research with the ultimate aim of improving professional practice and ultimately the educational experience provided for students. While action research has been applied in areas such as the processes of learning, teaching and assessment, school-based curriculum development, systemic planning, policy development, and personal and professional development, this chapter will focus on its use in educational settings.

There have been many definitions of action research. Carr and Kemmis (1986) provide a classic definition:

> Action research is simply a form of self-reflective enquiry undertaken by participants in social situations in order to improve the rationality and justice of their own practices, their understanding of these practices, and the situations in which the practices are carried out.
>
> Carr & Kemmis, 1986, p. 162

Koshy (2005, p. 2) defines it as an enquiry, undertaken with rigour and understanding so as to constantly refine practice. McNiff and Whitehead (2006, p. 7) argue that action research is a form of enquiry that enables practitioners everywhere to evaluate their work.

Action research has been seen as integral to the professional development of teachers and, indeed, for teaching to be classified as a profession. With specific reference to teaching as a profession, Lawton (1989, p. 89) holds that the claim of teaching to be a profession lies in the ability and opportunity for teachers to exercise their judgement over critical tasks involved in their role, namely curriculum development and teaching. In addition to action research developing the professionalism of teaching, Hopkins (2002, p. 33) suggests that teachers who engage in action research are involved in taking more control of their professional lives, developing their professional judgement and are moving towards independence and autonomy.

REFLECTION

Central to the implementation of an action research approach is the notion of reflection and experiential learning. Reflection describes a particular approach to learning and professional development. A conceptual model that attempts to describe what goes on in the process of reflection on experience has been developed by Boud, Keogh and Walker (1996).

Figure 16.1: The process of reflection

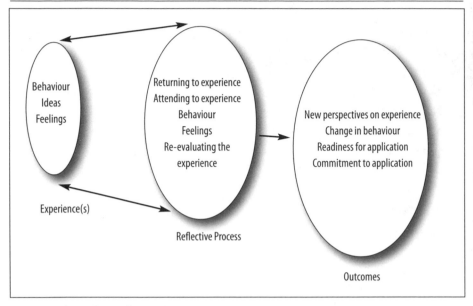

Source: Boud, Keogh & Walker, 1996, p. 52.

Reflection is central to action research and is highly relevant to the processes of learning and teaching. It is through reflection that self-awareness can be developed and it is through self-awareness of personal values and beliefs and the specific nature of their own situation that teachers are empowered to work with students from very different backgrounds and abilities.

Reflection also provides ways of linking different forms of knowledge, for example, academic and practical. In this sense, reflection involves reviewing everyday practice through academic knowledge and systematically assessing that knowledge in relation to experience of practice. In relation to teacher education, it is important to appreciate that developing the capability to reflect takes time and effort. Reflection can be both intellectually and emotionally challenging and supports should be in place to facilitate this process. In discussing the effects of using reflection in learning, Brookfield (1987, 1994) writes of discomfort and perplexity, Mezirow (1990) of disorienting dilemmas, uncertainties and dissatisfactions, and Butler (1996, p. 27) suggests that the dislodgement of personal theories, the breaking of the framework of understandings that govern personal and professional performance, and the creation of newer versions, involves, necessarily, a period of discomfort, when learning appears to be erratic and confused. In inclusive education, particularly, O'Hanlon (2003, p. 22) points out that action research that focuses on pedagogical issues encourages teachers to become reflective practitioners and that when practitioners become reflective, the processes of systematic and planned action can be integrated into personal and professional lives. For educational practice to become inclusive, she argues, it must first become reflective. Practitioners need to be reflective, to be theorists and to research their own practice using approaches appropriate to their particular professional area (Colin, 1998, p. 80).

EXPERIENTIAL LEARNING

Action research facilitates experiential learning. The notion of learning as a process and not a product (Bruner, 1996), and as contributing to the construction of personal and social meaning (Freire, 1974) offers a more dynamic concept of learning than the acquiring of concepts and facts that can be relied on to remain the same. It is now accepted that the concept of knowledge has changed from earlier static and transmitted contents to knowledge that is ever renewable and often construed jointly with other learners (Niemi, 2008, p. 185). Experiential learning makes learning more personal and, sometimes, stands in contrast to the interpersonal conventions of much academic education where the stress is on practical and technical knowledge. Experiential learning involves working out the tensions, and sometimes conflicts, between different ways of understanding, for example, concrete experience and abstract conceptualisation, and between active experimentation and reflective observation. Experiential learning facilitates the professional in moving beyond the 'technical-rationality model' (Schön, 1983) and developing an approach to practice that is localised, contextualised, and adopted to specific and unique situations. The role of action research in relating theory to practice and the production of new knowledge has been emphasised in the literature. Reason and Bradbury (2002, p. 5) make the point that action research is about working towards practical outcomes, and also about creating new forms of understanding. Koshy (2005, p. 9) considers action research as a constructive enquiry, during which the researcher constructs his or her knowledge of specific issues through planning, acting, evaluating, refining and learning from experience.

Such definitions would suggest that effective professional practice consists of much more than the application of academic knowledge to practice. Schön (1983, 1987) questioned the idea that professional work consists of the application of academic knowledge or method to practical problems. Rather, he suggests that that professional work is characterised by a knowing-in-action which is not the same as academic knowledge. It is modified by reflection-in-action, an ability to think about what one is doing while doing it. It is through such reflection that professional wisdom and skill are built up in the course of experience. These capacities are essential because real-world problems do not match the knowledge produced by research. Problems encountered by teachers are unique and specific and while theory can contribute to their resolution that is all it can do. Reflection on theory and how it can be applied in the unique context faced by the practitioner is necessary, a point made by Colin (1998, p. 89) when she states that 'theorists are generally too distant from the action to offer anything but yesterday's solutions'. Hirst (1993) argues that educational theory cannot encapsulate the whole range of considerations that have to be taken into account in professional activity. His conceptualisation of practice relates back to Aristotle. For Aristotle, wise practical conduct cannot take the form of the mere application of principles or rules. Particular situations must be assessed in terms of goals and values, but goals and values need also to be considered in the light of experience of particular situations. Only then can reasonable conclusions be reached about what it is appropriate to do.

Engaging in an action-research approach to practice by practitioners has an emancipatory effect. It empowers professionals. This emancipatory dimension has been emphasised by Carr and Kemmis (1993) who refer to the transformational attributes of action research, suggesting that it must transform educational practice through self-critical transformation of educational practitioners.

In summary, an action-research approach to teacher education models and facilitates practitioners in becoming self-aware, critically reflective, questioning, taking a research stance in relation to their practice, learning from experience, and combining academic and experiential knowledge to generate and construct new knowledge. This has a transformative and emancipatory function. It also has the potential for continuing personal and professional development and, thereby, enhances the quality of service offered to students. These are vital aspects of teacher education. Facilitating teachers in taking an action-research approach to their professional activities helps them to appreciate that professional development is a continuous process, a process supported by a self-critical approach to their work. The aim is to facilitate them in evaluating theory against practice and to integrate the two in solving practical issues related to their work.

THE CONTENT AND PROCESS OF ACTION RESEARCH

In action research, we do not need to have a problem in the strict, or negative, sense of the word. All we need to know is that there is something we would like to improve. It may be some aspect of professional practice, alternatively, we might wish to evaluate the effectiveness of a curriculum initiative based on a perceived need. The question about concerns may stimulate ideas for action research but may also relate to issues about the school's development plan, mission statement or aims and objectives, policy development, inclusive education and many others.

Working in collaboration with others, or alone, the considerations proposed by McNiff and Whitehead (2006) and McKiernan (1991) and one's own reflection on experience and knowledge of the present situation can lead to the identification of a general or an initial idea or an area of concern. This becomes the focus of the research. In choosing the areas to be researched using an action-research approach, it is important that it is something the researcher can do something about, is viable, and that it will facilitate professional development. It is beneficial to involve other interested parties in the research.

The concept of performance gap is useful in refining topics for action research. The identification of a gap between what is and what should be, or the situation as it is and the situation as the practitioner would like it to be provides motivation for change and improvement. It can provide a stimulus for a systematic approach to eliminate, or at least narrow the gap in the way things are and they way they should be. For example, in an evaluation of the Samaritans' suicide-awareness programme on the levels of awareness of suicide and related issues in transition-year pupils, Smyth Maguire (2001) noted a gap in the curriculum and, through her action research, attempted to fill this gap.

A focus emerges from critical reflection on experience which is then explored through research procedures. In other words, both the formulation and resolution of the research enquiry are grounded in the practitioner's experience. Lewin (1948) is generally credited as the person who coined the term 'action research'. His approach involves a spiral of steps, each of which is composed of a circle of planning, action and fact-finding about the result of the action. The basic cycle is shown in Figure 16.2.

Figure 16.2: The action-research cycle

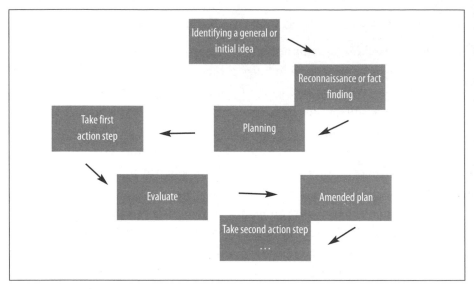

Source: Lewin, 1948, p. 206.

A range of specific considerations that will provide a framework to guide the action-research process have been suggested by different studies (for example, McNiff & Whitehead, 2006; McKiernan, 1991).

Like other forms of research, action research involves identification of a problem or something of concern, the collection of evidence, analysis of the data collected, the use of theory and the communication of findings to others. Action research is unlike more conventional research in the sense that most problems usually arise directly from practice. Its main purpose is to identify appropriate forms of action or intervention which may help to solve these problems. Once an appropriate form of action is identified, it must be implemented and its effectiveness evaluated. If the intervention is successful, it will involve a change in practice. This, in turn, may raise new problems which must be solved and so on. These recursive practices make up what may be termed the 'action research cycle'. In this sense, action research is ongoing and never fully completed. It is a continuous process.

Collaboration with all participants and other interested parties is an important feature of action research. The design and implementation of a curriculum initiative, for instance, would involve collaboration with students, parents, colleagues and other interested parties. This would involve seeking information about their perceptions at various stages of implementation and considering these in response to the ongoing implementation of the initiative.

Table 16.1: Considerations to guide the action research process

McNiff & Whitehead Initial questions	McKiernan Developing the process
What is my concern?	Examine problems deemed problematic by practitioners.
Why am I concerned?	Deem problems solvable.
What experience can I describe to show I am concerned?	Provide practical responses.
What can I do about it?	Suspend full definition of the situation until exploratory research is undertaken.
What will I do about it?	
What kind of data will I gather to show the situation as it unfolds?	Researcher should deepen own understanding of the problem.
How will I explain my educational influences in learning?	'Tell a story' about what is going on and how events hang together.
How will I ensure that the conclusions I come to are reasonable fair and accurate?	Report perceptions and beliefs of those in the setting .
	Use the language of participants' everyday discourse .
How will I evaluate the validity of the evidence-based account of my learning?	Validate in unconstrained dialogue with the participants.
How will I modify my concerns, ideas and practice in the light of my evaluations?	Enable free flow of information between actors in the project.

Source: McNiff & Whitehead (2006, p. 79); McKiernan (1991, p. 31).

The first step in action research is to describe the situation as it exists. This may take the form of a case study. This is followed by a carefully planned intervention calculated to improve the situation. This intervention is evaluated as the research progresses with changes being made on the basis of continuing evaluation. A well-established feature of action research is the notion of a 'critical friend'. A critical friend is an interested person with whom the researcher can discuss the process and receive constructive criticism as the research progresses. In other cases, an interested group of colleagues may be involved in order to provide feedback as the research progresses. The involvement of such a group may form part of the evaluation and validation process.

Action research is very versatile. Both quantitative and qualitative approaches may be used in conducting action research. The emphasis is on immediate application rather than the development of a theory or general application, although in a number of cases reflection on practice and action research does lead to the development of a theory. The research methods are selected to respond to the particular question that is proposed. Qualitative methods are more common with more of an emphasis on discovery and interpretation rather than quantitative method of hypothesis testing, correlation studies or other kinds of statistical analysis. It would be appropriate to describe the situation before the intervention takes place. This can take the form of a case study and techniques may include observation, interviews or photography which will provide a rich description of the situation.

As the research progresses, documentation might include, detailed descriptions of people, events and settings, field notes, interactive journals, memos, minutes of meetings, transcriptions, portfolios, photographs, audio tape recordings and video tape recordings. These data collection techniques provide valuable information which will form the basis for the validation of the data. Hopkins (2002) discusses helpful techniques that may be used in the action research process and these are summarised in Table 16.2.

A selective and small sample of action research undertaken in the UCD School of Education by experienced teachers engaged on postgraduate programmes illustrates how action research can contribute to the developmental processes of teaching, learning and curriculum development. McGrattan (1998) researched the development and implementation of a music programme with deaf children, some of whom were profoundly deaf. The research evaluated the programme as it progressed, the final outcomes, and the views of participants and other interested parties, including pupils, parents and teachers. It is a good example of the practical application of action research. Ryan (2000) did very worthwhile research with young pre-school children. The aim of this research was to develop their meta-cognitive skills and give them insight into, and help them to take responsibility for, their own learning. In addition to looking at the research process in the classroom, it also explored the extent to which meta-cognitive skills were generalised and used outside the classroom setting. Smyth Maguire (2001) undertook research in the area of suicide awareness and prevention. The stimulus for this research was the recognition of a gap in the curriculum, namely, suicide awareness among transition-year pupils. The study investigated the implementation of such a programme, with evaluation of the

Table 16.2: Advantages and disadvantages of techniques used in action research

Technique	Advantages	Disadvantages
Field notes	Simple Ongoing Personal Helps memory	Subjective Needs practice
Audio tape recordings	Versatile Accurate Provides ample data	Transcription difficult Time consuming May be inhibiting
Pupils' diaries	Provides pupils' perspectives	Subjective
Interviews and discussions	Provides participants' perspectives	Can be time consuming
Video tape recording	Visual and comprehensive	Can be intrusive, awkward and distracting
Questionnaires	Highly specific Easy to administer comparative	Time consuming to analyse Problems of response bias
Documentary evidence	Illuminate	Difficult to obtain Time consuming
Slide/Tape photography	Illuminative Promotes discussion	Difficult to obtain Superficial
Case study	Accurate Representative Uses range of techniques	Time consuming

Source: Hopkins (2002, p. 126).

programme as it was implemented. Changes were made to the programme on the basis of this evaluation. The study was a collaborative approach involving students, class teachers, form teachers, the principal and parents, and using their perceptions in the refinement of the programme. Cooney (2003), working with students with special needs, undertook an action-research initiative to facilitate and enhance the development of self-esteem in students. These research studies were characterised by a democratic and participative approach involving participants and interested parties and the validation of the results through triangulation,[1] i.e. through collating information from the participants and other interested parties utilising different methods. They could be classified as research with people rather than research on people.

These research studies illustrate how action research can be used effectively in school settings. Reading them will give a good indication of the rationale for the methodology and content, and process of action-research approaches.

VALIDITY

One criterion by which all research is evaluated is that of validity. The general question posed by a consideration of the validity of any research is: Does the research really do the things it claims to do and are the results valid (can they be believed)? In looking at the issues of validity, we consider a number of dimensions, namely descriptive, explanatory and external. Descriptive validity refers to whether or not a description captures the relevant and essential features of what is being described. It is important to be aware that descriptions are never total but some of the techniques mentioned previously, e.g. audio and video recording, photographs, and the involvement of a critical friend and peer group, will help to ensure the descriptive validity of the data collected.

Explanatory validity is concerned with whether an explanation captures accurately the set of causal factors that produced what is being explained. Rather than an emphasis on statistical analysis, action research concentrates on self-validation, peer validation, learner validation and validation from other interested parties, although statistical analysis can be a feature of action research. Triangulation (see footnote 1) is also an important tool in ensuring validity. McNiff and Whitehead (2006, p. 159) make the point that data obtained from discussion with a critical friend can be invaluable in demonstrating the integrity of the procedural aspects of the research. Validation groups are part of the procedure of an action-research enquiry. The task of the validation group is to listen to the individual researcher's claim to knowledge, offer constructive feedback, consider the evidence and agree that movement has, or has not, taken place. The evidence can be in the form of video or tape recordings, coupled with other written material. The validation group critically assesses the actions of the researcher and agrees criteria for examples in action that show the realisation of educational values in practice. In the context of learner validation, it is important to get on record the reactions of the clients themselves. This evidence is perhaps the researcher's strongest claim to knowledge. The material for learner evaluation may be provided by interviews, questionnaires, written statements, diaries, and video or tape recording.

In the context of evaluation, it is usual in action research to seek the evaluation of even those who are not directly involved in the research process. For instance, in the action research of both McGrattan (1998) and Smyth Maguire (2001) both asked for the opinions of teachers not directly involved in the research and the opinions of parents or guardians. This yielded some interesting findings. For example, teachers considered McGrattan's intervention so significant that they expressed a desire to learn the musical instrument themselves, and wanted her to teach them. In relation to Smyth Maguire's research, parents indicated that one of the effects of the programme was that it facilitated and enhanced communication between themselves and their teenage children, and that they wanted this to continue, indicating that they would like a programme for themselves similar to that provided for the participants in the research.

External validity refers to the extent to which the findings can be generalised to the wider population. One of the frequent criticisms of action research is its lack of generalisability. However, Koshy (2005, p. 205) makes the point that action research does not set out to be generalisable but to generate knowledge based on action within one's own situation. The lack of generalisability is compensated for by a detailed description of the situation, the intervention and whether or not it worked. It is possible that the findings of action research may have what has been termed a 'snowball effect', which would suggest areas that would benefit from investigation on a wider scale.

OBJECTIVITY

Criticisms have been made of the traditional conceptualisation of objectivity in educational research. However, there is general agreement that ontological objectivity in research is an ideal rather than an achievable goal. In considering the concept of objectivity in relation to action research, Carr and Kemmis argue that the aspiration to objectivity is mistaken in action research where the aim should be self-critical reflection which helps the practitioner to emancipate himself or herself from the dictates of habit, custom, precedent and coercive social structures (Carr & Kemmis, 1993, p. 236). Stenhouse has suggested that it is the researcher's subjective perception that is important rather than a concern with unobtainable objectivity:

It is the teacher's subjective perception which is crucial for practice since he [sic] is in a position to control the classroom. Accordingly we are concerned with the development of a sensitive and self-critical subjective perspective and not with and aspiration towards unobtainable objectivity.

Stenhouse, 1993, p. 228

This does not mean that action research is subjective. We have seen how data and results may be validated by the researcher, a critical friend, peers and colleagues and other interested parties, and through triangulation.

RELEVANCE

To be of value, research findings must not only be valid but also relevant. This chapter has attempted to show the relevance of action research. It is suggested that action research and its findings have relevance for the practitioners involved, their clients, colleagues and the wider community, and for the development of education.

CONCLUSION

Perhaps, in line with other professions in Ireland, such as counselling and psychology, evidence of continuing professional development may become mandatory for teachers. However, the absence of such a mandatory requirement at the present time should not take from the importance of such continuing professional development. Teacher educators are challenged to provide structures that will facilitate this.

The observations of Colin (1998) are relevant to teacher education, specifically with regard to introducing teachers in training to a wide range of theories and helping them to appreciate what these theories can contribute to practice through their own reflection on and critical evaluation of such theories in relation to practice. The emphasis on a continuing developmental awareness of their own practice is an important one. There is also an emphasis in the literature on teachers being familiar with the content and process of research:

> They [teachers] must have basic knowledge of research methods and some competence to evaluate the relevance and quality of research results. They need scientific literacy. Without these skills they are merely actors who are applying orders coming from outside their practice.

Niemi, 2008, p. 187

It is necessary to support teachers in establishing a research tradition which will help them research their own practice and improve it and thereby lead to a significant improvement in education. Stenhouse (1993, p. 233) argues that 'a research tradition which is accessible to teachers and which feeds teachers must be created if education is to be significantly improved'.

Professionals who take an action-research approach to their professional activity are not blindly applying theory and research but rather transforming theory and knowledge into something that is meaningful. Such an approach facilitates, empowers, and enhances professional development, and helps professionals to gain confidence in their professional activities. It helps them to learn about themselves, their students and colleagues, and to determine ways to improve their practice. They learn what it is they can influence which can have an empowering effect, facilitating them in the improvement of their own practice and student learning. Drudy (2008a) makes and important point in relation to teacher professional activity:

> Teachers are the only professional group who play a central role in the daily lives of the entire population in Western democracies, irrespective of class, creed or ethnic background. Teacher education plays a critical role in the formation of these professionals and in the setting of professional standards.
>
> Drudy, 2008a, p. 52

Inherent in the above is a requirement for teacher educators to engage in research into the content and process of what they offer to their students. Central questions arise as to whether or not what they are presenting is meeting the needs of their students and preparing them for the complexities of practice situations in which they find themselves. The perceived needs of other stakeholders are also important areas for consideration and analysis.

ENDNOTES

1   Cohen, Manion and Morrison define triangulation as the use of two or more methods of data collection in the study of human behaviour. It is a powerful way of demonstrating concurrent validity, particularly in qualitative research (Cohen et al., 2007, p. 141).

17

PUBLIC POLICY MAKING: THE EMERGING POLICY MAKING MODALITY AND ITS CHALLENGE FOR EDUCATION POLICY RESEARCH IN IRELAND[1]

Conor Galvin

POLICY MAKING IN TURBULENT TIMES

The emergence of new social, political and economic realities can have profound effects on how we make policy and indeed the nature of policy itself. Policy fields emerge or contract according to the changing context. Policy perspectives and approaches gain favour and then fall away. Policy players rise and fall in influence. We move from one-way to 'third way',[2] from *fiat* to light touch, from faith-based to evidence-based, and somewhere bound up in all of this is the perennial problem of academic policy research and its usages.

This, of course, is a somewhat simplistic reading of a complex and multidimensional process. But it serves to foreground an important point—the making of public policy, including education policy, is changing in line with a world that is changing rapidly.

At its most fundamental, public policy usually concerns the actionable outcome of some political decision to initiate or to furnish change—invariably described as 'improvement'—in a particular area of public interest. As an exercise in the analysis of policy and practice, the various contributions to this volume raise a number of profoundly significant points and concerns. The most salient relate to the nature of the authoring practices and political activity that surround and inform Irish education policy making today. These reflect the moment we find ourselves in as well as the journey here. We are living through the most serious financial meltdown in almost a century and the first to impact Ireland so deeply. Globally, dramatic and far-reaching changes in political and institutional arrangements are reshaping the structures and processes that make and shape policy. And so, today, more than ever, those with a critical interest in education in Ireland need a strong understanding of the policy-making process.

We also need to be strategic in our efforts to engage policy and the policy process. As educationalists, it is easy to forget that education policy is *only one* area of public policy and that academic policy research is also *only one* element in a complex matrix. Indeed, Schuller (2004) observes that the extent to which research evidence influences policy is subject to a number of factors, which he identifies as ranging from political opportunism to pressure of public opinion to the quality and capacity of the available research. Policy makers control this terrain. Consequently, there may be insights to be gained from considering the position of policy practitioners and thought leaders in the education-policy process and the roles of a variety of actors and institutions at the supranational, national and sub-national levels in the policy process. That is what this chapter seeks to do.

Two core dimensions of policy making are explored below to better place education policy making within this wider frame.

Policy as process rather than product

This has become such a truism that it is easy to overlook its significance. Nevertheless, the defining feature of successful public policy action is that it is *process* determined (Vestergaard, 2003). While, technically, it is the prerogative of government, policy does not simply issue and move seamlessly through implementation. It evolves. It changes as various factors from the target environment are worked in and as the original *meme* transforms through text and articulation/re-articulation. The importance to this of the broader environment, including the social, economic and political context within which the policy making is located, has long been recognised. Minogue (1983), for example, argued that policy is inescapably bound up with a process created by the interaction of decisions, policy networks, organisations, actors and events. This view would lean to the argument that research should be central to the task of creating policy and that the outturns must be robust enough to survive in the wild and sufficiently open to interpretative action to accommodate all key actors, but particularly those at street-level (Lipsky, 1983). In short, policy must be what Barthes (1975) has termed 'writerly'—i.e. open to local interpretation and contingent action—if it is to have any chance of wide adaption. In short, in democratic societies policy making is an open process that is accessible, amenable to the reasonable voice and iterative. Given the numbers of education researchers working in a human sciences/social sciences vein, it would be easy to assume that this is the only tenable view. It is not.

In contrast, the long-standing *policy science* view of public policy is that it is best conceptualised as a series of stages or steps in which proposals are systematically evaluated against clear, exogenous values and attainment criteria, and through which things rationally progress towards the realisation of the policy goal (Burton, 2006). In this view, it is restricted, rigorous and controlled. And this, arguably, is the mindset that many policy makers now bring to the education policy arena due to an increased 'policy professionalisation' and a homogenisation of role associated with shifts in governance and the reconstructing across in the developed world of notions of public service.

Put simply, the policy-making perspective has changed radically, and so too has the policy maker. Desmond King (2003) has suggested that this may, in large part, be due to the more recent structuring and restructuring of government funding agencies in the US and Britain. This has resulted in a series of major departures from how policy making has been 'traditionally' approached. The 'Beltway Man/Whitehall Man' of the 1950s and 1960s has given way to more corporate versions of the civil servant with a very different way of approaching policy formulation. A significant outturn from this, arguably, has been the emergence of alternative 'light' takes on policy research and policy development which effectively bypass the models central to research councils' thinking and practice and the researchers that these would probably involve. The practice of policy authoring as exemplified by the work of DEMOS, the influential, London-based think-tank, is a good example of this. Another good example is the 'policy unplugged' workshop model that has been sponsored by the UK Channel 4 television network in the past two or three years.[3]

It can be claimed with some justification that despite increased understanding of the new policy method and ongoing efforts on the part of academy-based researchers to build more flexible capacity in relation to policy research (e.g. Furlong & White, 2001), academic researchers remain reluctant to embrace wholly what is seen by many as a poisoned chalice. And perhaps with reason. Gardner and Gallagher (2007), and Gardner, Holmes and Leitch (2008) point to the possible ulterior political motivation of 'fast' research. Furthermore, there are other ideological and structural issues that divide commissioner from researcher, many of which have their roots in changing understandings of the role of the university itself. For instance, within the human and social sciences generally, research valuation exercises can significantly impact on the ability of schools/departments of education to engage in policy work (Galvin, 2007). Policy work/policy research takes time, and time is an increasingly scarce resource in the contemporary higher education setting. Consequently, while researchers and practitioners in the field of education policy are often aware of Minogue's (1983) sense of policy as the interaction of decisions, networks, organisations, actors and events, they frequently underestimate the cultural gap and contrasting expectations between those who commission policy work and those in the academy who are interested in pursuing it.

Policy as currency

The second concept that may prove useful in understanding new policy development and activity is that of *currency*. Donald Schön is widely valued in education circles for his work on reflective practice. There is another aspect to his work—his public-policy analysis—which is not so well known and which can be of considerable assistance in understanding policy dilemmas, such as the temporal dimensions of policy making discussed by Oates (2008) when he considers the significance of temporal discontinuity on policy making and, in particular, the problems that result for the arrangements and organisations that are meant to support that policy. Central to this analysis is Schön's view of the relationship of culture to the structural and contextual nature of change and the role of currency in this.

Schön (1971) articulates well the concept of culture as a set of *shared ideas* and related behaviours. He suggests that these shared ideas go through rising and falling levels of public support (what he terms '*shared agreement*') and sees well-supported ideas—*ideas in good currency*—as being a primary determinant of public policy. Relatively few ideas attain this stature and these change over time. They can also, Schön asserts, lag behind changing events and social realities. The essence of this argument is clearly evident in the following quotation, which is worth quoting at some length:

> Taken at any time, a social system is dynamically conservative in its structural, technological and conceptual dimensions. This last represents the 'system' of ideas in good currency. Characteristically, what precipitates a change in that system of powerful ideas is a disruptive event or sequence of events, which set up a demand for new ideas in good currency. At that point, ideas already present in free or marginal areas of the society begin to surface in the mainstream … The ideas become powerful as centres of policy debate and political conflict. They gain widespread acceptance through the efforts of

those who push or ride them through the fields of force created by the interplay of interests and commitments ...

When the ideas are taken up by people already powerful in society this gives them a kind of legitimacy and completes their power to change public policy. After this, the ideas become an integral part of the conceptual dimension of the social system and appear, in retrospect, obvious.

Schön, 1971, p. 120

Schön is particularly concerned with change in public policy in his model. In his view, society has room for only a limited number of ideas 'whose time has come' at any given time. Schön suggests that this is because society has limited attention-capacity so that when new disruptions appear, ideas for addressing some existing problem are simply displaced—especially if they are already proving to be limited or failing. As an account of why some ideas get picked-up or receive continuing support from politicians and policy makers while others do not—thought oftentimes seemingly more deserving in research terms—it would sit well with Pollard's account of why it is mistaken to consider research evidence as the sole active agent in policy articulation (Pollard, 2008). Policy research (where it exists) is always just one of a number of competing factors. 'Disruption' is, moreover, the province of politicians and policy makers, more usually than academics.

EDUCATION POLICY WORK AS NEW-MODEL POLICY MAKING

The preceding discussion raises a number of points concerning emerging activity relating to education policy making. Taken together, they represent a useful lens on the deep nature of the change that is coming upon the policy process. It is clear that genuine attempts are being made by some elements of the academy to understand the wider social implications of the policy model that is emerging and to position themselves so that the university can continue to contribute meaningfully to the policy process in various countries and settings. The work of Lawn and Lingard (2002) and Grek, Lawn, Lingard, Ozga, Rinne, Segerholm and Simola (2009) offer good examples of this. Nevertheless, a strongly technicist/managerialist perspective characterises much of the policy planning evident across the developed world, particularly the European Union (Antunes, 2006), and, most especially it would seem, in education policy formation in the United Kingdom (Ball, 2007) and here in Ireland (Lynch, 2008). This is reflected in underpinning policy rationales that are far more linear than cyclical, with the result that education initiatives frequently are progressed on a tight, 'command and control' model rather than on the lines of a more conventional cyclical/discursive, public-policy model.

The types of dilemma this tension turns up—particularly regarding evidence-informed policy/research informed practice—are well treated by Daugherty (2008) and by Nutley, Jung and Walter (2008). Daugherty (2008) suggests that researching to show direct evidence of effective approaches alone is a seriously limited view of the research possibilities of the social sciences, and that academic research is much less significant in its impact on policy making than most of us like to think. Nutley, Jung and Walter (2008) make a strong case for adding dimensions of research-based practitioner action, embedded research, and organisational excellence to the analysis of research usage. Their caution around the stress points in both rational-linear and interactive perspectives on such research usage is useful. So, too, is their suggestion of the value of considering best-fit to different circumstances as a way of explaining how research-informed practice may be approached more effectively. But what is not foregrounded in these, or in the other contributions, is the role of well-placed policy makers in facilitating or denying such usages, the systemic nature of the sanctioning operations they perform or the sorts of considerations that influence their activity. Increasingly, it would appear that there are commonalities to the way policy makers work that reflect time and evidence requirements, that suggest clear rationales about approach, and that point towards a convergence around business/corporate methods and values. All of which is a long way from how most academics in universities and colleges conceive of and operate around policy and policy research. Members of the education research community offer very little significant work that charts and challenges the emergence of this new policy orthodoxy—with the exception perhaps of Lawn and Lingard (2002), and Ozga (2009).

As a result, most academics would seem to be unaware of the increasing adoption by policy makers internationally of an emergent approach which has its origins in the work of a new generation of policy practitioners, most of whom are UK based. This *new-model policy making* centres around a 'third way' notion[4] of the social-investment state, and takes as its reference set the practice of a small group of highly innovative, London-based public policy makers—both collectives and individuals. These include influential think-tanks like DEMOS and IPPR, the Innovation Unit, the National School of Government, and leading figures in a number of DfES/DFSC 'spin-outs', such as the Learning and

Skills Development Agency (now the Quality Improvement Agency for Lifelong Learning (QIA)) and the Learning and Skills Network (LSN), NESTA (National Endowment for Science, Technology and the Arts) and, most recently, The Young Foundation. Various combinations and confederations of these groups are succeeding in driving the policy agenda in ways that most academic research could not hope to match. For instance, recent NESTA/Young Foundation/ National School of Government activity on Public Service Innovation is simply one example of such UK-based coalitions.[5]

There is now a broad literature in the area of third way and social-investment politics but surprisingly little has yet been published on the principled underpinnings of the public policy approach that supports the implementation of these ideas and drives their impact and reach. There are early indications of strong pressure to move towards a concerted displacement of older models of policy formulation and pursuit (*cf.* Bullock et al., 2001). But, until now, very little has been available in the public domain which deals authoritatively with the nature and detail of the alternatives embedded in this emergent model in public policy making. However, by drawing on recent articulations of his understandings and beliefs in regards to policy entrepreneurship and public policy making by Geoff Mulgan, who is a defining member of this set, it is possible to gain a certain amount of insight in this new model and its workings.[6] These are summarised below.

Firstly, new policy making clearly centres on policy science axioms concerning the nature of a policy field. Policy fields may, in this view, be grouped into three types: stable policy fields; policy fields in flux; and inherently novel policy fields. Stable fields are: '… composed of areas where knowledge is settled; governments broadly know what works; there is a strong evidence base; and the most that can be expected is some incremental improvement' (Mulgan, 2003, p. 3). Macro-economics and some areas of curative and preventative health are given as examples. Professional bodies in these areas and leading experts 'can be relied on to give good advice' (ibid.). Where a policy field is in flux, '… most people recognise that things need to change; that policies which once worked are no longer working' (ibid., p. 4). Education, welfare and pensions, and the organisation of public services are named as examples. Professionals in policy fields in flux are seen as '… often as much part of the problem as the solution, and may be resistant to criticism' their networks 'may be the last to recognise the need for change' (ibid.). Mulgan's third type of policy field—inherently novel fields—include those of new and emergent technologies and new forms of governance and regulation. These are seen as fields where: 'No one knows for sure what works or what doesn't because these are virgin territories ... the experts will only be just ahead of the amateurs' (ibid.).

Secondly, new policy making affords precedence to practice rather than theory. We are, Mulgan suggests, '... now in a phase when concepts are more promiscuous. Most governments profess to be more interested in what works than what makes ideological sense—and that means that there is likely to be a greater willingness to see practice rather than theory as the best source of ideas' (ibid., p. 3). Conceptual innovation is increasingly taking place in the context of practice and theorists are 'following behind, trying to make sense of what the practitioners are doing' (ibid.). The 'rather non-ideological climate' in which public policy is increasingly being made, may, in Mulgan's view, account for the particular truth of this claim. It would certainly accord with the pragmatism associated with a social investment view of state and concomitant policy pursuit. It would also help explain why Mulgan seems convinced that there is 'a great deal of fertility and experimentation' on the fringes or 'at the margins' from which good policy innovation emerges.[7]

Thirdly, it actively supports the implementation of a global policy commons. Where in the past the notion of *policy borrowing* would have attracted reactions ranging from scepticism to out-and-out hostility (*cf.* Finegold et al., 1992), new model policy brokerage would see this practice as an unequivocal strength. Mulgan describes it simply as 'learning from other countries', and a reflection of 'an emerging global market for ideas' (Mulgan, 2003, p. 1). It should be mentioned, of course, that there is a sophistication intended in this process that acknowledges '... concepts are not the same as their application. All policy ideas have to be adapted to different cultural and institutional environments, improved and reshaped ...' (ibid., p. 2). The locations from which policy concepts are drawn may surprise and increasingly reflect also what Mulgan terms 'a global commons—a shared space of knowledge, experiment and experience' (ibid., p. 5). He observes:

> ... the network of ideas has become more heterogeneous. Many of the best ideas and projects are now coming from smaller countries (such as Denmark, Netherlands, Sweden, Finland, Singapore and Korea), and within North America from states and provinces rather than the federal capitals.
>
> Mulgan, 2003, p. 4

It would also help to place Mulgan's claim that:

Some of this exchange has been helped by the multilateral organisations, which not only analyse and promote ideas in a very pragmatic way but have also pioneered methods of policy analysis and project design and appraisal which are now significantly more sophisticated than those used in the north [developed world].

Mulgan, 2003, pp. 4-5

In addition, new policy making is fast-paced and edgy. Mulgan consistently argues the value of looking to the periphery for the novel and the innovative—and of learning from this to author policies in what he terms 'the "hinterland" of the public sector—territory at one remove from the formal structures of accountability and control, where risks and imagination are easier, and where the future is most likely to take shape' (2007, p. 10). And, most tellingly perhaps, it is the natural domain of the *policy worker*—young, well-educated, task-orientated individuals who can be commissioned and decommissioned as required across the gamut of new policy formation—from authoring to valorisation, to dissemination and beyond.

EDUCATION POLICY AND POLICY MAKING IN IRELAND: TWO DEFINING FEATURES

It has been noted by Nic Craith (2009) that education is a constant in the policy agenda in Ireland and that the Irish education system is uniquely characterised by the presence and influence of strong interest groups, such as the Church, the vocational education committees and the teacher unions. She is not alone in this view. Our system has more than once been described as a historically complex and pluralist one (O'Sullivan 1989, 2006; OECD, 1991, 2003) within which policy and policy making has not always had a good history (Department of Education & Science/Cromien, 2000; Gleeson, 2004; Collins et al., 2007).

It is difficult to do justice to such complexity here. However, two defining features of our reality can usefully be outlined.

The first is to do with the unique role that the Organisation for Economic Co-operation and Development (OECD) has played in the seeding and orientation of education policy in Ireland across more that 40 years. The broad remit of the OECD is an economic one and its defining purpose is to build strong economies. Nevertheless, a series of OECD/CERI reports has at key moments helped to shape radically various Irish governments' education policy by leading to seminal funding and practice decisions. For example, the Irish government's *Investment in Education Report* (1965) (Department of Education, 1965) was based on the work of the OECD, and was the foundation of many later developments in education through the 1960s and 1970s. Similarly, the *Review of National Education Policies: Ireland* (OECD, 1991) provided the backdrop to many of the policy developments in this country throughout the 1990s and into this century. Although the OECD was invited initially to examine teacher education at the end of the 1980s, the effects of the latter report went well beyond teacher education. It influenced the Green Paper *Education for a Changing World* (Government of Ireland, 1992) which was followed by a public consultative process culminating in a National Education Convention in 1993 and the White Paper *Charting our Education Future* (Government of Ireland, 1995). By stimulating this consultative process, the OECD report also indirectly influenced legislation, such as the Education Act 1998 and the Teaching Council Act 2001. These are widely noted (*cf.* O'Sullivan 1989; Burke, 2004; Sugrue, 2008, inter alia). Other less obviously connected developments also followed; a White Paper on early childhood education in 1999 (Government of Ireland, 1999) and a White Paper on adult education (Government of Ireland, 2000b). A Universities Act was passed in 1997 (Government of Ireland, 1997). Education at primary and post-primary level was placed on a legislative footing in 1998. Further legislation followed with the 2000 Education (Welfare) Act, the 2001 Teaching Council Act and the 2004 Education for Persons with Special Educational Needs Act (EPSEN) (Government of Ireland, 2000a, 2001, 2004a). But what is less widely observed is the reason behind this recursive use of OECD publications: O'Sullivan (1989) commented on the power of the 'cultural stranger' role that the OECD brought to the table. But the reality is that the Department of Education and Science (DES) was simply not proactive in generating or driving policy-led change over the years involved, nor confident in its policy-making ability. Indeed, the landmark Cromien Report (Department of Education & Science, 2000) was swingeing in its criticism of the department in this regard. What followed was a radical restructuring of the DES and its approach to policy and policy making. This was at both an organisational and cultural level and it is to this restructuring that we now turn. And in this the influence of another supranational player—the European Union—is keenly evident.

The second defining feature of policy and policy making for education in this country relates to aspects of the 'new public management' (Tierney, 2006) that has in the past 15 years or so become the dominant ethos of the DES. This is part of a wider change agenda—one in which the European Union[8] has played a formative part which is neither as widely known nor understood as it might be (Collins et al., 2007). The role of the state and its relationship with the public is radically changing. According to McCarthy, Ireland 'came to statehood with a very traditional understanding of the role of the state as a nightwatchman state' (McCarthy, 2006, p. 80) but is now moving to become a *regulatory competition state*, which seeks to avoid direct service delivery, operates through regulation, privatisation and new public management and which delegates policy making and implementation to new actors at national and local levels. The resulting aggressive modernisation of the Irish public service has at its core the notion of a performance-oriented, 'customer-facing' service that is shifting from an ethic based on managing inputs such as personnel and funding to one driven by performance and results (OECD, 2008b). It utilises methodologies and tools, like customer service charters, regulatory impact analysis, value for money evaluations, performance management development systems and management information frameworks, to drive this change. In Ireland, the influence of this approach was evident in the strategic management initiative established through a co-ordinating group of secretaries of departments in 1994. *Delivering Better Government* (Government of Ireland, 1996) was the government's response to their report. More recently, drawing on the analysis and recommendations of an OECD review of the Irish public service, the Task Force on the Public Service produced an action plan: the *Transforming Public Services* programme (Department of the Taoiseach, 2008). These changes reflect in ongoing efforts to regulate, privatise and outsource public-service functions previously carried out by the state.

There are implications and challenges in both of these features of policy and policy making for anyone interested in pursuing the possibility of influencing or seeding policy. There are, in particular, issues around the nature of the research that are likely to be commissioned in support of a policy initiative (Lawn & Lingard, 2002), the stage(s) of a policy action that research is most likely to be required (Furlong & White, 2001) and the nature and utility of whatever research data is generated (Ozga, 2009).

A COUNCIL, A COLLEGE AND PERENNIAL PILOTS

A number of specific examples and recent instances from the Irish education arena may help to illustrate the growing reach of new policy making. These are necessarily brief but, hopefully, serve their purpose.

The first is to do with the establishment of The Teaching Council of Ireland in 2005. The design and configuration of the council itself resulted in significant measure from a broadly cast policy analysis of similar councils worldwide—essentially, accessing *the policy commons*. However, a close consideration reveals even deeper new policy model roots to both the function and staffing of the new entity; for example, the council's remit included two heretofore key DES functions (the registration of teachers and the application of discipline procedures against teachers where necessary). In effect, an agency arrangement was instituted and two particularly problematic, public-service functions 'spun-off' to the new body. Further dimensions include carefully designated ministerial appointments to the inaugural council—intended to bring the necessary 'business world' ethic to its work—and the marginalisation of higher education influence through the low number of teacher education representatives (four out of 37 members) contained in the Teaching Council Act in comparison to the level of representation on the Registration Council which was disestablished following commencement of the act.

The second example concerns the emergence of private, for profit, education in the field of teacher education. This development may be seen as exhibiting a particular tenet of new policy making. It comes from the 'fringes' in that it represents the application of a business/IT sector solution to a pressing and potentially expensive education sector 'problem'—the need to ramp-up the production of credentialed primary teachers without incurring substantial costs in doing so. Mulgan's observations on inherently novel policy fields and the imaginative margins come to mind. So, too, does his comment on new policy making's tendency to 'distrust' the field experts in an area of policy concern that is perceived as in flux or failing.

A third outworking of this new policy model relates to the area of teacher induction. There has been long-standing acknowledgment of Ireland's weakness in this area and a DES commitment to address it (Galvin, 2003; Nic Craith, 2009). Conway, Murphy, Rath and Hall (2009) have noted that there has been, until recently, a paucity of research into the practice of induction in Ireland. The National Pilot Project on Teacher Induction (see Chapter 12) and work on induction in County Dublin Vocational Education Committee schools (Galvin, 2003) addresses this lack of research. The concept of a professional continuum has not been contested; what has not yet occurred is a national rollout of induction as an entitlement for all newly qualified teachers as is the case in Northern Ireland, Britain and many other countries.

There are many other such instances of new policy modality and new public management with the education arena: the emergence and construction of secondary TPNs (teacher professional networks) and their primary equivalent; the use of consultancies to 'deliver' evaluations of essentially educational initiatives, such as the Liberties Learning Initiative or the CONNECT school project; the use of consultants in resolving disputes in some higher education institutions; the use of an economist to scope out the possible future shape and detail of non-university higher education provision in the greater Dublin area and the future of the National University of Ireland; the use of futures workshops/scenarios by the National Council for Curriculum and Assessment (NCCA) to 'foresight' future curriculum requirements; and, most visibly perhaps, the secondment of serving teachers to successive curriculum and continuing professional development (CPD) initiatives over the past 15 years, in such a way that these can be assembled and disassembled as needs and funding determine—rather than along pedagogical or educational system requirement lines.

What also becomes clear, from even a cursory consideration of the field, is that academic policy work is increasingly losing out to more edgy, new policy driven, short-timeframe managerialist activity. What Apple (2009b) terms the ideological assemblage that is teacher professionalism is being displaced by less substantial, less culturally, socially and educationally critical conceptions of what it means to be a professional. New policy making is a valuable and versatile tool in this regard.

CLOSING COMMENT

This chapter spotlights the public policy and policy action challenges increasingly being faced, especially by policy-focused educationalists. It considers the *new policy making* to show that, where education and public-policy making is concerned, academics are in the middle of a significant shift in policy modality. Those involved in academic policy research have a proven capacity to identify and address key, strategic and cross-cutting academic policy research from a medium to longer term perspective.

The emerging policy-making modality reflects times in which provocative questions are being asked about even the university and its role in society. So perhaps the greatest contribution that academic educators can now make to the wider university is to make their unique contribution to the national debate on the future of Irish education in the new Ireland now unfolding. This should be done in ways that 'assert the centrality of knowledge and content in higher education discourse' (Manning, 2009b, p. 2), that bring the policy discussion back to the importance of the relationship of professional teachers to learning, that create space for these issues to be considered in their own terms. To do this would be commendable and it is what the various chapters in this book have set out to do.

ENDNOTES

1   Parts of this chapter are based on papers read to the Political Studies Association of Ireland Annual Conference, Galway, October 2008, and the Campus Engage International Conference, Dublin, June 2009.

2   Anthony Giddens, one of the chief authors of the socio-political approach of the 'third way', describes the alternatives as follows: the 'first way' was the traditional left: traditional social democracy; the 'second way' was Thatcherism, or market fundamentalism—the belief that the realm of the market should be extended as far as possible; the 'third way' he describes as 'policy-rich'—it tries to hold the political centre-ground, tries to ensure the economy is strong, invests heavily in public services, but insists that this is coupled to reform, to make the public services more 'effective, responsive and transparent' (Giddens, 2007).

3   Given their political positioning, it is interesting to note that education and well being have been two of the areas included early in the series. See http://www.policyunplugged.net/inthewildchannel4.

4   See Giddens (1998) for a detailed exploration and analysis of the socio-political approach of the 'third way'.

5   See the National School of Government (UK) website for details of the initial event in this action: http://www.nationalschool.gov.uk/innovation/index.asp.

6   Geoff Mulgan was, until the autumn of 2004, Director of the Prime Minister's Strategy Unit (UK). Prior to this he was Head of the Performance & Innovation Unit in the UK government cabinet office and the British Prime Minister's personal adviser on social policy. He is currently the Chair of the Young Foundation, London.

7   See Mulgan (2006, 2007) for a comprehensive treatment of these issues.

8   This has been channelled through a variety of DGs particularly Education & Culture and Enterprise & Industry. Teaching and teacher education have increasingly become a focus of this work—see, for example, Commission of the European Communities, 2005, 2007.

REFERENCES

Abbott, L. (2006). 'Northern Ireland head teachers' perceptions of inclusion'. *International Journal of Inclusive Education*, 10(6), pp. 627–43.

Acker, S. (1994). *Gendered Education*. Buckingham, PA: Open University Press.

Adler, P.A. & Adler P. (1998). *Peer Power: Preadolescent Culture and Identity*. New Brunswick, NJ: Rutgers University Press.

Advisory Group on Post-Primary Teacher Education (2002). *Report of the Advisory Group on Post-Primary Teacher Education*. Dublin: The Stationery Office.

Agnus, A. (1993). 'The sociology of school effectiveness'. *British Journal of Sociology of Education*, 14(3) pp. 353–67.

Ainscow, M. (1999). *Understanding the Development of Inclusive Schools*. London: Falmer Press.

Ainscow, M. (2000). 'The next step for special education: supporting the development of inclusive practices'. *British Journal of Special Education*, 27 (2), pp. 76–80.

Ainscow, M. (2007). 'Taking an inclusive turn'. *Journal of Research in Special Educational Needs*, 7(1), pp. 3–7.

Akenson, D.H. (1970) *The Irish Education Experiment: The National System of Education in the Twentieth Century*. London: Routledge and Kegan Paul.

Akenson, D.H. (1975). *A Mirror to Kathleen's Face: Education in Independent Ireland, 1922–1960*. Montreal and London: McGill-Queen's University Press.

Aksu, M., Demir, C., Daloglu, A., Yildirim, S. & Kiraz, E. (In press: 2009). 'Who are the future teachers in Turkey? Characteristics of entering student teachers'. *International Journal of Educational Development*, doi:10.1016/j.ijdeudev.2009.06.005.

Alderson P. & Morrow V. (2004). *Ethics, Social Research and Consulting with Children and Young People*. Barkingside: Barnardos.

Allan, J. (2008). *Rethinking Inclusive Education*. Dordrecht: Springer.

Allport, G.W. (1954). *The Nature of Prejudice*. Cambridge, MA: Addison-Wesley.

American Psychiatric Association (1994). *Diagnostic and Statistical Manual of Mental Disorders* (4th edition). Washington, DC: American Psychiatric Association.

Anderson, L.W. & Pellicer, L.O. (1990). 'Synthesis of research on compensatory and remedial education'. *Educational Leadership*, 48(1), pp. 10–16.

Andersson, B. (1980). 'Some aspects of children's understanding of boiling point'. In: W.F. Archenhold, R.H. Driver, A. Orton & C. Wood-Robinson (eds), *Cognitive Development Research in Science and Mathematics* (pp. 252–9). UK: University of Leeds.

Andersson, B. (1990). 'Pupils' conceptions of matter and its transformations (age 12–16)'. *Studies in Science Education*, 18, pp. 53–85.

Andreotti, V. (2006). 'Soft versus critical global citizenship education', *Policy and Practice: A Development Education Review*, 3, pp. 83–98.

Ang, I. (1996). 'The curse of the smile: Ambivalence and the 'Asian' woman in Australian multiculturalism'. *Feminist Review*, 52, pp. 36–49.

Antunes, F. (2006). 'Globalisation and Europeification of Education Policies: routes, processes and metamorphoses'. *European Educational Research Journal*, Vol. 5(1), pp. 38–55.

Apple, M.W. (1996). *Culture, Politics and Education*. Buckingham, PA: Open University Press.

Apple, M.W. (2001). 'Will standards save public education?'. *Educational Policy*, 15 (5), pp. 724–9.

Apple, M.W. (2002). 'Does education have independent power? Bernstein and the question of relative autonomy'. *British Journal of Sociology of Education*, 23 (4), pp. 607–16.

Apple, M. (2009a). 'Markets, Standards, God, and Inequality in Education'. Lecture delivered in University College Dublin, 11 June 2009.

Apple, M. (2009b). 'Foreword'. In: S. Gerwitz, P. Mahony, I. Hextall & A. Cribb (eds), *Changing Teacher Professionalism: International Trends, Challenges and Ways Forward*. New York, NY: Routledge.

Arends, R.I., Winitzky, N.E. & Tannenbaum, M.D. (1998). *Exploring Teaching*. Boston: McGraw Hill.

Arnaiz, P. & Castejon, J.-L. (2001). 'Towards a change in the role of the support teacher in the Spanish education system'. *European Journal of Special Needs Education*, 16(2), pp. 99–110.

A.T. Kearney/Foreign Policy (2004). 'Measuring globalization: economic reversals, forward momentum'. Available at: http://www.foreignpolicy.com.

Atkinson, N. (1969). *Irish Education: A History of Educational Institutions*. Dublin: Allen Figgis.

Aubusson, P. (2002). 'An ecology of science education'. *International Journal of Science Education*, 24(1), pp. 27–46.

Australia (2001). *The Status and Quality of Teaching and Learning of Science in Australian Schools*. Report by D. Goodrum, M. Hackling & L. Rennie. Department of Education, Training and Youth Affairs.

Avramidis, E. & Kalyva, E. (2007). 'The influence of teaching experience and professional development on Greek teachers' attitudes towards inclusion'. *European Journal of Special Needs Education*, 22(4), pp. 367–89.

Baker, E.T., Wang, M.C. & Walberg, H.J. (1995). 'The effects of inclusion on learning'. *Education Leadership*, 52(4), pp. 33–5.

Baker, J., Lynch, K., Cantillon, S. & Walsh, J. (2004). *Equality: From Theory to Practice*. New York: Palgrave Macmillan.

Baker, J., Lynch, K., Cantillon, S. & Walsh, J. (2006). 'Equality: Putting the Theory into Action'. *Res Publica*. 12, pp. 411–33.

Ball, S.J. (2006). *Education Policy and Social Class*. London: Routledge.

Ball, S.J. (2007). *Education plc.: Understanding Private Sector Participation in Public Sector Education*. London: Routledge.

Ball, S.J. (2008). *The Education Debate*. Bristol: Policy Press.

Bank-Mikkelsen, N.E. (1976). 'The principle of normalization'. In: B. Nielson (ed.), *Flash 2 on Danish National Service for the Mentally Retarded* (pp. 45–50). Copenhagen: Person Training School.

Bannister, D. & Fransella, F. (1993). *Inquiring Man: The Psychology of Personal Constructs* (3rd edition). London: Routledge.

Bar, V. & Galili, I. (1994). 'Stages of children's views about evaporation'. *International Journal of Science Education*, 16, pp. 157–74.

Bar, V. & Travis, A.S. (1991) 'Children's views concerning phase changes'. *Journal of Research in Science Teaching*, 28, pp. 363–82.

Barkley, R.A., Fischer, M. & Edelbrock, C.S. (1991). 'The adolescent outcome of hyperactive children diagnosed by research criteria: 111 mother–child interactions, family conflicts and maternal psychopathology'. *Journal of Child Psychology and Psychiatry*, 32, pp. 235–55.

Barry, M. (2003). 'Getting Together: A Comparative Analysis of Inclusive Primary Education in the United States of America and the Republic of Ireland'. Unpublished Masters thesis, University College Dublin, Ireland.

Barthes, R. (1975). *S/Z: An Essay*. New York: Noonday Press.

Bartlett, M.S. (1954). 'A note on the multiplying factors for various chi square approximations'. *Journal of the Royal Statistical Society*, 16 (Series B), pp. 296–8.

Barton, L. (1996). 'Sociology and disability: some emerging insights'. In: L. Barton (ed.), *Disability and Society: Emerging Issues and Insights* (pp. 3–17). London & New York: Longman.

Barton, L. & Slee, R. (1999). 'Competition, selection and inclusive education: some observations'. *International Journal of Inclusive Education*, 3(1), pp. 3–12.

Basten, C. (1997). 'A feminised profession: women in the teaching profession'. *Educational Studies*, 23, pp. 55–62.

Baviskar, S., Hartle, R.T. & Whitney, T. (2009). 'Essential criteria to characterize constructivist teaching: Derived from a review of the literature and applied to five constructivist-teaching method articles'. *International Journal of Science Education*, 31 (4), pp. 541–50.

Bee, H.L. (2002). *The Developing Child* (9th edition) Boston: Pearson Custom Publisher.

Begeny, J. (2007). 'Inclusionary education in Italy: a literature review and call for more empirical research'. *Remedial and Special Education*, 28(2), pp. 80–94.

Bentley, M.L. (1998). 'Constructivism as a referent for reforming science education'. In: M. Larochelle, N. Bednarz & J. Garrison (eds), *Constructivism and Education* (pp. 81–103). Cambridge, UK: Cambridge University Press.

Bernstein, B. (1996). *Pedagogy, Symbolic Control and Identity: Theory, Research and Critique*. London: Taylor Francis.

Bigler, R.S. & Hughes, J.M. (2009). 'The nature and origins of children's racial attitudes'. In: J.A. Banks (ed.), *The Routledge International Companion to Multicultural Education* (pp. 186–99). New York: Routledge.

Birch, H.G., Richardson, S.A., Baird, D., Horobin, G. & Illsley, R. (1970). *Mental Subnormality in the Community: A Clinical and Epidemiological Survey*. Baltimore, MD: Williams & Wilkins.

Black-Hawkins, K., Florian, L. & Rouse, M. (2007). *Achievement and Inclusion in Schools*. Oxford: Routledge.

Blackmore, J. & Kenway, J. (eds) (1993). *Gender Matters in Educational Administration and Policy: A Feminist Introduction*. London: Falmer Press.

Bliss, J. (1993). 'The relevance of Piaget to research into children's conceptions'. In: P.J. Black & A.M. Lucas (eds), *Children's Informal Ideas in Science* (pp. 20–44). London: Routledge.

Block, D. (2003). *The Social Turn in Second Language Acquisition*. Edinburgh: Edinburgh University Press.

Bonati, M. (2006). 'The Italian saga of ADHD and its treatment'. In: G. Lloyd, J. Stead, & D. Cohen (eds), *Critical New Perspectives on ADHD* (pp. 128–55). London: Routledge.

Booth, T. (1996). 'A perspective on inclusion from England'. *Cambridge Journal of Education*, 26 (1), pp. 87–99.

Booth, T. & Ainscow, M. (eds) (1998). *From Them to Us: An International Study of Inclusive Education*. London: Routledge.

Booth, T. & Ainscow, M. (2002). *The Index for Inclusion*. Bristol: Centre for Studies on Inclusive Education.

Booth, T., Ainscow, M., Black-Hawkins, K., Vaughan, M. & Shaw, L. (2000). *The Index for Inclusion*. Bristol: Centre for Studies on Inclusive Education.

Boud, D., Keogh, R. & Walker, D. (1996). 'Promoting reflection in learning: a model'. In: R. Edwards, A. Hanson & P. Raggatt (eds), *Boundaries of Adult Learning* (pp. 32–56). London: Routledge.

Bourdieu, P. (1977). *Outline of a Theory of Practice*. Cambridge: Cambridge University Press.

Bourdieu, P. (1984). *Distinction: A Social Critique of the Judgement of Taste.* Cambridge: Harvard University Press.

Bourdieu, P. (1986). 'The forms of capital'. In: J. Richardson (ed.), *Handbook of Theory and Research for the Sociology of Education* (pp. 241–58). Westport: Greenwood Press.

Bourdieu, P. (1991). *Language and Symbolic Power.* Cambridge: Polity Press.

Bourdieu, P. (1998). 'The Essence of Neoliberalism'. *Le Monde,* December 1998. Available at: http://www.analitica.com/Bitblio/bourdieu/neoliberalism.asp (retrieved 27/06/2009).

Bourdieu. P. (2000). *Pascal Meditations.* Cambridge: Polity Press.

Bradbury, L. & Kobala, T. (2008). 'Borders to cross: identifying sources of tension in mentor-intern relationships'. *Journal of Teaching and Teacher Education,* 24 (8) pp. 2132–45.

Brembeck H., Johansson B. & Kampmann J. (eds) (2004). *Beyond the Competent Child.* Copenhagen: Roskilde University Press.

Brennan, M. (1935). *The Schools of Kildare and Leighlin.* Dublin: Gill & Son.

Brittan, G.G. (1978). *Kant's Theory of Science.* Princeton: Princeton University Press.

Britzman, D.P. (2003). *Practice Makes Practice.* New York: State University of New York Press.

Brookfield, S. (1987). *Developing Critical Thinkers; Challenging Adults to Explore Alternative Ways of Thinking and Acting.* Milton Keynes: Open University Press.

Brookfield, S. (1994) 'Tales from the dark side: a phenomenography of adult critical reflection'. *International Journal of Lifelong Education,* 13(3), pp. 203–16.

Brookhart, S.M. & Freeman, D.J. (1992). 'Characteristics of entering student teachers'. *Review of Educational Research,* 62 (1), pp. 37–60.

Bruner, J.S. (1986). *Actual Minds, Possible Worlds.* London: Harvard University Press.

Bruner, J.S. (1996). *Towards a Theory of Instruction.* New York: W.W. Norton.

Bullock, H., Mountford, J. & Stanley, R. (2001). *Better Policy-Making.* London: UK Government Centre for Management and Policy Studies.

Burke, A. (ed.) (2004). *Teacher Education in the Republic of Ireland: Retrospect and Prospect.* Armagh: Centre for Cross Border Studies.

Burns, J., Clift, J. & Duncan, J. (1991). 'Understanding of understanding: implications for learning and teaching'. *British Journal of Educational Psychology,* 61, pp. 276–89.

Burton, P. (2006). 'Modernising the Policy Process: making policy research more significant?'. *Policy Studies,* Vol. 27(3), pp. 173–95.

Butler, J. (1996). 'Professional development: practice as text, reflection as process, and self as locus'. *Australian Journal of Education,* 40(3), pp. 265–83.

Bryan, A. (2008). 'The co-articulation of national identity and interculturalism in the Irish curriculum: educating for democratic citizenship?'. *London Review of Education,* 6(1), pp. 47–58.

Bryan, A. (2009). 'The intersectionality of discourses on nationalism and interculturalism in the Republic of Ireland: teaching against racism?'. *Race, Ethnicity and Education*, 12(3), pp. 297–317.

Bryan, A., Clarke, M. & Drudy, S. (2009). 'A study of student teachers' perspectives on social justice and development education'. In: M. Liddy & J. O'Flaherty (eds), *Ubuntu Network Action Research and Other Projects to Integrate Development Education into Initial Teacher Education, 2006–2008.* Available at: http://www.ubuntu.ie (retrieved 20/08/09).

Bullen, E., Fahey, J. & Kenway, J. (2006). 'The Knowledge Economy and Innovation: Certain Uncertainty and the Risk Economy'. *Discourse: Studies in the Cultural Politics of Education*, 27(1), pp. 53–68.

Buzzi, I. (1995). 'Italy'. In: C. O'Hanlon (ed.), *Inclusive Education in Europe* (pp. 75–81). London: David Fulton Publishers.

Byrne, D., McCoy, S. & Watson, D. (2008). *School Leavers Survey Report 2007.* Dublin: Economic & Social Research Institute.

Cahill, E. (1940). 'The native schools of Ireland in the penal era'. *Irish Ecclesiastical Record*, 55, pp. 16–28.

Calderhead, J. (1989). 'Reflective teaching and teacher education'. *Teaching and Teacher Education*, 5(1) pp. 43–51.

Callan, T., Walsh J. & Coleman, K. (2005). 'Budget 2005: Impact on Income Distribution and Relative Income Poverty'. Available at: www.cori.ie/justice/budget/2005/index.htm (retrieved 29/06/2009).

Cambridge Primary Review (2009). *Towards a New Primary Curriculum: A Report from the Cambridge Primary Review.* Cambridge, UK: University of Cambridge.

Cameron, M. (2007). *Learning to Teach: A Literature Review of Induction Theory and Practice.* New Zealand Council for Educational Research.

Canale, M. & Swain, M. (1980). 'Theoretical bases of communicative approaches to second language teaching and testing'. *Applied Linguistics*, 1(1), pp. 1–47.

Carey, S. (1985). *Conceptual Change in Childhood.* Boston: MIT Press.

Carlaw, K., Oxley, L., Walker, P., Thorns, D. & Nuth, M. (2006). 'Beyond the hype: intellectual property and the knowledge society/knowledge economy'. *Journal of Economic Surveys*, 20(4), pp. 633–90.

Carpenter, B., Ashdown, R. & Boviar, K. (eds) (1996). *Enabling Access: Effective Teaching and Learning for Pupils with Learning Difficulties.* London: David Fulton Publishers.

Carr, W. & Kemmis, S. (1986). *Becoming Critical: Education Knowledge and Action Research.* London: Falmer Press.

Carr, W. & Kemmis, S. (1993). 'Action research in education'. In: M. Hammersley (ed.), *Controversies in Classroom Research.* Buckingham, PA: Open University Press.

Carrington, B., Francis, B., Hutchings, M., Skelton, C., Read, B. & Hall, I. (2007).

'Does the gender of the teacher really matter? Seven- to eight-year-olds' accounts of their interactions with their teachers'. *Educational Studies,* 33(4), pp. 397–413.

Carson, S. (1992). 'Normalisation, needs and schools'. *Education Psychology in Practice,* 7(4), pp. 218–22.

Central Statistics Office (2006). *Census 2006: The Irish language.* Available at: http://beyond2020.cso.ie/Census/ReportFolders/ReportFolders.aspx (retrieved 25/06/09).

Central Statistics Office (2007). *EU Survey on Income and Living Conditions (EU-SILC).* Available at: www.cso.ie/releasespublications/documents/ eu_silc/current/eusilc.pdf (retrieved 29/06/2009/2009).

Central Statistics Office (2008a). *Information Society and Telecommunications 2008.* Available at: http://www.cso.ie/releasespublications/documents/information_tech/ 2008/ictireland2008.pdf (retrieved 29/06/2009).

Central Statistics Office (2008b). *Non-Irish Nationals Living in Ireland.* Dublin: The Stationery Office.

Central Statistics Office (2009a). *Quarterly National Accounts, 30 June 2009.* Available at: http://www.cso.ie/releasespublications/documents/economy/ current/qna.pdf (retrieved 01/07/2009).

Central Statistics Office (2009b). *Live Register, 30 June 2009.* Available at: http://www.cso.ie/releasespublications/documents/labour_market/current/lreg.pdf (retrieved 01/07/2009).

Certeau, de, M. (1984). *The Practice of Everyday Life (Vol. 1). Arts de faire* (translator, Steven Rendall). Berkeley and London: University of California Press.

Certeau, de, M. Giard, L. & Mayol, P. (1989). *The Practice of Everyday Life (Vol. 2). Living and Cooking* (translator, Timothy J. Tomasik). Mineapolis: The University of Minesota Press.

Chambers, J.K. (2003). *Sociolinguistic Theory* (2nd edition). Oxford: Blackwell Publishing.

Champagne, A.B., Gunstone, R.F. & Klopfer, L.E. (1985). 'Effecting changes in cognitive structures among physics students'. In: L. West & A. Pines (eds), *Cognitive Structure and Conceptual Change* (pp. 163–87). Orlando: Academic Press.

Charlesworth, S.J. (2000). *A Phenomenology of Working Class Experience.* Cambridge, UK: Cambridge University Press.

Charter of University College Dublin 1910–11. Archives Department, University College Dublin.

Chuene, K., Luben, F. & Newson, G. (1999). 'The views of pre-service and novice teachers on mathematics teaching in South Africa related to their educational experience'. *Educational Research,* 41(1), pp. 23–34.

CILAR (Committee on Irish Language Attitude Research) (1975) *Report.* Dublin: The Stationery Office.

Clancy, P. (1995). 'Education in the Republic of Ireland: the project of modernity?'. In: P. Clancy, S. Drudy, K. Lynch & L. O'Dowd (eds), *Irish Society: Sociological Perspectives* (pp. 467–94). Dublin: Institute of Public Administration.

Clancy, P. (2001). *College Entry in Focus: A Fourth National Survey of Access to Higher Education,* Dublin: Higher Education Authority.

Clancy, P. & Wall, J. (2000). *Social Background of Higher Education Entrants.* Dublin: Higher Education Authority.

Clark, C., Dyson, A. & Millward, A. (eds) (1995). *Towards Inclusive Schools?* London: Routledge.

Clark, C., Dyson, A., Millward, A. & Robson, S. (1999). 'Theories of inclusion, theories of schools: deconstructing and reconstructing the 'inclusive' school'. *British Educational Research Journal,* 25 (2), pp. 157–77.

Clark, C., Dyson, A., Millward, A.J. & Skidmore, D. (1997). *New Directions in Special Needs: Innovations in Mainstream Schools.* London: Cassell.

Clough, E.E. & Driver, R. (1985). 'What do children understand about pressure in fluids'. *Research in Science & Technological Education,* 3, pp. 133–43.

Clynes, M. (2008). 'Changing Professional Development Needs of Teachers: An International Comparative Study'. Unpublished PhD thesis, School of Education, University College Dublin.

CNS Drug Discoveries (2004). Princeton, NJ: Epsicom.

Cochran-Smith, M. (2004a). 'Taking stock in 2004: teacher education in dangerous times'. *Journal of Teacher Education,* 55(1), pp. 3–7.

Cochran-Smith, M. (2004b). 'Stayers, leavers, lovers and dreamers: insights about teacher retention'. *Journal of Teacher Education,* 55(5), p. 387(386) [editorial].

Cohen, A. & Cohen, L. (1986). *Special Education Needs in the Ordinary School: A Sourcebook.* London: Harper & Roe.

Cohen, D. (2000). 'Social dynamics of stimulant prescription to school children in France and the United States'. *Pediatrics Grand Rounds.* Boston Medical Center.

Cohen, L., Manion, L. & Morrison, K. (2007). *Research Methods in Education* (6th edition). London and New York: Routledge.

Coleman, M. (2001). "The children are used most wretchedly': pupil responses to the Irish charter schools in the early twentieth century'. *History of Education,* 30(4), pp. 339–57.

Colin, A. (1998). 'Rethinking the relationship between theory and practice'. In: R. Edwards, R, Harrison & A. Tait (eds), *Telling Tales: Perspectives on Guidance and Counselling in Learning* (pp. 79–94). London: Routledge.

Collins, N., Cradden, T. & Butler, P. (eds) (2007). *Modernising Irish Government: The Politics of Administrative Reform.* Dublin: Gill & Macmillan.

Colum, M. (1947). *Life and the Dream.* London: Macmillan.

Combat Poverty Agency (1997). *Sharing in Progress*. Dublin: Combat Poverty Agency.

Comhairle na Gaeilge (1974). *Irish in Education*. Dublin: The Stationery Office.

Commission of the European Communities (Education and Culture) (2005). Testing conference on the common European principles for teacher competences and qualifications. Available at: http://ec.europa.eu/education/policies/2010/testingconf_en.html.

Commission of the European Communities (2007). Communication from the Commission to the Council and the European Parliament, Improving the quality of teacher education. {sec(2007) 931, sec (2007) 933 Brussles 3.8.2007., Com (2007) 392 final. Available at: http://ec.europa.eu/ dgs/education_culture/index_en.html (Chapter 16, retrieved, 29/06/2009).

Commission of Irish Education Inquiry (1825). *First Report of the Commission of Irish Education Inquiry*, 1825 (400) XII.

Commissioners of National Education in Ireland (1854). *Reading Book for Use of Female Schools*.

Commissioners of National Education in Ireland (1864). *Girls' Reading Book for Use of Schools*.

Commissioners of National Education in Ireland (1869). *Manual for Needlework*.

Commissioners of National Education in Ireland (1885). *Short Lessons in Domestic Science*.

Commission on the Status of People with Disabilities (1995). *A Strategy for Equality: Report of the Commission on the Status of People with Disabilities*. Dublin: The Stationery Office.

Conant, J.B. (ed.) (1957). *Harvard Case Histories in Experimental Science*. Cambridge, MA: Harvard University Press.

Connell, R.W. (1995). *Masculinity*. Sydney: Allen & Unwin.

Connell, R.W. & Messerschmidt, J.W. (2005). 'Hegemonic masculinity: rethinking the concept'. *Gender and Society*, 19(6), pp. 829–59.

Connolly P. (1998). *Racism, Gender Identities and Young Children*. London: Routledge.

Connolly, P. (2000). 'What now for the contact hypothesis? Towards a new research agenda'. *Race, Ethnicity and Education*, 3 (2), pp, 169–93.

Connolly P. (2004). *Boys and Schooling in the Early Years*. London: Routledge Falmer.

Conway, P., Murphy, R., Rath, A. & Hall, K. (2009). *Learning to Teach and its Implications for the Continuum of Teacher Education: A Nine-Country Cross-National Study. A Report Commissioned by the Teaching Council*. Maynooth: The Teaching Council of Ireland.

Coolahan, J. (1981). *Irish Education: Its History and Structure*. Dublin: Institute of Public Administration.

Coolahan, J. (ed.) (1994). *The Report of the National Education Convention*. Dublin: National Education Convention Secretariat/The Stationary Office.

Coolahan, J. (2003). *Attracting, Developing and Retaining Effective Teachers: Country Background Report for Ireland.* Paris: OECD. Available at: http://www.oecd.org (Chapter 12, retrieved 01/05/2009).

Coolahan, J. (2008). 'From Royal University to National University 1879–1908'. In: T. Dunne (ed.), *The National University of Ireland, 1908–2008*, pp. 3–18. Dublin: University College Dublin Press.

Cooney, A. (2003). ''I'm Stupid': An Action Research Intervention on Self-Esteem in a Special Educational Setting'. Unpublished MEd thesis, Education Department, University College Dublin.

Cooper, P. (2005). *AD/HD in Special Teaching for Special Children?* Maidenhead: Open University Press.

Cooper, P. & O'Regan, F.J. (2001). *Educating Children with AD/HD: A Teacher's Manual.* London: Routledge Falmer.

Cormack, R. & Osborne, R. (1995). 'Education in Northern Ireland: the struggle for equality'. In: P. Clancy, S. Drudy, K. Lynch & L. O'Dowd, *Irish Society: Sociological Perspectives* (pp. 495–528). Dublin: Institute of Public Administration.

Corsaro, W. (2005). *The Sociology of Childhood.* London: Pine Forge Press.

Cosgrove, J., Kellaghan, T., Forde, P., & Morgan, M. (2000). The *1998 National Assessment of English Reading.* Dublin: Educational Research Centre.

Cosgrove, J., Shiel, G., Sofroniou, N. & Kelly, A. (2001). *Ready for Life: The Literacy Achievements of Irish 15 Year Olds with Comparative International Data.* Dublin: Educational Research Centre.

Cosgrove, J., Shiel, G., Sofroniou, N., Saztrutski, S. & Shortt, F. (2004). *Education for Life: The Achievements of 15 Year Olds in Ireland in the Second Cycle of PISA.* Dublin: Educational Research Centre.

Council of Europe (2009). Available at: http://www.coe.int/T/E/ Social_cohesion/(retrieved 29/06/2009).

Cowne, E. (2005). 'What do special educational needs coordinators think they do?'. *Support for Learning,* 20(2), pp. 61–8.

Coyle, S. (2001). 'The resource teacher in primary schools'. *Learn: Journal of the Irish Learning Support Association,* 23, pp. 49–51.

Creegan, A. (2007). *From Difference to Disadvantage: 'Talking Posh' Sociolinguistic Perspectives on the Context of Schooling in Ireland.* Dublin: Combat Poverty Agency.

Croll, P. & Moses, D. (2000). *Special Needs in the Primary School: One in Five.* London: Cassell.

Cronbach L. (1951). 'Coefficient alpha and the internal structure of tests'. *Psychometrika,* 16, pp. 297–334.

Cullen, M. (1997) 'Towards a New Ireland: Women, Feminism and the Peace Process'. In: M.G. Valiulis & M. O'Dowd (eds), *Women and Irish History: Essays in Honour of Margaret MacCurtain* (pp. 260–77). Dublin: Wolfhound Press.

Cullen Owens, R., (2005). *A Social History of Women in Ireland, 1870–1970.* Dublin: Gill & Macmillan.

Cummins, J. (1982). 'A comparison of reading achievement in Irish and English medium schools'. *Oideas,* 26, pp. 21–6.

Cunningham, P. (2009). 'Science policy and evaluation: the Irish perspective'. Paper presented to *Evaluierunstag 2009,* Vienna, 23 March 2009. Available at: http://fteval.at/files/untitled/Cunningham.ppt#256,1,Science Policy and Evaluation: the Irish perspective (retrieved 28/06/2009).

Dahlman, C. (2004). Knowledge Strategies for Development: Challenges for Korea. Available at: http://siteresources.worldbank.org/EDUCATION/Resources/278200-1099079877269/547664-1099079956815/5476701128086743752/Pohang_KEDIWB_Dahlman_Feb04.ppt#727,1,Knowledge Strategies for Development: Challenges for Korea (retrieved 12/06/2009).

Dahlman, C. & Andersson, T. (2000). *Korea and the Knowledge-Based Economy: Making the Transition.* Washington: The International Bank for Reconstruction and Development/The World Bank and the Organisation for Economic Cooperation and Development/OECD.

Daly, M. (1979). 'The development of the national school system, 1831–40'. In: A. Cosgrave & D. MacCartney (eds), *Studies in Irish History* (pp. 151–63). Dublin: University College Dublin.

Darling-Hammond, L. (1995). 'Changing conceptions of teaching and teacher development'. *Teacher Education Quarterly,* 22(4), pp. 9–26.

Darling-Hammond, L. (2006). 'Constructing 21st-century teacher education'. *Journal of Teacher Education* 57(3), pp. 300–314.

Darling-Hammond, L. & Bransford, J. (eds) (2005). *Preparing Teachers for a Changing World: What Teachers should Learn and be able to do.* San Francisco: Jossey-Bass.

Darling-Hammond, L., Holtzman, D.J., Gatlin, S.J. & Heilig, J.V. (2005). 'Does teacher preparation matter? Evidence about teacher certification, teach for America, and teacher effectiveness'. *Education Policy Analysis Archives,* 13(42). Available at: http://epaa.asu.edu/epaa/v2013n2042/ (retrieved 12/04/2007).

Daugherty, R. (2008). 'Reviewing national curriculum assessment in Wales: how can evidence inform the development of policy?'. *Cambridge Journal of Education,* 38(1), pp. 73–87.

Davies, B. (2005). 'The (im)possibility of intellectual work in neoliberal regimes'. *Discourse: Studies in the Cultural Politics of Education,* 26 (1), pp. 1–14.

Davies, L. (2006) 'Global citizenship: abstraction or framework for action?'. *Educational Review,* 58(1), pp. 5–25.

Davis, P. & Florian, L. (2004). *Teaching Strategies and Approaches for Pupils with Special Educational Needs: A Scoping Study.* HMSO: Department for Education & Skills.

Deegan, J. (1996). *Children's Friendships in Culturally Diverse Classrooms*. London: Falmer Press.

Delpit, L. (2006). *Other People's Children: Cultural Conflict in the Classroom*. New York: The New Press.

DENI (Department of Education, Northern Ireland) (2008). 'Full-time equivalent (Fte) teachers for 2007/08 by area board and management type, Table 1'. Available at: http://www.deni.gov.uk/fte_teachers_by_board_ and_mantype-7.xls (retrieved 05/06/2009).

Department for Education (DfE) (1994). *Code of Practice on the Identification and Assessment of Special Educational Needs*. London: HMSO.

Department for Education & Skills (DfES) (2001). *Special Education Needs: Code of Practice*. London: HMSO.

Department of Education (1965). *Investment in Education*. Report of the survey team appointed by the Minister of Education. Dublin: The Stationery Office.

Department of Education (1993). *Report of the Special Education Review Committee (SERC Report)*. Dublin: The Stationery Office.

Department of Education (1994). *Circular M10/94*. Revision of Rule 46 of the 'Rules and Programme for Secondary Schools' in relation to exemption from Irish. Available at: http://www.education.ie/ servlet/blobservlet/ppc10 _94.doc (retrieved 10/9/2009).

Department of Education (1995a). *An Ardteistiméireacht: Gaeilge (Gnáthleibhéal agus Ardleibhéal) Na Siollabais agus an Córas Measúnachta*. Dublin: The Stationery Office.

Department of Education (1995b). *An Ardteistiméireacht: Gaeilge (Bonnleibhéal) An Siollabas*. Dublin: The Stationery Office.

Department of Education (1996). *Circular M12/96*. Revision to circular 18/79 on the exemption from the study of Irish in national schools. Available at: http://www.education.ie/servlet/blobservlet/pc12_96.doc (retrieved 10/9/2009).

Department of Education (1999). *Primary School Curriculum*. Dublin: The Stationery Office.

Department of Education & Science (2000). *Review of Department's Operations, Systems and Staffing Needs (The Cromien Report)*. Dublin: The Stationery Office.

Department of Education & Science (2002a). *Circular SP.ED 07/02. Applications for Full-Time or Part-Time Special Needs Assistant Support to Address the Care Needs of Children with Disabilities*. Available at:http://www.education.ie/servlet/ blobservlet/spedc07_02.pdf (retrieved 30/06/2009).

Department of Education & Science (2002b). *Circular SP.ED 08/02. Applications for Full-Time or Part-Time Resource Teacher Support to Address the Special Education Needs of Children with Disabilities*. Available at: http://www.into.ie/

ROI/InformationforTeachers/DESCirculars/DESCirculars2002/filedownload,428, en.pdf (retrieved 30/06/2009).

Department of Education & Science (2002c). *Guidelines on Traveller Education in Second-Level Schools*. Dublin: The Stationery Office.

Department of Education & Science (2005a). *Literacy and Numeracy in Disadvantaged Schools: Challenges for Teachers and Learners: An Evaluation by the Inspectorate of the Department of Education & Science*. Dublin: The Stationery Office. Available at: http://www.education.ie/servlet/blobservlet/insp_literacy_numeracy_05.pdf (Chapter 3, retrieved 27/06/2009).

Department of Education & Science (2005b). *DEIS: Delivering Equality of Opportunity in Schools*. Available at: http://www.education.ie/servlet/blobservlet/deis_index.html (Chapter 3, retrieved 19/06/2006) (Chapter 8, retrieved 30/04/2009).

Department of Education & Science (2005c). *Circular SP.ED 02/05. Organisation of Teaching Resources for Pupils who Need Additional Support in Mainstream Primary Schools and Special Education Needs: A Continuum of Support*. Available at: http://www.education.ie/servlet/blobservlet/sp02_05.doc (retrieved 30/06/2009).

Department of Education & Science (2005d). *Summary of all Initiatives Funded by the Department to Help Alleviate Educational Disadvantage*. Available at: http://www.education.ie/servlet/blobervlet/si_summary_02.doc (retrieved 30/04/2009).

Department of Education & Science (2006). *Department of Education and Science Annual Report 2006*. Dublin: The Stationery Office.

Department of Education & Science (2007a). *Irish in the Primary School (Inspectorate Evaluation Studies)*. Dublin: The Stationery Office/Evaluation Research & Support Unit.

Department of Education & Science/O'Connor, M. (2007b). *Sé sí—gender in Irish education*. Available at: http://www.education.ie/servlet/blobservlet/des_sesi_intro.html (retrieved 05/06/2009).

Department of Education & Science (2008a). *Main Estimate Features*. Available at: http://www.asti.ie/pdfs/budgetcuts.pdf (retrieved 12/06/2009).

Department of Education & Science (2008b). *Development of an Intercultural Education Strategy*. Paper presented at a consultation process for the development of an intercultural education strategy. Dublin: The Stationery Office.

Department of Education & Science (2008c). *Traveller Students Double in Post-Primary Schools in Six Years*. Available at: http://www.education.ie/home/home.jsp?maincat=&pcategory=10861&ecategory=10876&sectionpage=12251&language=EN&lin=link001&page=1&doc=42200 (retrieved 30/07/09).

Department of Education & Science (2009a). *Statistical Report 2005/2006*. Available at: http://www.education.ie/servlet/blobservlet/des_Statistics05 _EdSys.htm (retrieved 25/06/09).

Department of Education & Science (2009b). *Education Statistics 2006/2007*. Available at: http://www.education.ie/servlet/blobservlet/statistics_key_06 _07.pdf (retrieved 12/06/2009).

Department of Health & Children (2001). *Working Group on Child and Adolescent Psychiatric Services*. Dublin: The Stationery Office.

Department of Health & Children (2007). *Sectoral Plan under the Disability Act 2005 Year 1 Review*. Available at: http://www.dohc.ie/publications/fulltext/disability_ sectoral_plan/health_sectoral_plan_02.html (retrieved 30/06/ 2009).

Department of Justice, Equality & Law Reform (2005). *Planning for Diversity: The National Action Plan Against Racism 2005–2008*. Dublin: The Stationery Office.

Department of the Taoiseach (2008). *Transforming Public Services: Report of the Task Force on the Public Services*. Dublin: The Stationery Office. Available at: http:// www.taoiseach.gov.ie/eng/Publications/Publications_2008/Transforming_Public_ Services1.pdf.

Devereux, E., Breen, M. & Haynes, A. (2005). "Smuggling Zebras for Lunch': media framing of asylum seekers in the Irish print media'. *Études Irlandaises*, 30(1), pp. 109–30.

Devine, D. (2000). 'Constructions of childhood in school: power, policy and practice in Irish Education'. *International Studies in Sociology of Education*. 10 (1), pp. 23–41.

Devine D. (2003). *Children, Power and Schooling: How Childhood is Structured in the Primary School*. Stoke-on-Trent: Trentham Books.

Devine D. (2005). 'Welcome to the Celtic Tiger? Teacher responses to immigration and increasing ethnic diversity in Irish schools'. *International Studies in Sociology of Education*, 15, pp. 49–71.

Devine, D. (2007). 'Immigration and the Enlargement of children's social space in school'. In: H. Zeiher, D. Devine, A. Kjorholt & H. Strandell (eds), Flexible Childhood? Exploring Children's Welfare in Time and Space (pp. 143–69). Odense: University Press of Southern Denmark.

Devine, D. (2009). 'Mobilising capitals? Migrant children's negotiation of their everyday lives in school'. *British Journal of Sociology of Education*, 30(5), pp. 521–35.

Devine, D. (in press: 2010). *Immigration and Schooling in Ireland*. Manchester: Manchester University Press.

Devine, D., Kenny, M. & MacNeela, E. (2008). "Naming the other'—children's constructions and experience of racisms in Irish primary schools'. *Race Ethnicity and Education*, 11 (4), pp. 369–85.

Devine, F., Savage, M., Scott, J. & Crompton, R. (2005). *Rethinking Class: Culture, Identities and Lifestyles*. London: Palgrave Macmillan.

Donaldson, M. (1978). *Children's Minds*. London: Fontana.

Dörnyei, Z. (2001). *Teaching and Researching Motivation*. Harlow, England: Longman.

Driver, R. (1983). *The Pupil as Scientist?* Milton Keynes: Open University Press.

Drudy, S. (2006a). 'Gender differences in entrance patterns and awards in initial teacher education'. *Irish Educational Studies*, 29(3), pp. 259–73.

Drudy, S. (2006b). 'Change and reform in teacher education in Ireland: a case study in the reform of higher education'. In: P. Zgaga (ed.), *Modernization of Study Programmes in Teachers' Education in an International Context* (pp. 37–49). Ljubljana: Pedagoska Faculteta.

Drudy, S. (2008a). 'Professionalism, performativity and care: whither teacher education for a gendered profession in Europe?'. In: B. Hudson & P. Zgaga (eds), *Teacher Education Policy in Europe: A Voice of Higher Education Institutions* (pp. 43–62). Umea: University of Umea. Also available at: http://www.pef.uni-lj.si/tepe2008/documents/a-voice-from.pdf.

Drudy, S. (2008b). 'Gender balance/gender bias: the teaching profession and the impact of feminization'. *Gender and Education*, 20 (4) pp. 309–23.

Drudy, S. & Kinsella, W. (2009). 'Developing an inclusive system in a rapidly changing European society'. *International Journal of Inclusive Education*, 13(6), pp. 647–63.

Drudy, S. & Lynch, K. (1993). *Schools and Society in Ireland*. Dublin: Gill & Macmillan.

Drudy, S., Johnston, J. & Martin, M. (2003). *Patterns of Recruitment to Primary Teaching in the Republic of Ireland and Northern Ireland: A Comparative Analysis*. Report to the Royal Irish Academy, Dublin.

Drudy, S., Martin, M., Woods, M. & O'Flynn, J. (2005). *Men and the Classroom: Gender Imbalances in Teaching*. London and New York: Routledge.

Dunn, L. (1968). 'Special education for the mildly retarded: is much of it justifiable?'. *Exceptional Children* 35(1), pp. 3–22.

Dyer, R. (1988). 'White'. *Screen*, 29(4), pp. 44–65.

Dyhouse, C. (1981). *Girls Growing up in Late Victorian and Edwardian England*. London: Routledge & Kegan Paul.

Dyhouse, C. (1995). *No Distinction of Sex? Women in British Universities, 1870–1939*. London: Routledge.

Dyson, A. (2001). 'Special needs in the twenty-first century: where we've been and where we're going'. *British Journal of Special Education*, 28(1), p. 24.

Dyson, A. & Millward, A. (2000). *Schools and Special Needs: Issues of Innovation and Inclusion*. London: Paul Chapman.

Eivers, E., Shiel, G. & Shortt, F. (2004). *Literacy in Disadvantaged Primary Schools*, Dublin: Educational Research Centre.

Eivers, E., Shiel, G., Perkins, R. & Cosgrove, J. (2005). *The 2004 National Assessment of English Reading*, Dublin: Educational Research Centre.

Emanuelsson, I. (2001). 'Reactive versus proactive support coordinator roles: an international comparison'. *European Journal of Special Needs Education*, 16 (2), pp. 133–42.

European Commission (2005). *Common European Principles for Teacher Competences and Qualifications.* Available at: http://www.see-educoop.net/ education_in/pdf/01-en_principles_en.pdf (retrieved 01/06/2009).

European Commission (2007). Communication from the Commission to the Council and the European Parliament: improving the quality of teacher education, (sec(2007) 931, sec(2007)933 Brussels, 3.8.2007, Com (2007) 392 final. Available at: http://ec.europa.eu/dgs/education_culture/index_en.html (retrieved 01/06/2009).

European Commission (Economic and Financial Affairs) (2008). 'The economy of Ireland: whither the 'Celtic Tiger'?' *European Economy News,* Issue 11, October 2008. Available at: http://ec.europa.eu/economy_finance/een/011/article_7086_en.htm (retrieved 29/06/2009).

Evans, R.J. (1977). *The Feminists: Women's Emancipation Movements in Europe, America and Australasia, 1840–1920.* London: Croom Helm.

Evans, J., Lunt, I., Wedell, K. & Dyson, A. (1999). *Collaborating for Effectiveness.* Buckingham, PA: Open University Press.

Feiman-Nemser, S. & Remillard, J. (1996). 'Perspectives on learning to teach'. In: F.B. Murray (ed.), *The Teacher Educator's Handbook* (pp. 63–91). San Francisco: Jossey-Bass.

Fensham, P.J. (1994). 'Beginning to teach chemistry'. In: P.J. Fensham, R.F. Gunstone & R.T. White (eds), *The Content of Science: A Constructivist Approach to Its Teaching and Learning* (Chapter 2). London: Falmer Press.

Ferguson, D.L. (2008). 'International trends in inclusive education: the continuing challenge to teach each one and everyone'. *European Journal of Special Needs Education,* 23(2), pp. 109–20.

Finegold, D., McFarland, L. & Richardson, W. (eds) (1992). *Something Borrowed, Something Blue? A Study of the Thatcher Government's Appropriation of American Education and Training Policy, Part 1.* Didcot, UK: Symposium Books: Oxford Studies in Comparative Education series, Volume 2 (2).

Finn, I. (2000). 'Women in the Medical Profession in Ireland, 1876–1919'. In: B. Whelan (ed.), *Women and Paid Work in Ireland, 1500–1930* (pp. 102–19). Dublin: Four Courts Press.

Fish, J. (1985). 'Community, co-operation, co-partnership'. *Proceedings of the International Congress of Special Education.* Nottingham, UK.

Forest, M. & Pearpoint, J. (1990). 'Supports for addressing maladaptive behaviours'. In: W. Stainback & S. Stainback (eds), *Support Networks for Inclusive Schooling.* Baltimore: Paul H. Brooks.

Forlin, C. (2001a). 'The role of the support teacher in Australia'. *European Journal of Special Needs Education,* 16(2), pp. 121–31.

Forlin, C. (2001b). 'The role of the support teacher in regular schools—an international comparison'. *European Journal of Special Needs Education*, 16(2), pp. 83–4.

Foucault, M. (1979). *Discipline and Punish: The Birth of the Prison*. New York: Random House.

Foucault, M. (1980). *Michel Foucault: Power/Knowledge*. Hemel Hempstead: Harvester Wheatsheaf.

Foucault, M. (1988). *Power/Knowledge: Selected Interviews and Other Writings* (ed. C. Gordon). Hemel Hempstead: Harvester Wheatsheaf.

Foucault, M. (1991). *Discipline and Punish*. London: Penguin.

Fox, E. (2007). 'An investigation into the attitudes of fifth and sixth grade pupils and their teachers towards the Irish language as a subject at primary school. A study of five primary schools in Dublin'. Unpublished Masters thesis. University College Dublin, Dublin, Ireland.

Fraser, N. (2000). 'Rethinking recognition'. *New Left Review*, 3(May/June), pp. 107–20.

Fraser, S. (2004). *Doing Research with Children and Young People*. London: Sage/Open University Press.

Freeman, M., Marrais, de, K., Preissle, J., Roulston, K. & St Pierre, E.A. (2007). 'Standards of evidence in qualitative research: an incitement to discourse'. *Educational Researcher*, 36 (1), pp. 25–32.

Freire, P. (1974). *Education for Critical Consciousness*. New York: Continuum.

Fullan, M. (1991). *The New Meaning of Educational Change*. London: Cassell.

Furlong, J. & White, P. (2001). *Educational Research Capacity in Wales*. Cardiff: School of Social Sciences, Cardiff University.

Gaden, G. (1993). 'Integrated education, mental disability and respect for persons'. *Irish Educational Studies*, 12, pp. 57–72.

Gallagher, C.J. (2003). 'Reconciling a tradition of testing with a new learning paradigm'. *Educational Psychology Review*, 15 (1) pp. 83–99.

Galloway, D. M. & Goodwin, C. (1979). *Educating Slow Learning and Maladjusted Children: Integration or Segregation?* Harlow: Longman.

Galvin, C. (2003). *The Induction of New and Beginning Teachers to County Dublin Schools and Colleges: Capacity Building to Meet the Challenges*. Dublin: CoDubVEC.

Galvin, C. (2007). 'Contextualizing the emerging research and policy interface in Ireland'. A presentation to the Joint Academy of Social Sciences and Royal Irish Academy Seminar on *Assessing Research Quality in the Social Sciences*. Belfast, Friday, 22 June 2007.

Gannon, M. (2009). 'Frameworks for responding to diversity in schools'. In: G. Jeffers & U. O'Connor (eds), *Education for Citizenship and Diversity in Irish Contexts* (pp. 124–40). Dublin: Institute of Public Administration.

Gardner, J. & Gallagher, T. (2007). 'Gauging the deliverable? Educational research in Northern Ireland'. *European Educational Research Journal*, Vol.6(1), pp. 101–14.

Gardner, J., Holmes, B. & Leitch, R. (2008). 'Where there is smoke, there is (the potential for) fire: soft indicators of research and policy impact'. *Cambridge Journal of Education*, Vol.38 (1), pp. 89–104.

Gardner, R.C. (1985). *The Attitude/Motivation Test Battery: Technical Report*. Ontario: Department of Psychology, University of Western Ontario.

Gardner, R.C. & Lambert, W.E. (1959). 'Motivational variables in second language acquisition'. *Canadian Journal of Psychology*, 13, pp. 266–72.

Garner, S. (2007a). *Whiteness: An Introduction*. New York: Routledge.

Garner, S. (2007b). 'The uses of whiteness: what sociologists working on Europe can learn from North American work on whiteness'. *Sociology*, 40(2), pp. 257–75.

Giddens, A. (1998). *The Third Way: The Renewal of Social Democracy*. London: Polity Press.

Giddens, A. (2007). 'Its time to give the third way a second chance'. *Independent*. 28/06/2007.

Gill, M.G., Ashton, P.T. & Algina, J. (2004). 'Changing pre-service teachers' epistemological beliefs about teaching and learning: an intervention study'. *Contemporary Educational Psychology*, 29, pp. 164–85.

Gillborn, D. (2006). 'Critical Race Theory and Education: Racism and anti-racism in educational theory and practice'. *Discourse: Studies in the Cultural Politics of Education*, 27(1), pp. 11–32.

Gillborn, D. (2008). *Racism and Education: Coincidence or Conspiracy*. Routledge: London.

Goldstein, H., Moss, J. & Jordan, L. (1965). 'The efficacy of special class training on the development of mentally retarded children'. In: *Co-operative Research Project No. 619*. Washington, DC: Office of Education.

Gipps, C. & Murphy, P. (1994). *A Fair Test?* Buckingham, PA: Open University Press.

Giroux, H.A. (1983). *Theory and Resistance in Education: A Pedagogy for the Opposition*. London: Heinemann.

Giroux, H.A. (1997). 'Racial politics and the pedagogy of whiteness'. In: M. Hill (ed.), *Whiteness: A Critical Reader* (pp. 294–315). New York: New York University Press.

Giroux, H.A. (2001). 'Cultural studies as performative politics'. *Cultural Studies/Critical Methodologies*, 1 (1), pp. 5–23.

Giroux, H.A. & McLaren, P. (1989). *Critical Pedagogy: The State and Cultural Struggle*. New York: New York University Press.

Giroux, H.A. & McLaren, P. (1994). *Between Borders*. New York: Routledge.

Glasersfeld, von, E. (1996). *Radical Constructivism: A Way of Knowing and Learning*. London and Washington: Falmer Press.

Gleeson, J. (2004). 'Concurrent teacher education (post-primary) in the Republic of Ireland: Some issues and trends'. In: A. Burke (ed.), *Teacher Education in the Republic of Ireland: Retrospect and Prospect* (pp. 43–53). Armagh: Centre for Cross Border Studies.

Gleeson, J. & Ó Donnabháin, D. (2009). 'Strategic planning and accountability in Irish Education'. *Irish Educational Studies,* 28 (1) pp. 27–46.

Goffman, I. (1959). *The Presentation of Self in Everyday Life.* Middlesex: Penguin.

Goldstrom, J.M. (1972). *The Social Content of Education, 1808–1870: A Study of the Working Class School Reader in England and Ireland.* Shannon: Irish University Press.

Goodbody Economic Consultants (2001). *Review of the National Anti-Poverty Strategy Framework.* Dublin: Goodbody.

Goodson, I. (2003). *Professional Knowledge, Professional Lives: Studies in Education and Change.* Maidenhead and Buckingham, PA: Open University Press.

Government of Ireland (1986). *Combat Poverty Agency Act.* Dublin: The Stationery Office.

Government of Ireland (1992). *Education for a Changing World: Green Paper on Education.* Dublin: The Stationery Office.

Government of Ireland (1995). *Charting our Education Future: White Paper on Education.* Dublin: The Stationery Office.

Government of Ireland (1996). *Delivering Better Government.* Available at: http://www.onegov.ie/eng/Publications/Delivering_Better_Government_-_report.pdf.

Government of Ireland (1997). *Universities Act.* Dublin: The Stationery Office.

Government of Ireland (1998a). *Adult Education in an Era of Lifelong Learning: Green Paper on Adult Education.* Dublin: The Stationery Office.

Government of Ireland (1998b). *Education Act.* Dublin: The Stationery Office.

Government of Ireland (1998c). *Employment Equality Act.* Dublin: The Stationery Office.

Government of Ireland (1998, 2004). *Equality Act.* Dublin: The Stationery Office.

Government of Ireland (1999). *Ready to Learn: White Paper on Early Education.* Dublin: The Stationery Office.

Government of Ireland (2000a). *Education (Welfare) Act.* Dublin: The Stationery Office.

Government of Ireland (2000b). *Equal Status Act.* Dublin: The Stationery Office.

Government of Ireland (2000c). *Human Rights Commission Act.* Dublin: The Stationery Office.

Government of Ireland (2000b). *Learning for Life: White Paper on Adult Education.* Dublin: The Stationery Office.

Government of Ireland (2000c). 'Memorandum of understanding on education between the Government of the United States of America and the Government of Ireland'. Available at: http://historical-debates.oireachtas.ie/D/0521/D.0521.20000 6140116.html(retrieved 26/06/2009).

Government of Ireland (2000–2004). *Equal Status Acts.* Dublin: The Stationery Office.

Government of Ireland (2001). *Teaching Council Act.* Dublin: The Stationery Office.

Government of Ireland (2002). *Report on the Task Force on the Physical Sciences.* Dublin: The Stationery Office. Available at: http://irlgov.ie/educ/pub.htm and http://www.sciencetaskforce.ie/report (retrieved 16/07/09).

Government of Ireland (2004a). *Education for Persons with Special Educational Needs Act.* Dublin: The Stationery Office.

Government of Ireland (2004b). *Equality Act.* Dublin: The Stationery Office.

Government of Ireland (2005). *Disability Act.* Dublin: The Stationery Office.

Government of Ireland (2006). *Strategy for Science, Technology and Innovation 2006–2013.* Dublin: Department of Enterprise, Trade & Employment.

Government of Ireland (2008a). *Building Ireland's Smart Economy: A Framework for Sustainable Economic Renewal.* Dublin: The Stationery Office. Available at: http://www.taoiseach.gov.ie/eng/Publications/Publications_2008/ BuildingIrelandSmartEconomy.rtf (retrieved 06/06/2009).

Government of Ireland (2008b). *Looking at Junior Cycle Science: Teaching and Learning in Post-Primary Schools.* Dublin: Inspectorate, Evaluation Support and Research Unit, Department of Education & Science.

Government of Ireland (2009). *Growing Up in Ireland: National Longitudinal Study of Children: Key Findings 9 Year Olds.* Dublin: Economic and Social Research Institute and TCD (Children's Research Centre).

Grandy, R.E. (1998). 'Constructivisms and objectivity: disentangling metaphysics, from pedagogy'. In: M.R. Matthews (ed.), *Constructivism in Science Education* (pp. 113–23). Dordrecht, The Netherlands: Kluwer Academic Publishers.

Greaney, V., Burke, A. & McCann, J. (1987). 'Entrants to primary teacher education in Ireland'. *European Journal of Teacher Education,* 10 (2), pp. 127–40.

Green, A. (2006). 'Models of lifelong learning and the 'knowledge society''. *Compare,* 36(3), pp. 307–25.

Greenacre, M.J. (1993). *Correspondence Analysis in Practice.* London: Academic Press.

Grek, S. (2009). 'Governing by numbers: the PISA 'effect' in Europe'. *Journal of Education Policy,* 21 (1), pp. 23–37.

Grek, S., Lawn, M., Lingard, B., Ozga, J., Rinne, R., Segerholm, C. & Simola, H. (2009). 'National policy brokering and the construction of the European Education Space in England, Sweden, Finland and Scotland'. *Comparative Education,* 45(1), pp. 5–21.

Griffin S. & Shevlin, M. (2007). *Responding to Special Educational Needs: An Irish Perspective.* Dublin: Gill & Macmillan.

GTCS (General Teaching Council for Scotland) (2002). *Achieving the Standard for Full Registration: Guidance for New Teachers.* Edinburgh: GTCS.

Gunstone, R.F. (1995). 'Constructivist learning and the teaching of science'. In: B. Hand & V. Prain (eds), *Teaching and Learning in Science* (Chapter 1, pp. 3–20). Sydney: Harcourt Brace.

Haertel, E.H. & Lorié W.A. (2004). 'Validating standards-based test score interpretations'. *Measurement,* 2 (2), pp. 61–103.

Hage, G. (1998). *White Nation: Fantasies of White Supremacy in a Multicultural Society.* Annandale, NSW and UK: Pluto Press.

Hage, G. (2008). *The Weight of Words.* UpClose Podcast. The University of Melbourne. Available at: http://upclose.unimelb.edu.au/episode/143 (retrieved 30/07/09).

Hall, J. (1992). 'Segregation by another name?' *Special Children,* 56 (April), pp. 20–3.

Hall, S. (1998). 'Notes on deconstructing the popular'. In: J. Storey, *Cultural Studies and the Study Popular Culture: Theories and Methods* (2nd edition) (pp. 442–53). Edinburgh: Edinburgh University Press.

Hamilton, D. (1975). 'Handling innovation in the classroom: two Scottish examples'. In: A.W. Reid & D.F. Walker (eds), *Case Studies in Curriculum Change* (pp. 179–207). London: Routledge.

Hanafin, M. (2007). 'Minister Hanafin marks 200% increase in the number of autism specific classes available in schools throughout the country'. Ministerial press release, 16 November, 2007. Available at: http://www.education.ie (retrieved 19/06/2009).

Harford, J. (2005). 'The Movement for the Higher Education of Women in Ireland: Gender Equality or Denominational Rivalry?'. *History of Education* 34(5), pp. 497–516.

Harford, J. (2007). 'An Experiment in the Development of Social Networks for Women: Women's Colleges in Ireland in the Nineteenth Century'. *Paedogogica Historica,* 43(3), pp. 365–81.

Harford, J. (2008). *The Opening of University Education to Women in Ireland.* Dublin and Portland, OR: Irish Academic Press.

Hargreaves, A. (2007). 'Sustainable leadership and development in education: creating the future, conserving the past'. *European Journal of Education,* 42(2), pp. 223–33.

Hargreaves, A. & Fullan, M. (2000). 'Mentoring in the new millennium'. *Theory into Practice,* 39 (1), pp. 50–6.

Harre, R. (1993). *Social Being.* Oxford: Blackwell.

Harris, J. (1984). *Spoken Irish in Primary Schools: An Analysis of Achievement.* Dublin: Institiúid Teangeolaíochta Éireann.

Harris, J. (1989). 'The policy-making role of the Department of Education'. In: D.G. Mulcahy & D. O'Sullivan (eds), *Irish Education Policy: Process and Substance* (pp. 7–25). Dublin: Institute of Public Administration.

Harris, J. (2006). 'Conclusions and recommendations'. In: J. Harris, P. Forde, P. Archer, S. Nic Fhearaile & M. O'Gorman, *Irish in Primary Schools: Long-Term National Trends in Achievement.* Dublin: Department of Education & Science.

Harris, J., Forde, P., Archer, P., Nic Fhearaile, S. & O'Gorman, M. (2006). *Irish in Primary Schools: Long-Term National Trends in Achievement.* Dublin: Department of Education & Science.

Harris, J. & Murtagh, L. (1987). 'Irish and English in Gaeltacht primary schools'. In: G. Mac Eoin, A. Ahlqvist & D. Ó hAodha (eds), *Third International Conference on Minority Languages: Celtic Papers* (pp. 104–24). Clevedon: Multilingual Matters.

Harris, J. & Murtagh, L. (1988). 'National assessment of Irish-language speaking and listening skills in primary-school children: Research issues in the evaluation of school-based heritage-language programmes'. *Language, Culture and Curriculum,* 1 (2), pp. 85–130.

Harris, J. & Murtagh, L. (1999). *Teaching and Learning Irish in Primary School.* Dublin: Institiúid Teangeolaíochta Éireann.

Harris, M.K. & Johnson, P.E. (1998). 'A large-scale schools, higher education collaboration to implement systemic change in mathematics teaching and learning'. *International Journal of Mathematical Education in Science and Technology,* 29(5), pp. 697–707.

Hayden, C. & Dunne, S. (2001). *Outside Looking In: Children's and Families' Experience of Exclusion from School.* London: The Children's Society.

Hegarty, S. (1993). *Meeting Special Needs in Ordinary Schools: An Overview.* London: Cassell.

Hegarty, S. & Pocklington, K. (1981). *Educating Children with Special Needs in the Ordinary School.* Windsor: National Foundation for Educational Research—Nelson.

Heinz, M. (2008). 'The composition of applicants and entrants to teacher education programmes in Ireland: trends and patterns'. *Irish Educational Studies,* 27(3), pp. 223–40.

Henze, R., Katz, A. & Norte, E. (2000). 'Rethinking the concept of racial or ethnic conflict in schools: a leadership perspective'. *Race Ethnicity and Education,* Vol. 3, No. 2, pp. 195–206.

Heyer, den, K. (2009). 'Implicated and called upon: challenging an educated position of self, others, knowledge and knowing as things to acquire'. *Critical Literacy: Theories and Practices,* 3(1), pp, 26–36.

Higher Education Authority (2007). *National Office for Equity in Higher Education: Annual Report 2006, Outline Plans 2007.* Dublin: Higher Education Authority.

Higher Education Authority (2009). *Higher Education, Key Facts and Figures 07/08.* Dublin: Higher Education Authority.

Hirst, P. (1993). 'Educational theory'. In: M. Hammersley (ed.), *Educational Research: Current Issues* (pp. 149–59). London: Paul Chapman.

Holmes, R. (1995). *How Young Children Perceive Race.* Sage: London.

Hopkins, D. (2002). *A Teacher's Guide to Classroom Research* (3rd edition). Milton Keynes: Open University Press.

House of Commons, Education & Skills Select Committee (2006). *Special Educational Needs: Third Report of Session 2005, 2006*, Vol. 1. London: HMSO.

Howes, A., Booth, T., Dyson, A. & Frankham, J. (2005). 'Teacher learning and the development of inclusive practices and policies: framing and context'. *Research Papers in Education*, 20(2), pp. 133–48.

Huat See, B. (2004). 'Determinants of teaching as a career in the UK'. *Evaluation and Research in Education*, 18 (4), pp. 213–42.

Huberman, M., Grounauer, M-M. & Marti, J. (1991). *The Lives of Teachers* (translator, J. Neufel). London: Cassell.

Hudson, B. & Zgaga, P. (eds) (2008). *Teacher Education Policy in Europe: A Voice of Higher Education Institutions*. Umea: University of Umea, Faculty of Education.

Huggins, R., Izushi, H., Davies, W. & Shougui, L. (2008). *World Knowledge Competitiveness Index, 2008*. University of Wales Institute, Cardiff: Centre for International Competitiveness, Cardiff School of Management.

Hyland, A. & Milne, K. (1987). *Irish Educational Documents*, Vol. I. Dublin: CICE.

Hyland, A. & Moore, J. (2009). 'Child literacy and social inclusion', paper presented to the National Economic and Social Forum Conference on Child Literacy and Social Inclusion, 16 June 2009, Dublin. Available at: http://www.nesf.ie/en/default.asp (retrieved 19/06/2009).

Hymes, D. (1972). 'On communicative competence'. In: J.B. Pride & J. Holmes (eds), *Sociolinguistics*. Harmondsworth: Penguin.

Hytten, K. & Warren, J. (2003). 'Engaging whiteness: how racial power gets reified in education'. *Qualitative Studies in Education*, 16(1), pp. 65–89.

IAWG to the Chancellor and Senators of the National University (n.d.) NUWGA 1/3. Archives Department, University College Dublin.

Imants, J., Aalsvoort, van der, G., Brababder, de, C. & Ruijsssenaars, A. (2001). 'The role of the special services coordinator in Dutch primary schools'. *Educational Management & Administration*, 29(1), p. 13.

Incorporated Society for Promoting English Protestant Schools (1737). *Proceedings of the Incorporated Society for Promoting English Protestant Schools*.

International Monetary Fund (Fiscal Affairs Department) (2009). *The State of Public Finances: Outlook and Medium-Term Policies after the 2008 Crisis*. 6 March 2009. Available at: http://www.imf.org/external/np/pp/eng/ 2009/030609.pdf (retrieved 10/03/2009).

INTO (Irish National Teachers' Organisation) (1941). *Report of the Committee of Inquiry into the use of Irish as a Teaching Medium to Children whose Home Language is English*. Dublin: INTO.

INTO (Irish National Teachers' Organisation) (2004). *Gender Imbalance in Primary Teaching: A Discussion Document*. Available at: http://www.into.ie/ROI/Downloads/Publications/Other/filedownload,960,en.pdf (accessed 05.06.2009).

Jacobs, A. (2007) 'Examinations as Cultural Capital for the Victorian Schoolgirl: 'Thinking' with Bourdieu'. *Women's History Review*, 16(2), pp. 245–61.

Jacobs, J.A. (1993). 'Men in female-dominated fields'. In: C. Williams (ed.), *Doing 'Women's Work': Men in Nontraditional Occupations* (pp. 49–63). London: Sage.

James, A. & James, A. (eds) (2008). *European Childhoods: Cultures, Politics and Participation*. New York: Palgrave Press.

Jefferes, D. (2008). 'Global citizenship and the cultural politics of benevolence'. *Critical Literacy: Theories and Practices*, 2(1), pp. 27–36.

Jenkins, E.W. (2000). 'Constructivism in school science education: Powerful model or the most dangerous intellectual tendency?'. *Science and Education*, 9, pp. 599–610.

Johnson, O.G. (1962). 'Special education for the mentally handicapped: A paradox'. *Exceptional Children*, 29, pp. 62–9.

Johnson, P. (1998). 'Children's understanding of changes of state involving the gas state, Part 1: Boiling water and the particle theory'. *International Journal of Science Education*, 20 (5), pp. 567–83.

Johnston, J., McKeown, E. & McEwen, A. (1998). *Primary Concerns: Gender Factors in Choosing Primary School Teaching*. Report funded by the Equal Opportunities Commission for Northern Ireland. Belfast: Graduate School of Education, The Queen's University.

Johnston, K. & Hayes, D. (2007). 'Supporting student success at school through teacher professional learning: the pedagogy of disrupting the default modes of schooling'. *International Journal of Inclusive Education*, 11(3), pp. 371–81.

Jones, M.G. (1938). *The Charity School Movement*. Cambridge, UK: Cambridge University Press.

Joyce, B., Showers, B. & Rolheiser-Bennett, C. (1987). 'Staff Development and Student Learning: A Synthesis of Research on Models of Teaching'. *Educational Leadership*, 45(2), pp. 11–23.

Kaiser, H. (1970). 'A second generation Little Jiffy'. *Psychometrika*, 35, pp. 401–15.

Kaiser, H. (1974). 'An index of factorial simplicity'. *Psychometrika*, 39, pp. 31–6.

Kant, I. (1929). *Critique of Pure Reason* (translator, N. Kemp-Smith). London: Macmillan.

Kearns, H. (2005). 'Exploring the experiential learning of special educational needs coordinators'. *Journal of In-Service Education*, 31(1), pp. 131–50.

Kehily, M.J. (2002). *Sexuality, Gender and Schooling: Shifting Agendas in Social Learning*. London: Routledge Falmer.

Kellaghan, T., Weir, S., Ó hUallacháin, S. & Morgan, M. (1995). *Educational Disadvantage in Ireland*. Dublin: Department of Education/Combat Poverty Agency/Educational Research Centre.

Kelly, G.A. (1955). *The Psychology of Personal Constructs*. New York: Norton.

Kelly, S. (1970). *Teaching in the City: A Study of the Role of the Primary School Teacher.* Dublin: Gill & Macmillan.

Kewley, G. (1999). *Attention Deficit Hyperactivity Disorder: Recognition, Reality and Resolution.* London: David Fulton Publishers.

Killeavy, M. (1998). 'The professional development of primary teachers'. PhD thesis, Trinity College Dublin.

Killeavy, M. (2006). 'Induction: a collective endeavour of learning, teaching and leading'. *Theory into Practice,* 45(2), pp. 168–76.

Killeavy, M. & Moore, M. (2001). 'The lives of student teachers'. In: C. Day & D. van Veen (eds), *Educational Research in Europe Yearbook* (pp. 111–38). European Educational Research Association.

Killeavy, M. & Murphy, R., (2006). *National Pilot Project on Teacher Induction Report: Phase 1 & 2 Phase 2002–2004.* Dublin: Department of Education & Science.

King D. (2003). 'Social science research policy: the British experience'. A Presentation to The Royal Irish Academy's National Committee for Economics and Social Sciences (NCESS) and the Irish Research Council for the Humanities and Social Sciences Conference on Social Science Research Policy in Ireland. Dublin, 4 April 2003.

Kinsella, W. & Senior, J. (2009). *Policy, Legislation and Resource Allocation Models: A Review of National and International Practice.* Report compiled for the National Council for Special Education (NCSE).

Koshy, V. (2005). *Action Research for Improving Practice: A Practical Guide.* London: Paul Chapman Publishing.

Kuhn, T.S. (1962). *The Structure of Scientific Revolutions.* Chicago: University of Chicago Press.

Kyriacou, C. & Kobori, M. (1998). 'Motivation to learn and teach English in Slovenia'. *Educational Studies,* 24(3), pp. 345–51.

Labov, W. (2001). *Principles of Linguistic Change, Vol. 2: Social Factors.* Oxford: Blackwell.

Lalonde, R.N. & Gardner, R.C. (1985). 'On the predictive validity of the attitude/motivation test battery'. *Journal of Multilingual and Multicultural Development,* 6(5), pp. 403–12.

Lam, T.C.M. & Bordignon, C. (2001). 'An examination of English teachers' opinions about the Ontario grade 9 reading and writing test'. *Interchange,* 32 (2), pp. 131–45.

Lareau, A. (2000). 'Social class and the daily lives of children: A study from the United States'. *Childhood,* 7 (2), pp. 155–71.

Lareau, A. (2003). *Unequal Childhoods.* Berkeley LA: University of California Press.

Larochelle, M., Bednarz, N. & Garrison, J. (eds) (1998). *Constructivism and Education.* Cambridge MA: Cambridge University Press.

Lawler, S. (2005). 'Introduction: class, culture and identity'. *Sociology,* 39(5), pp. 797–806.

Lawn, M. & Lingard, B. (2002). 'Constructing a European policy space in educational governance: the role of transnational policy actors'. *European Educational Research Journal.* 1(2), pp. 290–307.

Lawson, A.E. (1995). *Science Teaching and the Development of Thinking.* Belmont, CA: Wadsworth Publishing Company.

Lawton, D. (1989). *Education, Culture and the National Curriculum.* London: Hodder & Stoughton.

Layder, D. (1997). *Modern Social Theory.* London: UCL Press.

Lee, O., Eichinger, D.C., Anderson, C.W., Berkheimer, G.D. & Blakesee, T.D. (1993). 'Changing middle school students' conceptions of matter and molecules'. *Journal of Research in Science Teaching,* 30, pp. 249–70.

Lewin, K. (1948). *Resolving Social Conflicts.* New York: Harper & Row Publishers

Lewis, A., & Norwich, B. (2001). 'A critical review of systematic evidence concerning distinctive pedagogies with pupils with difficulties in learning'. *Journal of Research in Special Educational Needs,* 1(1).

Lewis, A., & Norwich, B. (2004). *Special Teaching for Special Children?: Pedagogies for Inclusion.* Milton Keynes: Open University Press.

Lipsky, M. (1983). *Street Level Bureaucracy: Dilemmas of the Individual in Public Service* (2nd edition). New York: Russell Sage Foundation.

Lipsky, D. & Gartner, A. (1987). 'Capable of achievement and worthy of respect'. *Exceptional Children,* 54 (1) pp. 69–74.

Lloyd, C. (2008). 'Removing barriers to achievement: A strategy for inclusion or exclusion?'. *International Journal of Inclusive Education,* 12(2), pp. 221–36.

Lloyd, G. & Norris, C. (1999). 'Including ADHD'. *Disability and Society,* 14(4), pp. 505–17.

Lloyd, G., Stead, J. & Cohen, D. (eds) (2006). *Critical New Perspectives on ADHD.* London: Routledge.

Looney, A. & Klenowski, V. (2008). 'Curriculum and assessment for the knowledge society: interrogating experiences in the Republic of Ireland and Queensland, Australia'. *Curriculum Journal,* 19(3), pp. 177–92.

Lortie, D.C. (1975). *Schoolteacher: A Sociological Study.* Chicago: University of Chicago Press.

Lynch, K. (1989a). *The Hidden Curriculum: Reproduction in Education, a Reappraisal.* London: Falmer Press.

Lynch, K. (1989b). *The Hidden Curriculum.* Dublin: Gill & Macmillan.

Lynch, K. (2008). 'Care-less cultures: New managerialism and the care ceiling in higher education'. A Paper read at Critical Thinking: the Galway Symposium on the Future of Universities, NUI Galway, 5–6 June 2008.

Lynch, K. & Lodge A. (2002). *Equality and Power in Schools.* London: Routledge Falmer.

Lynch, K. & Moran, A. (2006). 'Markets, schools and the convertibility of economic capital: the complex dynamics of class choice'. *British Journal of Sociology of Education,* 27(2), pp. 221–35.

Lynch, K. & O'Riordan, C. (1996). *Social Class, Inequality and Higher Education: Barriers to Equality of Access and Participation Among School Leavers,* Dublin: Equality Studies Centre, University College Dublin.

Mac an Ghaill, M. (1994). *The Making of Men: Masculinities, Sexualities and Schooling.* Buckingham, PA: Open University Press.

McCarthy, D. (2006). 'Contextualising the state's response to global influences'. In: D. Jacobson, P. Kirby & D. Ó Broin, (eds), *Taming the Tiger: Social Inclusion in a Globalised Ireland.* Dublin: Tasc at New Island.

McCartney, D. (1999). *UCD: A National Idea: The History of University College Dublin.* Dublin: Gill & Macmillan.

McElwee, P. (1991). 'Transition from personal to scientific understanding'. *Journal of Research in Science and Technological Education,* 9, pp. 139–55.

McElwee, P. (1993). 'The conceptual understanding of scientific principles in Home Economics'. *International Journal of Technology and Design Education,* 3, pp. 5–17.

McElwee, P. (2005) 'Should teaching be based on research?'. *Chemistry in Action,* 75 (Spring), pp. 53–8.

McGrattan, M. (1998). An evaluation of the impact of a music programme on the social, emotional and cultural development of deaf children. Unpublished MEd thesis, Education Department, University College Dublin.

MacGréil, M. & Rhatigan, F. (2009). *The Irish Language and the Irish People. Report on the Attitudes towards, Competence in and Use of Irish Language in the Republic of Ireland in 2007–2008.* NUI Maynooth: Survey & Research Unit, Department of Sociology.

McIntosh, P. (1990). 'White privilege: Unpacking the invisible knapsack'. *Independent School,* 50(2), pp. 31–6.

Mackenzie, S. (2007). 'A review of recent developments in the role of the SENCo in the UK'. *British Journal of Special Education,* 34(4), pp. 212–18.

McKiernan, J. (1991). *Curriculum Action Research: A Handbook of Methods for the Reflective Practitioner,* London: Kogan Page.

McLeskey, J. & Waldron, N.L. (2000). *Inclusive Schools in Action: Making Differences Ordinary.* Alexandria, VA: Association for Supervision and Curriculum Development.

McManus, A. (2002) *The Irish Hedge School and its Books, 1695–1831.* Dublin: Four Courts Press.

McNeil, L. (2000). *Contradictions of Reform.* New York: Routledge.

McNiff, J. & Whitehead, J. (2006). *All You Need to Know About Action Research.* London: Sage Publications.

Mac Ruairc, G. (1997). "Big mad words' perceptions of language variation in schools: A sociological analysis'. Unpublished MEd thesis, University College Dublin.

Mac Ruairc, G. (2004). 'Schools, social class and children's perceptions of language variation'. In: J. Deegan, D. Devine & A. Lodge (eds), *Primary Voices*. Dublin: Institute of Public Administration.

Mac Ruairc, G. (2009). 'Dip, dip sky blue, who's it? NOT YOU: Children's experiences of standardised testing: A socio-cultural analysis'. *Irish Educational Studies*, 28 (1), pp. 47–66.

Mac Ruairc, G. (forthcoming). 'Leading DEIS schools: Exploring the work of school leaders in marginalised, disadvantaged communities, Report prepared for Leadership Development in Schools (LDS)'. Clare Education Centre.

Manning, M. (2009a) 'Foreword'. *Irish Human Rights Commission Annual Report*. Available at: http://www.ihrc.ie/_fileupload/publications/IHRC_AnnualReport_2008.pdf (retrieved 27/06/2009).

Manning, M. (2009b). Address by Dr Maurice Manning, Chancellor of the National University of Ireland, at the opening of the new UCD School of Education building, Belfield, 8 May 2009. Mimeo. Dublin: National University of Ireland.

Mannuzza, S., Klein, R.G., Bessler, A., Malloy, P. & Hynes, M.E. (1997). 'Educational and occupational outcome of hyperactive boys grown up'. *Journal of the American Academy of Child and Adolescent Psychiatry*, 6(9), pp. 1222–7.

Martinez, E. & Garcia, A. (2000). 'What is neoliberalism?: A brief definition for activists'. Available at: http://www.corpwatch.org/article.php?id=376 (retrieved 27/06/2009).

Masten, A.S. (1989). 'Resilience in development: Implications of the study of successful adaptation in developmental psychopathology'. In: D. Cicchetti (ed.), *Rochester Symposium on Developmental Psychology: The Emergence of a Discipline*. (Vol. 1, pp. 261–94). Hillsdale, NJ: Erlbaum.

Matthews, M.R. (1998). 'Introductory comments on philosophy and constructivism in science education'. In: M.R. Matthews (ed.), *Constructivism in Science Education* (pp. 1–10). Dordrecht, The Netherlands: Kluwer Academic Publishers.

Maybin, J. (2007). Language and Education. In: C. Llamas, L. Mullany & P. Stockwell (eds), *The Routledge Companion to Sociolinguistics* (pp. 157–63). Oxon, New York: Routledge.

Meiers, M. & Ingvarson, L. (2005). *Investigating the Links between Teacher Development and Student Learning Outcomes: Volume 1*. Australian Council for Educational Research.

Mezirow, J. (1990). *Fostering Critical Reflection in Adulthood: A Guide to Transformative and Emancipatory Learning*. San Francisco: Jossey-Bass.

Millar, R. (1989). 'Constructive criticisms'. *International Journal of Science Education*, 11, pp. 587–96.

Millar, R. (1990). 'Making Sense: what use are particle ideas to children?'. In: P.L. Lijnse, P. Lich, W. de Vos & A.J. Waarlo (eds), *Relating Macroscopic Phenomena to Microscopic Particles* (pp. 283–93). Proceedings of a seminar at Centre for Science and Mathematics Education, University of Utrecht.

Miller, J. (1996). *School for Women.* London: Virago.

Milne, K. (1997). *The Irish Charter Schools.* Dublin: Four Courts Press.

Minogue, M. (1983). 'Theory and practice in public policy and public administration'. In: M. Hill (ed.), *The Policy Process: A Reader* (pp. 10–29). Hemel Hempstead: Harvester Wheatsheaf.

Minor, L., Onwuegbuzie, A.J., Witcher, A.E. & James, T.L. (2002). 'Pre-service teachers' educational beliefs and their perceptions of characteristics of effective teachers'. *The Journal of Educational Research,* 96 (2), pp. 116–27.

Mittler, P. (1999). *Working Towards Inclusive Education: Social Contexts.* London: David Fulton Publishers.

Modood, T. (2007). *Multiculturalism: A Civic Idea.* Cambridge: Polity Press.

Montgomery, K. (2005). 'Banal race-thinking: ties of blood, Canadian history textbooks and ethnic nationalism'. *Paedagogica Historica,* 41(3), pp. 313–36.

Moore, V.A. (2001). '"Doing" racialized and gendered age to organize peer relations: observing kids in summer camp'. *Gender and Society,* 15 (6), pp. 835–58.

Moran, A. (2007). 'Embracing inclusive teacher education. *European Journal of Teacher Education',* 30(2), pp. 119–34.

Mulgan, G. (2003). *Global Comparisons in Policy-Making: The View from the Centre.* Available at: http://www.opendemocracy.net/debates/article-3-52-1280.jsp# (retrieved 15/06/03).

Mulgan, G. (2006). *Good and Bad Power: The Ideals and Betrayals of Government.* London: Allen Lane.

Mulgan, G. (2007). *Ready or Not? Taking Innovation in the Public Sector Seriously.* London: NESTA.

Murtagh, L. (2003) 'Retention and attrition of Irish as a second language: a longitudinal study of general and communicative proficiency in Irish among second level school leavers and the influence of instructional background, language use and attitude/motivation variables'. PhD thesis, University of Groningen.

Murtagh, L. (2006). 'Attitude/motivation, extra school use of Irish, and achievement in Irish among final-year secondary school (Leaving Certificate) students'. In: A. Gallagher & M. Ó Laoire (eds), *Language Education in Ireland: Current Practice and Future Needs.* Dublin: Irish Association of Applied Linguistics.

Murtagh, L. (2007). 'Out-of-school use of Irish: motivation and proficiency in immersion and subject-only post primary programmes'. *The International Journal of Bilingual Education and Bilingualism,* 10(4), pp. 428–53.

Musyck, B. & Hadjimanolis, A. (2005). 'Towards a knowledge-based economy: does the Cyprus R&D capability meet the challenge?'. *Science and Public Policy*, 32(1), pp. 65–77.

Myers, K. (2003). 'Critical voices: refugees, exclusion and schooling'. In: M. Shevlin & R. Rose (eds), *Encouraging Voices: Respecting the Insights of Young People who have been Marginalised* (pp. 254–73). Dublin: National Disability Authority.

Naiker, S.M. (1999). *Curriculum 2005: A Space for All—An Introduction to Inclusive Education.* Cape Town: Renaissance Tafelberg.

National Competitiveness Council (2009). *Statement on Education and Training.* Dublin: National Competitiveness Council.

National Council for Special Education (2006a). *Guidelines on the Individual Education Plan Process.* Available at: http://www.ncse.ie/publications/ final_report.pdf (retrieved 15/06/2009).

National Council for Special Education (2006b*). Plan for the Phased Implementation of the Education for Persons with Special Educational Needs Act, 2004.* Available at: http://www.ncse.ie/docs/ncse_imp_report.pdf (retrieved 15/06/2009).

National Educational Psychological Service (2007). *Mainstream Primary Schools and Special Education Needs: A Continuum of Support.* Available at: http:// www.education.ie/servlet/blobservlet/neps_special_needs_guidelines.pdf (retrieved 15/06/2009).

National Research Council (2006). *America's Lab Report; Investigations in High School Science.* Washington: The National Academies Press.

National Student (1910–15), James Joyce Library, University College Dublin.

NCCA (National Council for Curriculum and Assessment) (1999a). *Special Educational Needs: Curriculum Issues.* Dublin: NCCA.

NCCA (National Council for Curriculum and Assessment) (1999b). *Curaclam na bunscoile. Gaeilge: Teanga.* Dublin: The Stationery Office.

NCCA (National Council for Curriculum and Assessment) (2002a). *Draft Guidelines for Teachers of Students with Mild General Learning Disabilities.* Dublin: NCCA.

NCCA (National Council for Curriculum and Assessment) (2002b). *Draft Guidelines for Teachers of Students with Moderate General Learning Disabilities.* Dublin: NCCA.

NCCA (National Council on Curriculum and Assessment) (2005). *Intercultural Education in the Primary School:* Dublin: NCCA.

NCCA (National Council for Curriculum and Assessment) (2006). *Intercultural Education in the Post-Primary School: Guidelines for Schools.* Dublin: NCCA.

NCTAF (National Commission on Teaching and America's Future) (2003). *No Dream Denied: A Pledge to America's Children.* Washington, DC: NCTAF.

NCTAF (National Commission on Teaching and America's Future) (2005). *Induction into Learning Communities.* Washington DC: NCTAF.

Nic Craith, D. (2009). 'Policy for primary teacher education in 21st century Ireland'. A paper read to the Inaugural UCD/QUB Doctoral Studies Conference in Education, Dublin, 9 May 2009.

Nickerson, R.S. (1985). 'Understanding understanding', *American Journal of Education*, 93, pp. 201–39.

Niemi, H. (2008). 'Advancing research into and during teacher education'. In B. Hudson & P. Zgaga (eds), *Teacher Education Policy in Europe: A Voice of Higher Education Institutions* (pp. 183–208). Umea: University of Umea, Faculty of Education.

Nola, R. (1998). 'Constructivism in science and science education: a philosophical critique'. In: M.R. Matthews (ed.), *Constructivism in Science Education* (pp. 31–59). Dordrecht, The Netherlands: Kluwer Academic Publishers.

Nolan, B. & Smeeding, T.M. (2005). 'Ireland's income distribution in comparative perspective', *Review of Income and Wealth*, 51(4), pp. 537–60.

Nolet, V. & McLaughlin, M. (2000). *Accessing the General Curriculum: Including Students with Disabilities in Standards-Based Reform*. Thousand Oaks, CA: Corwin Press.

Norwich, B. (2008). 'What future for special schools and inclusion? Conceptual and professional perspectives'. *British Journal of Special Education*, 35(3), pp. 136–43.

Nunnally J. & Bernstein I. (1994). *Psychometric Theory* (3rd edition). New York: McGraw-Hill.

Nutley, S., Jung, T. & Walter, I. (2008). 'The many forms of research-informed practice: a framework for mapping diversity'. *Cambridge Journal of Education*, 38(1), pp. 53–71.

Oates, T. (2008). 'Going round in circles: temporal discontinuity as a gross impediment to effective innovation in education and training'. *Cambridge Journal of Education*, 38(1), pp. 105–20.

Ó Baoill, D.P. (2007). 'Origins of Irish-medium education: the dynamic core of language revitalisation in Northern Ireland'. *The International Journal of Bilingual Education and Bilingualism*, 10(4), pp. 410–27.

O'Brien, K. (1955). 'As to university life'. *University Review* I, No. 6, pp. 3–11.

O'Brien, J. & Christie, F. (2005). 'Characteristics of support for beginning teachers; evidence from the new induction scheme in Scotland'. *Mentoring and Tutoring*, 13 (2), pp. 191–205.

Ó Buachalla, S. (1988). *Education Policy in Twentieth Century Ireland*. Dublin: Wolfhound Press.

O'Donoghue v Minister for Health (et al.) (1996). 2 Irish Review 20, p. 65.

O'Dowd, L. (1995). 'Development or dependency? state economy and society in Northern Ireland'. In: P. Clancy, S. Drudy, K. Lynch, & L. O'Dowd, *Irish Society: Sociological Perspectives* (pp. 132–77). Dublin: Institute of Public Administration.

OECD (Organisation for Economic Co-operation and Development) (1991). *Review of National Policies for Education: Ireland.* Paris: OECD.

OECD (Organisation for Economic Co-operation and Development) (2003). *Attracting, Developing and Retaining Effective Teachers: Country Background Report for Ireland.* Paris: OECD.

OECD (Organisation for Economic Co-operation and Development) (2004a) *Education at a Glance: OECD Indicators 2004.* Paris: OECD. Available at: http://masetto.sourceoecd.org/vl=27112362/cl=12/nw=1/rpsv/cgi-bin/full textew.pl?prpsv=/ij/oecdthemes/99980037/v2004n11/s1/p1l.idx   (retrieved 28/06/09).

OECD (Organisation for Economic Co-operation and Development) (2004b). *Learning from Tomorrow's World: First Results from PISA 2003.* Paris: OECD. Available at: http://masetto.sourceoecd.org/vl=26917852/cl=18/nw=1/rpsv/cgibin/fulltextew.pl?prpsv=/ij/oecdthemes/99980185/v2004n23/s1/ p1l.idx (retrieved 28/06/09).

OECD (Organisation for Economic Co-operation and Development) (2004/2005). *Expenditure on Education.* Also OECD in Figures–2005 edition. Available at: www.oecd.org/edu/eag2004; http://ocde.p4.siteinternet.com/publications/doifiles/012005061T031.xls (retrieved 28/06/09).

OECD (Organisation for Economic Co-operation and Development) (2005). *Teachers Matter: Attracting, Developing and Retaining Effective Teachers, Education and Training Policy.* Paris: OECD: Centre for Educational Research and Innovation. Available at www.oecd.org.

OECD (Organisation for Economic Co-operation and Development) (2006). *Education at a Glance: OECD indicators 2006.* Paris: OECD.

OECD (Organisation for Economic Co-operation and Development) (2007). *Programme for International Student Assessment (PISA) 2006: Science Competencies for Tomorrow's World.* Paris: OECD. Available at: http://oberon.sourceoecd.org/vl=871191/cl=43/nw=1/rpsv/cgi-bin/fulltextew.pl?prpsv=/ij/oecdthemes/99980029/v2007n19/s1/p1l.idx (Chapter 3 retrieved 12/06/2009).

OECD (Organisation for Economic Cooperation and Development) (2008a). *Education at a Glance: OECD Indicators 2008.* Paris: OECD, Centre for Educational Research and Innovation. Available at: http://www.oecd.org.

OECD (Organisation for Economic Co-operation and Development) (2008b). *OECD Public Management Reviews: Ireland—towards an Integrated Public Service.* Paris: OECD.

OECD (Organisation for Economic Co-operation and Development) (2009a). *Society at a Glance 2009.* Paris: OECD.

OECD (Organisation for Economic Co-operation and Development) (2009b). *Creating Effective Teaching and Learning Environments: First Results from TALIS, Education and Training Policy.* Paris: OECD.

Ó Fathaigh, M. (1991). *Learning Irish in Second-Level Schools: Attitudes, Motivation and Achievement*. Dublin: Comhar na Múinteoirí Gaeilge.

O'Gorman, E. & Drudy, S. (2009). *Professional Development for Teachers Working in the Area of Special Education/Inclusion in Mainstream Schools*. Report submitted to the National Council for Special Education (Ireland).

O'Gorman, E., Drudy, S., Winter, E., Smith, R. & Barry, M. (2009). *Professional Development for Post-Primary SEN Teachers in Northern Ireland and the Republic of Ireland*. Armagh: Centre for Cross Border Studies.

O'Hanlon, C. (2003). *Educational Inclusion as Action Research: An Interpretative Discourse*. London: Sage Publications.

O'Hearn, D. (1999). 'Tigers and transnational corporations: pathways from the periphery?'. In: R. Munck, & D. O'Hearn (eds), *Critical Development Theory* (pp. 113–34). London and New York: Zed Books.

O Héideáin, E. (1967). *National School Inspection in Ireland: The Beginnings*. Dublin: Scepter Books.

O'Keefe, B. & O'Connor, P. (2001). "Out of the mouths of babes and innocents': Children's attitudes towards Travellers'. In: A. Cleary, M. Nic Giolla Phádraig & S. Quin (eds), *Understanding Children—Changing Experiences and Family Forms* (pp. 207–27). Dublin: Oak Tree Press.

Ó Laoire, M. (2000). 'Learning Irish for participation in the Irish language speech community outside the Gaeltacht'. *Journal of Celtic Language Learning*, 5, pp. 20–33.

Ó Riagáin, P. (1997) *Language Policy and Social Reproduction: Ireland 1893–1993*. Oxford: Clarendon Press.

Ó Riagáin, P. (2007) 'Relationships between attitudes to Irish, social class, religion and national identity in the republic of Ireland and Northern Ireland'. *The International Journal of Bilingual Education and Bilingualism*, 10(4), pp. 369–93.

Ó Riagáin, P. & Ó Gliasáin, M. (1994). *National Survey on Languages 1993: Preliminary Report*. Dublin: Institiúid Teangeolaíochta Éireann.

Osborne, J. & Dillon, J. (2008). *Science Education in Europe: Critical Reflections: A Report to the Nuffield Foundation*. London: King's College.

Osborne, J.F. (1996). 'Beyond constructivism'. *Science Education*, 80 (1), pp. 53–82.

Osborne, R. & Leith, H. (2000). *Evaluation of the Targeted Initiatives on Widening Access for Young People from Socio-Economically Disadvantaged Backgrounds*. Dublin: Higher Education Authority.

Osborne, R.J. & Cosgrove, M.M. (1983). 'Children's conceptions of the changes of state of water'. *Journal of Research in Science Teaching*, 20 (9), pp. 825–38.

O'Sullivan, D. (1989). 'Ideational base of policy'. In: D.G. Mulcahy & D. O'Sullivan (eds), *Irish Educational Policy* (pp. 219–74). Dublin: Institute of Public Administration.

O'Sullivan, D. (2006). *Cultural Politics and Irish Education Since the 1950s: Policy Paradigms and Power.* Dublin: Institute of Public Administration.

Ozga, J. (2009). 'Governing education through data in England: from regulation to self-evaluation'. *Journal of Education Policy,* 24(2), pp. 149–62.

Parkes, S. (ed.) (2004). *A Danger to the Men? A History of Women in Trinity College Dublin, 1904–*2004. Dublin: Lilliput Press.

Parkes, S.M. (ed.) (1978). *Irish Education in the British Parliamentary Papers in the Nineteenth Century and After, 1801–1920.* History of Education Society UK and Cork University Press: Guides to Sources in the History of Education No.5.

Pašeta, S. (1999). *Before the Revolution: Nationalism, Social Change and Ireland's Catholic Elite, 1879–1922.* Cork: Cork University Press.

Pašeta, S. (2000) 'The Catholic Hierarchy and the Irish University Question, 1880–1908', *History,* 85, No. 278, pp. 268–84.

Pavlenko, A. & Lantolf, J.P. (2000). 'Second language learning as participation and the (re)construction of selves'. In: J.P. Lantolf (ed.), *Sociocultural Theory and Second Language Learning.* Oxford: Oxford University Press.

Pearson, S. (2008). 'Deafened by silence or by the sound of footsteps? An investigation of the recruitment, induction and retention of special educational needs coordinators (SENCos) in England'. *Journal of Research in Special Educational Needs,* 8(2), pp. 96–110.

Pehkonen, E., Ahtee, M., & Lavonen, J. (2007). 'Explanations for the Finnish Success in PISA Evaluations'. In: T. Lamberg, & L.R. Wiest (eds), *Proceedings of the 29th Annual Meeting of the North American Chapter of the International Group for the Psychology of Mathematics Education.* Reno: University of Nevada.

Pence, D.J. & Fields, J.A. (1999). 'Teaching about race and ethnicity: trying to uncover white privilege for a white audience'. *Teaching Sociology,* 27, pp. 150–8.

Perry, P. (2002). *Shades of White: White Kids and Racial Identities in High School.* Durham: Duke University Press.

Pfundt, H. & Duit, R. (1994). *Bibliography of Students' Alternative Frameworks and Science Education.* Kiel: Institute for Science Education (IPN).

Picower, B. (2009). 'The unexamined whiteness of teaching: how white teachers maintain and enact dominant racial ideologies'. *Race, Ethnicity and Education,* 12(2), pp. 197–215.

Pijl, S.J., Meijer, C.J.W. & Hegarty, S. (1997). *Inclusive Education: A Global Agenda.* London: Routledge.

Pilkington, A. (1999). 'Racism in schools and ethnic differentials in educational achievement: a brief comment on a recent debate'. *British Journal of Sociology of Education,* 20(3), pp. 411–17.

Pinson, H. & Arnot, M. (2007). 'Sociology of education and the wasteland of refugee education research'. *British Journal of Sociology of Education,* 28(3), pp. 399–407.

Pollard, A. (2008). 'Knowledge transformation and impact: aspirations and experiences from TLRP'. *Cambridge Journal of Education*, 38 (1), pp. 5–22.

Pont, B., Nusche, D. & Hopkins, D. (2008). *Improving School Leadership (Vol. 1)*. Paris: Organisation for Economic Co-operation and Development.

Popper, K. (1972). *Conjectures and Refutations: The Growth of Scientific Knowledge* (4th edition). London: Routledge and Kegan Paul.

Powell, W. & Snellman, K. (2004). 'The knowledge economy'. *Annual Review of Sociology*, 30, pp. 199–220.

Prawat, R. (1992). 'Teachers' beliefs about teaching and learning: a constructivist perspective'. *American Journal of Education*, 100 (May), pp. 354–95.

Preece, J. (2000). *Online Communities: Designing Usability, Supporting Sociability*. Chichester, UK: John Wiley & Sons.

Putnam, R. (2000). *Bowling Alone: The Collapse and Revival of American Community*. New York: Simon & Schuster.

Rabbinge, R. (2009). 'A born-again CAP'. *Business and Finance*, 18 June 2009.

Radnor, H. (2002). *Researching your Professional Practice: Doing Interpretive Research*. Buckingham, PA: Open University Press.

Raftery, D. & Parkes, S.M. (2007). *Female Education in Ireland, 1700–1900, Minerva or Madonna?* Dublin and Portland, OR: Irish Academic Press.

Reason, P. & Bradbury H. (eds) (2006). *Handbook of Action Research*. London: Sage Publications.

Reay, D. (1998) 'Rethinking social class: qualitative perspectives on class and gender'. *Sociology*, 32 (2), pp. 259–77.

Reay, D. (1999). 'Making contact with teachers: habitus, cultural capital and mothers involvement'. In: M. Grenfell (ed.), *Pierre Bourdieu: Language, Culture and Education: Theory into Practice* (pp. 271–80). Berne: Peter Lang AG.

Reay, D. (2000). 'A useful extension of Bourdieu's conceptual framework?: emotional capital as a way of understanding mother's involvement in their children's education'. *The Sociological Review*, 48 (4), pp. 568–85.

Reay, D. (2001). 'Spice Girls', 'Nice Girls', 'Girlies' and 'Tomboys': Gender discourses, girls' cultures and femininities in the primary classroom. *Gender and Education*, 13, No. 2, pp. 153–66.

Reay, D. (2004). '"It's all becoming a bit of a habitus': beyond the habitual use of habitus in educational research'. *British Journal of Sociology of Education*, 25 (4), pp. 432–43.

Reay, D. (2005). 'Beyond consciousness? The psychic landscape of social class'. *Sociology*, 39 (5), pp. 911–28.

Reay, D. (2006). '"I'm not seen as one of the clever children': consulting primary school pupils about the social conditions of learning'. *Educational Review*, 58(22), pp. 171–81.

Renstrom, R., Andersson, B. & Marton, F. (1990). 'Students' conceptions of matter'. *Journal of Educational Psychology*, 82, pp. 555–69.

Richardson, P.W. & Watt, H.M. (2006). 'Who chooses teaching and why? Profiling characteristics and motivations across three Australian universities'. *Asia-Pacific Journal of Teacher Education*, 34 (1), pp. 27–56.

Roaf, C. & Bines, H. (1989). *Needs, Rights and Opportunities: Developing Approaches in Special Education*. London: Falmer Press.

Robins, J. (1980). *The Lost Children: A Study of Charity Children in Ireland, 1700–1900*. Dublin: Institute of Public Administration.

Roman, L. G. (1997). 'Denying (white) racial privilege: Redemption discourses and the uses of fantasy'. In: M. Fine, L. Weis, L.C. Powell & L.M. Wong (eds), *Off White: Readings on Race, Power and Society* (pp. 270–82). New York: Routledge.

Rutter, J. (2003). *Supporting Refugee Children in 21st Century Britain*. Trentham Books: Stoke-on-Trent.

Ryan, A. (2000). 'A critical evaluation of teaching, learning and meta-cognitive processes in young children'. Unpublished MEd thesis, Education Department, University College Dublin.

Schoen, L. & Fusarelli, L. (2008). 'Innovation, NCLB, and the fear factor; the challenge of leading 21st-century schools in an era of accountability'. *Educational Policy*, 22 (1), pp. 181–203.

Schön, D. (1971). *Beyond the Stable State: Public and Private Learning in a Changing Society*. London: Maurice Temple Smith.

Schön, D. (1983). *The Reflective Practitioner: How Professionals Think in Action*. London: Temple Smith.

Schön, D. (1987). *Educating the Reflective Practitioner*. San Francisco: Jossey-Bass.

Schuller, T. (2004). 'International policy research: 'Evidence' from CERI/OECD'. A round table paper read to ECER04 (the European Conference on Education Research), Crete, 4 September 2004.

Second Level Support Service (2009). 'Chemistry; atomic structure reactions & compounds; OC52, Investigating the activity series of metals'. Available at: http://www.juniorscience.ie.

Selley, N. J. (2000) 'Students' Spontaneous Use of a Particulate Model for Dissolution'. *Research in Science Education*, 30(4), pp. 389–402.

Shanahan, C. (2009). '3,500 children waiting for mental health services'. In: Headline, the national media monitoring programme for mental health and suicide. At: http://www.headline.ie/news/headline/2009/apr/ (accessed 15/06/09.

Shiel, G. (2006). 'The PISA assessment of reading literacy'. *Irish Journal of Education*, 37, pp. 79–100.

Shiel, G., Cosgrove, J., Sofroniou, N. & Kelly, A. (2001). *Ready for Life?: The Literacy*

Achievements of Irish 15-year olds with Comparative International Data. Dublin: Educational Research Centre.

Shiel, G., Perkins, R. & Gileece, L. (2009). *OECD Teaching and Learning International Study (TALIS): Summary Report for Ireland*. Dublin: ERC.

Sheils, J. (1988). *Communication in the Modern Languages Classroom*. Strasbourg: Council of Europe.

Shohamy, E. (2001a). 'Democratic assessment as an alternative'. *Language Testing*, 18, pp. 373–91.

Shohamy, E. (2001b). *The Power of Tests: A Critical Perspective on the Uses of Language Tests*. London: Longman.

Shore, S. & Halliday-Wynes, S. (2006). 'Preparing for the Professions: Practicalities and Politics of Teaching in Higher Education'. Discussion paper developed for the project Reflecting on Privilege in the Teaching Professions, University of South Australia. Available at: http://www. unisanet.unisa.edu.au/refpriv (retrieved 30/07/09).

Skrtic, T.M. (1991). *Behind Special Education: A Critical Analysis of Professional Culture and School Organisation*. Denver: Love.

Slavin, R.E. (2002). 'Evidence-based education policies: transforming educational practice and research'. *Educational Researcher*, 31 (7), pp. 15–21.

Slee, R. (1998). 'The politics of theorising special education'. In: C. Clark, A. Dyson & A. Millward (eds), *Theorising Special Education* (pp. 125–35). London: Routledge.

Slee, R. (2005). 'Education and the politics of recognition: inclusive education: an Australian snapshot'. In: D. Mitchell (ed.), *Contextualizing Inclusive Education* (pp. 139–65). London: Routledge.

Slee, R. (2006). 'Limits to and possibilities for educational reform'. *International Journal of Inclusive Education*, 10(2/3), pp. 109–19.

Smagorinsky, P. (2001). 'If meaning is constructed, what's it made from? Toward a cultural theory of reading'. *Review of Educational Research*, 71 (1), pp. 133–69.

Smith, R. & Barr, S. (2008). 'Towards educational inclusion in a contested society: from critical analysis to creative action'. *International Journal of Inclusive Education*, 12(4), pp. 401–22.

Smyth, E. (1999). *Do Schools Differ?* Dublin: Oak Tree Press.

Smyth, E., Darmody, M., McGinnity, F. & Byrne, D. (2009). *Adapting to Diversity: Irish Schools and Newcomer Students*. Dublin: ESRI Research Series, No. 8.

Smyth Maguire, L. (2001). 'An evaluation of the Samaritan's suicide awareness programme on the levels of awareness of suicide and related issues in transition year pupils'. Unpublished MEd thesis, Education Department, University College Dublin.

Society for Promoting the Education of the Poor of Ireland (1820). *Eighth Report of the Society for Promoting the Education of the Poor of Ireland*, App. VI.

Solomon, J. (1994). 'The rise and fall of constructivism'. *Studies in Science Education,* 23, pp. 1–19.

Solomon, R., Portelli, J., Daniel, B-J. & Campbell, A. (2005) 'The discourse of denial: how white teacher candidates construct race, racism and 'white privilege''. *Race Ethnicity and Education,* 8 (2), pp. 147–69.

Special Group on Public Service Numbers & Expenditures (2009). *Report.* Dublin: Government Publications.

Stanley, E.G. (1831). Letter from the Secretary for Ireland to His Grace the Duke of Leinster on the formation of a Board of Education; 1831–2 (196.) XXIX. 757.

State of Virginia (2009). *Regulations Governing Special Education Programs for Children with Disabilities in Virginia.* Available at: http://www.doe. virginia.gov/VDOE/Instruction/Sped/varegs.pdf (retrieved 07/08/2009).

Stavy, R. (1990). 'Children's conception of changes in the state of matter: from liquid (or solid) to a gas'. *Journal of Research in Science Teaching,* 27, pp. 247–66.

Stead, J., Lloyd, G. & Cohen, D. (2006). 'Widening our view of ADHD'. In: G. Lloyd, J. Stead & D. Cohen (eds), *Critical New Perspectives on ADHD* (pp. 1–11). London: Routledge.

Steele, J. & Mitchell, D. (1992). 'Special links with mainstream'. *Special Children,* 55 (March) pp. 14–16.

Stenhouse, L. (1993). 'The teacher as researcher'. In: M. Hammersley (ed.), *Controversies in Classroom Research,* (pp. 222–34). Buckingham, PA: Open University Press.

Stockman, I.J. (2007). 'Socio-political influences on research practices: examining language acquisition by African American children'. In: R. Bayley & C. Lucas (eds), *Sociolinguistic Variation* (pp. 297–317). Cambridge, UK: Cambridge University Press.

Su, Z., Hawkings, J.N., Zhao, C. & Huang. (2001). 'Choices and commitment: a comparison of teacher candidates' profiles and perspectives in China and the United States'. *International Review of Education,* 47 (6), pp. 611–35.

Suchting, W.A. (1992). 'Constructivism deconstructed'. *Science and Education,* 1(3), pp. 223–54.

Sugrue, C. (2008). 'The plate tectonics of educational change in Ireland: consequences for research quality, policy and practice?'. In: C. Sugrue (ed.), *The Future of Educational Change: International Perspectives* (pp. 48–72). London: Routledge.

Swain, M. (1995). 'Three functions of output in second language learning'. In: G. Cook & B. Seidlhofer (eds), *Principle and Practice in Applied Linguistics: Studies in Honour of H.G. Widdowson* (pp. 125–44). Oxford: Oxford University Press.

Swain, M. (2000). 'The output hypothesis and beyond: Mediating acquisition through collaborative dialogue'. In: J.P. Lantolf (ed.), *Sociocultural Theory and Second Language Learning.* Oxford: Oxford University Press.

Swan, G. (1994). 'Australia'. In: K. Mazurek & M. Winzer (eds), *Comparative Studies in Education*. Washington: Gallaudet University Press.

Tangen, R. (2005). 'Promoting inclusive education in secondary school in Norway: a national programme for teacher development'. *European Journal of Special Needs Education*, 20(1), pp. 57–70.

Task Force on Autism (2001). *The Report of the Task Force on Autism*. Dublin: The Stationery Office.

Thalhammer, E., Zucha, V., Enzenhofer, E., Salfinger, B. & Ogris, G. (2001). *Attitudes Towards Minority Groups in the European Union: A Special Analysis of the Eurobarometer 2000 Survey*. Vienna: European Monitoring Centre on Racism and Xenophobia.

The Lanthorn, December 1942, Vol. X, No. 3. Magazine of the Dominican College, Eccles Street, Catholic Central Library, Dublin.

Thomas, G. & Loxley, A. (2001). *Deconstructing Special Education and Constructing Inclusion*. Buckingham, PA: Open University Press.

Thomas, G. & Loxley, A. (2007). *Deconstructing Special Education and Constructing Inclusion* (2nd edition). Maidenhead: McGraw-Hill/Open University Press.

Thomas, G. & Vaughan, M. (2004). *Inclusive Education: Readings and Reflections*. Maidenhead: Open University Press.

Thomas, G., Walker, D. & Webb, J. (1998). *The Making of the Inclusive School*. London: Routledge.

Thomas, L., Wareing, S., Singh, I., Peccei, J.S., Thornborrow, J. & Jones, J. (2004). *Language, Society and Power* (2nd edition). London and New York: Routledge.

Thurstone, L.L. (1947). *Multiple Factor Analysis*. Chicago: University of Chicago Press.

Tierney, W.G. (ed.) (2006). *Governance and the Public Good*, Albany, NY: SUNY Press.

Timperley, H., Wilson, A., Barrar, H. & Fung, I. (2007). *Teacher Professional Learning and Development (BES)*. Wellington: Ministry of Education New Zealand.

Titley, E.B. (1983). *Church, State and the Control of Schooling in Ireland, 1900–1944*. Kingston and Montreal: McGill-Queen's University Press.

Tomlinson, S. (2005). 'Race, ethnicity and education under New Labour'. *Oxford Review of Education*, 31(1), pp. 153–71.

Tormey, (2007). 'Education and Poverty'. In M. Cousins (ed.), *Welfare, Policy and Poverty* (pp. 169–200). Dublin: Combat Poverty Agency.

Totterdell, M., Woodroffe, L., Bubb, S. & Hanrahan, K. (2004). 'The impact of NQT induction programmes on the enhancement of teacher expertise, professional development, job satisfaction or retention rates: a systematic review of research on induction'. In: *Research Evidence in Education Library*. London: EPPI-Centre, Social Science Research Unit, Institute of Education.

Trier, J. (2003). 'Inquiring Into 'techniques of power' with pre-service teachers through the 'school film' *The Paper Chase'. Teaching and Teacher Education,* 19(5), pp. 543–57.

Trier, J. (2005). 'Sordid Fantasies: Reading Popular Culture 'Inner City' School Films as racialised texts with pre-service teachers'. *Race, Ethnicity and Education,* 8(2), pp. 171–89.

Troyna, B. & Hatcher, R. (1992). *Racism in Children's Lives—A Study of Mainly-White Primary Schools.* Routledge: London.

TTA (Teacher Training Agency) (1998). *National Standards for Special Educational Needs Coordinators.* London: TTA.

Tytler, R. (2000). 'A comparison of year 1 and year 6 students' conceptions of evaporation and condensation: dimensions of conceptual progression'. *International Journal of Science Education,* 22 (5), pp. 447–67.

Tytler, R. & Peterson, S. (2000) 'Deconstructing Learning in science: young children's responses to a classroom sequence on evaporation'. *Research in Science Education,* 30 (4), pp. 339–55.

United Kingdom (1695). An Act to Restrain Foreign Education (7 Will. c.4).

United Kingdom (1697a). Banishment Act (9 William III, c.2).

United Kingdom (1697b). Registration Act (2 Anne c.7).

United Kingdom (1703). An Act to Prevent the Further Growth of Popery (2 Anne c.6).

United Kingdom (1709). An Act for Explaining and Emending an Act Entitled. An Act to Prevent the Further Growth of Popery (8 Anne c.3).

United Nations (1983). *World Programme of Action Concerning Disabled Persons. Available at: www.un.org/documents/ga/res/38/a38r028.htm* (retrieved 07/09/ 2009).

United Nations (1989). *Convention on the Rights of the Child.* Available at: http:// www.unicef.org/crc/ (retrieved 29/06/2009).

United Nations (2006). *Convention on Rights of Persons with Disabilities.* Available at: http://www.un.org/disabilities/default.asp?navid=12&pid=150 (retrieved 29/06/2009).

United States (1975). Education for All Handicapped Children Act [Public Law 94–142]. Available at: http://www.eric.ed.gov/ERICDocs/data/ericdocs2sql/ content_storage_01/0000019b/80/39/e2/b6.pdf (retrieved 09/06/2009).

United States (1990, 1997). Individuals with Disabilities Education Act and Amendments. Available at: http://idea.ed.gov/ (retrieved 09/06/2009).

United States (2001). No Child Left Behind Act, Washington: US Government publication. Available at: http://www.ed.gov/policy/elsec/leg/esea02/index. html (Chapter 7, retrieved 09/06/2009) (Chapter 15, retrieved 27/07/ 2009).

United States Supreme Court (1982) *Board of Education v. Rowley,* 458 U.S. 176. Available at: http://supreme.justia.com/us/458/176/case.html (retrieved 07/09/2009).

University College Dublin Calendar 1910–11, Archives Department, University College Dublin.

UNESCO (United Nations Educational, Scientific and Cultural Organisation) (1994). *The Salamanca Statement and Framework for Action on Special Needs Education.* Paris: UNESCO. Also available at: http://www.eric.ed.gov/ERICDocs/data/ericdocs2sql/content_storage_01/0000019b/80/13/82/96.pdf (Chapter 5, retrieved 29/06/2009) (Chapter 7, retrieved 09/06/2009).

UNESCO (United Nations Educational, Scientific and Cultural Organisation) (2000). Dakar Framework for Action. *Education for All: Meeting our Collective Commitments.* Paris: UNESCO.

Varma-Joshi, M., Baker, C. & Tanaka, C. (2004). 'Names will never hurt me?'. *Harvard Educational Review,* 74(2), pp. 175–208.

Vaughn-Cook, A.F. (2007). 'Lessons learned from the Ebonics controversy: Implications for language assessment'. In: R. Bayley, & C. Lucas (eds), *Sociolinguistic Variation* (pp. 254–75). Cambridge, UK: Cambridge University Press.

Velleman, P.F. & Wilkinson, L. (1993). 'Nominal, ordinal, interval, and ratio typologies are misleading'. *The American Statistician,* 47:1, pp. 65–72.

Vestergaard, E. (2003). 'Humanities and social sciences research policy: The European experience'. A Presentation to The Royal Irish Academy's National Committee for Economics and Social Sciences (NCESS) and the Irish Research Council for the Humanities and Social Sciences Conference on Social Science Research Policy in Ireland, Dublin, 4 April 2003.

Vlachou, A. (2006). 'Role of special/support teachers in Greek primary schools: a counterproductive effect of 'inclusion' practices'. *International Journal of Inclusive Education,* 10(1), pp. 39–58.

Vosniadou, S. (1996). 'Towards a revised cognitive psychology for new advances in learning and instruction'. *Learning and Instruction,* 6(2), pp. 95–109.

Waldron, F. & Sikes, P. (2006). 'What does it mean to be Irish? Children's constructions of national identity'. *Irish Educational Studies,* 25(2), pp. 231–53.

Walsh, B. (2007). *The Pedagogy of Protest: The Educational Thought and Work of Patrick H. Pearse.* Oxford: Peter Lang.

Walsh, C. (2005). Mary Lavin (1912–1996). In: A. Roche (ed.), *The UCD Aesthetic: 50 Years of UCD Writers* (pp. 122–9). Dublin: New Island.

Warnock Report (1978). *Report of the Committee of Enquiry into the Education of Handicapped Children and Young People.* London: HMSO.

Wearmouth, J., Paige-Smith, A. & Soler, J. (2004). 'Computer Conferencing with Access to a 'guest expert' in the professional development of special educational needs coordinators'. *British Journal of Educational Technology,* 35(1), pp. 81–93.

Wedell, K. (2008). 'Confusion about inclusion: patching up or system change?'. *British Journal of Special Education*, 35(3), pp. 127–35.

Weir, S. Archer, P. & Flanagan, R. (2004). *A Review of School-Based Measures Aimed at Addressing Educational Disadvantage in Ireland Report to the Educational Disadvantage Committee.* Dublin: Educational Research Centre.

Weiss, G. & Hechtman, L.T. (1993). *Hyperactive Children Grown Up: ADHD in Children Adolescents and Adults* (2nd edition). London: Guilford Press.

Westbury, I., Hansen, S-E., Kansanen, P. & Bjorkvist, O. (2005). 'Teacher education for research-based practice in expanded roles: Finland's experience'. *Scandinavian Journal of Educational Research*, 49(5), pp. 475–85.

White, P., Gorard, S. & Huat See, B. (2006). 'What are the problems with teacher supply?', *Teaching and Teacher Education*, 22(3), pp. 315–26.

Whitty, G. (2006). 'Education(al) research and education policy making: is conflict inevitable?'. *British Educational Research Journal*, 32 (2), pp. 159–76.

Wideen, M., Mayer-Smith, J. & Moon, B. (1998). 'A critical analysis of research on learning to teach: making the case for an ecological perspective on inquiry'. *Review of Educational Research*, 68, pp. 130–78.

Wilgosh, L. (1992). 'Integration of children with special needs'. *The International Journal of Education Management*, 6 (5) pp. 8–14.

Wilkerson, T.E. (1976). *Kant's Critique of Pure Reason.* Oxford: Clarendon Press.

Wilkinson, W.K. (2003). *Straight Talk about ADHD: A Guide to Attention/Deficit Hyperactivity Disorder for Irish Parents and Professionals.* Cork: Coleman Press.

Williams, C.L. (ed.) (1993). *Doing 'Women's Work': Men in Nontraditional Occupations.* Newbury Park, CA: Sage.

Williams, C.L. (1995). *Still a Man's World: Men Who do Women's Work.* Berkeley, California: University of California Press.

Willis, P. (1990). *Common Culture: Symbolic Work at Play in the Everyday Cultures of the Young.* Milton Keynes: Open University Press.

Wilson, J.M. & Marcotte, A.C. (1996). 'Psychosocial adjustment and educational outcome in adolescents with a childhood diagnosis of ADHD'. *Journal of the American Academy of Child and Adolescent Psychiatry*, 35, pp. 579–87.

Winter, E., Fletcher-Campbell, P., Connolly, P. & Lynch, P. (2006). 'Resource Requirements for the Diagnosis and Assessment of Special Educational Needs in Ireland'. Unpublished Research Report. Trim, County Meath: National Council for Special Education.

Witherell, C. & Noddings, N. (1991). *Stories Lives Tell: Narrative and Dialogue in Education.* Teachers College Press, New York.

Wolfendale, S. (ed.) (2000). *Special Needs in the Early Years: Snapshots of Practice.* London: Routledge Falmer.

Wong, H.K., Britton, T. & Ganser, T. (2005). 'What the world can teach us about new teacher induction', *Phi Delta Kappan*, 86 (5), pp. 379–84.

Woodin, T. (2005). 'Muddying the waters: changes in class and identity in a working class cultural organisation'. *Sociology*, 39 (5), pp. 1001–18.

World Bank, (2004). *2005 World Development Report: A Better Investment Climate for Everyone*. New York: World Bank and Oxford University Press.

World Bank (2007). *WDI Online: World Development Indicators*. Available at: http://ddp-ext.worldbank.org.eproxy.ucd.ie/ext/DDPQQ/report.do?method=showReport (retrieved 30/07/2009).

World Bank (2009). *Education for the Knowledge Economy*. Available at: http://web.worldbank.org/WBSITE/EXTERNAL/TOPICS/EXTEDUCATION/0,,contentMDK:20161496~menuPK:540092~pagePK:148956~piPK:216618~theSitePK:282386,00.html (retrieved 12/06/2009).

Wrigley, T. (2008). 'School improvement in a neo-liberal world'. *Journal of Educational Administration and History*, 40 (2), pp. 129–48.

Yager, R.E. & Penick, J.E. (1983). 'Analysis of the current problems with school science in the United States of America'. *European Journal of Science Education*, 25, pp. 463–9.

Ysseldyke, J.E. & Algozzine, B. (1995). *Special Education: A Practical Approach for Teachers*. New York: Houghton Mifflin Company.

Ysseldyke, J.E., Algozzine, B. & Thurlow, M.L. (2000). *Critical Issues in Special Education*. New York: Houghton Mifflin Company.

Zanting, A., Verloop, N., Vermunt, J.D. & Van Driel, J.H. (1998). 'Explicating practical knowledge: an extension of mentor teacher's roles'. *European Journal of Teacher Education*, 21(1), pp. 50–55.

Zeiher, H., Devine, D., Kjorholt A. & Strandell, H. (eds) (2007). *Flexible Childhood? Exploring Children's Welfare in Time and Space*. Odense: University Press of Southern Denmark.

INDEX